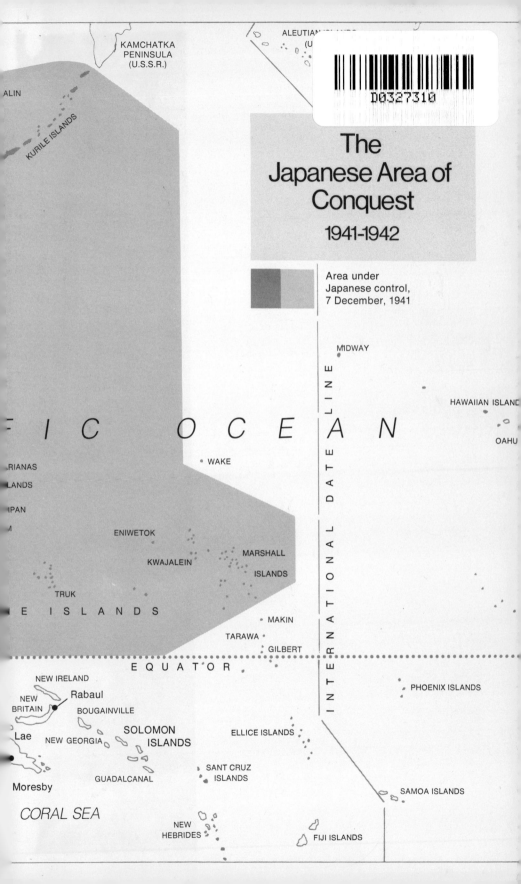

The Japanese Area of Conquest

1941-1942

Area under
Japanese control,
7 December, 1941

KAMCHATKA
PENINSULA
(U.S.S.R.)

ALEUTIAN ISLANDS
(U

ALIN

KURILE ISLANDS

MIDWAY

HAWAIIAN ISLAND

OAHU

IC OCEAN

WAKE

RIANAS
LANDS

PAN

ENIWETOK

KWAJALEIN

MARSHALL

ISLANDS

TRUK

E ISLANDS

MAKIN

TARAWA

GILBERT

INTERNATIONAL DATE LINE

EQUATOR

NEW IRELAND

NEW
BRITAIN

Rabaul

BOUGAINVILLE

PHOENIX ISLANDS

Lae

NEW GEORGIA

SOLOMON
ISLANDS

ELLICE ISLANDS

GUADALCANAL

SANT CRUZ
ISLANDS

SAMOA ISLANDS

Moresby

CORAL SEA

NEW
HEBRIDES

FIJI ISLANDS

Titans of the Seas

By the same authors:

Corregidor: *The Saga of a Fortress*
Typhoon of Steel: *The Battle for Okinawa*

HARPER & ROW, PUBLISHERS

New York

Evanston

San Francisco

London

James H. Belote
William M. Belote

TITANS
OF THE SEAS

*The Development and Operations of
Japanese and American Carrier Task
Forces During World War II*

This volume is dedicated to the memory of
Franklin Charles Palm and Raymond J. Sontag

TITANS OF THE SEAS: THE DEVELOPMENT AND OPERATIONS OF JAPANESE AND AMERICAN CARRIER TASK FORCES DURING WORLD WAR II. Copyright © 1975 by James H. Belote and William M. Belote. All rights reserved. Printed in the United States of America. No part of this book may be used or reproduced in any manner whatsoever without written permission except in the case of brief quotations embodied in critical articles and reviews. For information address Harper & Row, Publishers, Inc., 10 East 53rd Street, New York, N.Y. 10022. Published simultaneously in Canada by Fitzhenry & Whiteside Limited, Toronto.

FIRST EDITION

Designed by C. Linda Dingler

Library of Congress Cataloging in Publication Data

Belote, James H
  Titans of the seas.
  Bibliography: p.
  Includes index.
  1. World War, 1939–1945—Pacific Ocean.
2. Aircraft carriers.   3. World War, 1939–1945—Naval operations.   4. World War, 1939–1945—Aerial operations.   I. Belote, William M., joint author.
II. Title.
D767.B47   940.54′4   74–1971
ISBN 0–06–010278–0

75 76 77 78 79 10 9 8 7 6 5 4 3 2 1

Contents

Photographs follow page 150

Maps

Preface

When Admiral Chuichi Nagumo's carrier task force struck Pearl Harbor on that fateful Sunday morning of December 7, 1941, precipitating war between Japan and the United States, a dramatically new and effective weapons system burst into the mainstream of naval warfare. This book tells the story of the evolution of that weapons system, the fast carrier task force, from its inception in World War I to its evolution into a supreme instrument in World War II. Carrier warfare reached its zenith in the decisive Battle of the Philippine Sea, fought on June 19 and 20, 1944. In this penultimate contest the real decision of the Pacific war was reached. More fully than has been done heretofore, the authors have traced the planning and execution of the Japanese attack on Pearl Harbor, their subsequent sweep of the southwest Pacific and Indian oceans, the great carrier battles of 1942—Coral Sea, Midway, Eastern Solomons, Santa Cruz—the American task-force attacks on Japanese bases during 1943, and the details of the showdown contest in the Philippine Sea.

The after-action reports of the Japanese and American warships and air groups involved, written soon after the events by participants, are the primary sources for this book. A list of these and other materials is at the end of this volume.

Although the authors bear full responsibility for the conclusions drawn in this book, their debt to others is considerable. To Vice Admiral Edwin B. Hooper, USN (ret.), the U. S. Navy's Director of Naval History, the authors owe thanks for genial encouragement and access to the raw materials of carrier task-force history. To Dr. Dean Allard, the able Chief Archivist of the Naval History Division, the authors are grateful for wise counsel as well as "logistical" support. Besides suggesting the *raison d'être* for this book—that the action reports of the carrier units contain a rich treasure trove of material not heretofore fully utilized—Mrs. Kathy Lloyd of the Naval History Division tirelessly searched the records for information, obscure and otherwise, that is the spice as well as the foundation of naval history. Special thanks are due Rear Admiral Clarence E. Dickinson, USN (ret.), for permission to quote from his excellent book, *The Flying Guns.*

The authors also wish to thank numerous colleagues in the craft of naval history for encouragement and valuable ideas, especially Professors E. B. Potter, Neville Kirk and William Darden of the U. S. Naval Academy, and Professor Clark G. Reynolds of the University of Maine. Dr. Reynolds' penetrating analysis of the command relationships among America's top naval airmen prior to and during World War II is "must" reading for any serious student of naval warfare. To Captain Harold Wells, USN (ret.), of Elsah, Illinois, the authors are especially grateful. His personal knowledge of events and of fellow naval aviators involved in the Guadalcanal and other actions was valuable—and unique. A helpful research assistant was John A. Belote.

Finally, as was the case with their previous joint-authored books, *Corregidor: The Saga of a Fortress* and *Typhoon of Steel: The Battle for Okinawa*, the authors are indebted to their editor, Mr. Marion S. Wyeth, Jr., of Harper & Row, for expert assistance and sagacious advice. And of their wives, Mrs. Edith W. Belote and Marilyn P. Belote, the authors can only say that without their encouragement and assistance with typing and proofreading this book could not have appeared.

JAMES H. BELOTE
WILLIAM M. BELOTE

1. Pearl Harbor

Sunday morning, December 7, 1941. Clouds rushed overhead as six big aircraft carriers, escorted by a pair of fast battleships, three cruisers, and a covey of destroyers, slammed through heavy seas at 24 knots. Their course was due south, their destination a point in the ocean 275 miles north of Pearl Harbor, close enough to launch an air strike on this main base of the U. S. Pacific Fleet.

Leading the left-hand column of three flattops was the veteran *Akagi,* pride of the Imperial Japanese Navy. Behind her was her near-sister, *Kaga,* followed by the *Hiryu.* Leading the right-hand column was the *Soryu,* the smallest of the six at 15,900 tons displacement. Behind *Soryu* were the new twins *Shokaku* and *Zuikaku.* This task force comprised all of the first-line attack carriers of the Japanese Navy. Also it was the strongest carrier task force ever assembled. Never before had six flattops, embarking more than 400 planes in their air groups, sailed on a war mission.

Commanding the Pearl Harbor attack force, called the First Air Fleet, was a gray-haired, stoutish veteran seaman, Vice Admiral Chuichi Nagumo. Nagumo was not a flyer himself. His only prior aviation experience had been as a light-carrier skipper in 1929. Moreover, he disapproved of the Pearl Harbor operation and during the planning stages had opposed it as being too risky. He considered his carriers to be extremely vulnerable ships, loaded as they were with an antithetical combination of volatile aviation gas and high-explosive bombs and ammunition. Any enemy hit short of a dud might blow one up. Nevertheless, Nagumo had accepted the command of the First Air Fleet and had decided to press home the attack. Rear Admiral Ryunosuke Kusaka, his Chief of Staff, was confident that the air crews would find eight battleships in Pearl Harbor. That was enough for Nagumo. If his flyers could sink or disable the battle wagons of the U. S. Pacific Fleet, he would have scored a success.

Commander Minoru Genda, Nagumo's air-operations officer, always had been an enthusiast for the Pearl Harbor strike. He believed that it would surprise the enemy and succeed, probably at an acceptable cost. He had been, however, sorely disappointed that the Japanese consulate in

1

Honolulu had reported no American carriers in port. He was hoping that the carrier *Enterprise* would return to Pearl before the attack and that the new flattops *Hornet* and *Wasp* would arrive from the Atlantic. "If that happens," Genda said, "I don't care if all eight of the battleships are away."

With just a trace of a smile Nagumo had listened tolerantly, as usual without comment. Though every inch a Samurai, of a warrior family from Yamagota on northern Honshu, he was a kindly man, as his benign countenance showed. He could not share Genda's views; to him, battleships outranked carriers in the hierarchy of sea power. But he could appreciate his aviator's ardor and fighting spirit.

Now it was nearing 6:00 A.M. on X-Day, December 7, Hawaii time. There could be no waiting for the heavy sea to abate. If the Pacific Fleet was to be hit before being alerted the planes would have to be launched as scheduled. Nagumo summoned his Air Unit Commander, an intense, dynamic thirty-nine-year-old veteran pilot named Mitsuo Fuchida. He grasped Fuchida's hand firmly and said, "I have confidence in you." He then accompanied Fuchida to the *Akagi's* briefing room. Fuchida, a commander in rank, called his assembled pilots to attention and saluted Captain Hasegawa, the *Akagi's* skipper. Hasegawa issued the final order, a simple "Take off according to plan." The great ship heeled into the northerly wind, fluttering signal flags denoting her turn.

Minutes later a lamp on the flight deck twirled a circle of green. The first Zero fighter, piloted by Lieutenant Commander Shigeru Itaya, rolled slowly, gathered speed, then lifted abruptly into the air as the flight deck dipped from beneath it. Another followed—the other carriers also were launching—and within 15 minutes the entire first strike of 183 fighters, dive bombers, and torpedo and high-level bombers was in the air. Only one plane, a fighter, had crashed on takeoff despite the heavy sea and lack of a distinct horizon for the pilots to see. The most skilled naval airmen in the world flew these planes, many combat-experienced from Japan's continuing war with China.

The now assembled formation circled the task force once, then turned due south at a leisurely 125 knots indicated air speed. In a few minutes all planes—Zero fighters above and Val dive bombers and Kate torpedo planes beneath—had broken through dense clouds to emerge into brilliant early-morning sunlight at 6,000 feet. In little less than two hours' flying time they would be over Oahu and Pearl Harbor.

Some 300 miles to the south and west about 210 miles from Oahu, another carrier also had begun launching its planes at 6:00 A.M. This was the U. S. S. *Enterprise*, Genda's hoped-for prey, a relatively new ship commissioned in 1938. At 19,900 tons displacement the "Big E" was slightly larger than Japan's *Hiryu*. It embarked Air Group 6, which, like Japan's larger counterparts, was made up of squadrons of fighters, dive bombers, and bomber-torpedo planes. The *Enterprise* was not on a patrol mission; rather, it was the nucleus of a small task force returning to base after ferrying a squadron of Marine fighters to Wake Island. U. S. S. *Lexington*, the only other carrier then operating from Pearl, was nearing Midway Island on a similar mission.

The orginal schedule had called for the *Enterprise* to enter port on the afternoon of December 6. But because reinforced trade winds had slowed the destroyer screen and delayed its refueling, the task force commander, Vice Admiral William F. Halsey, had decided to postpone arrival until Sunday noon. Halsey was a born fighter and ready for trouble. His ships had all of their antiaircraft guns manned around the clock. If the task force encountered a Japanese ship, Halsey had ordered his crews to sink it. The reason the *Enterprise* was launching planes was to search ahead and make sure that the way into Pearl Harbor was clear.

Neither Halsey nor Commander Howard L. Young, the skipper of Air Group 6, had been pleased with the performance of the dive-bomber pilots in recently concluded exercises. The pilots had dropped bombs all around—but not on—their towed target. Most had much less experience than Nagumo's airmen. The average flight time of a U. S. Navy pilot in December 1941 was 305 hours against an average of 700 in the entire Japanese Navy and up to 2,000 in the Pearl Harbor strike force.

Operation of the *Enterprise* as the core ship of a task force was standard American practice. Only occasionally had American carriers operated together. If war came the current battle plan called for the three Pacific Fleet carriers—*Saratoga* (which was operating out of San Diego on December 7), *Enterprise* and *Lexington*—to operate independently, two in separate forces containing battleships as their main component, the third with a scouting force of heavy cruisers. American doctrine did not envisage the massing of carriers. Indeed, with only seven flattops in the entire fleet and with four of the seven operating in the Atlantic, the U. S. Navy scarcely could afford to hazard several at once, even if doctrine had called for it.

Weighty measures of strategy hardly burdened Commander Young as he orbited the *Enterprise* in his scout bomber. He was more concerned with the immediate problem of leading 18 SBDs (Douglas Dauntlesses) of Scouting and Bombing Squadrons 6 into Pearl Harbor's Ford Island airfield. Flying wing on him in airplane 6-S-2 was a young ensign, Perry L. Teaff. Young did not really expect to encounter enemy ships. En route to Oahu he saw what he had expected to see, tanker *Pat Doheny* of the Richfield Oil Company and submarine *Thresher* exercising with an old four-piper destroyer of World War I vintage, the U. S. S. *Litchfield*. After circling the last-named ships Young flew on, heading for landfall near Barbers Point on Oahu's southwest coast.

Japanese sources agree that Admiral Isoroku Yamamoto, the commander-in-chief of the Japanese Combined Fleet, originated the idea of attacking Pearl Harbor. From at least January 1941 and possibly earlier than that, Yamamoto had been convinced that only by crippling the U. S.

Pacific Fleet at its home base would Japan have any chance to win a war with America.

The factors that underlay Yamamoto's conviction can only be surmised. The admiral has left no record himself. He was air-minded; indeed it was his rigorous training that had brought Japan's naval air force to its peak of perfection. He also was well acquainted with Admiral Heihachiro Togo's surprise torpedo-boat attack on a Russian naval squadron at Port Arthur in 1904. As a young officer he had served under Togo in the famous battle of the Tsushima Strait that followed. But it may have been a successful surprise British torpedo-plane attack on an Italian battleship squadron at Taranto, Italy, late in 1940 that convinced him of the feasibility of raiding Pearl Harbor. On hearing of the attack he had immediately cabled Japan's naval attaché in Rome for details.

Yamamoto had ordered preliminary planning for Plan Z, as the Pearl Harbor strike was called, in January 1941. He relied on Rear Admiral Takajiro Onishi and Commander Minoru Genda, then both of the 11th Air Fleet, and on his own operations officer, Captain Kameto Kuroshima, to sketch an outline of the attack. All three had agreed that an air raid on Pearl Harbor was workable though risky.

By May 1941 the Pearl Harbor plan had acquired both a formal status as a proposal and a determined opponent. Its detractor was Admiral Osami Nagano, chief of the Naval General Staff in Tokyo. His approval was necessary before an attack could be launched. To Nagano Plan Z represented but one of many operations that the Japanese Navy must undertake in the event of a war. If Japan's six large fleet carriers were diverted to a Pearl Harbor attack, only four small light carriers would be available for all other operations. These, he believed, were not enough.

Despite Nagano's opposition, and though many of his own staff came to doubt Plan Z, Admiral Yamamoto remained stubbornly hopeful. He already had concentrated the big fleet carriers in the First Air Fleet, and in August 1941 he ordered detailed planning and training to begin. The showdown between the two admirals came in September and early October. Faced with Yamamoto's threat to resign unless he approved Plan Z, Nagano finally yielded his consent.

In the meantime training continued. High-level bombing tests beginning on October 24 and lasting two weeks bolstered Yamamoto's confidence in his air crews. The Kate high-level bombers scored from 10,000 feet a phenomenal 50 percent hits or better on a stationary target the shape and size of the U. S. S. *California*. Against the target ship *Settsu* maneuvering at 16 to 18 knots, the Val dive bombers scored an average of 40 percent hits. The torpedo-plane pilots, practicing in a cove in Kagoshima Bay that closely resembles Pearl Harbor, learned to drop their "tin fish" at 100 knots from as low as 30 feet at 4.5-degree angles of incidence to a stationary 600-foot target, scoring close to 100 percent hits. The Zero fighter pilots practiced formation dogfighting until their flights of three could maintain tight Vs while warding off attacks by six opponents. All pilots practiced deck landings on their carriers. About half became qualified to land at night.

When on November 26, 1941, it steamed from Hitokappu Bay in the Kuriles to execute Plan Z, the First Air Fleet was in the highest state of readiness. Every pilot had his assigned target and had been trained to perfection to hit it.

In contrast the American command on Oahu was grossly unprepared. The U. S. Army, bearing responsibility for defense against air attack, had radar and enough fighter planes—99 P-40s and 39 P-36s—to have given the first wave of Commander Fuchida's attackers a real scrap. But on December 7 the radar was still on training status and not operational. No radio commo system existed to vector fighters to intercept an attack. Not a single fighter was in the air or ready to take to the air. All were on four-hour flight notice. The planes either were lined up infantry style or gathered in clusters for easy guarding on the ground. The Army commander, Major General Walter C. Short, considered sabotage by Hawaii's civilians of Japanese nationality to be the main threat and seems not to have taken seriously the threat of a massed carrier strike.

The aviators of Marine Air Group 21 at Ewa airfield were as unready as their Army comrades. They had lined up their 49 planes, including 11 modern fighters and 32 dive bombers, wing tip to wing tip down either side of the single runway.

Admiral Husband E. Kimmel, the Pacific Fleet's commander, had none of his seven airborne Catalina patrol planes searching to the north in the direction from which Nagumo's attack was coming. Yet studies prepared months earlier had envisaged an attack from that quarter by a maximum of six carriers as the most likely possibility. Most of the Catalinas were sitting helplessly at their Kaneohe base. Kimmel's most effective defense measure was having a quarter of the ships' antiaircraft batteries on alert status around the clock. This meant that the crews were supposed to be near the five- and three-inch batteries so assigned. The only guns constantly manned were a pair of .50-caliber machine guns on the foretop of each battleship.

In a theoretical way Admiral Kimmel and General Short were expecting war because of the deteriorating relations between Japan and America. But they did not expect the enemy to hit *them*.

Concern about his enemy's state of alert was not Mitsuo Fuchida's main worry as he flew toward Oahu. He was much more disturbed about the weather. If the solid cloud cover below extended over Pearl Harbor it would greatly hinder his attackers. Glancing back, Fuchida could see in formations of five the 49 Kate high-level bombers under his personal command. To his right and a little below were the 40 Kate torpedo planes under Lieutenant Commander Shigeharu Murata of the *Akagi*'s air group. These were the planes expected to do the most damage. To his left and slightly above were Lieutenant Commander Kuichi Takahashi's 51 Val dive bombers. Their mission was to blast American airfields. Droning well above were 43 Zeros commanded by the veteran *Akagi* fighter pilot Lieutenant Commander Shigeru Itaya. If the American pilots rose to challenge the formation, Itaya's eager boys would bounce them. If none was aloft, the fighters would join the dive bombers in attacking the airfields, strafing with their machine guns and 20-mm. cannon.

That he would be attacking an unwarned foe in peacetime on a Sunday morning aroused in Fuchida no sense of remorse. His God, as he recalled later, "was the Emperor"; his religion, "the Navy and the glory of Japan." He felt no fear, even though he expected to lose perhaps 30 percent of his men. His one concern was to succeed in his assigned mission. As professional Japanese warriors all of the pilots shared their leader's views and determination.

Back on the Japanese carriers, plane handlers already were bringing up from the hangars and muscling into place on the flight decks the second strike of planes, readying them for takeoff an hour after Fuchida's departure. This group, led by Lieutenant Commander Shigekazu Shimazaki, consisted of 170 Kates, Vals, and Zeros targeted against cruisers, destroyers, the American airfields, and—if any were present—aircraft carriers.

At 7:30 A.M., after being airborne for an hour and a half with no break in the clouds, Fuchida suddenly noticed them scattering up ahead. Next he saw a long white line of surf. A few minutes later he was crossing the north coast of Oahu over Kahuku Point exactly as scheduled. Pearl Harbor lay dead ahead across the island's mountains.

Ten minutes later, at 7:30 A.M., Fuchida slid back the hatch of his plane—he was sitting in the observer's center seat and not flying the Kate —and fired one "black dragon" signal flare. This meant "deploy for surprise attack." Moments later, noting that Itaya and the fighters had apparently missed his signal, he fired another. This time Itaya spotted the flare and his Zeros deployed, veering toward their preassigned targets.

Fuchida had almost caused a slip-up. Seeing the second flare and knowing that two "black dragons" meant surprise lost, Commander Takahashi had immediately turned his Val dive bombers toward the airfields. The original plan had called for him to orbit to allow the torpedo planes to go in first with unobstructed runs. Takahashi led a force himself toward Ford Island in Pearl Harbor and nearby Hickam Field. Lieutenant Akira Sakamoto headed another toward the main U. S. fighter base at Wheeler Field in the center of the island. Itaya's Zeros, seeing no enemy planes in the air, followed both groups of Vals, some splitting off to strafe also the Marine base at Ewa and the Navy patrol-plane station at Kaneohe. The first bombs fell almost simultaneously on Hickam and Wheeler fields and on Ford Island, alongside which, in pairs, were moored the battle wagons of the Pacific Fleet.

Hell erupted on the airfields. Screeching to as low as 400 feet, the Vals dropped their bombs on hangars and along the flight lines. At Ford Island parked PBYs leaped and blazed and hangars burst abruptly apart. At Hickam Field circular knots of B-18 bombers, so parked to allow easier guarding against sabotage, tumbled in all directions as bombs landed amidst them. At Wheeler, after circling the field, the Zeros following the dive bombers strafed densely packed rows of P-40s and P-36s, setting afire plane after plane with quick, deadly bursts. In less than 20 minutes most of the planes on all three fields had either been destroyed or so damaged as to be unflyable.

Strafers ruined the Catalinas at Kaneohe and the Marine fighters and scout bombers at Ewa. Lieutenants Suganami and Okajima, commanding nine and six Zeros respectively, circled Ewa in a deadly daisy chain, diving to as low as 20 feet, shooting up one plane after another. In 30 minutes they had destroyed or put out of commission nearly every one of the 49 planes on the field. With no established air defense, unable to get a single plane into the air, the best the Marines could do was to wrench machine guns from damaged SBDs and break out others from ordnance shops, setting them up on fuel drums and other improvised mounts. But Suganami and Okajima were gone before they could hit. At Kaneohe it was, if anything, worse. Eleven Zeros commanded by Lieutenants Kaneko and Sato, aided by some Val dive bombers, destroyed or wrecked every one of the 33 operational patrol planes at the base.

Seeing the dive bombers attacking first and fearing that smoke might obstruct the vision of his torpedo-plane pilots, Commander Murata took a short cut through Oahu's mountains, dropping his torpedo within two minutes after the explosion of the first bomb. One by one, floating in very low and slow from either side of Ford Island, his pilots following released torpedoes equipped with wooden vanes to prevent their diving into the mud of the shallow harbor. Some planes barely cleared the hangars of adjacent Hickam Field. Others dodged around the masts of cruisers, destroyers, and auxiliaries while lining up their runs. Flight Petty Officer Juzo Mori of the *Soryu* flew directly over Ford Island from the north, dodged the foretop of a cruiser, circled the harbor, and dropped his "fish" at the *California*. He then flew directly over the battleship to bank away as instructed to the south, the opposite direction from his carrier. Machine-gun bullets holed his plane but did not bring it down.

Six planes, confused apparently by the flat-deck appearance of the target ship *Utah* and mistaking her for a carrier, wasted their torpedoes on this elderly ex-battleship, capsizing her. But most of the pilots found their preassigned targets and dropped their "tin fish" as precisely as if on a practice run in Kagoshima Bay. Every battleship exposed to torpedoes was hit. So too were cruisers *Helena* and *Raleigh*, anchored near the *Utah* on the other side of Ford Island. Over half of the 40 torpedoes carried scored. Only a plane or two fell before it could drop.

One of the first ships hit was the *Oklahoma*. Five to seven missiles ripped her side wide open below the armor belt, causing her to capsize and bury her masts in Pearl Harbor's mud. *West Virginia* was horribly hurt by at least six and possibly seven hits, but efficient counterflooding enabled her to settle to bottom on nearly an even keel. *California* took only two hits, but these proved enough to sink her also on even keel. *Arizona* took a single hit and *Nevada* another. Nevertheless, this one hit on the *Nevada* ripped in her bow a hole 45 feet long and 30 feet high, attesting to the exceptional power of the warheads of the Japanese torpedoes.

Approaching with his high-level bombers and seeing the explosions below, Commander Fuchida was convinced that the dive bombers and Zeros had caught the enemy by surprise. To the *Akagi* he radioed "*Tora! Tora! Tora!*" (Tiger! Tiger! Tiger!), the prearranged code word meaning "surprise attack successful."

Passing the southern tip of the island at 10,000 feet, Fuchida turned back, leading the Kates in a long line toward Ford Island and battleship row. At 8:05 A.M., preparing to drop, he noted the first ominous puffs of antiaircraft fire. The five-inch guns on the ships below had gone into action far sooner than Fuchida had expected. One plane of Fuchida's five was damaged. Streaming gasoline, it dived toward the harbor, then disintegrated from a direct hit. The other four planes continued and after two passes finally released their heavy bombs at the *Maryland*, one of the battle wagons moored inboard of others and so untouched by torpedoes.

Dropping to the floor of his plane, Fuchida followed the bombs down to note a pair of faint flashes which he took to be direct hits. He, Lieutenant Mitsuo Matsuzaki, his pilot, and radioman Shigenari Mazuki all cheered frantically. Fuchida was correct. Two bombs had hit the *Maryland*. One 1,760-pound (800 kilogram) missile had exploded with a low order of detonation that did little damage; the other had passed into the ship below the waterline to explode—also with a low order of detonation—and flood several compartments.

Moments after Fuchida's Kate had dropped, a tremendous explosion erupted from battleship row. A bomb—either a 1,760-pounder from a Kate or an equally effective 550-pounder (250 kilogram) from a Val— had exploded near the forward magazine of the battleship *Arizona*. It ignited a hot black powder fire that had spread to the magazine. The terrific blast of tons of powder in the magazine caused the ship to appear to leap from the water. It settled back with its forward half wrecked and burning and its foremast toppled forward. Four-fifths of the crew, 1,123 men, perished in an instant. Tremendous fires now spread among the battleships, fed from the *Arizona* and the torpedoed ships, igniting the thick blanket of bunker oil lying on the water.

By about 8:25 most of the attackers of the first wave had left, flying south to clear the island before turning back to their assembly point off the north coast of Oahu. Fuchida and his crew continued to orbit, assessing the damage, waiting for the second strike to arrive.

At 8:20 A.M., about the time Fuchida was finishing his bomb run, Commander Howard Young of the *Enterprise* was passing Barbers Point in his SBD Dauntless. Sight of a squadron of planes circling Ewa stirred his curiosity, but he assumed they were U. S. Army fighters and gave them a wide berth. Years of flying since his graduation from the U. S. Naval Academy in 1923 had made the forty-year-old Young a careful, cautious leader.

Halfway between Ewa and Ford Island, his destination, Young was rudely alerted. A Zero suddenly flashed by him from the rear, guns winking from wings and cowling, bright red ball gleaming on its fuselage. Sight of its insignia brought home to Young an incredible truth. A Japanese fighter of a new, unknown type had attacked him!

Slamming the stick forward, Young sent the dive bomber in a twisting path toward the ground with Ensign Teaff hugging his wing. At 800 feet above sugarcane fields north of Pearl City the pair began to circle. They were, Young realized, in a desperate fix. To climb and engage the enemy fighter would be folly. Nor did he have enough fuel to return to the *Enterprise*. Any course would carry him and Teaff through antiarcraft fire bursting in every direction. Finally, Young decided to stay "on the deck" and fly right through to Ford Island. He made it, landing at 8:35 with antiaircraft machine-gun bullets whizzing all around and through his plane. Teaff landed just behind. A few minutes later other SBDs began landing, thirteen of the eighteen making it safely. Two or three of the others were shot down by Zeros. One Zero fell to the rear-seat guns of Radioman William C. Miller, just before Miller himself was killed by a burst. Miller's pilot, Lieutenant Clarence E. Dickinson, Jr., watched the Zero fall before bailing out of his own flaming plane. American antiaircraft fire downed at least one SBD.

By this time the AA gunners were firing at everything in the air, paying no attention to recognition signals or the shapes and sizes of planes above. They fired at a dozen B-17 heavy bombers from a squadron from California that had the misfortune to arrive during the attack. Though totally surprised, confused, and harassed by Zeros as well as the AA gunners, the Flying Fortress pilots managed to get all of the big four-engined planes down. One landed on a golf course. The others made airfields, though one was strafed and burned at Wheeler and another badly shot up at the end of a short strip at Bellows Field, a subsidiary base the Japanese strafed but did not bomb.

Aside from their brushes with the SBDs and the B-17s, Plan Z had thus far been no contest in the air for Commander Itaya's Zeros. Nothing had risen to challenge them. Nine planes from Fuchida's first attack wave had been shot down, three Zeros, a Val dive bomber, and five Kates, all but two or three by AA fire. Intrepidity had cost one Zero pilot his life. In dropping low to strafe Hickam Field, he hit the ground, crushing his belly tank, then skipped off to crash in the hills beyond the field.

At 8:45 A.M. Lieutenant Commander Shimazaki led in the second attack wave. His strike consisted of 54 Kate horizontal bombers targeted against airfields and 80 Vals assigned to bomb the remaining shipping. Thirty-six Zeros commanded by Lieutenant Saburo Shindo, a veteran of dogfights over China, flew cover, with orders to strafe the airfields in the absence of enemy fighters.

The Kates concentrated on hangars and installations, causing much damage and loss of life among American ground crews at Wheeler, Hickam, Kaneohe, and Ford Island air bases. Many of the Vals, though given cruisers as primary targets, appear to have concentrated on the battleship *Nevada*. This elderly ship, despite the gash in her bow caused by the torpedo, was trying to steam out to sea. The Vals badly hurt her with five hits, setting her afire, threatening her magazines, and forcing Lieutenant Commander Francis J. Thomas, USNR, the senior officer aboard, to beach the ship near Hospital Point to keep her from sinking in the narrow channel.

Other dive bombers went after the unhit flagship of the Pacific Fleet, the battleship *Pennsylvania*, resting in drydock with a pair of destroyers. They got only one hit on the *Pennsy* but blew the bow off the destroyer *Shaw* and wrecked and burned the *Cassin* and *Downes*. But like the other planes of the second strike, they encountered very heavy antiaircraft fire, especially from the now alert cruisers and destroyers in Pearl Harbor. Two groups also encountered fighter opposition.

This came from a pair of well-trained Army pilots, Lieutenants George Welch and Kenneth Taylor. When the attack began both men drove to Haleiwa airstrip, a sod auxiliary field that the Japanese either did not know about or had overlooked. They roared off in formation about 8:30 A.M. in a pair of P-40Bs, planes that could outrun a Zero at low altitude. Over Barbers Point they found nothing, the strafing Zeros having retired from the nearby Ewa area.

Returning to Wheeler Field, they dodged through their own AA fire and landed to get .50-caliber ammunition for their nose guns. Taking off again, they veered right into a string of orbiting Vals. Taylor shot down one and would have been shot down himself by another on his tail had not Welch picked it off. Both then headed again for Barbers Point, found another group of Vals orbiting, and piled in. Welch, a deadly shot, got three and Taylor another.

The pair returned again to Wheeler, where Welch took off a third time with Lieutenant John L. Dains flying wing in a P-36. They found no more of the enemy, but American antiaircraft fire picked off Dains over Schofield Barracks.

Other defenders gave Lieutenant Shindo's escorting Zeros at least one good scrap. Shindo's antagonists were five obsolescent P-36 fighters that had managed to get into the air from Wheeler Field at 8:50 A.M. Climbing to 8,000 feet, as steeply as their slow planes would allow, they plunged into a formation of nine Zeros near Bellows Field. Lieutenants

Lewis M. Sanders and Philip M. Rasmussen each bagged an enemy, but one Zero, a dogfight machine without peer, flipped into the tail of Lieutenant Gordon H. Sterling, Jr., and shot him down. Sterling was the fourth Army fighter pilot killed that day, the others being Dains and two brave airmen downed by strafers while trying to take off in P-40s from Bellows Field.

In all, Commander Shimazaki's second wave of attackers lost 20 planes, six Zeros and 14 Vals. Lieutenant Fusata Iida of the *Soryu,* a battle-hardened veteran of three years of the China war, deliberately dove his plane onto Kaneohe Air Station. Antiaircraft had holed his fuel tanks. Knowing that he could not get back to the carrier, Iida had elected to become the war's first Kamikaze. Before departure Iida, an only child, had written to his mother, "Please don't weep if I die in battle. Take good care of yourself and live to a ripe old age."

Last to leave were Fuchida and his crew, who headed north at about 10:00 A.M. They returned to the *Akagi,* landing aboard at 1:00 P.M.

Fuchida left behind massive ruin. Of his main targets the battleships *Oklahoma* and *Arizona* were finished, wrecked beyond repair. *West Virginia, California,* and *Nevada* were so damaged and burned that each had to be refloated and rebuilt. Only *Maryland, Tennessee,* and *Pennsylvania* were lightly damaged and quickly repairable.

The airfields had been hit so hard that no possibility remained of flying a thorough search for the enemy carriers. Most of the Army's 231 aircraft had been destroyed or damaged. Not one Marine combat plane was serviceable, and the Navy had only a handful of patrol planes plus the surviving *Enterprise* scout bombers.

Just one American combat organization remained in the Hawaii area capable of attacking the enemy. This was the bulk of Air Group 6 aboard the *Enterprise.* But no one on the Big E, from Admiral Bill Halsey on down, knew where the Japanese were. Nor could Pearl Harbor tell him. Halsey therefore operated his task force near Kaula Rock about 160 miles westward of Pearl Harbor all day December 7, ready to strike either north or south of Oahu as soon as he located the enemy.

He missed two vital cues. The first came from the *Enterprise's* newly installed radar. It picked up blips over Oahu at 288,000 yards—more than 160 statute miles from *Enterprise*—that probably were Japanese planes. Later, the operators tracked some of the blips to the northward of Oahu. But at this stage no one had much experience with the radar or confidence in it. Consequently, Halsey did not launch either a search or his air group due north of Oahu. Had he done so his scouts might have encountered at extreme range Nagumo's retiring carriers.

Another cue was missed for want of timely reporting. Among other reconnaissance planes dispatched by Halsey's task force were a pair of small, slow SOC float planes catapulted from the heavy cruiser *Northampton.* Their mission was to search a vector out to 150 miles to the northward. Fifteen miles west of Kauai, a major Hawaiian island west and slightly north of Oahu, a Zero fighter suddenly attacked them at 11:35 A.M. It made seven passes at the biplane SOCs, which maintained tight formation and made easy turns at 80 knots to give the gunners good aim from their rear seats. The Zero pilot hit one plane 14 times and the other 11, but on his last pass he "squashed" down above the SOCs and was himself hard hit. He left steaming smoke. Both scouts continued their search out to 150 miles, but neither spotted the carriers or any more Zeros. Halsey did not learn of their adventure until the next day.

On his return to the *Akagi* Commander Fuchida went first to the carrier's ready room to see his pilots, then to the bridge of the flagship to see Admiral Nagumo. There he found the entire staff awaiting his report. His friend, Commander Minoru Genda, wore a broad smile.

Yet Fuchida sensed a note of discord. He realized that the staff had been arguing heatedly among themselves about the advisability of rearming the planes and launching a third strike. Quickly he related his estimate of damage: four battleships sunk, all others hit, at least 250 enemy planes destroyed. Then: "It would be unwise to assume we have destroyed everything. There are still many targets remaining which should be hit. I recommend that another attack be launched."

Nods made it obvious that many of the staff agreed. Pearl Harbor held dozens of ships, including five cruisers and twenty-nine destroyers that had not been damaged. Also, the prize target of all, the oil-tank farm at the naval base, stood exposed and helpless within sight of burning battleship row. Its destruction and a heavy bombing of the drydocks and repair shops might have prevented all American naval operations for months. The Kates and Vals could attack these targets assured of virtually no fighter opposition.

Though he looked at Fuchida admiringly, Nagumo did not answer his junior's plea. Instead he asked him to recount once again his list of damage. Then at 1:30 P.M. he ordered the First Air Fleet to retire to Japan. "We may conclude that anticipated results have been achieved."

Probably Nagumo's strongest reason for leaving was to avoid damage to his own force. He had performed his mission as a Samurai; he had attacked Pearl Harbor successfully against his better judgment with the remarkably low loss of just 29 planes and 55 air crew. That was quite enough.

In terms of traditional sea power Pearl Harbor was a crushing Japanese victory. If World War I-class slow battleships were to be the naval backbone of a Pacific war, then the operation could be accounted a complete success. Japan had halved the strength of the American battle line for more than a year to come. But if the carrier with its deadly air group was to be the decisive weapon, then the Pearl Harbor attack had been literally "no contest." No American carrier had been sunk because none was present.

In their initial flush of victory few Japanese, not even Admiral Yamamoto, could see the Pearl Harbor outcome in perspective. Nor could the Americans clearly assess it in the sting and humiliation of the worst naval defeat in their national history.

2. Sticks, Wires, and Former Battle Cruisers

Summertime dawn came early to the crew of the H. M. S. *Furious* as the carrier plowed through the North Sea toward the German coast. A converted battle cruiser of 22,450 tons, *Furious* was the world's first true aircraft carrier. Clustered on its forward flying platfom were seven flimsy stick-and-wire Sopwith Camels with a 50-pound bomb attached to either lower wing. A group of Royal Flying Corps officers, sheepskin-coated and goggled, were moving toward the little biplane fighters preparatory to taking off. "Attack the Zeppelin sheds at Tondern," their orders read. This day, July 19, 1918, they would try.

Soon after 3:00 A.M. the Camels wobbled up from the racing *Furious,* a flight of three leading, a second of four following, and headed toward the coastline of northern Germany. But soon the trailing flight also numbered three. One of the unreliable Clerget engines sputtered, stopped, and a Camel glided into the North Sea. A nearby destroyer peeled off to rescue the pilot.

First to arrive was Captain F. W. Dickson. Near Tondern he spotted a huge, half-buried structure and dropped a 50-pounder. Banking away, he looked back and saw a flash, some smoke, but no other effect. Probably, he realized, he had bombed a humble potato storage shed. Glancing upward and ahead, he saw Captain W. D. Jackson and Lieutenant N. E. Williams diving toward a pair of huge wooden structures five miles to the north. He opened throttle and climbed to join their attack.

Arriving first, Jackson released two bombs into the northernmost of the big hangars. Dickson and Williams added three more. Flames burst from the shed, then erupted into a hydrogen-fed ball of fire that shot a thousand feet into the air, marking the end of German naval airships L.54 and L.60.

For the Camel pilots the flight back was disastrous. Unable either to rendezvous or to locate the *Furious* in the gathering mist, three flew into neutral Denmark and internment. A fourth, Lieutenant W. A. Yeulett, spun into the North Sea and vanished, the victim, probably, of vertigo. Only Dickson and Captain B. A. Smart reached the carrier, Smart electing to ditch alongside a destroyer for rescue rather than to try a landing on its after landing platform. Nevertheless, though deeply regretted, the loss of four pilots had been a cheap price for the British Admiralty to pay for the L.54 and L.60. By any standard the world's first carrier air strike had been a success.

United States naval officers had noted with great interest the success of the *Furious* in the Tondern raid. After the First World War had ended, in order to have a carrier as soon as possible, they agreed to the conversion of the collier *Jupiter* into a carrier. She was slow (14 knots) and inferior to the *Furious* either for flying strikes or scouting missions, but she could mount a 500-foot full-length flight deck, and the high headroom of her coal holds offered possibilities for storing and repairing aircraft. But to nonflying Navy line officers she looked odd indeed, with a flat wooden deck and no superstructure at all, not even a rudimentary island. At a loss to think how else to describe her, they dubbed her "the Covered Wagon." Officially, on recommissioning on March 20, 1922, she became the U. S. S. *Langley*, CV-1.

In the meantime, while *Langley* was converting in early 1922, a naval disarmament conference had been meeting in Washington, D.C. At its conclusion each of the three major participants—the United States, Great Britain, and Japan—were allowed to convert two big gunnery ships each into fast fleet carriers. The British were allotted the *Courageous* and *Glorious*, former battle cruisers the size of the *Furious*. The Japanese were allowed to convert the *Akagi*, also started as a battle cruiser, and the *Kaga*, begun as a battleship. The United States was authorized to convert the *Saratoga* and *Lexington*, large battle cruisers with hulls 30 percent complete. This outcome was welcomed in all three nations as a money-saver; in fact, it probably increased expense. The conference also allowed each of the powers enough additional tonnage to build a limited number of new carriers.

Until *Lexington* and *Saratoga* were ready, a process consuming nearly six years, *Langley*, the "Covered Wagon," served as the only U. S. flattop. For three years it rested mostly at dockside while tedious experiments tested almost every imaginable type of arresting gear for landing aircraft aboard. Favored at first was a system of horizontal wires laid port to starboard across the stern like a series of tenement wash lines. The trouble was that when a plane landed "out of the groove"—that is, to one or the other side of the flight deck—the uneven pull of the wire was likely to swerve the plane to the side. Finally, a hydraulic mechanism was devised capable of compensating for the uneven drag, and by 1927 the system was sufficiently reliable to dispense entirely with longitudinal wires.

In Fleet Problem V of 1925, the fifth of 20-odd annual U. S. Navy fleet exercises conducted between World Wars I and II, the *Langley* earned a "well done" for launching ten planes in 13 minutes. Yet it was clear to all that the Covered Wagon's 14-knot speed was too slow for fleet work.

The entire U. S. Navy, not just the aviators, now waited impatiently for the big new *Lex* and *Sara* to finish training their air groups.

Saratoga had run up her commissioning pennant on November 16, 1927, at the yard of the New York Shipbuilding Company at Camden, New Jersey. *Lexington* followed just 29 days later on December 15. Both had proven to be tremendously costly, consuming a whopping $44,000,000 each. The big sisters displaced 36,000 tons, had flight decks 106 feet wide and over 800 feet long, and could carry 83 planes each. Both also had eight eight-inch guns in four twin turrets mounted fore and aft of a huge funnel and island superstructure on their starboard sides. Everything aboard them ran by electricity—their galleys, their two elevators apiece to carry planes to and from the hangar deck to the flight deck, even the windlass and steering gear. Twelve five-inch guns mounted in bays along each side of the flight deck furnished protection against enemy planes.

Because the big flattops retained their battle-cruiser machinery, both were very fast. In late 1928, with her engines turning out 209,710 horse-power—well above her designed power of 180,000—the *Lex* slammed through swells off San Pedro, California, at 34.82 knots. Not to be out-done, the *Sara* shaved the *Lexington*'s world speed record for big ships the next month by reaching 34.99 knots with her steam turbines putting out 213,000 horsepower.

The early morning of January 25, 1929, found the *Saratoga* speeding easily through whitecapped Pacific swells at 30 knots. Receding in the distance behind her were the Galapagos Islands, fabled for iguanas, giant tortoises, and variously evolved Darwin finches. Four days before at 8:00 A.M. *Sara* had left behind her accompanying force of battleships, the main body of a "Black" aggressor force, and now was nearing her launching point for a surprise attack on the Panama Canal. The "Black" commander, astute Admiral William V. Pratt, had accepted the advice of his aviators: He was sending the flattop on a long "end run" around the "Blue" defenders. Pratt hoped that by approaching the canal from the south the *Saratoga* would escape detection and that its planes could bomb the Miraflores and Pedro Miguel locks. To put the canal out of business was the main task of his "Black" aggressors.

Saratoga had on board her own and the *Langley*'s planes. She carried 54 stubby Boeing F2B and F3B biplane fighter-bombers, 18 cumbersome Martin T4M torpedo-bombers, and 15 reliable Vought 02U scouts. To press home an attack on the canal these planes would have to overwhelm 13 Army biplane fighters.

Some 90 miles from the entrance to the canal, the *Saratoga* launched a striking force of 30 fighters, 17 fighter-bombers, and three radio-communication planes. Escorted by the fighters, the bombers flew to their targets undetected. Over the Miraflores locks the Boeings hurtled into vertical dives from 9,000 feet to pull out with Wasp engines howling at 500 feet. They streaked on at low altitude to strafe with blank ammunition

Fort Clayton, the coast artillery base, and nearby Albrook airfield. One pilot, Lieutenant James H. Carrington, dropped in addition to his "administrative" bomb a real airmail letter addressed to his wife back home in San Diego.

Near Panama City some of the F3Bs met 12 Army fighters and engaged them in a tumbling, swirling dogfight. After outmaneuvering and outclimbing their antagonists, they joined the retiring bombers and returned to the *Saratoga*.

The *Saratoga*'s attack had been a success. It had demonstrated the ability of an air group from a carrier to deliver an overwhelming surprise attack on a key objective. It had also demonstrated the Navy's confidence in its radial, air-cooled engines and the ability of its planes to mix it up with land-based fighters. Just one plane had to ditch, a fighter that had lost fuel pressure and had landed in the ocean alongside the *Saratoga*. Rescuers had picked up Lieutenant (jg) M. E. Arnold unharmed.

But the exercise had also illustrated inadvertently the great vulnerability of a carrier. While maneuvering and waiting to recover her planes, the *Saratoga* through a navigational error had blundered onto a division of defending "Blue" battleships. Three "took her under fire" at short range and, in the opinion of the accompanying umpire, "sank" her. A few minutes later she ran afoul of a "Blue" submarine that administratively "launched" four torpedoes from only 1,200 yards' range. Before the morning had ended planes from her sister ship *Lexington*, operating with the "Blue" fleet, found her and dive-bombed her flight deck. *Saratoga* theoretically sank for the third time in one day. In actual combat it seemed likely that a carrier's life would be eventful but short.

Subsequent fleet problems confirmed the workability of the carrier task-force concept, the relative vulnerability of the carrier as compared to other ships, and the need for many more in the fleet. After Fleet Problem XI in 1930, Vice Admiral Cyrus W. Cole commented that a carrier task group should ideally consist of a flattop, four cruisers, and eight destroyers.

Yet never in any U. S. fleet exercise did more than two carriers operate together. Carriers usually operated in single-ship task forces. This led Rear Admiral Harry E. Yarnell to comment in 1932 that most engagements inevitably degenerated into an attempt by each force to "get" the other's flattop. For a trans-Pacific war, he noted, the United States would need at least six. Were the enemy to use six fleet carriers in a single mass strike, he warned, grave harm could be done to any U. S. installation from San Diego to Bremerton. He reiterated what already had become a standard refrain: The Pacific Fleet needed more carriers.

Getting them proved to be extraordinarily difficult despite the clearly seen and accepted need. Congress had grudgingly accepted in February 1929 a Navy General Board request for a small flattop numbered CV-4 (*Langley* was CV-1, *Lex* and *Sara* CVs 2 and 3) and then had balked at more. Nor was this ship fully satisfactory when finally commissioned in

1934 as the U. S. S. *Ranger*. At 14,500 tons it was less than half the size of the *Saratoga* and had a top speed of only 29 knots. Stringent need to reduce costs had reduced its elevator capacity and ammunition storage and had eliminated the deck catapults. Although its plane capacity of 75 equaled the other carriers and it had an efficient arresting gear, the *Ranger*'s deficiencies induced the Navy to confine her combat to the Atlantic throughout World War II.

Experience with the *Ranger* disillusioned the General Board with small carriers. In 1932 the Board asked for two 20,000-ton ships, the minimum effective size for a flattop, it now believed. The request failed, but the next spring a former Assistant Secretary of the Navy was in the White House. President Franklin D. Roosevelt diverted already voted Public Works Administration emergency relief funds for the construction of CVs 5 and 6, named on launching in 1936 the *Yorktown* and *Enterprise*. Both were fine ships of nearly 20,000 tons, with good underwater protection, 32-knot speeds, three elevators, and hangar decks devoted exclusively to plane stowage. Their flight decks, like those on the *Langley* and *Ranger*, were of teakwood mounted on a steel frame. Armored flight decks, the Bureau of Ships had concluded, would reduce plane capacity and add so much top weight as to jeopardize stability.

The General Board had now run out of carrier tonnage permitted by the Washington Treaty. Reducing the slow *Langley* to tender status, however, would leave approximately 15,000 tons of the 135,000 available for use. The Board in 1934 therefore approved one more ship of an improved *Ranger* type, CV-7. It became the U. S. S. *Wasp*. Long delayed in both design and construction, the *Wasp* did not commission until April 1940. Nevertheless, in terms of "bang for the buck," the Navy had come up with a winner. On a displacement of only 14,700 tons *Wasp* had the speed of the bigger carriers, embarked an air group as large, and would compile a brilliant war record in a short career in World War II.

In 1935, with four carriers in commission, counting *Langley*, and three more authorized or building, the General Board dropped all consideration of new flattops. It planned only to replace the *Lex* and *Sara* when the ex-battle cruisers reached their age limits in the late 1940s. Neither Japan's announcement of intent to disregard treaty limits nor its aggressive move in China in 1937 produced any change in the Board's decision even after the Washington Treaty had expired at the end of 1936. The Board stood pat until May 17, 1938, when Congress finally authorized a 20 percent increase in the Navy above the treaty limit, boosting allowable carrier tonnage to 175,000. Thus prodded—and with great reluctance— the Board authorized one ship similar to the *Enterprise* and *Yorktown*, recording huffily while doing so that it was ". . . not in favor of constructing this carrier at this time." Thus was the last of America's prewar flattops, U. S. S. *Hornet*, CV-8, more or less forced on the U. S. Navy. The Board could have allowed a second new ship like *Hornet*, but it wanted an improved new design not yet ready in 1938. The new ship would belatedly appear as the U. S. S. *Essex*.

Without fanfare but with a single-minded determination characteristic of their nation, the Japanese seized the world's leadership in naval aviation following World War I. With resources inferior to both the British and the Americans, with less industrial capacity, the Japanese carried on a much greater aviation program. By the mid-1930s they had conducted more experimentation, had built more planes and ships than either of their future antagonists.

Japanese carrier aviation began with the commissioning of I. J. S. *Hosho*, a little flush-decked ship of 7,470 tons and 25 knots ordered in 1919 and completed on December 27, 1922. Though small, the *Hosho* could carry 26 planes. Used mostly for training before and during World War II, the *Hosho* served well its initial purpose of providing experience invaluable in the construction of later ships. She was also employed in much the same manner as the *Langley* in annual fleet problems remarkably similar to those of the U. S. Navy.

Japan's naval leaders had swallowed in bitterness the Washington arms-limitation agreement. This restricted the tonnage of Japan's battleships and carriers to three-fifths the total of tonnage of either the British or the Americans. Yet Japanese naval aviation and even the Japanese Navy in general benefited from the Washington Treaty. Japan could not hope to win a naval-tonnage race with the United States, and the treaty did make available the surplus, incomplete hulls of the *Kaga* and *Akagi*.

Both were enormous ships. At 38,200 tons standard displacement the *Kaga* was the largest flattop in the world. Not much smaller was the *Akagi* at 36,500 tons. Both were thus larger than America's contemporary *Lexington* and *Saratoga*. To the world the Japanese Navy Department blandly announced the tonnage of the ships as 26,900 tons each, a gross fabrication. But the world chose to accept it, enabling the Japanese to save nearly 21,000 tons of the tonnage allocated by the Washington Treaty. *Akagi* was completed in March 1927, *Kaga* a year later.

Neither at first equaled their American rivals as floating airfields, being capable of operating only about 60 planes apiece. The Japanese nonidentical twins bore a marked resemblance to Britain's *Furious*, with no islands and upper and lower flight decks terminating well short of their bows. At great cost both had to be removed from service and rebuilt, *Kaga* in 1935 and *Akagi* two years later. The lower flying decks were suppressed in favor of single flight decks as on the *Lex* and *Sara*, plane capacity was increased to about 90 planes each, including spares, and smallish island structures were added, starboard side on *Kaga*, port side on *Akagi*. Because of her battle-cruiser origin, *Akagi* shaded *Kaga* in speed, 31 knots to 28 for her half-sister. Like the United States, Imperial Japan had invested much in just two ships.

By 1931 the Japanese Navy had *Hosho*, *Kaga*, and *Akagi* in service and was completing a fourth carrier. This latter was the *Ryujo*, a light ship of 10,600 tons that could nevertheless fly off the remarkable total of 46 aircraft. Japan also had 17 naval aircraft squadrons and 284 naval aircraft in service—more than the strength of Britain's Fleet Air Arm nearly a decade later. Already, by seizing Manchuria from China in 1931, Japanese military authorities had embarked on a course of national expansion that would culminate in total war.

The Manchurian campaign of 1931 coincided with the first of six Naval Rearmament Replenishment Plans adopted by the Japanese Admiralty prior to World War II. In the first two the Naval Staff strove to complete the build-up of the Navy to the maximum allowable by the Washington Treaty. In the last four—implemented after treaty limitations had expired on December 31, 1936—its intent was to keep pace with U. S. naval expansion. In neither of the first two plans could Japan build battleships. Enough treaty tonnage remained, however, to allow Japan to lay down two more aircraft carriers. These were the *Soryu* and *Hiryu*, listed as displacing 10,050 tons each. This combined total of 20,100 tons coincided precisely with the remaining aircraft-carrier tonnage allowed Japan by treaty. As commissioned, however, *Soryu* was 15,900 tons and *Hiryu* 17,300, large enough for each to carry 73 planes and operate as a fleet carrier. On completion the *Soryu* and *Hiryu* would give Japan four large fleet carriers (CVs) and two light carriers (CVLs), at least matching the anticipated U. S. total.

In comparison to contemporary British and American flyers, Japanese air crewmen drilled ruthlessly hard. One reason was the attitude of an ambitious rear admiral, Isoroku Yamamoto. As the commander of an air flotilla in 1930 and later as head of the Navy's technical arm during the next several years, Yamamoto demanded and had gradually obtained excellence from his flyers. He once told a group of pilots, "The Japanese fleet lags a long way behind the West. . . . That is why I regard death in training the same as a hero's death in action. The Japanese spirit should not fear death." In his coat pocket he always carried a notebook containing the names of men killed under his command in training. He also had his pilots salute a list of deceased comrades before every takeoff. The list was long. Takeoffs and landings from carriers took many lives, as did flights over water in single-engined aircraft.

As early as December 1934 Japan had announced her intention of ignoring the arms clauses of the Washington Treaty after December 31, 1936, the date of the treaty's expiration. The denunciation was followed by the assassination by Army extremists of an octogenarian finance minister hostile to increased military appropriations and by attempts on the lives of other civil officials believed to be opposed to military and naval expansion. A new cabinet took office in March 1936, pledged to begin full-scale preparations to conquer China. Japan was about to test her carriers and naval aviation in the crucible of battle.

3. American, Japanese, and British Naval Air Power

On August 17, 1937, Lieutenant Commander Iwai, commanding the air group of I. J. S. *Kaga,* roared down her flight deck in his ponderous Type 89 biplane torpedo bomber. Eleven others followed, their mission to blast Chinese airfields at Hangchow on the China mainland. The Sino-Japanese "incident"—in reality a full-fledged war—had begun. The Japanese Navy's mission was to transport troops to China, to carry out landing operations, and to join with the Japanese Army Air Force in destroying Generalissimo Chiang Kai-shek's Chinese Air Force.

That Japan's naval air arm was not yet fully ready for combat became apparent when only one of Iwai's 12 bombers returned. Only Lieutenant Tanaka landed aboard the *Kaga,* his Type 89 splattered with bullet holes. China's defending miscellany of fighters—Curtiss Hawk IIIs, Boeing export model P-26s, British-made Gloster Gladiators, and Russian-built I-15s and I-16s—had won the first round. Lost with ten of his fellow pilots was Commander Iwai. The disaster happened, Lieutenant Tanaka told his superiors, because the bomber squadron had failed to rendezvous with its protecting fighters and had attacked unescorted.

Protected missions were flown later from the *Kaga* and from the smaller *Ryujo* and *Hosho* (*Akagi* was still reconstructing), but these did not turn out well, either. The *Kaga's* Type 90 biplane fighters were highly maneuverable but slower than many of the Chinese planes. The *Kaga* therefore hurried back to Sasebo to embark the Mitsubishi company's new Type 96 (A5M1), later code-named "Claude" by American intelligence.

The trim little Claude had been test-flown in 1935 but was so revolutionary that the Navy's leaders had hesitated to order it into production. Many veteran pilots dismissed it because it was a low-wing monoplane and less maneuverable than the Type 90 biplane. It also was all-metal, flush-riveted, and had a split flap to reduce its landing speed. With a 750-hp engine the Claude could make 281 mph, much more speed than any other carrier fighter then flying. It had a nonretractable but trim and neatly designed landing gear. To a superlative degree the Claude possessed three of the essentials of a champion fighter plane. Besides being fast it had excellent acceleration to high speed and could outclimb anything else flying. Its only serious weaknesses were its relatively short cruising radius and light construction.

Equipped with a squadron of these formidable little machines, the *Kaga* steamed resolutely back into action. On September 18 its air group raided the main Chinese airfield complex near Nanking. The next day 12 Claudes commanded by Lieutenant Yamashita piled into a formation of more than 20 Curtiss Hawks and Russian-built I-15s and I-16s over Nanking. The first large-scale air-to-air battle fought in Asia erupted and ended with the Japanese pilots claiming 14 confirmed kills of Chinese planes against no losses of their own.

This one strike quite literally broke the neck of Chiang Kai-shek's painfully accumulated Chinese Air Force. In the next few weeks the *Kaga* pilots struck ten times more at the Nanking complex, forcing their enemy to resort to hit-and-run tactics. The *Kaga*'s Second Combined Air Flotilla had flown 291 sorties and had destroyed 42 planes. The Japanese public had an authentic hero in Flight Petty Officer Koga, who had downed four Chinese planes in two engagements.

The performance of the *Kaga*'s Claudes had ended the debate between the rival advocates of the maneuverable biplane and the fast monoplane. From henceforth the monoplane was supreme in the Japanese naval service.

The China "incident" in the months that followed seemed to vindicate Japanese naval-aviation doctrine and practice. It proved the value of carrier air power but by no means suggested the obsolescence of surface warships. Combat losses after the opening days of the Shanghai campaign were light, but operational accidents were numerous, and aircraft production in Japan was much too low. Also, too few pilots were being trained. Until the outbreak of World War II the Japanese Navy's qualifications for naval air cadets and its attrition rate in flying school remained the world's highest, and its pilot reserves—partly in consequence—were relatively low.

When young Saburo Sakai, destined to become Japan's leading surviving ace, entered training in late 1937 at Tsuchiura near Tokyo, he discovered that only 70 of more than 1,500 aspirants had been accepted. Before his arduous ten-month course had ended, 45 of his class had been "washed out," many for reasons totally unrelated to flying. In his training Sakai swam 50 meters under water and clung by one arm from a pole for 20 minutes. His experience illustrates why as few as 100 pilots a year became full-fledged naval aviators in the mid and late 1930s, nowhere near enough for an adequate war reserve.

A few air-power zealots in Japan of junior rank, Minoru Gerda included, argued for a massive build-up of carrier-based and land-based air power at the expense of surface-ship construction. But of high-ranking officers only Admiral Yamamoto, in 1937 the deputy chief of the Naval General Staff, appears to have partially favored their ideas. Though already powerful because of his charismatic personality, Yamamoto could not by himself transfer emphasis from the battleship to the carrier in Japan's future building plans; probably he did not want to.

In her Third Replenishment Plan covering the period from March 1937 to March 1942 Japan emphasized the construction of gunnery ships heretofore banned by treaty. The core of the plan centered around two monster new battleships, the *Yamato* and *Musashi*. Each weighed in at 64,000 tons standard displacement, was heavily armored, and carried nine 18.1-inch guns as its main battery, an armament vastly superior in hitting power to the nine 16-inch weapons projected for the new U. S. S. *Washington* about to start building in the United States.

For air power the Third Plan projected 14 more air squadrons for a total of 53 and carriers *Shokaku* and *Zuikaku*. This projection of but two carriers constituted a firm rebuttal of Genda's ideas. The Japanese Naval Staff preferred a policy of only maintaining parity with the U. S. in flat-tops. As the staff saw it, the carrier might or might not be an all-important weapon. Probably it would not, and unless war experience proved otherwise, the battleship must remain the supreme weapon of naval warfare. Thus the Naval Staff's reasoning in Tokyo was precisely that of the General Board's in Washington. Nevertheless, the *Shokaku* and *Zuikaku* represented the optimum in Japanese carrier design. At 25,675 tons standard displacement apiece, each was more than 5,000 tons larger than America's new *Enterprise* and *Yorktown*. Each could carry 96 aircraft, including spares, and steam at the very high speed of 34 knots.

In addition to designing the *Shokaku* and *Zuikaku*, the Imperial Navy's technical branch had already ordered some excellent new carrier planes, worthy monoplane successors to the revolutionary little Claude. First of a trio that would be standard by 1941 was the Nakajima Type 97 B5N1, an "attack" plane that represented a milestone in torpedo-bomber development. Combining high speed with a thousand-mile range and excellent flight characteristics, the Type 97 (Allied code name "Kate") entered service in 1937. This sleek-looking low-wing plane would imperil any ship afloat when armed with Japan's reliable Type 91 1,764-pound, 21-inch aerial torpedo. Like all planes produced that early, the Kate lacked armor and self-sealing tanks.

An effective dive bomber was the Aichi company's D3A1, the bat-winged Type 99 "Val." It entered service in 1939, two years after the Kate. This rugged and reliable monoplane approximated Nazi Germany's notorious Stuka in performance. With a 550-pound bomb it touched 241 mph at 9,000 feet. As a fleet scout it could fly 1,250 miles, far enough for normal carrier operations.

The Nakajima A6M—Zero-sen to its pilots, "Zeke" to its Allied foes—was an altogether exceptional airplane, the world's first true strategic fighter. Its better than 1,200-mile range, twice that of contemporary American fighters, may well have been an essential precondition for the Pearl

Harbor attack. Had not the Zero been capable of covering from Taiwan General MacArthur's Luzon-based American Air Force in the Philippines, Yamamoto might have been forced to use his fleet carriers for the task, thus abandoning his project of striking at Pearl.

The Zero's short fuselage and light wing-loading made it equal— or nearly so—to the Claude in maneuverability. Trim lines and low drag gave it 320 mph at 15,000 feet. Its armament was heavy, a pair of machine guns in the nose and a 20-mm cannon in each wing. Like the Claude, it had excellent acceleration and climb. Its Sakae radial engine of close to a thousand horsepower was beautifully fitted to the fuselage and was reliable in performance and easy to maintain. Of all the fighters in the Pacific at the outbreak of war, the Zero was probably the only machine that could approach the performance of Britain's Spitfire or Germany's Me-109.

The Zero nevertheless had serious weaknesses. At the insistence of Japan's aggressive fighter pilots, its designer, thirty-eight-year-old Jiro Horikoshi, had not incorporated armor or self-sealing tanks. These would have added weight and reduced performance. Scorning these as defensive, the pilots wanted the maximum speed, climb, and firepower attainable from the airframe and engine. Consequently, the Zero was lightly built, unable to withstand either heavy battle damage or a terminal velocity dive and sharp pullout.

In 1939 and 1940 the Japanese Naval Staff authorized two additional *Yamato*-class battleships and many more cruisers, destroyers, and submarines but only one new carrier. This was the 29,300-ton *Taiho*, a remarkable vessel that featured an armored flight deck, a 33-knot speed, and a planned complement of 94 planes. The staff planners realized that they risked losing the lead in carriers to the American Navy, but they reckoned that any probable U. S. increase in flattops could be offset—if necessary— by converting merchant ships and fleet tenders into acceptable fleet carriers. Their future moves would be geared to American decisions.

Also, the Japanese Naval Staff was taking less risk than it might seem, even in retrospect. In 1938–39 the U. S. Navy's General Board—despite the China incident and the imminence of war in Europe—was envisaging only four more carriers for the *entire decade* of the 1940s. One, of a new 27,000-ton *Essex* class, would be completed in 1943, two in 1945, and one more in 1946. And two of these would merely replace the overage *Sara* and *Lex*. The Board was satisfied if the number of U. S. flattops should roughly equal Japan's in tonnage. Like the Japanese, it was much more interested in battleships, which it still regarded as the backbone of the fleet, and was projecting 15 more of three new classes. U. S. Navy airpower enthusiasts had a good case for their heated accusations that the conservative Board seemed to be much more interested in battleships than in carriers.

In common with most U. S. aviators, veteran flyer Captain Marc A. Mitscher, destined to become the first skipper of the new *Hornet*, had long been more concerned by the scarcity of pilots than of carriers. Important legislators fortunately had shared his concern, and Congress had passed in 1935 an act authorizing Naval Aviation Cadets. No longer must a flyer be a Naval Academy graduate or long-service professional. On graduating from a recognized college or university a physically qualified young man could apply for aviation training at the Navy's flying school at Pensacola, Florida. Graduating as a naval aviator, he would serve three years on active duty with the fleet before entering the Naval Reserve. By mid-1936 the initial 50 cadets had completed training, a vanguard of thousands to follow. The U. S. Navy was not committing Japan's error—training too few.

In 1937, while the Japanese were putting the Claude into service, the U. S. Navy was finally replacing its reliable Boeing F4B fighters with another biplane, the stubby Grumman F2F "flying barrel." Equipped with a more powerful engine and a retractable landing gear, the F2F could outrun the 188-mph Boeing F4B-4. But a 280-mph Claude monoplane would have left it far behind at any altitude.

The first monoplane ordered by the U. S. Navy, ironically enough, was its least successful one. In 1937 the carrier torpedo squadrons exchanged their sturdy old Great Lakes TG-2 biplanes for the Douglas TBD Devastator, a three-seat monoplane featuring a partly retractable landing gear and a huge, broad low wing. Though of the same vintage as the Japanese Kate, the inappropriately named Devastator was inferior in every respect. Whereas the Nakajima plane could reach 229 mph at 7,000 feet— roughly the speed of the F2F fighter—the Douglas plane could reach less than 200 mph at a similar altitude. The Kate had more than double the range of the Devastator, which could fly at most 450 statute miles with a torpedo or 700 with bombs. Fortunately, a high-performance replacement was at hand in 1941. Prior to Pearl Harbor day the Grumman company had tested its TBF Avenger and would deliver 145 of these speedy, powerful replacements during the first half of 1942.

In 1938 Jack Northrop, a brilliant aircraft designer, offered the Bureau of Aeronautics another monoplane, the BT-1 dive bomber. As extensively redesigned by the Douglas company and put into mass production, it became the famous SBD Dauntless, a plane easily the peer of Aichi's Val though slower to enter service. In December 1941 the SBD-3 was aboard most U. S. carriers. It had a top speed of about 250 mph and a range with bomb load of about 1,300 statute miles. Like Val, the SBD-3 lacked self-sealing gasoline tanks.

The "Iron Works"—as the Grumman company came to be nicknamed because of the sturdiness of its products—finally saved the day for the U. S. Navy in fighters. By 1938 the Navy had belatedly recognized that any biplane, no matter how powerful, simply could not keep pace with a monoplane of equal power. It had therefore turned to a company new to the aviation business, Brewster, for its first monoplane fighter, the chunky F2A Buffalo. Though capable of a fairly good performance by 1938 standards in both speed and maneuverability—the Buffalo could outrun a Claude—the relatively light Buffalo rapidly deteriorated in fighting qualities when weighted down with armor, extra guns, and radio equipment. Also, when tested aboard the *Lexington* by the veteran enlisted pilots of Fighting Squadron 2, its undercarriage proved too tender for the slam-bang landings normal to carrier operations.

Grumman, in competition with Brewster, had originally submitted a biplane design for its F4F Wildcat fighter. But realizing that the plane would lack speed, Roy Grumman had hurriedly ordered his designers to revamp the F4F as a monoplane featuring a sturdy barrel fuselage and retractable landing gear that folded into the belly. The result was no Zero, no optimum design, but the Wildcat equaled the Buffalo's speed and proved more maneuverable than the Brewster's overweight versions. The Wildcat also carried two-stage supercharging for its Twin-Wasp R-1830 engine, giving it good performance between 15,000 and 20,000 feet. The Wildcat's top speed about equaled the Zero's at altitude, but it had much less acceleration, speed of climb, and maneuverability when compared with Jiro Horikoshi's lightweight fighter, especially low down. But a Wildcat could outdive a Zero from any height, carried a heavier armament of four to six .50-caliber machine guns, and with its rugged airframe could withstand much greater punishment. Like the Zero, early models lacked armor and self-sealing tanks.

By the time of Pearl Harbor nearly all fighter squadrons aboard carriers were flying the F4F-3 Wildcat. Only the enlisted "Chiefs" of Fighting 2 aboard the *Lexington* still were flying the Buffalo.

Wise indeed was the man who coined the phrase "airplanes do not an air force make." Japan by 1941 had somewhat better aircraft than the United States. But her naval air superiority lay mainly in the superb experience of her air-crew personnel. Japan also possessed a weapon of great consequence in its Type 91 torpedo. The Japanese torpedo could be dropped by a Kate flying at nearly top speed at an altitude of several hundred feet. In contrast, the American Mark 13 Bliss-Leavitt 21-inch torpedo suffered from at least 12 defects, some serious. It could not be dropped from a height of more than 200 feet or at a speed greater than 130 miles per hour. With a speed of only 33.5 knots it was slow in the water compared to the Japanese weapon, enabling moving ships to dodge it, and if it struck a target the chances were considerably better than even that it would fail to explode. It is hardly an exaggeration to say that the performance of the Mark 13 was so bad (until finally improved in 1944) as to make American torpedo-plane attacks well nigh futile. Fortunately, the standard American 500- and 1,000-pound bombs were reliable, though at war's onset doctrine erroneously called for use of instantaneous rather than delayed-action fuses.

By contrast the United States displayed commendable foresight and initiative in putting radar (short for "Radio Detection and Ranging") into service by Pearl Harbor day. As early as March 1941 a XCAM radar set was aboard the U. S. S. *Yorktown*. Experiments showed that a fighter-direction officer (FDO) could vector a standing Combat Air Patrol to an interception "quickly and reliably," as a *Yorktown* report had it. The new carrier *Hornet*, entering service in late 1941, had a "radar plot" in a special darkened compartment where on a transparent screen radar data could be evaluated. By December 1941 reliable performance in detecting planes up to 50 miles out was expected of the XCAM, but the altitude of an incoming flight had to be partially guessed at. For their part, the Japanese were entirely dependent on obtaining direction fixes on enemy radio transmissions; as yet they had no radar even under service test. The Japanese began to deploy radar only in the fall of 1942 and fought nearly all of the major carrier battles of that year without its aid.

It took the fall of France to Nazi armies to drive the United States into an all-out naval expansion. The Senate and House of Representatives hastily voted in June 1940 an authorization for 61 new warships, including three more fleet carriers—though strictly speaking only two. The *Hornet*, part of the two-ship authorization of May 17, 1938, had been laid down, but the second ship, the *Essex*, had been held up while the Navy's experts tried to come to an agreement concerning her design. For simplicity *Essex* is counted here because she was the first of the new wartime CVs.

As the implications of the Nazi victory sank deeper into public consciousness and as Britain was threatened with invasion, Congress the next month passed a "Two Ocean Navy Bill" that called for 202 more surface combat vessels, eight carriers, and a 15,000-plane naval air force. The tally of authorized large flattops now was 11.

To these moves by Congress President Franklin Roosevelt added a stroke of his own. In a fireside chat to the American people he broadcast his Administration's intent to build the Army and Navy air arms to 50,000 planes. With antisubmarine warfare in mind the President also privately requested the Navy to begin immediately to convert modern cargo ships into escort carriers. Navy officialdom, which had recently held that the high performance of modern planes made them unsuited to the small flight decks of merchantman converts, hastily changed its collective mind. Altered immediately from a merchant hull was the "jeep carrier" U. S. S. *Long Island*, the first of dozens of CVEs to follow. While these "Combustible, Vulnerable, and Expendable" ships (CVE actually stood for "Aircraft Carrier, Escort") were not intended for high-seas battles, they freed the large carriers for purely fleet work. *Long Island* commissioned in June 1941, but a lengthy delay followed while she was tested in service before others were converted. Next to commission were *Sangamon*, *Santee*, and *Nassau* more than a year later.

A long delay, too, was inevitable between the commissioning of the *Hornet* on October 20, 1941, and the *Essex*, the first of the new fleet carriers. All 11 of the new ships had been promptly ordered between July and September 1940, but the keel of the name ship had not been laid down until April 28, 1941. Since the best previous time for completion of a fleet carrier had been 25 months, it took no genius to discern that *Essex* would take at a minimum more than 18 months to complete. Authorizations of December 1941 and July 1942 added two and 19, respectively, new *Essex*-class carriers to the U. S. program. In 1943 and 1944 a veritable flood of new flattops would enter service.

Faced with an American warship program that they understandably termed "astronomical," unable even to keep their current Fourth Armament Plan on schedule, the shaken planners of Japan's Naval Staff could respond only by improvising.

To augment carrier strength the staff already had ordered converted into light carriers (CVLs) three fast fleet tenders. Of these, *Zuiho*, a ship of 11,200 tons, was commissioned in late 1940 and sister *Shoho* just after Pearl Harbor. The third ship, *Ryuho*, of 13,360 tons, was delayed and completed in December 1942. Each of these 28-knot ships could carry about 30 planes. Better suited to fleet carrier duties, though somewhat slower at 25.5 knots, were two ocean liners requisitioned for conversion. Both had been laid down for Japan's N.Y.K. Line, but each had been designed with double hulls, extra height between decks, and provision for plane elevators. The first ship, *Junyo*, commissioned in time to take part in the Aleutian occupation of June 1942. Sister *Hiyo* commissioned two months later. Both were large, 19,000 tons in naval standard tonnage, about the size of the *Enterprise* and slightly larger than the *Hiryu*, and each could carry 50-plus planes. Three final ships ordered converted were the *Kasuga Maru*, the *Nitta Maru,* and the *Yawata Maru*. These were sizable 22-knot liners well suited to escort carrier (CVE) duties. The *Kasuga Maru* commissioned as the 17,830-ton *Taiyo* on August 25, 1941. The other two were still in dockyard at war's outbreak.

When a "senior statesman's conference" in the presence of Emperor Hirohito made the final decision for war with the United States on November 30, 1941, many senior naval officers realized that Nippon was gambling its future with the long-term odds against success. To intimates Admiral Yamamoto expressed his doubts approximately thus: "For the first year [of war] I will run wild; after that I can guarantee nothing." Other Japanese admirals agreed. No conceivable string of victories could erase the coming superiority in naval strength that the Americans would surely possess by 1943 or 1944. But almost to a man the junior officers of Yamamoto's Combined Fleet held no such reservations. Did not Japan have better combat planes and ships than America? Did not "spiritual strength," the willingness of the ordinary Japanese to die for his Emperor, mock the well-known moral weakness of the Anglo-Saxon foe?

Japan's naval air force was inferior to America's in terms of raw numbers but not otherwise. Japan's total of carriers numbered 11, counting *Shoho*, to America's eight. In embarked aircraft numbers of planes were about even. Much of the U. S. Navy's air strength in December 1941 of 5,260 planes and 6,750 pilots was in trainers and student pilots. Japan had 3,202 naval aircraft, of which 1,762 were in operational squadrons. Some 1,035 were carrier-type planes. Flying personnel, including pilots, bombardiers, navigators, radiomen, and gunners, tallied about 7,000.

A long shadow of what would come had been cast by British experience in World War II prior to Pearl Harbor. The flattop with its air group had already proven itself a potent naval weapon even though Britain's Fleet Air Arm was too weak to demonstrate naval air's full potential.

After the conversion of the *Courageous* and *Glorious* in the 1920s the British had commissioned just one more flattop, H. M. S. *Ark Royal,* launched in 1937. Fortunately, when World War II broke out the Royal Navy had in advanced stages of construction four new carriers of the 23,000-ton *Illustrious* class. All were either complete or nearly so by December 7, 1941. Their steel flight decks proved to be resistant to light bombs and later to Kamikazes.

Had the British faced first-class carrier aviation opposition this stout island people might have been defeated. But Adolf Hitler never completed Nazi Germany's *Graf Zeppelin,* launched in 1938, and Benito Mussolini ignored the requests of Italy's admirals for flattops, listening instead to his airmen who said land-based aircraft were enough. The British were able to capitalize on German and Italian naval air weakness to score two smashing victories.

As early as the Ethiopian crisis of 1935–1936 the British had contemplated using carriers to attack Italy's main naval anchorage at Taranto at the instep of the Italian boot. With Italy and Britain at war, the scheme was revived in the fall of 1940. The new carrier *Illustrious* had arrived in the eastern Mediterranean in September, giving the British forces offensive potential. Planes were in short supply, but by November 1940 enough Swordfish torpedo planes were available with trained crews to make a night torpedo attack feasible.

Aided by aerial photographs, Operation Judgment, as the attack was code-named, was meticulously rehearsed. The location of defending torpedo nets and barrage balloons was plotted from aerial reconnaissance and the pilots given courses to avoid them.

On the night of November 11–12 the *Illustrious*'s Swordfish struck, flying in two waves launched an hour apart. Despite heavy antiaircraft fire from the alert enemy ships, the first six of the antiquated torpedo-carrying biplanes, rumbling across the harbor at only 80 knots, banked and deployed to drop their tin fish. First to release was squadron commander Lieutenant Commander Kenneth Williamson. His 18-inch torpedo barely missed a destroyer and plowed into the battleship *Conte di Cavour.* This one hit proved lethal; the crew of the 23,000-ton ship could not check the flooding, and the battleship sank at anchor, out of the war for good. Three other planes managed an "anvil" attack on the new 35,000-ton *Littorio* and hit her twice, once on either side. The five Swordfish of the second wave scored equally well. One pilot hit the wounded *Littorio* and another the *Caio Duilio*, forcing her to be beached. Eleven obsolete planes, flown with great skill and bravery, had put out of action for many months three of the seven battleships of the Italian Navy. In terms of lasting results they had achieved almost as much as Nagumo would gain at Pearl Harbor a year later. Just two planes fell, including Williamson's, but with his observer the commander survived the war as a POW.

Nevertheless, Operation Judgment was a specialized raid, not a full-scale carrier strike on the order of Pearl Harbor. At no time in the Mediterranean did the British have the air strength to hit hard by daylight a strong enemy base.

The second great success of the war for British carrier aviation came in May 1941 when the new 42,200-ton German battleship *Bismarck* broke out into the Atlantic on a raiding mission. Initial attempts to bring her to bay went astray on May 23 when she blew up the battle cruiser *Hood*, Britain's largest ship, and severely damaged the *Prince of Wales*, a brand-new 35,000-ton battleship. *Bismarck* then escaped, tailed by British cruisers that shadowed her with radar.

The *Bismarck* next drew attention from the *Victorious*, a just-commissioned carrier loaded with a shipment of crated Hurricanes intended for Gibraltar. Her only operational aircraft, flown by green crews, were nine Swordfish and six fighters, but the torpedo planes nevertheless managed a hit on the German ship. This fish struck amidships in a heavily protected spot and did little harm.

But more trouble was coming for the *Bismarck* in the form of the carrier *Ark Royal*, steaming up from Gibraltar with a powerful surface squadron. Found by a Catalina flying boat near mid-ocean after eluding the cruisers, the *Bismarck* next underwent attack by 15 Swordfish from the *Ark Royal*. Despite very bad weather and low cloud, but assisted mightily by their accurate altimeters and airborne radar, the obsolete biplanes got two and possibly three hits on the speeding, zigzagging ship. One torpedo struck far aft, wrecking her steering gear and jamming her rudder. This doomed the *Bismarck*. She now became a circling cripple and was blasted into wreckage by the powerful rifles of the *Ark Royal*'s consorts, battleships *King George V* and *Rodney*.

The *Bismarck* chase seemed to cast the flattop in a new light. Operating singly in company with battleships, *Victorious* and *Ark Royal* not only had extended the vision of their respective task forces by hundreds of miles but with their planes they had furnished the means of bringing the *Bismarck* to bay. Neither carrier had possessed the striking power to sink the German giant. But by slowing her and destroying her ability to maneuver, they had converted her maiden voyage into her last.

The year 1941 ended with the British carriers the dominant offensive naval weapons both in the Mediterranean and the North Atlantic. At sea, beyond the range of the single-seat fighter and short-range dive bomber, they had been supreme.

The uses of Britain's carriers had seemed endless. They had hunted down enemy raiders and supply ships, escorted important convoys, attacked special land targets, conducted ocean sweeps and patrols, and—not least—had ferried land-based aircraft to such critical fighting zones as Egypt, Malta, and Murmansk. In sum, British World War II experience had shown the fleet carrier to be the one type of heavy warship most needed, even though the Royal Navy had never employed its flattops in powerful, multicarrier task forces. It had been left to Yamamoto to do that at Pearl Harbor.

4. Sledgehammer at Rabaul

To the pilots of Vice Admiral Chuichi Nagumo's First Air Fleet, retiring aboard their carriers from their attack on Pearl Harbor, the biplane era of aviation exemplified by Britain's Swordfish seemed decades past. Though proud of their ability and their planes and normally high-spirited, they also had that matter-of-factness requisite to good pilots. Many resumed their prewar custom of running laps around the flight decks of the carriers. Others dozed in their ready rooms, read magazines, or waited for the evening meal, the best of the day.

On December 23, with the carriers nearing Kyushu Island, the pilots drew lots for a large bottle of sake, the better to commemorate their nearing end of abstinence from alcohol that Commander Fuchida had imposed. Then most of them took off and searched ahead of the task force en route to their home airfields.

On arrival at their Kyushu bases they learned the details of some startling news. Their comrades of the 22nd Air Flotilla, operating twin-engine bombers from the Saigon area in French Indochina, had attacked, torpedoed, and sunk on December 10 the new British battleship *Prince of Wales* and an accompanying battle cruiser, the *Repulse*. In a feat rivaling that of the First Fleet at Pearl Harbor, these land-based flyers at one blow had broken the back of Allied naval power in the western Pacific. From henceforth, the only naval opposition in Malayan, Philippine, and Netherlands East Indies (Indonesian) waters would come from a handful of Dutch, British, Australian, and American cruisers and destroyers, plus a few submarines and land-based planes.

Coming so soon after Pearl Harbor, the loss of the two great ships proved tremendously shocking to the British and American publics. Even more stunned were the admirals. Air cover obviously was imperative for any surface force operating within range of Japanese torpedo planes. The shock extended to Japan also. Admiral Yamamoto had not expected to deal with the *Repulse* and *Prince of Wales* so handily; neither had the conservative admirals on the Naval Staff. But being on the giving rather than the receiving end, they accepted less readily the lessons of this disaster to their foe. They continued to regard the battle-wagon force at Hashirajima anchorage at Kyushu as the core of the Japanese fleet rather than Nagumo's six fast carriers of the First Air Fleet.

Admiral Yamamoto already had decided how next to use Nagumo as the First Air Fleet's flattops steamed into Hashirajima on Christmas Day, 1941, receiving the frantic cheers of the crews of Japan's assembled battleships. Nagumo would support landings in the Australian-mandated islands of New Britain, New Ireland, and New Guinea, and then support Vice Admiral Takahashi's Third Fleet and Vice Admiral Kondo's Second Fleet in the occupation of the Philippines, Borneo, the Celebes, and Java. Seizure of these islands, plus Malaya and Burma, would complete Japan's initial conquests, carving out the Southern Resources Area from which Japan would draw the oil, tin, rice, and other necessities to sustain a long war.

After a few days of fuel and supply replenishment and rest for the crews, the *Kaga, Akagi, Zuikaku,* and *Shokaku* would steam south to Truk Atoll in the Caroline Islands and from there support landings in the South Pacific. The *Soryu* and *Hiryu,* returning separately to Japan after being used to support a landing on Wake Island, would operate in the Celebes as a separate force.

As to Japan's moves after that, Yamamoto was undecided. Further expansion would in any case involve negotiations at the highest levels between the leaders of the Army and Navy. Some sort of offensive action seemed desirable that surely would require the entire First Air Fleet. In the meantime, Nagumo would be used to back up already scheduled operations.

To Mitsuo Fuchida, still commanding the airmen, Yamamoto's decision made little sense. With the American and British fleets defeated, he saw no need to use the First Air Fleet to support landing operations. He wanted to sail right back to Pearl Harbor, this time to get the U. S. carrier force. But Yamamoto knew that Admiral Nagumo would have no part of a second mission, which would be totally bereft of surprise. As he explained to his staff, to go through with another raid on Pearl would require him to relieve Nagumo, who would then be forced to commit suicide. Besides, Yamamoto was convinced that the Pearl Harbor job had been done, that the U. S. fleet could not menace Japanese operations in southeast Asia or threaten the homeland. In these views he had the hearty concurrence—for once—of Admiral Nagano, the commander of the Navy General Staff. Moreover, Allied air power in Australia and the Netherlands Indies might not be strong, but it must be wiped out before Japanese troops could land safely on New Britain Island and in New Guinea. So Nagumo and the First Air Fleet would act as the exterminators, softening up both targets for landings.

Had Yamamoto realized just how weak the Royal Australian Air Force was in New Guinea and on New Britain he might have spared

Nagumo his cruise, leaving the job to light fleet carriers *Ryujo* and *Zuiho* and land-based Nells of the 25th Air Flotilla based at Truk.

Yamamoto may have been influenced by several daring reconnaissance flights flown by Aussie pilots under terribly primitive conditions from Rabaul on New Britain and Kavieng on New Ireland. Flight Lieutenant R. A. Yeowart took off from Kavieng on January 8 in a heavily laden, camera-equipped Lockheed Hudson, a small, twin-engine reconnaissance land plane. At 5:44 A.M., after flying 700 miles, he reached fabled Truk Lagoon in the Carolines. Truk was suspected to be a major Japanese base because all Westerners had been barred from it in peacetime. Yeowart and his crew counted in the lagoon three merchant ships, 12 warships of cruiser-destroyer size, one large warship, and 27 bombers of the 25th Air Flotilla lined up on an airfield excavated from a small island. He managed two photo runs before fighters rose after him, then dived away into the dubious "safety" of a nasty rain squall that buffeted the Hudson severely. He made it back with his precious photos, the only ones the Allies would obtain of Truk for many long months.

With his four carriers Nagumo left Hashirajima on January 5, steamed southwest toward Taiwan, and then headed southeast toward Truk. Iki Kuramoti, a young 25-mm. antiaircraft gunner aboard the flagship *Akagi*, was glad to go. He had celebrated New Year's in his homeland; now he wanted to see the fabled "Southern Seas." As he wrote, "I stood at my lookout station watching while scenes of silver and gold waves and naked natives dancing in the shadow of coconut trees floated before my eyes." Reality soon dissolved his dream. Sweltering in his winter uniform, he suffered from the blazing tropical sun and the steaming heat below decks on the flagship. He was glad to reach Truk and change into a summer uniform. Yet the tropics had their appeal. The vegetation, he noted, "grew luxuriantly directly down to the beating waves," reflecting its contours in the intensely blue water. "Adding the moon to this [made] the mid-day heat seem like a dream."

At Truk all ships loaded supplies. Kuramoti and the other gunners mounted armored shields on their light AA guns, and the First Air Fleet sailed once more bound for Rabaul and Kavieng.

To defend Kavieng the Aussies had nothing but some light anti-aircraft. At Rabaul they had eight Wirraways, slow two-seater monoplanes modeled after a North American basic trainer design. In a foolish decision the RAAF had adopted these as its main fighter-bomber. Trouble began for the Rabaul garrison on January 20, 1942, when Commander Fuchida led 90 attackers against it shortly before noon. Coast watchers on small islands north of Rabaul reported his formation, and the Australians scrambled all serviceable Wirraways. Flying Officer Lowe and his gunner, Sergeant C. A. Ashford, who had been on patrol, bravely turned into the huge formation at 10,000 feet, only to have six of Commander Itaya's Zeros pounce on them. Twisting and turning, finding themselves hopelessly outclassed in speed, maneuverability, firepower, and everything else, the two Aussies managed to survive until they reached 5,000 feet. Then the Wirraway burst into flames and fell in a long funeral pyre into the sea. Survival of two of the Wirraways cannot be accounted for by negligence on the part of Itaya's Zeros. The Aussie pilots managed to find scattered cloud cover and play hide and seek until the Zeros tired of the game and left.

Watching the operation from above, as he had done over Pearl Harbor, Commander Fuchida could take little satisfaction. He saw only the Wirraways and one ship in harbor, the Norwegian merchantman *Herstein,* which the Val dive bombers hit and set afire. The two Aussie airstrips already seemed pretty well beat up from previous attacks by Nells, and so Fuchida led his entire formation of Kate bombers over a six-inch gun emplacement at Praed Point that the Australians had neglected to camouflage, saturating it with bomb bursts. Just one plane fell to the anti-aircraft fire, a Nell from the 25th Air Flotilla that also participated in the attack.

The next day Fuchida's airmen attacked Kavieng with planes from the *Akagi* and *Kaga,* while others from the *Shokaku* and *Zuikaku* attacked civilian grass airstrips at Lae and Salamaua on New Guinea. They met no opposition other than ground fire at Kavieng. Most of the few planes they destroyed were civilian craft, an odd collection that included Ford and Junker trimotors used to fly supplies for New Guinea's gold. mines. On January 22 all four carriers hit Rabaul again, a final softening-up strike in preparation for a landing the next day, but the pilots could find nothing worthwhile to bomb or even to strafe. The First Air Fleet then retired to Truk, its work done.

A disgusted Fuchida felt that the whole operation had been a waste of time. He wrote later, "All in all, [our] employment . . . in this operation struck me as extravagant. If ever a sledgehammer had been used to crack an egg, this was the time."

Had it known exactly what Nagumo was up to, a disorganized American command at Pearl Harbor might well have agreed with Fuchida. Orders from the Navy Department had transferred command of the Pacific Fleet temporarily to Vice Admiral William S. Pye, who had been Admiral Kimmel's Commander, Battle Force, in administrative charge of Pacific Fleet battleships. Pye gave way on Christmas Day to Admiral Chester W. Nimitz, who as Chief of the Bureau of Navigation had been directing the Navy's personnel assignments. Although never an aviator, since his graduation from the Naval Academy's Class of 1905 Nimitz had compiled a distinguished career in destroyers, submarines, cruisers, and battleships. Now the white-haired, distinguished-looking Texan had to step into a role —Commander Pacific Fleet—in which by default carriers had become the main reliance in holding the line against further enemy attacks. At once Nimitz began expunging the gloom and defeatism he found prevalent at

Pacific Fleet headquarters. His operational orders would follow in due course, though not as soon as some carrier enthusiasts hoped. Until then the Japanese Navy and Nagumo's flattops would continue to dominate the headlines.

5. Riposte in the Marshalls

Admiral Bill Halsey was disgusted. Dammit! When was the U. S. Navy going to fight? He had wanted to steam the *Enterprise* to the Marshalls to try to catch the Pearl Harbor attackers, but orders from Hawaii had kept him chasing shadows south of Oahu for several days after the blow. Now he was to steam north and east of Oahu and hunt enemy submarines. This was not, in Halsey's view, either a rewarding or particularly safe job for a carrier. But the chain of remarkable good luck that was to bless the Big E through the war had begun. On two occasions torpedoes passed close aboard and missed, and Halsey's flyers found and sank submarine I-170.

In the meantime carrier *Saratoga* had arrived from San Diego to join *Lexington* and *Enterprise* in patrols. All three flattops operated in separate task groups and kept planes constantly aloft on routine searches. Inevitably, operational losses resulted.

Saratoga, with Air Group 3 embarked, was already earning a reputation as a hard-luck ship. Ordered to ferry some Marine Corps fighters to Wake Island, she was nearing her launch point when word came on December 22 to scrub the mission. Vice Admiral Pye, who by now had temporarily relieved Admiral Kimmel as Pacific Fleet Commander, knew that carrier planes had attacked Wake, that the Japanese had landed there, and that the issue on the island was "in doubt." He feared that the *Saratoga* might blunder into a superior enemy force—possibly into a battleship squadron, as she had done in Fleet Problem IX. He could not risk losing her. Thus Wake fell with no carrier support. But lose *Saratoga* the Navy did anyway on January 11, 1942, for five critical months. While slowing to 13 knots to recover patrolling SBDs, the *Sara* took without warning a submarine torpedo in her side. Counterflooding checked a six-degree list, and *Sara* made Pearl under her own power, but she had to go to Bremerton in Puget Sound for repair and a refit that removed her top-heavy 8-inch turrets.

The Japanese were jubilant. The submarine identified the *Sara* as the *Lexington* and reported her sunk from two hits. Coming so soon after Pearl Harbor and the sinking of the *Repulse* and *Prince of Wales*, the report was accepted in Tokyo at face value. Wrote the newspaper *Osaka Mainichi*, "It may well be that this exploit is equivalent to the sinking of three [battleships] of the enemy."

The torpedoing of the *Saratoga* was the least of the bad news flooding into Washington, D.C., in December of 1941 and January of 1942. Christmas Day had seen Japanese troops lodged in the Philippines and the city of Manila abandoned to the enemy. Hong Kong had fallen, and the British were being driven back rapidly in Malaya and Burma. On January 11 the Japanese landed in the Celebes, threatening to cut off the Netherlands East Indies from Australia. And off the U. S. East Coast German submarines were fouling the beaches of Florida and the Carolinas with thick, gummy oil from sunken tankers. The only good war news was from Russia; Hitler's drive on Moscow had been checked, and Siberian troops from Marshal Zhukov's Red Banner Far East Army were counterattacking in subzero cold.

Admiral Nimitz, the new Pacific Fleet commander, took the news bad and good with apparent calm. He had an enormous capacity for the type of detailed, clear-headed planning that his job required. Tactful, patient, basically optimistic about the war's ultimate outcome, not a worrier, Nimitz had quietly been restoring the self-confidence of others. He kept Admiral Kimmel's staff and reassured the members. He had been exactly the man needed to bolster a dispirited, apprehensive Pearl Harbor.

Nimitz knew that he would have to stand basically on the defensive. He would have to hang onto Midway Island guarding Hawaii's approaches from the west, and he would have to maintain the communication line from Hawaii through Samoa and Fiji to Brisbane in Australia. To accomplish these goals he could not allow the Japanese to remain undisturbed in the Marshall Islands; he would have to hit them with his only offensive weapons, the carrier task groups. The obvious man to send was Halsey, the fighter, already known to the *Enterprise*'s crew as "Wild Bill."

Accordingly, in late January he ordered Halsey to attack the Marshalls with Task Force 8, built around the *Enterprise* and the *Yorktown* that had just arrived at Pearl from the Atlantic. In selecting Halsey Admiral Nimitz had chosen a seagoing version of George Patton. Halsey was no intellectual; he had graduated well down the list of the U. S. Naval Academy's Class of 1904. But he had a solid seagoing record that had continued after he had switched from destroyers to naval aviation in the early 1930s.

Halsey's target, the major islands of the Marshall group, form on a chart a rough parallelogram, about 200 miles on each side and 125 miles on each end. All lie within fighter range of one another and thus are self-supporting. Wake Island lies 600 miles almost due north of Kwajalein. American-owned Howland and Baker islands lie some 900 miles southeast. Due south of Mili, within fighter range, lies Makin in the Gilberts, a New Zealand mandate.

Probably not many Americans could have correctly identified the

Marshalls in early 1942 or have guessed that they lay some 2,000 nautical miles from Pearl Harbor. Nor could they have described their typical coral atoll nature. All were coral reefs formed atop volcanic uprisings. Kwajalein encircled a large lagoon, thus forming a safe anchorage for ships. At Roi Island on the atoll's northern side, the Japanese were completing an airfield with three intersecting runways. On Taroa Island at Maloelap Atoll they had completed a fine new air base, more modern than Ford Island at Pearl, with two heavy-duty coral runways, one 4,920 feet long. Together, Roi and Taroa supported the Chitose Naval Air Group of the 24th Air Flotilla, equipped with Claude fighters and Nell medium bombers. Jaluit Atoll and Kwajalein Island proper based Kawanishi four-engine H6K "Mavis" flying boats and smaller float planes. All of the major islands had antiaircraft and coast defense gun protection and naval garrison troops serving as infantry.

Of the precise nature of the Japanese defenses Halsey was innocent. His latest information consisted only of periscope observations made in late January by submarine *Dolphin*. He therefore decided to hit all known targets simultaneously, dividing his force into three groups. *Enterprise*, with three destroyers as a screen, would attack Wotje, Taroa Island in Maloelap Atoll, and Roi and Kwajalein islands in Kwajalein Atoll. Rear Admiral Raymond A. Spruance would peel off with heavy cruisers *Northampton* and *Salt Lake City* to bombard Wotje. *Chester* would bombard Maloelap. *Yorktown*, operating under Rear Admiral Frank Jack Fletcher as Task Force 17 with cruisers *Louisville* and *St. Louis* and four destroyers, would attack Jaluit and Mili in the southern Marshalls and newly occupied Makin in the Gilberts.

The *Enterprise* and *Yorktown* sailed together from Samoa and on January 31, 1942, separated for fast 500-mile run-ins to their separate targets. An easterly wind forced the *Enterprise* to steam to within 36 miles of Wotje, dangerously close, to launch its planes.

In order to hit as many targets at once as he could, Commander Howard L. Young, Air Group 6's skipper, planned to lead personally 36 SBD dive bombers against the Roi airfield, while nine TBD Devastators blasted from high level the seaplane base and naval anchorage at Kwajalein. To prevent attacks from the known airfields at Wotje—not yet operational, it turned out—and Maloelap's Taroa airfield, Young set up strafing and light bombing attacks by 12 Wildcats. Armed with machine guns and pairs of hundred-pound bombs, six would attack each field. The Wildcats would take off about an hour after the Dauntlesses and Devastators; their greater speed and the shorter distance to their targets would allow them to arrive at the same time as the larger, slower planes. All air attacks and the cruiser bombardment would begin simultaneously. The remaining six Wildcats of Fighting 6 would orbit the *Enterprise* on Combat Air Patrol (CAP).

At 4:43 A.M., in total darkness, Commander Young roared down the flight deck of the Big E in a dangerous takeoff. All of the SBDs followed, 18 from Bombing 6 and 17 from Scouting 6, and headed for Roi. The heavy Devastators followed at 5:08 and the Wildcats at 6:10. Ill-luck dogged the fighters; one veered over the side, pilot and plane lost.

When finally in formation all planes began a slow, steady climb to 15,000 feet, normal dive- and glide-bomb altitude, air speed 110 knots. Nearing Roi, they orbited to get their bearings, thereby alerting the Japanese defenders and giving them time to man their antiaircraft and warm up their Nakajima Claude fighters.

At about 7:00 A.M. the lead planes tipped over and dove, glide-bombing at a shallow angle to drop on the airfield the pair of hundred-pound bombs each Dauntless carried. Most pilots, as ordered, saved their single 500-pounders for bigger game. Leading the pack was Lieutenant Commander Halstead L. Hopping, the skipper of Scouting 6. He dove too soon and had to level off short of the airfield, crossing it at a speed no greater than his straining 1,200-hp Wright Cyclone engine could pull him. Behind him a Claude scooted down the field, leaped nimbly into the air, and climbed to pounce on his tail. Either it or the antiaircraft shot Hopping down into the sea.

Ten Claudes, airborne already or dodging bomb bursts to zoom from the field, whirled after the SBDs that were completing their dives. With no fighter escort the Dauntlesses were on their own. Fortunately, most planes had built up good speed and managed to zoom into scattered clouds at 3,000 feet before the Claudes could catch them. Inexperience cost the life of one Claude pilot. He jumped from above and behind the SBD of Ensign William P. "Willie" West. Radioman John W. Snowden, West's gunner, whirled his twin .30-caliber mount and got the plane when its pilot pulled up instead of diving past the Dauntless. The Claude had "squashed out," offering Snowden an easy target. Two others attacked Lieutenant Clarence Dickinson, in formation with two other pilots. But when the three rear-seat gunners fired, the Japanese pilots broke away and began to stunt. "They looped together," Dickinson recalls, "and followed with an elegant slow roll. . . . I can't guess what was in their minds. . . ." Since another Claude pilot did the same this day, it may be that some of the Japanese were observing a tactical doctrine that called for stunting as a method of luring enemy aircraft into dogfights. In that event they did well to shoot down three SBDs.

The Americans did well, too, in their first combat dives. They hit grounded planes and hangars, causing considerable damage at Roi, though not nearly enough to knock out the airfield or all operational planes.

Orbiting above, Commander Young heard one of his TBDs attacking Kwajalein Island report naval targets in the lagoon suitable for heavy bombs. He therefore ordered Bombing 6's Dauntlesses to break off attacking Roi and begin a 40-mile climb at full military power to Kwajalein's anchorage. Dickinson and two pilots of Scouting 6 also heard Young's call and followed on their own, hoping to drop their 500-pound bombs on an enemy flattop. On sighting the anchorage Dickinson was disappointed. He saw some anchored large ships—three tankers or engines-aft cargo ships, a large transport, a light cruiser, what appeared to be old cruiser-mine-layer *Tokiwa,* and a cluster of seven submarines—but no carrier. Bombing 6 was already diving, plunging vertically from 14,000 feet, perforated dive brakes wailing to induce a terror below that can be fully appreciated only by one who has been under dive-bomber attack himself.

In the lead plane, carefully adjusting his dive, eye glued to his tele-scope sight, was Squadron Commander William R. Hollingsworth. With cool detachment he noted that his target, the light cruiser, was shooting ten large and many smaller guns at him. Releasing and pulling out sharply, he banked away, looked back, saw smoke boiling up from the ship, the training cruiser *Katori,* and assumed he had scored a hit. (The "hit" may—or may not—have been smoke from AA fire. Throughout the war pilots confused bomb hits with puffs from heavy antiaircraft guns. Pilot observa-tion almost always exaggerated the number of hits.) Two other pilots also claimed hits on her; the others picked other targets. Lieutenant Dickinson, one of the last to dive, aimed at large transport *Yasukuni Maru* with a plane on its stern and claimed a hit. Hit also, the pilots believed, were the tankers, several cargo ships, and two submarines. All regretted that their bombs had instantaneous rather than delay fuses, which meant that they exploded on contact rather than deep inside their targets.

Sweeping low across the harbor, one pilot banked to strafe a launch racing toward one of the ships from the shore. On seeing him coming, all hands prudently dove overside, leaving the launch to turn in circles. Several other pilots strafed a pair of Mavis flying boats moored on the water.

Afterward Lieutenant Commander "Holly" Hollingsworth was pleased with his men. They had displayed, he pridefully reported to Admiral Halsey, "intelligence and initiative in choosing their objectives" and had pressed home their dives "boldly and with disregard of AA fire."

In the meantime each of the nine cumbersome TBD Devastators had dropped its three 500-pound bombs from high altitude, using the Navy's famed Norden bomb sight. The skipper of Torpedo 6, Lieutenant Com-mander Eugene E. Lindsey, already had decided that the setup at the anchorage was ideal for torpedo attack and had radioed to the Big E for a strike by the nine remaining TBDs of his squadron. Led by Lieutenant Commander Lance E. Massey, the squadron's "exec," the planes lumbered off, each with a 2,000-pound torpedo. After what seemed to the pilots an eternity—long after the SBDs had left—the slow-flying planes arrived at the anchorage. On sighting the enemy ships, several of which were burn-ing, Massey yelled over his radio, "Get that cruiser that's headed off to the right. Take them home, boys, take them home!"

Three pilots banked to "box" the *Katori,* which had gotten under way and was trying to limp to sea, bomb damage clearly visible. One torpedo "prematured," exploding short of the cruiser, but one other appeared to hit and explode. Continuing on across the lagoon, Massey and his other five pilots flew their slow planes into the teeth of the ack-ack, which was flinging out red balls of 25-mm. tracer. All pilots closed to 400–500 yards, point-blank range, released their torpedoes at the *Yasukuni Maru* and *Toa Maru*, zoomed over the enemy ships, then banked sharply away, noting that the rattled Japanese were inadvertently shooting into each other's ships. Massey circled out of range to assess the damage, noting that the *Katori* had stopped and was down at the bow and that three other ships were listing, surrounded by huge pools of oil. The *Yasukuni Maru*, his own personal target, was down by the stern and had swung toward the beach, evidently intent on grounding itself to keep from sinking. Postwar Japanese records show that the *Toa Maru* was heavily damaged also. Several other ships were hit, but only one ship, the *Shonan Maru No. 10*, was permanently lost. Submarine I-23 was damaged, as was minelayer *Tokiwa*.

In the meantime, six of the 12 Wildcats sent to strafe and bomb Wotje and Taroa airfields had stirred up a hornet's nest. At Wotje the Wildcats found the airfield incomplete and no enemy planes evident. But at Taroa they found a fully developed base with 11 Claudes aloft on defensive patrol, others on the ground, and a strong force of bombers in neat rows on the field. With flight leader James S. Gray in the lead, all six pilots dove in hard and fast, strafing and dropping their hundred-pound bombs along the flight line. They realized at once that unless they raised hell with that base the enemy might get away a strike at the *Enterprise*. Banking steeply after their runs, they swept back to strafe the base again, regretting that their lack of incendiary ammunition prevented them from setting afire many of the grounded planes. Five Claudes then jumped Lieutenant Gray, who ran for it and tried to turn into the enemy attacks. He claimed two, including one that crashed onto the airfield in a long trail of flame and wreckage, and Lieutenant W. E. Rawie another. The pilots made no attempt to dogfight when they discovered the rapid climb and maneuverability of the Claudes. Fortunately, the Wildcat was much faster. Improvised boiler-plate armor installed behind Gray's seat had saved his life. Fifteen dents attested to hits from the 7.7-mm. (approximately 30-caliber) guns of the Claudes. Gray's flight was lucky to escape without loss.

The *Chester* also discovered the hard way the strength of Taroa air base. After blasting Maloelap following Gray's fighter sweep, Captain T. M. "Tommy" Shock's heavy cruiser drew the unwelcome attention of eight Nells. Despite frantic maneuvering, one bomb dropped from high level hit the ship well aft, tearing a six-foot hole in the main deck and killing eight and wounding 11 men. *Chester* was not badly hurt and remained fully operational.

Because the Taroa airfield obviously needed more attention, Admiral Halsey authorized two attacks by SBDs, one at 10:30 A.M., the other an hour later. Commander Hollingsworth led out nine rearmed and refueled Dauntlesses over the field in the first, diving away from the Claude defenders at 13,000 feet, each plane dropping a "ripple" salvo of two 100-pound and one 500-pound bombs. Hollingsworth's gunner, on pullout, watched his pilot's bombs blast apart two of a dozen bombers rowed up precisely on the apron. Other pilots set afire two more Nells and three of eight Claudes refueling on the field. Lieutenant Joe R. Penland and Ensign C. R. Walters hit hangars. The SBDs then sped away, with only two planes suffering fighter attack.

The next nine Dauntlesses, coming in an hour later, encountered an angry enemy. The Japanese had sent up all surviving Claudes, and this time they jumped the SBDs during their dives. They concentrated on "tail-end Charlie," Ensign John J. Doherty, last to dive, who pulled ahead and beneath Lieutenant John J. Van Buren. Spotting a Claude on Doherty's tail, Van Buren adjusted his dive, got the enemy fighter in his sight, and set it afire with his two .50-caliber synchronized nose guns. After pulling out, the pilots found themselves literally "jinking"—weaving back and forth—for their lives. Doherty vanished with three fighters on his tail after yelling defiantly over his radio, "This Jap will never get me." Absence of self-sealing tanks and armor in his SBD-3 may have contributed to his loss.

Lieutenant Edward J. Kroeger, flying plane 6-B-11, took a bullet in his left foot. Despite this he managed to hold his plane steady as his gunner, Radioman Achilles A. Georgiou, got the fighter. Georgiou then took a bullet himself that ripped open his arm from wrist to elbow. Though giddy from pain and loss of blood, Kroeger managed to land the badly damaged dive bomber safely, fainting after bouncing onto the deck.

The battered condition of the Dauntlesses and the number of Claudes still defending Taroa airfield made it obvious to Admiral Halsey that his *Enterprise* had no business continuing to steam back and forth almost in sight of Wotje Atoll. The Big E therefore pulled out, racing north at 30 knots, with a Combat Air Patrol from Fighting 6 still overhead. Not a single enemy plane had yet appeared.

In the meantime the *Yorktown*, with Air Group 5 aboard, was having bad luck in the southern Marshalls and at Makin in the Gilberts. Admiral Fletcher's plan called for simultaneous strikes at Jaluit, Mili, and Makin from distances of 140, 71, and 127 miles respectively.

Against Jaluit, the main target, the *Yorktown* launched at 4:55 A.M. 11 TBDs and 17 SBDs. The pilots expected to bomb a reported airfield, the seaplane base, docks, and shipping. In darkness and bad weather they utterly failed to form up. After 40 minutes Lieutenant Commander R. G. Armstrong, leading the scout bombers, set out with what planes he could locate—about 20—for Jaluit. Others proceeded independently in pairs and treys. Squalls and vicious thunderheads plagued the flight. Bad weather over the atoll broke up the formation, and a ceiling dropping to as low as 3,000 feet over the anchorage prevented most of the SBDs from dive-bombing. The pilots found two large ships and a seaplane base but not the airfield Intelligence had said was there. Attacking first, Lieutenant William S. Guest at 7:01 A.M. planted his bomb squarely on the stern of a 5,000-ton freighter. All pilots following spotted the resulting fire and glide-bombed the ship repeatedly without a single additional confirmed hit. Many pilots noted a defect that would bother the dive bombers later. In the humid weather their plexiglass canopies fogged up, as did their gunsights, when the planes dove from cool into warm air. Reported Lieutenant J. L. Neilson curtly, "Windshield fogged badly at 4,000 feet on dive. Impossible to see through. Bomb missed." Many of the Devastators failed to drop at all; they could not find a break in the clouds. Others glide-bombed, a risky business in these slow, big-winged planes without armor or self-sealing tanks. Fortunately for all of the American pilots, AA fire was very light.

The return to the *Yorktown* was a "sweat." Without the new "YE-ZB" radio homing equipment recently installed on the flattop most of them would never have made it. As it was, two TBDs had to ditch off Jaluit, radioing that they were landing together. Another ran out of fuel 20 miles from the *Yorktown*. Three other planes, two SBDs and a TBD, simply vanished without a trace. None of the pilots was recovered. Lieutenant Edwin B. Parker, flying Devastator 5-T-4, got aboard the carrier with just two gallons of fuel in his tanks. The *Yorktown's* plane losses equaled the *Enterprise's*, and probably every loss was the result of the bad weather.

The nine SBDs sent against Makin attacked in trail what they took to be a seaplane tender and a pair of Mavis patrol planes anchored in the lagoon. They destroyed the hapless flying boats with machine-gun fire but got only one hit on the tender, scored by the flight leader, Lieutenant Commander William O. Burch. As they left the disappointed pilots noted that the ship was on an even keel and not sinking.

Five SBDs sent against Mili found nothing to shoot at. One pilot attacked a pair of tanks set back from the island's village, reporting afterward, "I observed no fires so concluded I had destroyed the natives' supply of fresh water."

A bitter Commander Curtis S. Smiley, Air Group 5's skipper, could report very little for the loss of six of his planes and crews. Only two ships, one at Jaluit and the other at Makin, had suffered certain hits. The enemy had no airfield on the islands and no installations worth risking a second attack through bad weather. Nor did he believe that the pre-dawn takeoff had been a good idea. "We have," Smiley concluded, "been working under false premises in our peacetime operation of aircraft at night. Large numbers of planes, completely darkened or with only dim running lights, *cannot* be effectively rendezvoused in the vicinity of a practically invisible carrier on a dark ocean."

The early afternoon of February 1 found both the *Yorktown* and *Enterprise* steaming east at high speed, exercising what was known as "retirement" to Admirals Halsey and Fletcher and "getting the hell out of here" to the crews. *Yorktown's* patrolling Wildcats found at 1:15 P.M. a patrolling Mavis and splashed it.

Shortly afterward, at 1:39, some 360 miles to the north and west, the radar of the *Enterprise* picked up more dangerous opposition, six enemy Nells from either Roi or Taroa. Leading this flight was Lieutenant Kazuo Nakai, a veteran of 50 combat missions in China and six against Wake Island before its fall. This was Nakai's second mission of the day. The first had been the morning attack that had scored a hit on the *Chester*. Nakai was typical of Japan's best Navy flyers. Born in Tokyo, a graduate of Japan's Naval Academy at Eta Jima, he had gone on to excel in flight school at Kasumigaura air base northwest of Tokyo.

The Americans could detect Nakai's approach through the clouds but could not fire on him because the *Enterprise's* radar had as yet no fire-control capacity. Reports came in "Bogie at 35,000 yards," "Bogie at 21,-000 yards," and so on until—as Commander E. B. Mott, the Big E's gunnery officer, recalled—"Pop! Right through the clouds came six twin-engine enemy bombers in a glide." At 3,000 feet the planes were too low for easy tracking by the five-inch and just out of range of the .50-caliber machine guns. They were in perfect range of the four-barreled 1.1-inch pompoms that fired savagely. One plane fell; others, including Nakai's, took hits that knocked pieces from them, but all dropped three bombs apiece that missed to port as the *Enterprise* twisted away. One bomb exploded close, splattering the ship with fragments, touching off a brief but spectacular fire from gasoline from a severed fuel hose. One man, Boatswain's Mate Second Class G. H. Smith, suffered a fatal wound.

On passing astern of the *Enterprise*, knowing that he could not get home in his damaged Nell, Lieutenant Nakai banked his big plane about and dove at the stern of the ship, aiming for the bulky stack and island squarely below Commander Mott in Sky Control. About 300 yards out the .50s and 1.1s bit directly into the cockpit, wounding or killing Nakai and causing the Nell to drift to port. The plane, burning fiercely, flew right up the carrier's flight deck, clipped the tail from an SBD from which a mechanic was firing its free guns, and plunged into the sea, striking off a wing on a forward gun gallery, but causing no harm or loss. As the plane passed Mott could see Nakai slumped over the controls. The brave Japanese professional had barely missed. The crash of his blazing Nell into the *Enterprise's* stern or on the flight deck could have resulted in a serious fire and heavy casualties among the crew. Gasoline—either from the Nell or the cloven SBD—splattered Mott's face 60 feet above the flight deck.

The *Enterprise* was not yet out of danger. Radar picked up other snoopers, and at 4:00 P.M. two more Nells appeared, flying at 14,000 feet, the Wildcats of the CAP climbing frantically behind trying to reach them. Ignoring the five-inch guns, which fired consistently behind the planes, the Japanese bombardiers dropped four heavy bombs with precision. These would have hit had not Captain George D. Murray ordered a sharp turn to port. All four fell harmlessly into the water. At least one of the Japanese pilots paid for his daring. Commander Wade McClusky and Lieutenant Daniels flying CAP in Wildcats caught up with him, set his plane afire with repeated attacks, and finally tumbled it into the ocean.

Neither Halsey nor Captain Murray was pleased. The antiaircraft had mostly missed on both attacks, and the ammunition belts in the Wildcats on CAP had shown a tendency to jam when the planes maneuvered sharply. All of the Nell pilots had displayed courage and determination. Had he known of it Halsey would have been the first to grant grudging approval of Lieutenant Nakai's promotion—posthumously—to lieutenant commander for his daring attempt to Kamikaze the *Enterprise*.

At 7:00 P.M., 25 minutes after sunset, the Big E landed her last CAP of the day, and the exhausted fighter pilots stumbled off to their bunks. During the night she found *"Enterprise* weather," the sort that would bless this happy ship for the next nine months of the war. She steamed into a cold front carrying rain and low clouds and followed it for hundreds of miles until well clear of Japanese reconnaissance planes. *Yorktown* also retired without incident.

On February 6 the *Enterprise*, with Halsey on the bridge, steamed back into Pearl. Word of the exploits of Task Force 8 had preceded her. At Fort Kamehameha and from Hickam Field soldiers cheered, as did doctors, nurses, and patients at Hospital Point. From the grounded *Nevada* grimy sailors waved frantically. The crew of each ship in harbor cheered in turn as the *Enterprise* slid by. For them and in the eyes of the American public the Big E and the *Yorktown* had delivered the first installment of revenge for Pearl Harbor.

In truth, the damage was considerably less than the excited American pilots had reported. The only ship totally destroyed was the hapless subchaser *Shonan Maru No. 10*. But a considerable number of others were badly damaged. Had the American bombs carried delay fuses others undoubtedly would have sunk. Destroyed were nine grounded planes at Taroa and Roi, and three Claudes were shot down. Killed were 90 men, including Rear Admiral Yashiro of the 6th Base Force.

Seen in retrospect, Halsey's raid was daring to the point of recklessness. He had attacked the entire Marshall group and Makin in the Gilberts with just two carriers, estimating that he would have to deal with at least four enemy airfields and several seaplane bases. He had steamed the *Enterprise* most of the day in a five-by-25-mile rectangle off Wotje within range of three of the airfields. He was lucky to get off with only one bomb hit, that not on his carrier but on the *Chester*.

Although American doctrine did not at this time call for carriers to operate together, Halsey would have been better advised to have had the *Enterprise* and *Yorktown* attack the northern Marshalls together. Damage to the enemy would have been much heavier and likelihood of a counterblow therefore less. Had a strike at the southern Marshalls and Gilberts been deemed necessary, *Lexington* could have been used. To put the matter in terms of theory, the principle of concentration of force—of hitting the enemy in overwhelming strength—should have been followed. The Americans had not repeated Yamamoto's strategy at Pearl Harbor.

The attack proper had disclosed many needs. All planes had to have armor and self-sealing tanks, plus IFF (Identification Friend or Foe) to insure safe return. The fighter complement of 18 planes to a squadron was not enough. Howard Young, skipper of Air Group 6, wanted the numbers of SBDs and Devastators reduced to permit embarking at least 27 fighters. Except for the Wildcats, all planes had too low a performance, especially the big Devastators. "Fortunately in this action," Young said, "VT-6 encountered no air opposition, but it is certain that their mission would have [failed] . . . had they been intercepted by enemy fighters which were in the near vicinity."

Yet undeniably the Marshalls raid was worth the cost of 12 planes. Halsey's success in the face of great odds showed as perhaps nothing else could the tremendous striking power of even a single-carrier air group. Also it pointed up an underlying Japanese weakness. At no point among her numerous islands could the Japanese air defense be more strong than a U. S. carrier task force massed against it. Tokyo Radio attempted to dismiss the Marshalls raid as "aerial guerrilla warfare." But neither Admiral Yamamoto nor the Navy General Staff could ignore for too long the danger posed by America's roving flattops, now quite literally the only effective American naval weapon systems besides submarines.

6. Darwin, Marcus, New Guinea

At his Combined Fleet Headquarters, now aboard the new battleship *Yamato* in the Hashirajima anchorage, Admiral Yamamoto took the sound view that Halsey's bold thrust was intended to divert Japan from completing the conquest of the Netherlands East Indies. He did not intend to be diverted. The best use for Nagumo's carriers, he believed, was to continue supporting the Japanese invasion forces. Port Darwin, on Australia's northern coast, must be knocked out. Darwin was the build-up point for support of the Allies in Java, with airfields, supply dumps, and thousands of tons of shipping. Yamamoto, however, could not entirely ignore Halsey, and so he ordered detached from Nagumo the new flattops *Zuikaku* and *Shokaku* to cruise in waters to the east of Japan and fly defensive patrols. The *Hiryu* and *Soryu* would join Nagumo at Palau Island and participate in the Darwin strike. The First Air Fleet's strength for the Darwin operation would be four carriers, two fast battleships, three cruisers, and nine destroyers, by itself a unit more powerful than anything that the British or the Americans could now assemble in the Pacific. It would be attached to Vice Admiral Nobutake Kondo's Southern Area Force.

Seaman Iki Kuramoti of the *Akagi* enjoyed his brief stay at Palau in the western Carolines. The island was, he noted, "the most civilized among the various South Sea Islands." It was the seat of government for the Caroline group and boasted stores, parks, shrines, and elementary schools. "It reminded me of a country town at home." Kuramoti managed to meet a pair of native girls and found himself ". . . amazed at their skill in Japanese, at their simplicity and naïveté, and at the intelligence of their profiles."

He had no opportunity to cultivate a friendship. On February 15 the First Air Fleet left Palau, steamed south of Mindanao, the southern-most Philippine island, past the Japanese-occupied Celebes to a point some 220 miles north-northwest of Darwin. There, on February 19 at 7:00 A.M., Fuchida led out against Port Darwin a massive strike of 71 Vals, 81 Kates, and 36 Zero fighters, a flight of nine from each carrier. One Zero flight led by Lieutenant Nikaido flew direct escort for the bombers. Commander

Shigeru Itaya, the China war and Pearl Harbor veteran, led the other three ahead to sweep the air clear of enemy fighters.

To defend Darwin the Australians were almost as badly prepared as at Rabaul. Darwin had Bachelor Field, also used by civil aviation, and RAAF Station Darwin. Neither had more than rudimentary facilities or a permanently attached fighter wing. The main defense for the port and the two airfields, aside from a few Hudsons and Wirraways useless for air-to-air combat, consisted of 18 antiaircraft guns manned by twenty-year-old youths of the Australian militia. The guns had no fire-control equipment, and the crews had never fired a live round. For close-in defense they had a few air-cooled Hotchkiss .30-caliber machine guns and some .50s from the United States. Several of the 47 merchant and naval ships in harbor had antiaircraft, including the largest warship, the U. S. S. *Peary,* an old four-piper World War I-class destroyer.

Passing through Darwin en route to Java were ten P-40s of the U. S. Army's 33rd Pursuit Squadron under Major Floyd Pell. Their fighting capacity was slight, because most of the pilots had only a few hours on a P-40, some as few as 12.

At 9:15 A.M. on February 19, with Fuchida's striking force already under way, Pell led his green pilots off for Java, only to turn back ten minutes later after learning by radio that the weather had closed down over Timor, his initial destination. Returning to Darwin, he took his own flight of five in to land, leaving Lieutenant Robert G. Oestreicher, his only other experienced pilot, to patrol with five planes over the harbor. Oestreicher was at 8,000 feet, climbing to his patrol altitude of 15,000, the top fighting ceiling for a P-40, when he suddenly yelled into his mike, "Zeros, Zeros, Zeros!" But it was too late; Commander Itaya and his veterans already were pouncing on them, diving from out of the sun.

Two P-40s fell into the ocean, while the Japanese machine-gunned the pilots dangling in their parachutes. Itaya's Zeros ran down another P-40 ten miles out in the bay, but Lieutenant Max R. Weeks managed to bail out, escape the strafing of his chute, and find a floating tree on landing in the water. He got back safely after dark. Second Lieutenant William R. Walker, with a bullet through his shoulder, managed to land at Bachelor Field, ground-loop, and run away from his plane before it was shot to pieces. Oestreicher got into cloud cover and later claimed a Val.

In the meantime Pell and his four pilots had tried to take off again, with the major and two of his men being cut down just as they were getting into the air. Lieutenants Burt H. Rice and John G. Glover turned into the attacks and managed to reach 5,000 feet, but Rice then had to jump, and Glover, badly shot up, barely managed a crash landing. Ten P-40s, caught by surprise and flown by green pilots, had been no match for 36 Zeros.

In the meantime Fuchida had arrived with his Kate high-level bombers and Takashige Egusa with the Vals. Against undirected antiaircraft fire they could be fussy about selecting their targets. The Vals concentrated on the *Peary*, which was under way, getting five hits and sinking the little ship. They also attacked the light seaplane tender *Preston*, but this ship had improvised a formidable battery of .50-caliber AA machine guns from spares for its brood of PBY flying boats. Consequently, Egusa's pilots inflicted only nonlethal damage. They destroyed the largest ship in the harbor with several hits, the U. S. Army transport *General M. C. Meigs* of 12,568 tons, and a smaller trooper, the *Mauna Loa*. A hit on her cargo of depth charges blew in two the *Neptunia*, a 6,000-ton coaster; also sunk were the *British Motorist*, a tanker, and the *Zealandia* of 6,683 tons. Hospital ship *Manduna* took a hit but survived. In Darwin town some 200 civilians lost their lives from bombing and vicious strafing. Itaya lost one Zero strafer. Trooper Max Grant, with a machine gun, dropped a Zero that crashed ashore, killing its pilot and scattering enough wreckage to furnish a goodly supply of souvenirs. The only other plane lost was a Val dive bomber. The defenders had lost 11 P-40s, six Hudsons, a Wirraway, and three PBY flying boats, half on the ground or water.

The attack on Darwin on February 19 had begun the worst month of the Pacific war for the Allies. This same day had seen the small Allied fleet in Netherlands East Indies waters, commanded by Dutch Rear Admiral K. W. F. M. Doorman, defeated in a brush with Japanese cruisers and destroyers covering a landing on Bali. A week later on February 27, Doorman's five cruisers and 11 destroyers lost the Battle of the Java Sea to a Japanese cruiser force near Surabaya. Two Dutch cruisers and three British and Dutch destroyers went down. On this day also the old "Covered Wagon," the U. S. S. *Langley*, configured as a tender with half of its flight deck chopped off, yielded to horizontal bombers off Tjilatjap while trying to ferry fighter planes to Java. On March 1 the damaged U. S. heavy cruiser *Houston* tried to escape from the Java Sea into the Indian Ocean with the Australian light cruiser *Perth*. Both went down that night in the Sunda Strait after steaming into the middle of a Japanese landing force.

Nagumo's First Air Fleet contributed to this holocaust. It operated between February 25 and March 5 in the Indian Ocean south of Java, claiming two destroyers and eight merchant ships in antishipping sweeps and launching a very destructive air strike at Tjilatjap on Java on March 5. Victims of Fuchida's pilots included U. S. destroyers *Edsall* and *Pillsbury*, gunboat *Asheville*, and oiler *Pecos*, the latter sunk by a Val south of Christmas Island. The only remaining refuges for Allied warships in the Far East were Fremantle near Perth in Australia and Ceylon off the coast of India.

Though they had recognized the political necessity of supporting the Dutch, neither Admiral Nimitz nor Admiral Ernest J. King, now the U. S. Chief of Naval Operations, dared send U. S. carriers into Netherlands East Indies waters. But Halsey's Marshalls raid had disclosed the feasibility of surprise carrier strikes elsewhere, and it was toward Rabaul, bent on such a mission, that Captain Frederick C. "Ted" Sherman's *Lexington* was steaming. The "Lady Lex" was part of a task force commanded by Vice Admiral Wilson Brown. While Fuchida's airmen were attacking Port Darwin, Brown's ships were beginning a high-speed run-in toward their target. Admiral Nimitz hoped that a successful blow by Brown's airmen might divert the Japanese from attacking Port Moresby on New Guinea's south coast. Radio intercepts had revealed this Japanese purpose.

Despite the tense war situation and the risk of steaming so boldly through dangerous waters between the Solomons and Gilberts, the routine of the big flattop scarcely differed from peacetime. Pilots off duty lounged in their ready rooms or wardrooms, getting "sack time" in their chairs, writing letters, drinking endless cups of "jamoke," the Navy's incredibly strong coffee, and playing acey ducey (a form of backgammon) or bridge, sometimes for high stakes. Captain Sherman seemed to be always on the bridge, usually with a searching eye on the nearby destroyers. On the flight deck highly trained plane handlers, clad in different-colored sweat shirts (red designated crash and repair crews; yellow, men who directed moving planes; blue, the "pushers" who moved about parked planes), lounged about but ready to dash into motion the moment the loudspeaker should bellow, "Now launch planes!"—the signal to send off another Dauntless or Wildcat on patrol. When a Wildcat raced the prescribed 194 feet down the flight deck into a 25-knot wind the carrier's supreme moment had come. The plane, banking slightly to the right to clear the ship as it struggled for altitude, was the *Lexington*'s only reason for being.

Condition "A," the call to General Quarters, would send every man to his battle station. It could mean that a radar operator had detected a suspicious blip, that a destroyer's sonar had echoed from an underwater object, or that Captain Sherman had laid on just another drill to keep everyone alert. Chow time meant excellent, well-prepared food at the beginning of a cruise and rather too much extracted from cans toward the end, after the ship had depleted its refrigerated stocks.

Landing a CAP brought into action a key man on the ship, the LSO, Landing Signal Officer, himself usually an experienced pilot. The carrier would head into the wind to get the desired 25 knots of breeze from the bow, a plane-guard destroyer would take position astern, and the LSO would climb onto his platform, holding his paddles or flags straight out from his shoulders. Then he would guide the plane in, dipping to the right or left, suddenly dropping the paddles when the plane was about to snag the arresting gear and slam onto the deck in a typically rough carrier landing. Or, if the pilot was not "in the groove," he might frantically start crossing his paddles over his head, the signal for a "wave off," instruction to the pilot to "pour on the coal" and go around again for another try. Even the best of pilots occasionally got wave-offs; and it was not unusual for a frightened or rattled pilot to get five or six and to spend the better part of an hour trying to land.

At dusk with the sun setting the *Lexington* was at its most beautiful.

It no longer appeared to be top-heavy and lopsided, and the planes bunched on the stern appeared to be etched against a reddening sky. For 2,500 men it was home, something familiar and solid if not really safe.

While about 400 miles northeast of Rabaul on February 20, the *Lexington*'s radar picked up a blip. A few minutes later lookouts spotted a four-engined Mavis flying boat. The skipper of Fighting 3, Lieutenant Commander John S. "Jimmy" Thach, shot it down in his first combat action, noting that the Japanese crew made no effort to bail out and continued to shoot at him even with their plane on fire. The 20-mm. cannon shells fired from its turrets looked to Thach "like Roman candles—a black center with a fiery corona." (After war began *Lex*'s old Fighting 2, made up of enlisted pilots, was disbanded. Thach and Fighting 3 joined the *Lex* after *Sara* was torpedoed.)

That this Mavis or another, also shot down, had spotted the *Lex* became clear at 4:50 P.M. when the radar picked up nine twin-engine high-performance Mitsubishi G4M Bettys approaching at 11,000 feet. Lieutenant Noel Gayler's division on CAP got four but not before some of the Japanese bombardiers had released. Captain Sherman bided his time, let them take good aim, then threw the *Lexington* into a violent turn at the moment of release, insuring clean misses by all bombs at a comfortable distance. Thach and his section went after the escaping bombers.

Then came trouble. Behind the first flight, undetected by the radar as a separate group, came nine more Bettys. Only two Wildcats were in position to intercept. The guns of one jammed, leaving Lieutenant Edward H. "Butch" O'Hare to tackle them alone. This he did in overhead, high-side, and low-side approaches, weaving through the formation, firing short deflection bursts, knocking down five of the Bettys in six minutes, most of them in flames. Thach went after the rest. "We had to chase them quite a distance from the ship," he recorded later, "but I wanted to make it a hundred percent if I could." Counting the two Mavises, Fighting 3 claimed 19 of 20 Japanese planes attacked this day. This was close to correct, for a postwar Japanese count cites 13 shot down and two force-landed of 17 Betty attackers, plus three Mavises lost. Thach believed his squadron's success confirmed his ruthless concentration on gunnery in practice. "Our victory was due to our ability to hit the target and make every bullet count."

The second formation of Bettys also had managed to release their bombs, coming closer than the first but failing to hit. One plane tried a crash dive, giving the flattop's .50s and 1.1s a workout. It hit the water 75 yards to the rear of the ship.

The Japanese press reported this stiff repulse ambivalently. The *Osaka Mainichi* recorded that Japan's "wild eagles" had inflicted "fatal damage" on a U. S. carrier, type unspecified. But it recorded also the pilot's reports of heavy AA fire and the loss of nine of the attackers. Failing to return was the squadron leader, Lieutenant Commander Takuzo Ito, a Japanese Naval Academy graduate of the Class of 1928, and Lieutenant Commanders Yogoro Seto and Masayoshi Nakagawa from the Academy's classes of 1933 and 1938. The hero who had tried to crash the *Lex* was Lieutenant Noboru Sakai. The Japanese claimed ten Wildcats; in fact they got two, with one man lost. These pilots had tried to attack from dead astern, flying straight into the 20-mm. tail "stinger" carried in a "greenhouse" in the tail of each Betty. Noel Gayler's life was saved when a bullet from a Betty gunner failed to penetrate his bulletproof windscreen.

Despite their heavy losses, which demonstrated that the relatively fast and long-range Betty was vulnerable and extremely flammable, Commander Ito's pilots had saved Rabaul from attack. Realizing that his task force had lost the advantage of surprise and that he might draw another attack that included dive bombers, Admiral Brown canceled the mission and retired. Rabaul held no targets, he believed, worth risking the loss of the precious *Lexington*. "Butch" O'Hare's expert shooting netted him the title of "ace" in his first air combat, wide popular acclaim when the exploit became known, and a Congressional Medal of Honor.

Strategically, the *Lexington*'s sortie toward Rabaul had one extremely important result. It convinced the Japanese Navy command at Truk that landing operations scheduled against Port Moresby and Tulagi, set to go in early March as soon as Lae and Salamaua on New Guinea had been occupied, would be too risky. It therefore deferred both until Admiral Yamamoto would see fit to dispatch carrier elements to the southeast area. This was not to be until the end of April.

While the *Lexington* was returning, Bill Halsey was steaming for Wake Island in the *Enterprise*. Aboard he still had Commander H. L. Young's veterans of Air Group 6. The plan was simple: Protected by Wildcats, the Big E's Dauntlesses and Devastators would blast enemy installations early on the morning of February 24, after which cruisers and destroyers would bombard the atoll.

Bad weather complicated and delayed the launch. Lieutenant Perry Teaff's Dauntless went over the side, striking a five-inch gun and plunging into the water. This ended the war for Commander Young's Pearl Harbor companion. He was recovered, an eye badly injured, but his gunner was lost. Consequently, the bombardment began first at 7:10 A.M. and then was followed by the air strike instead of vice versa. Good targets were scarce. The best were three of the big Mavis flying boats found and destroyed, one in the air. Ensign Percy W. Forman was lost, being last seen when his Dauntless was at low altitude, descending, with its engine smoking badly. "It is assumed," Commander Young reported to Admiral Halsey, "that the pilot made a water landing some ten miles east of Wake." Fire from ground-based AA machine guns holed six other SBDs, and a piece of hinge fitting, bearing the date "1938," from an exploding Mavis struck and damaged Lieutenant Roger Mehle's Wildcat.

The late takeoff disappointed Commander Young because it meant forfeiture of surprise. In reporting to Halsey he reiterated again the need for at least 27 fighters on a carrier and the necessity of having "at least" 50 percent spare pilots to man the planes. But 52 planes had successfully attacked despite the weather, the bombing had been accurate, and the Wildcat escort had promptly dispatched the one enemy plane in the air.

In her retirement the lucky *Enterprise* again found a weather front to hide in while steaming in the direction of Midway Island. She still was enjoying its protection when the Pearl Harbor radio offered a new target. Admiral Nimitz radioed to Halsey, "Desirable to hit Marcus if you think it possible." Wild Bill was happy to oblige. Marcus, not an atoll but an isolated mountain top in the ocean, lay to the northwest about halfway between Wake and Iwo Jima near the Japanese Bonin Islands. It was about a thousand miles from Tokyo, close enough, Nimitz hoped, to jolt the Japanese high command when it was attacked.

Off Midway Halsey refueled from the fleet oiler *Sabine* and, without returning to Pearl, headed directly for Marcus. Bad weather induced him to drop off his destroyers, which could not keep up in heavy seas, and to run in at high speed with just the cruisers *Salt Lake City* and *Northampton* as escorts, accepting the risk of a chance encounter with an enemy submarine. He took a bigger chance on March 3, risking a loss of surprise, when his SBDs bombed two submarines and forced them to submerge. A less bold commander would have turned back. Finally, at 4:46 A.M. on March 4, Commander Young led into a solid overcast at 4,000 feet a strike of 32 Dauntlesses and six Wildcats. The slow Devastators stayed behind; Halsey wanted to throw one quick, hard punch and then get out.

Emerging on top of the overcast at 15,000 feet, the pilots found that they had become separated. Young was ahead with Bombing 6, followed by Scouting 6 and trailed by Scouting 6's commander, Wilmer Earl Gallaher, leading three Dauntlesses. Luck rode with them. Over Marcus a long rift several miles wide opened in the clouds. Snapping on his radio, Young barked, "There it is! Below us. Attack, Holly. Commence your attack."

At 6:30 A.M. Lieutenant Commander Hollingsworth dove, leading down Bombing 6. Scouting 6 followed as black puffs of AA fire began, supplemented by long trains of 25-mm. tracer. Gallaher with his four-plane flight brought up the rear of the attackers.

Last man to dive was a worried Lieutenant Clarence Dickinson. The AA fire, he noted, was much heavier than at the Marshalls and at Wake, and now every shell and bullet seemed aimed at him. On the way down he stayed in the cover of one of two enormous columns of smoke rising from petroleum fires set by the first attackers. He veered out to drop his bomb from 1,500 feet at what appeared to be a wood structure in the hangar area of Marcus's small airfield. After pulling out at 600 feet he dove again to keep his speed up, leveled off just above the water and zigged and zagged away from the island with the antiaircraft trailing off behind him. He recalled afterward:

I enjoyed that trip back to the carrier about as much as any ride I've ever had. It was as if I were coming back from my own funeral with God's assurance it had been just a mistake. . . . I was alive!

He called over the intercom to his gunner, "Are you all right back there, De Luca?"

"Yes, Mr. Dickinson. And how!"

Less fortunate was Dickinson's roommate, Lieutenant Hart Dale Hinton. Hit by flak, his plane totally aflame, Hinton had crash-landed off Marcus and with his gunner was taken prisoner by the enemy's garrison.

In strictly military terms the results of the Marcus raid were dubious. Thirty-two Dauntlesses had planted a bomb apiece on a small enemy outpost at the cost of one of their number. No follow-up strikes had been flown, not even a photo-reconnaissance mission. Not a single enemy plane had been attacked or even seen. Yet Nimitz and Halsey had achieved their purpose; they had forced the Japanese to pay attention to them. Word of the Marcus attack touched off a blackout in Tokyo.

The continuous operations of the Big E since Pearl Harbor had been very hard on Air Group 6. On March 6, after returning from a routine antisub and scouting patrol, Dickinson made a bad landing. The SBD hit hard, bounced high, and spun sideways. Afterward Flight Surgeon "Doc" Jordan came up to Dickinson.

"How do you feel, Dick?"

"I'm just as tired as I can possibly be. I want some sleep."

"Well, Gee! You just scared me to death. You're grounded!"

Dickinson didn't argue. All hands on the *Enterprise* needed a rest, and so did Admiral Bill Halsey.

While Dickinson had been making his "Chinese" landing on the *Enterprise*, Rear Admiral Frank Jack Fletcher of the *Yorktown* task group had been conferring with Vice Admiral Wilson Brown and Captain Ted Sherman of the *Lexington* group. Since a direct approach on Rabaul had not been safe, the three American commanders decided to attack Japanese forces about to land on New Guinea. But instead of sailing close, within easy range of the Base Air Force now entrenched at Rabaul, they would attack across the big bird-shaped island from the Gulf of Papua. To insure inflicting heavy damage, both flattops would operate together, something not without precedent in the American Navy but rarely done in peacetime maneuvers. Thus was formed *ad hoc* what a naval historian later called "the most effective force which had [yet] been assembled within the American Navy." Captain Sherman was designated "Commander Air Force" for the operation, though the title meant little. The attack date was set for March 10, by which time it was expected that the Japanese would have landed.

Intelligence was right. The Japanese had begun landing, virtually un-opposed, at Lae and Salamaua, due north of Port Moresby on March 8.

The Japanese wanted both as outposts to protect their main southern bastion at Rabaul. The forces were small—a Navy battalion at Salamaua, an Army one at Lae, plus supporting artillery and AA units. Commanding the landing force was Rear Admiral Sadamichi Kajioka with the light cruiser *Yubari*, six destroyers, seaplane tender *Kiyokawa Maru* with 13 float planes of the Yokosuka air unit, and assorted minesweepers, patrol boats, and transports. Offshore in support was Rear Admiral Aritomo Goto with four heavy and two light cruisers and destroyers. Kajioka's force still was there supporting an almost bloodless landing on the morning of March 10.

At 7:49 A.M., from approximately 150 miles distant in the Gulf of Papua, the *Lexington* began launching, followed 20 minutes later by the *Yorktown*. Between them the carriers launched 104 planes, the heaviest American strike yet, of 61 SBDs and 25 TBDs with 18 Wildcats for cover. The trick of the operation was to get the heavily laden Devastators, some with torpedoes, some with bombs, over the 12,000- to 16,000-foot Owen Stanley Mountains. They would have to fly through a 7,500-foot pass between Mt. Stanley and Mt. Lawson, being unable to climb high enough to get over any other way. Anxiously watched by Commander William B. Ault, the skipper of the *Lex*'s air group, they made it and roared down the northern slope of the mountains toward an enemy 45 miles away.

The *Lexington*'s 13 Devastators carrying torpedoes went in first, attacking anchored transports and claiming three hits, their crews noting that the *Yubari* and the destroyers had slipped anchor and were fleeing out to sea. The Dauntlesses tipped over next, plummeting almost straight down from 14,000 feet, aiming for three large transports anchored at Lae as well as the warships. Hit by ground AA fire at 400 feet on pullout, Ensign Joseph Philip Johnson's Dauntless crash-landed in the water. The Wildcats found and shot down a Dave float plane that had been harassing the Devastators, then wheeled out to sea to strafe repeatedly the *Yubari* and the destroyers.

Yorktown's Devastators found the *Kiyokawa Maru* with four aircraft on its stern 25 miles at sea. Bombing from 13,000 feet, they loosed a pattern that scored one or more hits on the maneuvering ship. Air Warrant Officer Kumesaka Nemoto recorded the result in his diary: "Our ship was badly damaged. I clearly realized how helpless a ship could be without an air unit. . . . [We] may have to dock at Yokosuka." He concluded—erroneously if understandably—"[It was] our biggest loss since the beginning of the war." Fortunately for Nemoto, *Yorktown*'s Dauntlesses did not find the damaged *Kiyokawa Maru*; instead they attacked and wrecked a pair of auxiliary minesweepers.

The bombing of the pilots was rather better than their warship identification. Postwar Japanese sources record damage to the *Yubari*—described as "medium"—to a pair of destroyers, to minelayer *Tsugaru*, to tender *Kokai*, to the 6,863-ton *Kiyokawa Maru*, and to two converted minesweepers. Sunk was the Army transport *Yokohama Maru*, and run aground and burned out was the Navy transport *Tenyo Maru*. Killed were 126 Navy men, with another 240 wounded. The claims of the *Lexington* pilots to have sunk a pair of heavy cruisers were purely fancy. Either they mistook the *Yubari* and the destroyers for bigger game, or they attacked (and missed) some of the units of Admiral Goto's covering force. The *Yorktown* pilots reported no enemy heavy cruisers as present.

In terms of numbers of ships sunk as compared to those damaged, the raid paralleled the Kwajalein strike. Captain Elliott Buckmaster, the exceptionally acute and able skipper of the *Yorktown*, may have put his finger on the reason in his after-action report. Instantaneous fuses, he noted, had been used on the bombs. This, he believed, was a mistake, the bombs having exploded without penetrating to the vitals of the ship. "It is considered," he wrote in accepted Navy language, "that the use [in the future] of delayed action fuses is essential against surface vessels. The advantage to be gained by fragments of near misses is far outweighed by the disruptive internal damage when a direct hit [with a delay fuse] is obtained." The bombing had apparently been accurate, and without question the pilots had pressed home their attacks. No fewer than eight of the *Lexington*'s SBDs and three of its Devastators came home with battle damage, mostly from rifle caliber fire, in addition to Ensign Johnson's plane lost. That meant they had come in very low. In their first attack on an enemy naval landing force both the *Lexington* and *Yorktown* pilots had acquitted themselves well.

7. Ceylon and Tokyo

While Admirals Brown and Fletcher were retiring from the Gulf of Papua satisfied with their Lae–Salamaua strike, Admiral Nagumo was returning to Staring Bay in the Celebes. He was content with the bag from his antishipping sweep south of Java. His entry into the bay on March 11 coincided with the collapse of Dutch resistance on Java and British resistance in central Burma. Nagumo now could replenish his ships and rest his air crews, while a lesser Japanese force seized Port Blair in the Andaman Islands. By this move Admiral Yamamoto was thrusting Japanese imperial power into the Indian Ocean and threatening India.

From his anchorage at Hashirajima Yamamoto already had decided that Nagumo's First Air Fleet should next attack the big island of Ceylon off the Indian subcontinent. An air strike at Colombo, the island's chief port, and another at the British naval anchorage at Trincomalee might well "Pearl Harbor" the Royal Navy's Indian Ocean fleet. This was a worthy target. Japanese Intelligence guessed that the fleet included two carriers, three battleships, 15 cruisers, and a goodly swarm of destroyers. Additionally, an attack should sink a lot of merchant shipping.

In accord with Yamamoto's order Vice Admiral Nobutake Kondo, the Southern Area Force commander and now Nagumo's immediate superior, ordered him to carry out "Operation C," with "C-day" set for April 5. Nagumo was to leave Staring Bay at his own convenience, sail by way of Djakarta and Sunda Strait, locate the British fleet based at Ceylon, attack it, and then return via the Strait of Malacca and Singapore. Nagumo would take with him flagship *Akagi*, the *Soryu* and *Hiryu*, and also the *Shokaku* and *Zuikaku* that had arrived after patrolling uneventfully in waters east of Japan. The *Kaga* needed engine repairs and would sit out this mission. Otherwise, the same all-powerful carrier striking force that had attacked Pearl Harbor would be united once more.

Protecting the flattops would be all four of Japan's fast battleships—*Kongo*, *Haruna*, *Hiei*, and *Kirishima*—plus heavy cruisers *Tone* and *Chikuma*, with their useful scouting seaplanes, and light cruiser *Abukuma* and a brood of destroyers. In a separate striking force light carrier *Ryujo* would raid shipping with heavy cruisers and destroyers along the Indian coast between Madras and Calcutta. About Ceylon and as far away as Bombay seven submarines would provide reconnaissance and also sink shipping.

Neither Vice Admiral Sir Geoffrey Layton, commanding the British naval establishment at Ceylon, nor Admiral Sir James Somerville, commanding the British Eastern Fleet from at sea, was anxious for a showdown with Nagumo, though their force was considerably stronger than the Japanese had estimated. It consisted of the new armored deck carriers *Indomitable* and *Formidable*, the light carrier *Hermes*, built in the early 1920s, the battleship *Warspite* fresh from repair and refit at Bremerton in the United States, and four slow old "R"-class battleships, *Ramillies, Revenge, Resolution*, and *Royal Sovereign*. Also included were the heavy cruisers *Cornwall* and *Dorsetshire*, five light cruisers, and 16 destroyers. This agglomeration of ships was, however, more powerful on paper than at sea and no match for Nagumo. The captains had not trained together, and the carriers had only 57 strike aircraft, mostly slow biplane Swordfish and Albacores. Few of the 40 fighters embarked had enough performance to tackle a Zero. Somerville reckoned, probably correctly, that his only hope was to shadow the Japanese force and catch it with a surprise night torpedo attack with the Swordfish and Albacores. In a daylight standoff he stood to suffer a repeat of what had happened to the *Repulse* and *Prince of Wales*.

Somerville therefore elected to keep the main body of his fleet well away from the enemy's obvious targets at Colombo and Trincomalee. He chose to operate from bleak Addu Atoll in the sun-scorched Maldive Islands, south of and well to the west of Ceylon. Though Addu Atoll lacked antiaircraft guns and antisubmarine nets, Somerville could refuel and train his command there, hopefully out of knowledge of the Japanese, while waiting for Nagumo to appear.

At Colombo on Ceylon the Royal Air Force had two squadrons of Hurricane Mark Is and Mark IIs, fast modern fighters, and another at Trincomalee. To these 50 planes the Royal Navy added a dozen clumsy two-seat Fulmar fighters that belonged to the old light carrier *Hermes*, plus some Swordfish and Albacores. The only force available to bomb the Japanese was a Canadian squadron of a dozen twin-engine Blenheims, land planes suitable only for high-level bombing. A handful of Catalina flying boats identical to U. S. Navy PBYs rounded out the none too robust defense. Perhaps the worst deficiency was the lack of operational early-warning radar either at Colombo or Trincomalee.

At 8:00 A.M. on March 26 the First Air Fleet stood out from Staring Bay with *Akagi* leading. This time even Commander Fuchida was satisfied; he knew that his pilots should have some worthwhile targets, and he hoped for another resounding and glorious victory. But the Japanese did not sail undetected. Evidently through the interception and deciphering of

Yamamoto's orders, Admiral Somerville learned of Nagumo's projected departure. He therefore maneuvered his force south of Ceylon between March 30 and April 2, hoping to locate Nagumo with reconnaissance planes and to launch a night attack. Finally, concluding either that Intelligence had been mistaken or that Nagumo had abandoned his plans, he retired to Addu Atoll to let his ships take on fuel and fresh water. Foolishly he also ordered the heavy cruiser *Dorsetshire* to return to Colombo to complete some repairs in company with her sister ship *Cornwall*. The *Hermes* went back to Trincomalee with destroyer *Vampire* to pick up her planes, all of which had been operating from land bases.

Somerville was just entering Addu Atoll late on the afternoon of March 4 when his communications officer handed him a message radioed from a patrolling Catalina. From RAF Squadron Leader Birchall it reported battleships, aircraft carriers, and destroyers to the southeast of Ceylon—then broke off in mid-sentence. Six alert Zeros of Commander Itaya's combat air patrol led by Flight Petty Officer Matsuyama had forced Birchall down, destroyer *Isokaze* rescuing him and his crew. But as Nagumo had feared, Birchall had reported the force.

Somerville made no attempt to close the enemy. He was some 600 miles to the west. But Admiral Layton at Colombo ordered the *Cornwall* and *Dorsetshire* to leave at once for Addu Atoll to join Somerville and the planeless *Hermes* to clear Trincomalee and operate to the northwest. He fully expected a carrier strike on either Colombo or Trincomalee the next morning.

For his part Admiral Nagumo was profoundly dissatisfied with his own intelligence. His submarines had told him little, and he did not know where Somerville's British fleet was. He reasoned that Colombo on Ceylon's west coast would more likely harbor the British than Trincomalee on the exposed east side and so closed Ceylon from the south on the night of April 4–5.

At 6:00 A.M. on April 5 the *Akagi* and *Soryu*, leading the Japanese carrier columns, turned into the wind to launch planes. Commander Itaya took off first, followed by 35 Zeros. Then came 38 of Commander Egusa's trusty Vals. Finally, 53 Kates took the air led by Fuchida himself. En route and nearing their target they had a lucky break. Far below Fuchida spotted a formation of ten Swordfish biplanes armed with torpedoes. He motioned to Itaya to go after them with his Zeros. This the commander did in a swift, merciless pass, shooting down eight. These were *Hermes* planes from 814 Squadron, Fleet Air Arm, flying into Colombo from Trincomalee. Itaya had caught them within sight of their destination.

Coming up on the target, deploying to attack, Fuchida noted with regret that Colombo held few naval craft and not much shipping. But he ordered the Vals to dive at craft in the harbor and led his Kates against Colombo's airfield and shipyard installations. This time, for the first time, his pilots ran into a real fight.

Though still on the ground when the Japanese were sighted, 36 Hurricanes and six Fleet Air Arm Fulmars managed to get into the air. One Hurricane squadron tore off from the race track, where it had established itself on an improvised runway, and barged into Egusa's Vals over the harbor. They mauled them, shooting down several and damaging others, before Itaya's Zeros could dive to the rescue and entangle them in dogfights. The result was then a lopsided Japanese victory. Fuchida's airmen claimed more than 50 planes down—in fact they brought down 20 against only one Zero lost—and proved that the Zero could easily outperform a Hurricane in a dogfight. Nevertheless, although the Vals had sunk two small naval vessels and fired a merchant ship against the loss of six of their number, they had signally failed to achieve Yamamoto's hope of destroying the British Indian Ocean fleet. It was not there.

Now the almost fantastic good fortune that had continuously favored Nagumo since Pearl Harbor came to his aid again. A slow scout plane from the cruiser *Tone*, flying a routine search, sighted the fleeing *Cornwall* and *Dorsetshire* and reported. On landing and refueling Commander Egusa of the *Soryu* led out 53 Vals against these ships that had no air cover. He approached his victims out of the sun from bow on so that few antiaircraft guns could bear or crews see. Diving from 12,000 feet and bombing with an accuracy probably unparalleled in any operation in the entire Pacific war, Egusa's pilots put both of the speeding, maneuvering ships under in a half hour. The pilots claimed 31 hits on the *Dorsetshire* and 15 on the *Cornwall* (in fact they got eight on her), with not a single Val shot down. To *Dorsetshire* seaman A. G. Elsegood the veritable shower of bombs seemed to lift his ship and "shake her bodily." Fortunately, he was unhurt, the water was warm, no sharks were about, and light cruiser *Enterprise* and two destroyers picked up 1,122 men of the crews of both ships the next day. Nevertheless, 422 jack-tars had been killed or drowned.

In the late afternoon a report from patrolling Zeros jolted Nagumo. The pilots, Flight Petty Officers Noguchi and Hino from *Hiryu*, sighted a pair of Fairey Albacores 350 nautical miles south of Ceylon, shooting down one. These, Nagumo reasoned correctly, could only have come from one of Somerville's carriers that was somewhere in his vicinity. He therefore decided to retire eastward for the night to get out of range, then return the next morning, fly off a search, find his elusive enemy, and bring him to battle.

For his part Admiral Somerville had been trying all day to avoid battle. While keeping a strike of Albacores ready on his decks and flying off search planes that included the lost pair, he had steamed far to the south of Addu Atoll, turning back only at dusk to be ready for a night attack should his or land-based scouts locate the enemy. When they failed to do so, he put about after dark and steamed toward Addu Atoll, reluctant even to enter his anchorage. He feared it might become a target should Nagumo discover that he had been using it.

By continuing these Fabian tactics Somerville completely frustrated Nagumo's search planes on the morning of April 6, though the admiral sent them out as far as 230 nautical miles from the *Akagi*. Nor did Somerville try to close, even though his radar on occasion picked up the strong Japanese air patrols as they reached the limits of their searches.

Tiring of the game, uneasy at the failure of his reconnaissance, Nagumo abandoned his search on the afternoon of the 6th and then steamed east to get outside a 500-nautical-mile search radius from Ceylon. His staff began planning another strike, this one against Trincomalee set for April 9.

In the meantime, small carrier *Ryujo* had been cruising along the Indian coast between Madras and Calcutta, causing havoc among unprotected merchant shipping. On April 4 ten of her Type 96 biplane torpedo planes sighted and attacked 14 ships, sinking three. On the 6th four Type 96s attacked 12 merchant ships near Cocanada, claiming the phenomenal result of two sunk and six damaged and left burning, plus destruction ashore of two oil tanks and two warehouses. "Our damage," a Japanese officer reported, "was only a few planes struck by enemy bullets." Nevertheless, the depredations of the Japanese cruisers and destroyers accompanying *Ryujo* were more serious, resulting in more than a dozen sinkings.

April 8 found Nagumo and the First Air Fleet steaming west again, keeping to economical speed in view of the shortage of bunker oil in the destroyers, approaching once more the 500-nautical-mile radius from Ceylon. The weather continued good. The often rough Indian Ocean was as docile as Japan's Inland Sea.

When Nagumo was 400 miles from Trincomalee on the late afternoon of April 8, a RAF Catalina spotted the task force. Itaya's Zeros tried to destroy it, but by dodging in and out of clouds and flying low over the water, the pilot skillfully evaded all attacks. Though certain beyond a doubt that he had been detected, Nagumo nevertheless held course to attack Trincomalee in the morning. There was always the chance that the British fleet might be in port or nearby.

At first light on April 9 all carriers launched, Fuchida leading out 90 Kates armed with bombs, escorted by 38 of Itaya's fighters. Nagumo held back all of Egusa's Vals. He hoped that his battleship and cruiser float planes, fanning out in wide searches to 150 nautical miles, still might find the British carriers.

British ground observers spotted the Japanese coming in, and 22 Hurricanes and Fulmars, all of the fighters available at Trincomalee, scrambled and began fighting for altitude. Itaya's Zeros gave them a ferocious scrap, keeping them away from all but one section of the Kates and shooting down eight Hurricanes and three of the Navy Fulmars for the loss of only three of their number and one Kate. A rueful Fleet Air Arm pilot recorded of his dogfight with a Zero, "The Fulmar was far too slow for these little bastards, who could turn on a sixpence, pull up into a stall, do a roll off the top, and cock ten thousand devils of a snook at you."

The damage at Trincomalee was heavy enough even without the Vals. A Kate hit and blew up the bomb-storage depot at the airfield at China Bay; others dropped on merchant shipping in the harbor, claiming three ships sunk. Shore installations suffered heavily. Only two Kates were lost, one in combat and one by forced landing, with five air crew.

Nagumo's foresight in sending out the cruiser float planes paid off handsomely. Sixty-five miles south of Trincomalee, from whence it had fled the night before, was light carrier *Hermes*. It still was without its planes, and just one destroyer was keeping it company. An old Type 95 scout plane from the battleship *Haruna* found the veteran flattop and reported her. Nagumo ordered an attack, and Lieutenant Commander Takahashi, commanding the *Shokaku*'s air unit, led out a crushingly powerful attack force of 85 Vals with a few protecting Zeros for cover.

At 10:30 A.M. the Vals attacked, getting no fewer than 40 hits, by British estimate, in ten minutes. Within another ten the 10,500-ton ship was under water. Fifteen Vals dove on destroyer *Vampire*, hit her despite her desperate maneuvering, and sank her also. Loss of life from both ships totaled 315.

Nagumo continued his air search until satisfied that the *Hermes*, which his pilots had positively identified and photographed, was alone. Then he began to retire. His fuel situation forbade any more attacks on Ceylon or nearby India, and he had done well enough by sinking a pair of heavy cruisers and the *Hermes*. Merchant-ship losses to his and the *Ryujo* task forces had totaled 23. Now he would enjoy one final bit of luck.

After returning from his bombing mission, Commander Fuchida was standing on the deck of the *Akagi* when the air-raid alarm sounded. Almost simultaneously a string of water spouts leaped into the air near the ship. Glancing up, he saw nine twin-engine bombers passing overhead. This was Canadian No. 11 Squadron with its Blenheims that had found and surprised its enemy only to miss with its bombs. Itaya's Zeros of the CAP went after them and shot down five. They lost Flight Petty Officer Makino, his Zero being the seventeenth and last Japanese plane shot down in the entire operation.

In the meantime, while the Japanese were attacking Trincomalee, Admiral Somerville, who had proven himself to be a gallant and daring officer in the Atlantic and Mediterranean, was far away, literally fleeing. The day before, April 8, he had risked entering Addu Atoll to fuel and then had hauled out with his entire force for Bombay and the east coast of Africa. In this wise decision he had full Admiralty support. Until such time as his carriers had full complements of modern planes, until his crews had been well trained in task-force operations, he dared not fight the Japanese Navy. The dispatch of the *Cornwall*, *Dorsetshire*, and *Hermes* to Ceylon had been a costly blunder.

By April 13 the First Air Fleet was nearing Singapore, having received orders to return to Japan. Including the attack on Pearl Harbor, it had performed stupendous feats, sinking five battleships, an aircraft carrier, two heavy cruisers, seven destroyers, and tens of thousands of tons of naval auxiliaries and merchant ships. In addition it had destroyed hundreds of enemy aircraft while spanning the Pacific and Indian oceans.

Nagumo had lost not a single ship; he had been attacked only once from the air and had fewer than 60 planes downed in combat. His pilots had set a standard for dive-bombing that neither their enemies nor their own successors would approach later in the war.

That the First Air Fleet's successes should have generated euphoria among its crews was inevitable. Seaman Iki Kuramoti expressed the prevailing sentiment in his description of the raid on Trincomalee. The fleet, he recorded, had bombed shore installations until "there were none remaining." After that it had dispatched the *Hermes* and a destroyer "in the work of a moment." He concluded, "We seemed to be inspired with superhuman powers." Fuchida and his pilots shared Kuramoti's "victory disease." Actual war had been so easy! Bombing and sinking enemy ships, shooting down enemy planes had been hardly more difficult or dangerous than peacetime maneuvers.

At 1:00 P.M. on April 18 the First Air Fleet was passing the northern tip of Luzon in the Philippines. All hands were relaxed, excepting those watching for enemy submarines. None was prepared for the incredible news that abruptly came cracking through the *Akagi*'s radio receivers high above the flight deck. Tokyo had been bombed! Reports followed of raids on Yokohama, the naval base at Yokosuka, Kobe, Osaka, and Nagoya.

Recalls Commander Fuchida, "Such widespread action came as a distinct shock, and we did not know what to make of it." The only possible source of an air attack had to be enemy carriers. But how could they hit so many targets at once? Seaman Kuramoti shared the greater chagrin of the enlisted men. "We wept bitter tears and were filled with indignation. . . ." At once the task force increased speed to 20 knots and rushed east to try to intercept the enemy. But when it became clear that the raids were on a very small scale and that no repeat attacks were likely, the First Air Fleet turned sharply north and headed for the Hashirajima anchorage.

The Tokyo raid that had dazzled Fuchida and distressed Kuramoti was "Special Bombing Project One," a brain child of Admiral Ernest J. King, the U. S. Navy's Chief of Naval Operations, and General Henry H. Arnold, commanding the U. S. Army Air Forces. The idea had been simple: Steam an aircraft carrier close to Tokyo, launch a deckload of 16 Army B-25 bombers, bomb Tokyo and other cities, and then fly the planes 1,093 more miles to Chuchow airfield in eastern China. There the planes would refuel, take off again, and fly on to the interior of China for delivery to Chiang Kai-shek's air force.

It was one of those concepts that had sounded crazy at first. But the more King's staff had studied it, the more feasible it had looked. New carrier *Hornet*, completing her accelerated shakedown trials, was scheduled to go to the Pacific. The Tokyo raid could be her first war mission. Tests had proved that a B-25 Mitchell, a new, fast, twin-engine bomber with enough range, could take off from the *Hornet*. Available to lead the mission was a genuine charismatic hero, Lieutenant Colonel James H. "Jimmy" Doolittle, the famous racing pilot. The mission obviously entailed enormous risks for the air crews but might pay handsome dividends. A surprise attack on Tokyo should produce great loss of "face" to both the Japanese Army and Navy, but far more important would be the tremendous boost given to the badly shaken morale of the American people. Damage to targets would be incidental; 16 planes carrying four 500-pound bombs apiece could hardly inflict significant military damage.

On April 2, 1942, with Captain Marc A. Mitscher in command, the *Hornet* left San Francisco Bay with cruisers *Nashville* and *Vincennes* and a division of destroyers. Everyone hoped that any enemy agent lurking atop Telegraph Hill and spotting the B-25 perched awkwardly on the big flattop's stern would assume that the ship was on a ferry mission—as in a sense it was.

On April 12 at 6:00 A.M. the *Hornet* joined Task Force 16 containing Admiral Halsey's familiar *Enterprise, Northampton, Salt Lake City,* and destroyers. The Big E's crew was mystified. Why Army bombers on a carrier? Why, also, an obviously northwesterly heading for the task force? Halsey finally cleared up the rumors by sending a terse signal to all hands: THIS FORCE IS BOUND FOR TOKYO. The cheers that resounded throughout all ships masked a certain alarm. This was the craziest thing Wild Bill had done yet.

The original plan had called for an approach to within 500 miles of Tokyo, a late-afternoon launch, and a night attack on Japan. The B-25s would then cross or skirt Japan, fly southwesterly from Kyushu to China, and arrive at Chuchow by daylight. The plan seemed foolproof—provided that the *Hornet* could get close enough.

On April 17, 1,000 miles east of Tokyo, Task Force 16 refueled and began a high-speed run-in. At 3:10 A.M. on the 18th the *Enterprise*'s surface search radar picked up two blips, ships ahead. Admiral Halsey altered course to evade. At 7:15 A.M. a patrolling SBD flew over the deck and dropped a message. Its pilot had spotted a patrol boat 42 miles ahead and believed that its lookouts had seen him. Wild Bill pressed on. Finally, at 7:44 A.M., lookouts sighted a fishing-type boat equipped with a powerful radio and another nearby. This was the *Nitto Maru No. 23*, which reported the task force. Cruiser *Nashville* finally sank it after expending 924 shells. The gunners had found the *Nitto* almost an impossible target, as it dipped from sight beneath heavy swells. It now was obvious that the Japanese had established a strong chain of surface patrols 650 miles out from their shores.

After clearing by message with Doolittle, Halsey decided to launch. He could not risk coming any closer. A launch this soon meant not only arrival over Tokyo at about noon but it added a critical 170 miles more to fly. Worse, it meant a night arrival over China with fuel critically low, if, indeed, Doolittle and his pilots could get that far.

At 8:20 A.M. Doolittle launched, racing down 467 feet of clear flight deck ahead of him. He made it, as did all of the 15 other pilots. Most stalled off their heavily laden planes, which they need not have done since the wind velocity over the flight deck was about 50 miles per hour. But after wallowing along nose high, they built up speed and headed straight for their targets. Tokyo was 668 miles away.

With the B-25s gone Task Force 16 put about. *Hornet* began launching her own SBDs and Wildcats to spell the *Enterprise* patrols already in the air. They took out their spleen on the Japanese picket boats that had almost frustrated their mission, while the carriers and cruisers steamed east at 25 knots. They attacked 16 and sank several, finding that the .50-caliber guns on the Wildcats were the best weapons. Radar picked up a patrolling enemy plane at 35 miles, but after the Japanese pilot had closed to 32 miles he turned back and so missed contact. Other Japanese pilots from the 26th Air Flotilla, sent on search by the *Nitto Maru*'s warning, sighted two of the B-25s approaching at low altitude but concluded that they must be Japanese flying boats.

Due to necessarily chancy navigation, the planes assigned to bomb Yokohama, Yokosuka, and Tokyo arrived north and south of the target area between about 12:00 noon and 1:00 P.M. Consequently, they attacked from various headings, thoroughly confusing the defenders as to the direction from which they had come. From Admiral Halsey's standpoint on the retiring task force this was a blessing. Racing in "on the deck," climbing briefly to 2,000 to bomb, and then dropping down again, the pilots were amazed to encounter light resistance from both antiaircraft and fighters. The Japanese were on the alert, but few of the Army Type 97 "Nate" fighters attacked. Flying high and without radar aid, the pilots missed seeing the camouflaged B-25s roaring in low. Those pilots who attacked found that they could not catch a Mitchell once it had dropped its bombs. Gunner Mel Gardner in Plane Number 11 shot down one diving fighter in flames. Since none of the B-25s was lost and the Japanese claimed several planes downed, it may be that they picked off by mistake several of their own airliners.

Lieutenant Edgar McElroy's plane hit the Japanese coast 50 miles off course. He corrected and raced over his target, the workshop and building-slip area of the Yokosuka Navy Yard, Japan's largest. One of Bombardier Sergeant Bourgeois' bombs toppled a crane; another hit a ship on a repair slip. His 500-pound incendiary cluster burst apart over the naval base, scattering smaller thermite missiles. His fourth bomb and some of the incendiaries made the prize hits of the raid, striking directly on the *Ryuho*, the new light aircraft carrier under conversion, causing enough damage to delay its completion until November 1942.

From a strictly military standpoint it might have been best to have targeted all aircraft against the Yokosuka yard. But since the mission was mainly psychological in intent the damage inflicted hardly mattered. The pilots tried to find their assigned targets, which included power plants, oil-tank farms, steel mills, and aircraft factories, but if they could not they picked the nearest likely-looking installation and dropped. Japanese anti-aircraft fire aimed at the low-flying planes may well have caused as much damage and as many civilian casualties as the bombs.

Among the installations recorded by the Japanese as damaged were the Nagoya Aircraft Factory, the Mitsubishi Company, Factory No. 1 of the Japan Steel Company, an oil-tank farm, several power plants, and, perhaps inevitably under the conditions, six schools and six wards of an Army hospital. Fifty people died; 252 were wounded. Fires gutted 90 miscellaneous buildings.

All planes succeeded in leaving Japan, and to that point the mission had been an unqualified success. But as they flew into storm and darkness south of Japan, the pilots realized that they would have no chance to find their airfield. Some, low on fuel, crash-landed on the China coast. Most crews flew inland until their fuel ran out and then parachuted blindly into cloud and darkness. One plane flew near Vladivostok in Soviet Russia and landed, whereupon the plane was confiscated and the crew interned. Perhaps the most surprising feature was that most of the crews survived and were aided by Chinese guerrillas to safety. Including Colonel Doolittle, 71 of 80 air crew lived. Four were killed, three of eight captured were executed by the Japanese as war criminals, and one died in prison.

As Admiral King and General Arnold had hoped, the Tokyo raid gave a tremendous boost to American morale. With his superb ability to provide the right touch, President Roosevelt suggested to inquiring reporters who pressed him as to the source of the planes that the raiders had come from "Shangri-La," James Hilton's idyllic, fictional Asian paradise. Those who paid the dearest price for the raid were the people of East China. In revenge for their helping the downed airmen, the Japanese Army launched an offensive into the area, leveling cities and villages, killing an estimated 250,000 Chinese, and thoroughly justifying Chinese leader Chiang Kai-shek's skepticism voiced prior to the raid as to its wisdom. Nevertheless, a victory it was, and a significant one, in the grim history of the Pacific war.

8. The Coral Sea

Jimmy Doolittle's daring raid on Tokyo had profoundly shocked Admiral Yamamoto. He recognized that the attack was a stunt, but it reminded him forcefully of America's enormous potential. In two or three years the United States would have enough carriers to carry out massive bombing raids on Japan's combustible capital. Also, Doolittle and his pilots had directly threatened the life of Japan's Divinity, Emperor Hirohito. Under no circumstances could Yamamoto tolerate a repeat performance.

The raid had demolished a continuing debate on future strategy. Yamamoto and Navy staff chief Nagano had agreed on a general course of action, but their subordinates had continued to haggle bitterly over details. Doolittle's feat had abruptly ended further wrangling and had forced the Combined Fleet and the Naval General Staff to rush to completion plans for a second-stage Japanese offensive in the Pacific.

As early as mid-January 1942 Yamamoto had ordered his Combined Fleet Headquarters to start thinking about future operations. Rear Admiral Matome Ugaki, his chief of staff, favored an invasion of Hawaii. Japan's carrier superiority, he believed, plus an overwhelming advantage in battleships, would make an occupation feasible. He therefore proposed seizing Midway, Johnston, and Palmyra islands in June, followed by landings in the Hawaiian islands.

Detailed study, however, revealed his plan to be too ambitious. Japan lacked enough carrier air strength to dominate totally Hawaiian skies. Also, heavy American coast artillery batteries covered all key harbors. Reluctantly, Ugaki abandoned his dream that would indeed have given Japan great leverage in any peace negotiations.

He next proposed seizing Ceylon and invading India. This time war-gaming disclosed no insuperable difficulties, and in mid-March an Army–Navy conference at Imperial General Headquarters in Tokyo reviewed an official Navy proposal for these "western operations." Here the Navy's scheme was scuttled. The Army representatives would not agree to an amphibious invasion of Ceylon, a mandatory preliminary of the plan. The necessity of guarding against Soviet forces, they said, left the Army without troops to spare. Since the Army could decide where and when to employ its men, that ended it. The Navy had no real equivalent of U. S. Marine Corps divisions with which to invade Ceylon. Its own Special Naval Landing Forces were each battalion-sized and too few for the job.

Meanwhile, Admiral Nagano's Naval General Staff had been devising an Australia-first strategy. The easy capture of Rabaul and the Bismarck Archipelago had disclosed Australia's military weakness. But an Australian venture was no more acceptable to the Army than Ugaki's Ceylon invasion had been. Again, the Army claimed it to be impossible to muster the ten divisions needed to conquer northern Australia. This time the Navy planners sensed why. The Army was expecting Hitler's spring and summer offensive of 1942 to defeat Soviet Russia and to bring down Stalin's government. The Army wanted divisions available to occupy the Soviet Far East.

Realizing that the Army never would provide strong ground forces for anything they dreamed up, the Naval General Staff planners now concocted a strategy to semi-isolate Australia from the United States. After the forthcoming seizure of Port Moresby that the Lexington's approach to Rabaul had deferred, amphibious forces would seize the New Hebrides, New Caledonia, the Fiji Islands, and Samoa. By July, with these operations complete, America's lifeline between the Hawaiian islands and Australia would be cut or at least bent. Because it would require few Army troops, this plan presumably would be acceptable. But now Admiral Yamamoto rebuffed Nagano's planners.

Having dropped his plan to seize Ceylon, Yamamoto's Chief of Staff Ugaki had devised a less ambitious version of his original Hawaiian proposal. He proposed near simultaneous seizure of the outer Aleutian Islands, including Kiska and Attu, and Midway Island just 1,130 miles from Oahu. From bases on these, he reasoned, American sorties from Pearl Harbor could be surveilled and blunted. Johnston and Palmyra islands could next be taken to sever the America–Australia lifeline. But to Admiral Yamamoto, Ugaki's scheme had a supreme advantage: It should force the inferior American carrier fleet into decisive battle. If the American carrier force was destroyed, then invading Hawaii might be practicable.

Working out details in Tokyo and aboard the Yamato proved exasperatingly difficult. The Aleutians–Midway operation was much the largest ever planned by the Japanese Navy. It would consume as much bunker oil—to name just one major supply item—as the fleet had consumed in an entire year of peacetime cruising. Getting the carrier air groups ready in time would be touch and go. And finally the problem remained of first making the Port Moresby landing now rescheduled for early May before the Midway operation could begin. But Jimmy Doolittle's raid cut short all further debate. Another surprise raid on Tokyo might succeed unless patrol planes based in the Aleutians and at Midway could "close the gap" in the North Pacific.

When the flattops of Admiral Nagumo's First Air Fleet steamed into the Hashirajima anchorage in April, ships intended for the vast Midway operation had already begun to assemble. From the *Yamato* and from powerful stations ashore wirelessed movement orders already were crackling out—coded, of course, for secrecy.

The Japanese should have realized the danger. They had been using essentially the same code system since December 1, 1940, a system they designated Naval Code D and American and British codebreakers JN25b. Use of the same code for so long was dangerous, especially since in January 1941 the Naval Staff in Tokyo had learned that the British somehow had traced supposedly secret movements of the carrier *Soryu*.

In truth, the Allied codebreakers had long ago cracked into the basic system. They were able to read enough of most ordinary naval messages (about 15 percent) to get the essence. Also, the Japanese did not attempt to encrypt call signs designating the originators and recipients of the messages. On the war's outbreak Japan's commo experts had merely modified the JN25 code, frustrating the codebreakers only temporarily. They were planning to issue a new codebook on April 1, 1942, but inability to get it delivered in time to all addresses had caused them to retard its activation date first to May 1 and then to June 1.

The consequence was that Yamamoto was sending out his Combined Fleet orders in a code that by April his enemies again were reading. He had not done so with Plan Z to attack Pearl, using instead landline and messenger to transmit his orders. But with Operation "AF" (Midway) and for its preliminary subsidiary, the plan to seize Port Moresby, designated in communications Operation "MO," orders went by radio.

American cryptographers at Pearl Harbor, with important help from Melbourne and Colombo, first caught on to Operation MO. Messages from Yamamoto to Truk and Rabaul began detailing the elaborate operation. By April 20 Lieutenant Commander Joseph J. Rochefort's hard-working specialists at Pearl Harbor had made enough sense from their "take" to know that 11 transports with new light carrier *Shoho* and four heavy cruisers as escort would sail through the Coral Sea to Port Moresby, arriving about May 8. They knew, too, that two fleet carriers would accompany them.

The intercepts also furnished hints of other features of the plan, a plan so complicated as to make Admiral Nimitz suspicious, concerned that the Japanese might be deliberately deceiving him. An invasion group consisting of the minelayer *Okinoshima*, two destroyers, a transport, and smaller craft would seize undefended Tulagi Island in the Solomons to establish a naval station. A support group with seaplane carrier *Kamikawa Maru* would establish a seaplane base in the Louisiade Islands. Finally, the First Air Fleet's Carrier Division 5, *Zuikaku*, *Shokaku*, a pair of heavy cruisers, and six destroyers, would perform four distinct missions. It would steam from Truk to Rabaul ferrying new Zero fighter planes to the Base Air Force stationed there. Then it would round the eastern side of the

Solomons chain to cover the Tulagi landing. Entering the Coral Sea south of Guadalcanal, it would search out and attack a defending American squadron that Yamamoto's planners assumed would include a carrier. It would find and destroy this force in approximately the middle of the Coral Sea. Finally, the force would approach Townsville on Australia's northeast coast and destroy enemy planes there and at four other air bases, thus furnishing indirect air protection to the transports off Port Moresby. Basic to the plan was the assumption that the Americans would be surprised. Yamamoto's staff had no inkling that secrecy had been lost.

In light of his forewarning and given the circumstances, it might have been good strategy for Admiral Nimitz to have withdrawn his carriers from the South Pacific, leaving the defense of Port Moresby and Australia to a confident U. S. Army Air Force. At Townsville on the base of the Cape York Peninsula, the Japanese carrier pilots would have to contend with the 22nd Medium Bombardment Group equipped with 92 B-25s and B-26s and the 8th Fighter Group with 50 P-39 fighters. At nearby Charters Towers airfield was the 3rd Light Bombardment Group with 19 more B-25s, 14 fast A-20s, and 19 A-24 dive bombers, the last being Army versions of the Navy's SBDs. Although the Army pilots were green and the in-commission rate of the planes below later wartime standards, the Zeros on *Zuikaku* and *Shokaku* were not numerous enough to handle 50 fighters and 144 bombers. American air strength in this remote section of northern Australia already dwarfed that of the British on Ceylon against which the entire First Air Fleet had been committed.

Even so, Nimitz dared not leave the defense entirely to the Air Force. He could not allow Port Moresby to be taken; otherwise, the Japanese might try to seize northern Australia. Nimitz had no way of knowing that the Japanese Army had killed this plan.

Nimitz therefore decided to send into the Coral Sea, just where the Japanese expected to find them, carriers *Lexington* and *Yorktown* even though food supplies on the *Yorktown* had begun to run short. Admiral King in Washington backed Nimitz's decision. The flattop's crew, the hard-boiled King commented, would have to eat "hardtack and beans" until the operation was over. Tanker *Neosho* would keep the ship filled with black oil. Nimitz also wanted to commit *Enterprise* and *Hornet* to the fight. But these ships did not return from Tokyo to Pearl until April 25, too late to reach the Coral Sea in time. Nimitz hurried them southward anyway, hoping that the Japanese might not meet their projected timetable.

May 1 found *Yorktown* and *Lexington* steaming into perhaps the most beautiful body of salt water in the world, the blue-green Coral Sea. Rear Admiral Frank Jack Fletcher aboard the *Yorktown* was in charge as Commander, Task Force 16.

Fletcher began refueling from *Neosho* on May 2, a process that con-sumed most of the day, then separated while Rear Admiral Aubrey W. Fitch in the *Lexington* drained oiler *Tippecanoe*. With flagship *Yorktown*

Fletcher steamed slowly west, having left Fitch with orders to catch up as best he could. Fletcher thus had only one carrier when he learned at 7:00 P.M. on May 3 that the Japanese were landing on Tulagi. Deciding he could not wait for Fitch, he dashed north at 27 knots to clobber the landing with *Yorktown's* Air Group 5.

Fortunately, during an all-night high-speed run, Fletcher steamed into a hundred-mile-deep cold front that concealed him from Rabaul's search planes. At 7:01 A.M. from southward of Guadalcanal, he launched his first strike of 12 Devastators with torpedoes and 28 Dauntlesses with bombs. No fighters went along, which made little difference because the enemy had neither land- nor carrier-based aircraft nearby. Fletcher kept his Wildcats aboard, wisely concluding that he would need all 18 if the *Shokaku* and *Zuikaku* showed up.

The squadrons made no attempt to coordinate their attacks. Lieutenant Commander William O. Burch's faster Dauntlesses arrived first and tipped into near vertical dives from 14,000 feet. They met little antiaircraft fire from the surprised Japanese aboard a pair of destroyers, the 4,000-ton minelayer flagship *Okinoshima*, transports, and assorted small craft below. But they encountered a pesky foe met before in the Gilberts and Marshalls. Most of the SBD-3s windscreens and gunsights fogged when the temperature rose sharply as the Dauntlesses plummeted into heavy, warm lower air. Many pilots dropped high, others "by guess and by God." Burch bitterly estimated afterward that the accuracy of his pilots had been reduced by 75 percent. That they hit the destroyer *Kikuzuki* and forced her onto the beach a total loss may have been a stroke of luck, given the circumstances.

A few minutes later Lieutenant Commander Joe Taylor's Devastators lumbered awkwardly in, dropping 11 torpedoes for only one hit and that on a lowly minesweeper. More SBDs arrived from Bombing Squadron 5, but, like Scouting 5, they also suffered badly from fogged windscreens and sights.

Admiral Fletcher sent the SBDs back for two more strikes—a risky thing to do—but the fogging curse continued. The pilots sank four landing craft, and accompanying Wildcat pilots strafed and damaged the fleeing destroyer *Yuzuki*, killing her captain and most of the bridge crew. The pilots made rather extravagant claims of ships sunk, but sober analysis revealed bomb damage light compared to the tonnage dropped.

Air Warrant Officer Kumesaka Nemoto of the Yokosuka Air Group, who was aboard a transport and was bombed for the second time by U. S. carrier planes, was surprised at their inaccuracy. "Ten enemy planes," he noted contemptuously in his diary, "were continuously dive-bombing *Koei Maru* while she was unloading . . . but not a single bomb hit her."

In three strikes Fletcher's airmen had sunk only destroyer *Kikuzuki*, cargo ship *Kingosan Maru*, and four small craft against the loss of three planes. They also damaged and forced aground the *Okinoshima*, which got

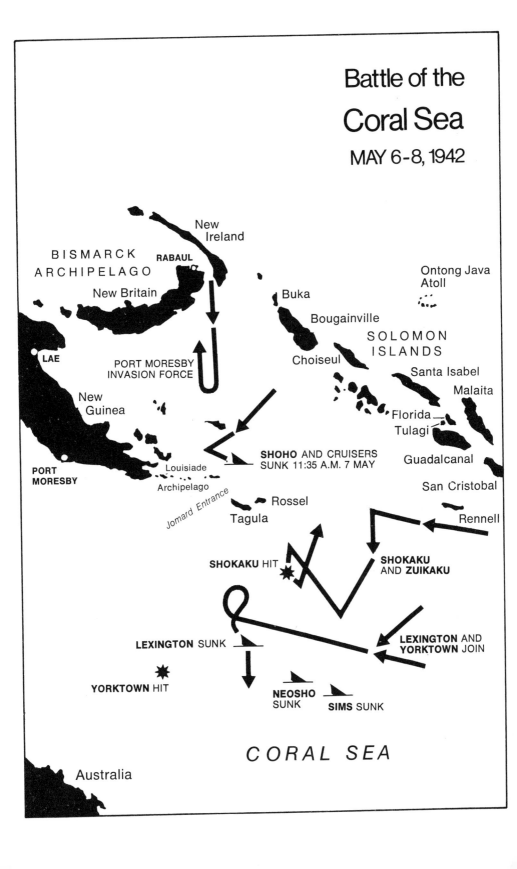

Battle of the Coral Sea

MAY 6-8, 1942

New Ireland

BISMARCK ARCHIPELAGO

RABAUL

New Britain

Buka

Ontong Java Atoll

Bougainville

SOLOMON ISLANDS

PORT MORESBY INVASION FORCE

LAE

Choiseul

Santa Isabel

Malaita

New Guinea

Florida

Tulagi

SHOHO AND CRUISERS SUNK 11:35 A.M. 7 MAY

Guadalcanal

PORT MORESBY

Louisiade Archipelago

Jomard Entrance

Rossel

San Cristobal

Rennell

Tagula

SHOKAKU HIT

SHOKAKU AND **ZUIKAKU**

LEXINGTON SUNK

LEXINGTON AND **YORKTOWN** JOIN

YORKTOWN HIT

NEOSHO SUNK

SIMS SUNK

CORAL SEA

Australia

away but was sunk a few days later by a submarine while trying to limp to Rabaul. That the *Okinoshima* survived the thousand-pound bombs that hit her may have been because the Americans were using 1/100 second near instantaneous fuses.

If the performance of *Yorktown*'s pilots (and also of Frank Jack Fletcher) had been less than spectacular, the Japanese certainly had done no better. Rear Admiral Kiyohide Shima, commanding the Tulagi occupation force, had been a "sitting duck." Had Fletcher managed to complete his fueling rapidly and to keep his Task Force 17 together, *Lexington*'s planes might have insured the loss of all of Shima's ships. Also, Vice Admiral Takeo Takagi with *Shokaku* and *Zuikaku* had been conspicuously absent where and when he was most needed. Instead of covering the landing as planned, he had been loitering at the northwest tip of the Solomons chain, unable to close in time to catch the lonesome *Yorktown*. Frank Jack had proved one thing: He had guts—and luck.

May 5 found the *Yorktown* joining the *Lexington*, refueling destroyers in a process maddeningly—and dangerously—slow. The next day, May 6, found Takagi and his carriers in the Coral Sea, and the rival task forces searched for each other all day without success. Nor did PBY Catalinas flying from Nouméa in New Caledonia find Takagi. The best information for Fletcher came from Pearl Harbor, which reported from communications intelligence that Japanese carriers had entered the Coral Sea. Pearl could not, however, pinpoint their location. Nevertheless, the evening of May 6 brought a near miss. Moving faster and overhauling Fletcher from astern, Takagi closed to within 70 miles before turning the *Shokaku* and *Zuikaku* sharply north into a front of squally and overcast weather. He had had a very bad break when a patrol plane from Rabaul spotted Fletcher and reported, but word failed to reach him.

Dawn on May 7 found the *Lexington* and *Yorktown* steaming westward in bright, clear, sparkling weather. Their approach to the Louisiade Island group and Jomard Passage was timely. Through the Jomard Passage the Japanese landing force headed from Rabaul to Port Moresby must pass. The invasion force already had been sighted by Australian-based planes. Fletcher's aim was to pinpoint, strike, and cripple it with Task Force 17. For his part, assuming that Fletcher had not ventured so far west, Admiral Takagi sent scouting Kates directly to the south, hopefully to find and destroy Fletcher, before turning west himself to cover the advancing Port Moresby force. Both sides launched scouts simultaneously and both found targets—but not each other.

At 7:36 A.M. one of Takagi's searching Kates located tanker *Neosho* and its escorting destroyer *Sims*. This once the well-trained Japanese airmen muffed their ship recognition and erroneously reported these vulnerable ships as a carrier and a cruiser. On the strength of this report Rear Admiral Tadaichi Hara, who commanded the air groups of the *Shokaku* and *Zuikaku*, launched a full strike of planes. Twenty-five bomb-carrying Kates attacked first and missed both ships. But the arrival of

36 Vals doomed them. The twisting, squirming *Sims* took three 500-pound bombs, broke in two, and vanished with most of her crew. The *Neosho*, her fuel tanks empty, took seven hits that set her afire and eventually gutted her but failed to sink her. The result was a tactical victory, a "can" and a valuable fleet oiler in exchange for the loss of six planes, but when his pilots reported Hara realized that he had committed a serious blunder. He had wasted most of a precious day against lesser game.

Admiral Fletcher did much better. One of his planes spotted the support force for the Port Moresby invasion group and through an encoding error recorded his find as "two carriers and four heavy cruisers." The pilot had meant to report two cruisers and two destroyers. His mistake was a good thing. Fletcher launched at 10:00 A.M. a full strike of 93 Dauntlesses, Devastators, and escorting Wildcats. He retained 47 planes aboard to protect his force.

At about 10:50 A.M., shortly after passing Tagula Island in the Louisiades, Lieutenant Commander Weldon L. Hamilton of *Lexington*'s Scouting 2 sighted from 15,000 feet 25 to 30 miles away the light carrier *Shoho** and its accompanying four heavy cruisers of Rear Admiral Goto's covering group. Commander Bill Ault, the *Lex*'s Air Group Commander, promptly diverted all planes to hit the carrier. *Shoho* had survived the attention of high-level B-17s from Australia the day previous; but now her number was up.

Arriving first over the little carrier at about 11:07 was Bill Ault with his two wing men. The trio deployed into line and dove, fighting off harassing Zeros on CAP and near missing with bombs that blew overside five planes from the CVL's deck. Three minutes later came ten *Lexington* SBDs with 500-pounders. All dove and none hit, though one bomb exploded within 30 yards. The shuddering, racing *Shoho*, drenched with salt water, managed to straighten course long enough to launch three Zeros. Then Captain Ishinosuke Izawa starboarded his helm to try to avoid Torpedo 2's Devastators sweeping in from the right. This time there was no escape. The "torpeckers" and vertically plunging Dauntlesses of Bombing 2 attacked simultaneously and both hit. At 11:20 two bombs struck near the after elevator, crashing through the flight deck and exploding just inside the rear hangar. One or more Mark 13 torpedoes hit and at least one exploded against the stern starboard, knocking out steering and propulsion. Fires progressed through the hangar deck as the ship coasted to a stop.

The *Shoho*'s six Zeros on CAP had tried bravely to save her. They had chased down Ault and the first of *Lexington*'s SBDs throughout their 250-mph, 12,000-foot, 40-second dives. They got one but themselves were

---

* *Shoho*, a sister to CVL *Zuiho*, carried 30 Zeros and Kates. She commissioned in December 1941, carried out trial runs in January, and on February 1, 1942, was dispatched to Truk. She returned from Truk in April and was in Yokosuka when Doolittle's raiders attacked. She sortied after the *Hornet*, failed to make contact, and on return was again sent to Truk. On May 2 she joined the Port Moresby attack force north of Bougainville.

jumped on pullout by escorting *Yorktown* Wildcats that shot down three. Lieutenant Commander Jimmy Flatley got a Zero just off the water by "walking" a torrent of tracer and .50-caliber ball ammo into the lightly built plane. The remaining three escaped to ditch at Deboyne Island, where the *Kamikawa Maru* had anchored.

At 11:25 *Yorktown*'s entire strike showed up and began attacking the blazing, helpless ship. Five more Mark 13s struck and 13 bombs, almost tearing the *Shoho* to pieces. At 11:31 Captain Izawa ordered "Abandon Ship!" and at 11:35 she was gone, leaving on the water blazing oil and gasoline, flotsam, and the bobbing heads of the surviving crew. Not even the humidity had succored the *Shoho*; the air was dry, and the canopies and sights of the Dauntlesses had not fogged.

Navy reporter Amefuji recorded *Shoho*'s end in a story eventually published in Japan. While he was standing on the bridge a bomb explosion had knocked him down and wounded him in the thigh and head. Amefuji had struggled to his feet and had just time to shout to his cameraman Yashikoa, "Hey, let's go together," when "Abandon Ship" was called. Rising waves swept him overside and under. Surfacing amid blazing oil, swimming clear as the ship upended and sank, he could hear swimming crewmen shouting, "Banzai!" Others joined a young sailor in singing the "Gunkan," the Navy march. A saddened Ensign Toshio Nakamura aboard a nearby destroyer recorded in his diary, "She fought bravely until the very last."

Amefuji was among just 204 of 736 crewmen rescued. He stayed in the water nine hours on a raft made from debris until picked up by destroyer *Sazanami* at dusk.

The last departing American pilots had seen the *Shoho* go under. Snapping on his radio, Lieutenant Commander Bob Dixon of the *Lexington*'s Scouting 2 had barked, "Scratch one flattop! Dixon to carrier. Scratch one flattop!"

For Vice Admiral Shigeyoshi Inouye, commanding the Port Moresby invasion from Rabaul, the *Shoho*'s loss was quite enough to warrant aborting the landing. Now his transports were without their air cover and subject to attacks from the American carriers as well as B-17s. He ordered all ships to reverse course toward Rabaul. Fletcher, too, was content with the destruction of the *Shoho*. He decided against striking the carrier's cruiser escort, because his pilots would have to return after dark.

As the *Yorktown* and *Lexington* planes were streaming back to their welcome decks, three Allied cruisers, operating independently, were rushing westward toward Jomard Passage under the command of genial Rear Admiral J. G. Crace, R. A. N. These were the Aussie cruiser *Australia*, the New Zealand *Hobart*, and the U. S. S. *Chicago*, plus two escorting destroyers. Originally attached to Task Force 17, Crace's ships had been sent ahead to block the passage and destroy any Japanese vessels that might try to slip through.

Now, at 1:58 P.M., less than two hours after the loss of the *Shoho* while Crace's squadron was nearing the passage at 25 knots, a formation of Bettys from Rabaul crossed at high level, dropped bombs, and missed. Next appeared twelve Nells sweeping in low, each armed with a torpedo. Heavy AA fire, radical maneuvering, and good fortune enabled the cruisers to dodge and escape the fate of the *Prince of Wales* and *Repulse*. Last came twelve more Nells, escorted by Zeros, that also missed from high altitude. Finally, three bombs exploded close aboard *Farragut*, being dropped, the destroyer's irate crew afterward realized, by three U. S. Army B-26s from Townsville. Crace's force had survived the unwelcome attention of 44 enemy and three "friendly" planes with no losses. It had shot down four planes and had forced another to crash-land. It had riddled five more with shrapnel and bullets. More important, it had diverted planes that otherwise might have attacked Fletcher's carriers.

On the return of his carrier planes from their attacks on the *Neosho* and *Sims*, Admiral Tagaki—who by now had learned of the attacks on the *Shoho*—was more anxious than ever to find the U. S. carriers. Despite the danger inherent in a late-afternoon launch, he sent out a special search-strike force of 15 Kates and 12 Vals commanded by his Carrier Group 5 skipper, Lieutenant Commander Shigekazu Shimazaki. The pilots included those best trained for night flying, for Shimazaki realized that all would have to make night landings on return. Hampered by worsening weather, including rain squalls and poor visibility, the planes searched to the limit of their combat radius, then jettisoned bombs and torpedoes and put about.

In returning they stumbled near dusk onto Task Force 17. After being spotted on ships' radar, they first took a severe mauling, losing a Val and eight Kates to the *Lexington*'s CAP. Lost on the American side were two Wildcats. Forming up again as best they could, the 18 surviving planes flew after sunset at 7:00 P.M. right past the *Yorktown*. Assuming it was their own carrier, they began to orbit and blinkered in Morse a request to land. The puzzled carrier blinkered back until both sides realized their error. The Americans then fired, and the Japanese hastily raised flaps and wheels and sped off. Radar tracked them due north and then orbiting at 30 miles' distance. They were not, however, over their carriers, as the Americans believed; they were lost. Only six planes, including Lieutenant Commander Shimazaki's, finally managed to land safely on the *Shokaku* and *Zuikaku* at 9:00 P.M. Eleven planes and crews splashed out of fuel, all hands lost.

May 7 had been disastrous for Admiral Tagaki. He had failed to protect the Port Moresby force; he had missed locating Task Force 17 and had lost 21 of his best planes and air crew. He thought of trying to find and attack the American force with his destroyers and cruisers on the night of the 7th but decided against an attempt. Admiral Fletcher also considered seeking a night surface action, but as he said later, "The best plan seemed to be to keep our force concentrated and prepare for a battle with the enemy carriers next morning." He might, however, have tried a night torpedo attack with the Devastators of *Lexington*'s Torpedo 2. All of these pilots had trained in night landings and with their YE homing gear would have been able to get back to their flattop. But in view of the deficiency of the Mark 13 torpedoes, the short range of the Devastators, and the difficulty of finding the enemy, who at the closest was 95 miles eastward, it probably was best no attempt was made.

May 8 dawned as the day of decision. Concluding that his scout planes certainly would find the enemy early in the morning, Admiral Hara began launching 60 planes at 8:22 A.M., even before the scouts reported in. A less confident Fletcher launched a full 360-degree search of 18 SBD scouts from the *Lexington* two hours earlier and held his strike force ready on the carrier decks.

Each side logged the success of its search almost simultaneously. At 8:28 A.M. a Kate pilot, Flight Warrant Officer Kenzo Kanno, found the *Lexington* and reported her position in a message intercepted aboard the carrier. Ten minutes later Lieutenant Joseph G. Smith reported the *Shokaku* and *Zuikaku* operating 175 miles northeastward of Task Force 17 in a cold front of squally weather. Luck was with Fletcher, as it had been several times earlier. Had Lieutenant Smith missed the enemy in a squall the forthcoming battle would have been one-sided. Fletcher, operating in clear, windy weather with ceiling and visibility unlimited, would have undergone attack, while Hara would not.

At 8:38 A.M., immediately on receipt of Smith's message, Fletcher ordered his carriers to launch. At 9:15 A.M. 30 *Yorktown* Dauntlesses and nine Devastators, with an escort of 14 Wildcats, set out for the enemy's reported position. *Lexington*'s strike of 24 Dauntlesses, 12 Devastators, and 10 Wildcats followed ten minutes later. Both sides now had strikes in the air.

What had happened was something that conservative Japanese and American admirals had feared would after years of observing maneuvers. The vulnerable flattops of both sides, each a combination ammunition ship and high-octane gasoline tender, had gotten away virtually simultaneous attacks. Each was destined to be hit, and if the pessimists were right, the result might be mutual annihilation. This would also be the first naval battle in history in which the opposing warships never sighted each other.

In contrast to the more skilled Japanese, the Americans had their usual trouble keeping together. *Yorktown*'s planes, flying without a strike commander, made no attempt to wait for *Lexington*'s, and when both air groups entered a front of bad weather some 55 miles northeast of TF-17, the torpedo planes, flying low and slow, became separated from the dive bombers, cruising at 16,000 feet.

At 10:32 the *Yorktown*'s dive bombers spotted the *Shokaku* and *Zuikaku* operating several miles apart. Rather than dive immediately on their target, they orbited for 20 minutes, waiting for the Devastators, giving the *Shokaku* time to turn into the wind and launch more Zeros and the *Zuikaku* an opportunity to disappear into a heavy rain squall and evade attack.

The Devastators, first to attack, pressed in courageously as the defending Zeros tangled with their Wildcat escort. The *Shokaku* circled sharply right and then left. Since they had not deployed for an "anvil" attack from either bow, all Devastators missed. Commander Burch's Dauntlesses then dove from 17,000 feet, harassed by Zeros but bothered even more by the fogging of their canopies and gunsights. Nevertheless, they managed two hits with 1,000-pounders. One landed forward, tearing up the end of *Shokaku*'s flight deck and destroying the anchor windlass room. The second struck aft, destroying the flattop's aircraft-engine repair shop. A towering gasoline fire set by the first hit induced the air crews to conclude (wrongly) that the *Shokaku* was finished. In fact her crew quickly quenched the fire, and she still could land planes, though none could take off from the damaged bow.

About ten minutes later the *Lexington*'s Devastators arrived, attacking *Shokaku* simultaneously with four Dauntlesses led by the *Lex*'s air group skipper, Bill Ault. Again the torpedo planes missed, but one of the SBDs landed a bomb that caused additional damage and raised the casualty roster to 108 killed and 40 injured. Six accompanying Wildcats got into a terrific scrap with the Zero CAP, losing three of their number but claiming two Zeros shot down. The Zero pilots had performed very poorly in protecting their carrier. They had failed to press their attacks on the Dauntlesses, had allowed the Devastators to approach unmolested, and had let themselves be lured into fights with the Wildcats. Nor was the AA fire of escorting surface ships effective. The Japanese cruisers and destroyers had scattered to maneuver independently when the American planes appeared, leaving the *Shokaku* on her own.

The other 20 *Lexington* dive bombers, which had become separated from Ault, failed completely to find the enemy. They flew a box search about the enemy's reported position, which was 25 miles south of his true one, then jettisoned bombs and returned.

American bombing accuracy was very poor. Thirty-four Dauntless attackers had scored only three nonlethal hits and eight near misses. All 20 Mark 13 torpedoes launched by the Devastators had missed. The Japanese noted that the torpedoes had been launched from too far out; also that they ran so slowly in the water as to be easily avoidable. Nevertheless, the *Shokaku* was out of the Pacific war until July, and perhaps a half dozen of the 15 to 18 Zeros on CAP had fallen either to the Wildcats or the surprisingly tough Dauntlesses.

The Americans had lost 14 planes—three Wildcats, two Devastators, and nine Dauntlesses. Ault, wounded, his plane badly damaged, was in radio touch with the *Lexington* after the attack but failed to make her deck. Losses would probably have been much heavier had not a providential nearby rain cloud hid the TBDs and SBDs after they completed their attacks.

Though they had launched earlier, the Japanese striking force of 18

Kates, 33 Vals, and 18 Zeros under Lieutenant Commander Kuichi Takahashi arrived at their targets an hour later than the Americans. The planes
had scattered widely after takeoff to search the waters ahead. Luck rode
with Takahashi. En route he had encountered Warrant Officer Kenzo
Kanno, the scout who had found the *Lexington* and *Yorktown*. Though too
short of fuel to fly back to his own carrier if he joined the attackers, Kanno
immediately formed up with Commander Takahashi to lead him to Task
Force 17. The delay had come in recalling and reassembling all planes.

The *Yorktown*'s radar picked up the oncoming Japanese formation
68 miles out at 10:55 A.M. Both she and the *Lexington* immediately adopted
Condition Zed with all watertight doors dogged and guarded. *Lexington*'s
skipper, Captain Ted Sherman, was not at all surprised. He had been
expecting an attack at about 11:00 A.M., based on knowledge derived from
the monitoring of Takahashi's and Kanno's airborne radio traffic. Each
carrier dispatched eight Wildcats on CAP and sent a number of SBDs
several thousand yards out as an antitorpedo-plane patrol.

Because Lieutenant F. F. "Red" Gill, the TF-17 air traffic controller
based on the *Lex*, could not determine accurately the height of Takahashi's
formation, he failed to get the Wildcat CAP high enough for an effective
intercept. About half of the fighter pilots missed the enemy altogether as
the Japanese flew in overhead. Only three pilots intercepted at the favored
distance of 15 to 20 miles out.

Commander Takahashi, with Warrant Officer Kanno on his wing, attacked at 11:18 A.M. He had deployed his 18 Kates against both the *Lex*
and *Yorktown*. The planes dived at their targets from about 7,000 feet at
40 to 50 degrees after zipping right over the 23 Dauntlesses on antitorpedo-
plane patrol and outrunning them. Stopping the attack thus fell to the AA
gunners of the two carriers and of the escorting cruisers and destroyers.

One five-inch weapon scored a direct hit on the Kate of either Commander Takahashi or Warrant Officer Kanno. As the plane disintegrated
the Americans aboard a nearby cruiser could see the bodies of the three
crewmen tumbling through the air. Commander Shigekazu Shimazaki, who
led the *Zuikaku*'s Kates, recalled his own run two weeks after the battle:

> Never in all my years have I even imagined a battle like that! When we
> attacked the enemy carriers we ran into a virtual wall of antiaircraft fire; the
> carriers and their supporting ships blackened the sky with exploding shells and
> tracers. . . . I dove almost to the water's surface and sent my torpedo into the
> *Saratoga*-type carrier [*Lexington*]. I had to fly directly above the waves to
> escape the enemy shells and tracers. In fact, when I turned away from the
> carrier, I was so low that I almost struck the bow of the ship, for I was flying
> below the level of the flight deck. I could see the crewmen staring at my plane
> as it rushed by.

When the first torpedo dropped about 1,500 yards out, Captain Ted
Sherman, hands clasped behind his back, ordered full rudder to port,
sending the cumbersome *Lexington* into a slow, wide turn. This Type 91

missile ran straight and fast but missed ahead. Other Kates dropped, and two fish running from astern passed on either side of the ship, forcing Sherman to hold course. Two more running deep passed directly under the *Lex.*

At 11:18 A.M., only moments after the attack began, a torpedo hit on the port side just forward of the island. To Lieutenant Commander George L. Markle, the Chief Chaplain, the shock seemed to "raise the ship up as if going over a hump." But to Signal Officer G. O. Hansen, "the explosion didn't feel very heavy." At full load the *Lex* displaced about 41,000 tons, quite a bulk for a few hundred pounds of explosives to jar.

At 11:20, two minutes later, another Type 91 hit near the gig boat pocket also on the port side. Seconds later an attacking Kate banked and brazenly flew up *Lexington*'s side just above flight-deck level, drawing tracer from every 20-mm. and 1.1-inch gun that would bear. The concentrated fire knocked the Kate into a double snap roll from which it splashed just under the flare of the big ship's bow.

The final torpedo hit—which apparently caused little damage—came at 11:20 from a Type 91 that broached a hundred yards out, dove under the water, and then struck the extreme forward part of the bow. (Men below decks counted four distinct shocks and assumed that four torpedoes had hit. But one shock may have been from a very near miss from a bomb. One officer thought that the second hit was from two torpedoes running parallel and striking simultaneously. The best guess would therefore seem to be that the *Lex* was hit by at least three and perhaps five torpedoes, all on the port side. Assuming that only nine Kates attacked, this was excellent marksmanship.) The *Lexington* was by no means in serious trouble. Her antitorpedo bulges had saved her. Three fire rooms had to be abandoned temporarily, but the ship listed only six degrees and at 11:22 was making 30 knots.

The smaller and more nimble *Yorktown*, lacking the bulges but able to turn in half of the radius of the *Lex*, fared much better. Skipper Elliott Buckmaster ordered "RIGHT FULL RUDDER" when he saw the first of three attacking Kates drop, followed by "EMERGENCY FLANK SPEED!" Cruisers *Astoria, Portland,* and *Chester* and destroyers *Russell, Hammann, Aylwin,* and *Dewey** helped by keeping station, ignoring the torpedo drops, and pouring out rapid AA fire on their own. Three torpedoes ran past the *Yorktown* on the port side and four others missed farther out. The gunners claimed six of the Kates before they could launch, plus another that crashed and burned after dropping, but this seems exaggerated since probably only nine Kates attacked.

In the meantime the Val dive bombers had simultaneously begun their steep glide attacks with but slight fighter opposition. Only Lieutenant McCormick and Ensign Walter A. Haas of the *Yorktown* managed a

---

* *Lexington*'s escorts were cruisers *Minneapolis* and *New Orleans* and destroyers *Morris, Anderson, Phelps,* and *Monaghan.*

successful intercept. At 13,000 feet the pair spotted a string of 15 Vals spaced perfectly at four-second intervals in a single attack column. The lead planes already had begun their dives. "I rolled over on my back," McCormick reported afterward, "and made an overhead attack on the fifth plane in column." He missed, but—"I pulled out sharply and came back in again. I slid in behind one farther back and closed to point-blank range. He didn't smoke, but ship personnel confirmed that he crashed without releasing his bomb." Haas in the meantime had overshot his target, but he shot down a Val that was pulling away.

Cursing his luck and the air controller was Commander Jimmy Flatley, the *Yorktown*'s fighter squadron skipper. Caught too low, Flatley found that his Wildcat climbed too slowly to intercept either the Vals or the Kates. He caught an unwary Zero after the attack and shot it down in a savage burst, then recklessly attacked three more. Unable to dogfight them, he had to break off and dive away. A pilot alone, he conceded in his after-action report, was a dead duck against Zeros. The only safe tactic for American pilots to adopt was to stay in pairs, dive from superior altitude, zoom up, and try for another run.

Against the *Yorktown* the Vals scored better than the theoretically more lethal Kates. The Vals began plunging at 11:24. Skipper Buckmaster turned into the direction of the dives, hoping to induce the pilots to drop "over." Some did, but no fewer than 11 or 12 bombs near missed, two so close as to dish in the hull plating and riddle the carrier's side with fragments. Two others lifted the screws of the 20,000 ton flattop from the water. One bomb hit at 11:27 and passed through the flight and hangar decks deep into the bowels of the ship. It burst just above a fireroom, filling it with smoke and denting but not rupturing the overhead. Calling below, Buckmaster asked, "Shouldn't we slow?" "Hell no," the Black Gang replied. "We'll make it." The *Yorktown* continued at 24 knots. Pardonably, the Val pilots reported on return that they had probably sunk the ship with "more than" eight bomb and three torpedo hits.

Against the *Lexington* the dive bombers scored twice or perhaps thrice. One bomb hit the lip of the huge stack, killing several 20-mm. gunners on catwalk mounts nearby and severing the cord of the ship's steam siren, setting it off in a screeching, uncontrolled blast. Another bomb, much more damaging, struck near the Number Six five-inch gun manned by Marines, wiping out its crew and starting a fire in the ship's admiral's cabin. A third bomb, which may have near missed, struck at or near the gig-boat pocket and caused some casualties. No bomb penetrated into the hangar deck, the vital area of the ship. On *Lexington* the Japanese pilots reported they had scored with ten bombs and nine torpedoes.

At 11:40 the attack was over, and both the *Yorktown* and the torpedoed *Lexington* still were making 25 knots. Neither was hurt badly enough to discontinue flight operations. Battle-damaged SBDs of the anti-torpedo-plane patrol that had tangled fiercely with the Zero escort and had lost four of their number began landing immediately on both carriers.

Lexington's log at 12:00 noon recorded the ship to be "steaming as before." Wrote Captain Sherman, "We felt like throwing out our chests at our condition." All fires were out except the one smoldering in admiral's country, and it was under control.

Records the U. S. Navy's official historian, Rear Admiral Samuel Eliot Morison, "If the Coral Sea score had been frozen then and there, the United States could justly have claimed a victory." The Japanese had lost a light carrier, a destroyer, and several auxiliaries against an American loss of only the *Neosho* and *Sims*. *Yorktown* and *Lexington* had been damaged—Lady *Lex* would need a navy-yard overhaul—but so would the crippled *Shokaku*, already on its way home. The Japanese had lost 29 planes in their final attack—six Zeros, 15 Vals, and eight Kates—and others operationally when planes had to be pushed over the side of the *Zuikaku* to make room for 40 of the surviving planes of the attack group. Six ditched alongside destroyers. The next day would see only 39 planes fit for combat aboard the *Zuikaku*, including 24 Zeros and only nine Vals and six Kates. Lost had been 12 Zeros, 27 Vals, and 18 Kates. Worse than the loss of planes was the loss of skilled pilots. The air crew of Carrier Division 5 were Pearl Harbor veterans. About half, including Commander Takahashi, were gone. Including crew losses from the *Shoho*, Japanese casualties numbered 1,074 killed or wounded.

By 12:47 P.M. the *Lexington* had corrected her list and was preparing to land her returning air group. The fire in the admiral's cabin now was out. Suddenly, with no warning, a terrific explosion rent the ship, much more severe than any of the torpedo hits. Though the cause was not definitely known, a later board of inquiry concluded that "All evidence indicates that the violent explosion . . . resulted from an accumulation of gasoline vapor in the I. C. Motor Generator Room, in the presence of operating electrical machinery which was capable of producing electrical sparks." Evidently, the torpedo hit forward of the island had ruptured the ship's gasoline tanks. The gas had vaporized, seeped into the motor room, and exploded. This caused more gasoline to leak, more explosions, and fires that soon put the ship in gravest jeopardy. The crew discovered that the *Lexington* lacked enough foamite fire-fighting equipment to check the oil- and gasoline-fed flames.

Nevertheless, for the next two hours flight operations continued, and the returning strike was recovered, the Devastators an hour after they should have been out of fuel. But finally at 4:30 P.M. it got too hot below, and Captain Sherman reluctantly had to order the engine-room crews to secure the machinery. *Lexington* slowed to a stop. At 5:07 P.M. Admiral Fitch called down to Captain Sherman, "Well, Ted, let's get the men off." The men left slowly, reluctantly, as cruisers and destroyers closed to lower boats and pick up crewmen from the water. The sea was warm, some 80 degrees, wave action was negligible, and few if any perished in the abandonment.

Lexington continued to explode and blaze in an awesomely beautiful display as darkness fell, going down from a *coup de grâce* delivered by destroyer torpedoes at about 10:00 P.M., ten and a half hours after being attacked. Seaman Jack Smith said, "I couldn't watch her go, and men who had been with her since she was commissioned in 1927 stood with tears streaming." One after-action explosion, touched off by a sparking electric motor, had converted a tactical victory for the United States Navy into a tactical defeat.

Personnel losses aboard the *Yorktown* had totaled 66 killed and seriously injured. Captain Sherman estimated *Lexington's* fatalities, including lost aviators, as 26 officers and 190 men out of 2,951 aboard. American losses on all ships, including *Neosho* and *Sims*, totaled 564 killed and 140 wounded. One unfortunate airman, captured, died as a POW.

Strategically, victory clearly belonged with the Americans. Operation MO, the Japanese invasion of Port Moresby, had to be postponed once more, and both the *Shokaku* and *Zuikaku* were scratched from the Midway operation because of battle damage and air-crew losses.

Neither side had fought well. Against first-class American fighter and AA opposition the best of Japan's airmen had suffered very heavily in their unprotected planes, and their bombing accuracy, perhaps as a consequence, was far below that of their Indian Ocean operations. The performance of the American attack groups had been poor. Fogging of the Dauntless windscreens and the subpar performance of the slow and short-range Devastators and their Mark 13 torpedoes had resulted in much too little damage to the enemy. The Wildcats, on the other hand, had performed well against the Zeros when handled properly, although they lacked enough range to be good escort fighters. The use of radar to vector the American CAP had been a flat-out failure; the director had kept the CAP too low. And everyone on the American side, from Admiral Fletcher down to air group commanders, had yet to learn how to coordinate operations launched from more than one flattop.

On the Japanese side the main responsibility for defeat lay squarely with Admiral Yamamoto and his Combined Fleet Staff. Possessed of numerical superiority over his enemy, he had failed to use it and mass his forces. The isolated *Shoho* had been overwhelmed and lost, removing a light flattop that would have been a very useful companion to sister ship *Zuiho*, destined to compile an excellent war record. The *Shokaku* and *Zuikaku* had fought the *Yorktown* and *Lexington* on no better than even terms. Only the after-action explosion on the *Lexington* had tipped the balance. For Japan even the trade of CVL *Shoho* for the massive *Lexington* was not acceptable. So long as the bulk of the big flattop's skilled crew survived to man the new ships of the *Essex* class—one of which would bear the name *Lexington*—her loss hardly mattered over the long-term course of the war, whereas Japan could not afford to lose a single ship.

Following the battle, Admiral Nimitz, who had been keeping in touch by radio, ordered Admiral Fletcher to clear the Coral Sea. He knew from intercepted commo that the Japanese invasion force had turned back and saw no point in risking the damaged *Yorktown* further. He had only three operational carriers now that the *Lexington* was gone. He allowed the *Enterprise* and *Hornet* to continue southwest and to operate eastward of Efate and Santa Cruz from May 12 to 16 but then recalled both to join the *Yorktown* in hot-footing it back to Pearl.

The more aggressive—and probably less well-informed—Admiral Yamamoto at midnight on May 8 ordered the plane-shy *Zuikaku* to "annihilate" the remaining enemy forces. He had been told that the *Lexington* had been sunk and the *Yorktown* either sunk or crippled. Pilots from Rabaul also had reported heavy losses to Admiral Crace's cruiser force. The *Zuikaku* zigzagged about the Coral Sea until May 10 before returning to Truk and then Japan. She would not sortie again on a war mission until June 12—after the Battle of Midway.

9. Midway: The Battle Joined

At 6:00 A.M. on May 27 Admiral Nagumo's First Air Fleet again was standing out to sea. Leading the way from the Hashirajima anchorage was flagship *Akagi*, followed by the *Kaga, Soryu,* and *Hiryu.* Escorts included fast battleships *Haruna* and *Kirishima,* heavy cruisers *Tone* and *Chikuma* with their useful Type O "Jake" scouting float planes, light cruiser *Nagara,* and 12 destroyers. Except for the damaged *Shokaku* and the replenishing *Zuikaku,* Nagumo had practically the same force that had struck Pearl Harbor in January. He was to blast Midway Island in preparation for a landing, and if the American carrier fleet showed up he was to sink it. Yamamoto's Operation "AF," the seizure of Midway, was under way.

On the *Akagi*'s bridge the mood was jauntily optimistic, though none of Nagumo's staff had taken part in drafting this "AF" plan. The staff, as Commander Fuchida later recalled, was "fully confident" that it could "carry out any mission which Combined Fleet assigned." Nagumo himself paid scant attention to details; he seemed to assume his force was unbeatable.

In complexity the AF operations plan far outdid the ill-fated MO plan for the seizure of Port Moresby, now postponed until July because of the Battle of the Coral Sea. Though he had enough surface ships and carrier-borne planes to sail directly to Midway and take it, Yamamoto nevertheless elected to devise a complex indirect approach and to make surprise a key feature.

First, Yamamoto's plan called for a force built around the newly commissioned carrier *Junyo* and the veteran CVL *Ryujo* to attack Dutch Harbor in the Aleutians. This would take place on June 3. Yamamoto intended this subsidiary attack to draw Admiral Nimitz's attention to the Aleutians and induce him to send his carriers and heavy cruisers racing northward. On the next day, June 4, the Nagumo force would bomb Midway from a point approximately 200 miles to the northwest. This would destroy the island's defenses, confuse Nimitz, and perhaps send his forces charging back south.

When the American carriers arrived after the bombing of Midway,

Yamamoto hoped to trap and sink them, using not only Nagumo's carriers but also his battleships steaming on their first combat mission of the war. Operating in distant support of the Aleutians force would be slow battle wagons *Ise, Hyuga, Fuso,* and *Yamashiro.* Supporting Nagumo's carriers, a few hundred miles to their rear, would be the mighty new *Yamato* with Yamamoto himself aboard and the fast and powerful *Mutsu* and *Nagato.* Old light carrier *Hosho* would fly antisubmarine patrols for the battleships.

Approaching Midway from the west and southwest would be Admiral Kondo's Midway Occupation Force. Kondo himself would command from a separate covering group consisting of fast battleships *Kongo* and *Hiei,* light carrier *Zuiho,* and four heavy cruisers, plus screening destroyers. Yet another force, composed of the oversized heavy cruisers *Suzuya, Kumano, Mogami,* and *Mikuma,* would operate independently under Rear Admiral Takeo Kurita. Its mission would be to bombard Midway in preparation for the landing of troops.

Though Yamamoto was supposed to be air-minded, his AF plan gave at least as much prominence to battle wagons as to carriers. Moreover, by scattering the carriers all over the northern Pacific instead of concentrating their striking power, it made them subject to possible piecemeal defeat by enemy land- and carrier-based air. Surprise was vital; if it was not attained, then Yamamoto's failure to concentrate could possibly lead to serious trouble. It apparently never occurred to Yamamoto that his foe might be forewarned.

The total acreage of Yamamoto's target, Midway Atoll, was less than that occupied by the decks of his 140 warships, transports, and auxiliaries. Its coral reef, six miles in diameter, surrounded two small islands comprising all of the usable land mass. Sand Island, the larger, contained the seaplane base, cable station, and lighthouse, plus the majority of the U. S. Marine defenders. The smaller Eastern Island contained the 5,300-foot airstrip for land planes and most of the goony birds, the raucous local albatrosses.

Planes on the island numbered 121, all the airstrip could handle. They included a squadron of fighters, two of dive bombers, one of B-17 heavy bombers, and 32 Catalina patrol planes. At the last minute four Army B-26 bombers equipped to drop torpedoes arrived, as did six new Grumman TBF Avenger torpedo planes. Backed up by two efficient air-search radars, Midway's air defenses when counted in numbers alone should have been extremely formidable. But only the PBY search crews were well trained. The other crews either were inexperienced or cursed with such obsolete planes as the Marines' F2A Buffalo fighters and slow SB2U Vindicator dive bombers. Nevertheless, Midway's planes would make a vital contribution to the approaching battle, and though he knew it not, Nagumo had fewer aircraft than his enemy. The four Japanese carriers had 93 Zeros, plus 24 more ·being ferried as part of the Midway occupation force, 86 Val dive bombers, and 93 Kate torpedo planes. The American carriers had

79 Wildcat fighters, 112 Dauntless dive bombers, and 44 Devastator torpedo planes. Midway added 27 F2A-3 and F4F-3 fighters, 16 SBD Dauntlesses, 11 SB2U Vindicators, six TBF Avengers, four B-26 Marauders, and 19. B-17 Flying Fortresses. Counting the ferrying Zeros, the Japanese planes numbered 296. Counting 32 Catalina search planes, the American aircraft numbered 348.

Wisely, Nimitz decided not to go to sea himself. He stayed in Pearl Harbor, where his communications were centered. To defend Midway he elected to use the *Hornet* and *Enterprise* organized into Task Force 16. *Yorktown* would join with its escorting cruisers and destroyers as Task Force 17 as soon as crash repair of its Coral Sea bomb hit was complete. To defend against the subsidiary threat in the Aleutians, Nimitz dispatched a force of five cruisers under Rear Admiral Robert A. Theobald, who flew his flag in light cruiser *Nashville*.

Nimitz would have liked to have used carrier *Saratoga*, just repaired from her torpedo hit in January and now training a new air group off San Diego. But a cruiser-destroyer escort could not be rounded up in time. Nimitz considered but decided against using Task Force One, six slow battleships operating out of San Francisco Bay. These ships would, he concluded, only interfere with the fast-stepping carrier-cruiser task forces besides complicating his refueling problems. In contrast to Yamamoto, Nimitz was much more inclined to forgo traditional surface naval power and to rely on his carrier air groups to repel a vastly superior enemy.

Nimitz regretted not being able to use his most aggressive carrier admiral, Bill Halsey, who had been hospitalized with a skin ailment. In his place as commander of Task Force 16, *Enterprise* and *Hornet*, he had appointed Rear Admiral Raymond A. Spruance, who had never before commanded carriers but who had been commanding Halsey's cruisers.

Nimitz's orders to Spruance and to Frank Jack Fletcher, who was commanding TF-17 and was designated overall force commander, were to hit the approaching Japanese hard "by employing strong attrition tactics." Translated into practical terms, this meant carrier air strikes. Both admirals were to operate according to the principle of "calculated risk" and to avoid getting overwhelmed by superior forces.

On May 28 the *Enterprise* and *Hornet* steamed from Pearl Harbor, leaving behind an agonized Bill Halsey, who had to bid them Godspeed from a hospital bed. *Yorktown* with Fletcher sailed on May 30, having had her bowels restored to order in an incredible two days by the workmen at Pearl Harbor's Navy Yard. She carried an air group made up partly of her own veterans of Air Group 5 but mostly of Air Group 3 that had stayed behind at Pearl Harbor when the *Sara* left for Bremerton to have her torpedo damage repaired in January.

Fletcher had orders to rendezvous with the *Enterprise* and *Hornet* at "Point Luck," a square in the ocean about 200 miles north and slightly east of Midway. There he would assume overall command of Task Forces

16 and 17, and the Japanese would be given the privilege of making the first move. With proper positioning, and if the Midway planes managed to spot and track the Japanese, he might be able to hit their carriers while their planes were away bombing Midway.

Perhaps because all of their operations had been so easy thus far, Admiral Nagumo and his planning officer, Commander Genda, were hardly concerned about the danger of a surprise carrier strike from north of Midway, even though this was about the only way the Nagumo force could be defeated. The United States, they assumed, could not base more than the equivalent of one carrier air group on Midway, and their flyers should destroy it outright without much trouble. They knew, too, that a prevailing bad weather front would conceal their advance until almost within launching distance of Midway. They should, therefore, escape detection by PBYs and take the defenders by surprise. Nimitz could not have more than three carriers—more likely two—because two presumably had been sunk in the Coral Sea. Genda's and Nagumo's scenario for the forthcoming Battle of Midway ran thusly: (1) Attack and destroy the enemy air forces based on Midway, hopefully catching them on the ground; (2) sink the counterattacking American fleet that should not contain more than two carriers. The only difference between their reasoning and Yamamoto's was that they intended to destroy the Americans before Yamamoto could get there in *Yamato*.

As the *Akagi* steamed toward its launch point northwest of Midway a few telltale indicators emerged that should have given Nagumo pause. Unusually heavy radio traffic from Pearl Harbor, though unreadable, suggested an American alert. A long transmission from an American submarine operating near Japan deviated from the usual pattern of short messages. Finally, on June 2, while operating in dense fog, Nagumo had to send a course change to his ships by wireless, thus breaking radio silence. Yet Nagumo continued to assume that he would achieve total surprise and adhered strictly to the preset plan.

Combat action in the Midway area began a full day sooner than the AF plan called for. At 9:00 A.M. on June 3, a full day in advance of Nagumo's strike, Ensign Jack Reid in command of a PBY picked up nearly 700 miles west of Midway Admiral Kondo's transports of the Midway Occupation Force. On learning of this contact, Nimitz warned Fletcher: "This is not, repeat not, the striking force." Nine B-17s missed these ships with bombs, but four night-flying PBYs equipped with torpedoes got a hit on oiler *Akebono Maru* at 1:00 A.M. the next morning. Admiral Yamamoto aboard his flagship learned of these attacks, but he decided not to break radio silence to warn Nagumo or to order the First Air Fleet to take special reconnaissance measures. The Occupation Force brushed aside the attacks and kept coming; even the damaged oiler stayed in formation.

At 2:50 A.M. on June 3 Rear Admiral Kakuji Kakuta's 2nd Mobile Force, consisting of light carriers *Ryujo* and *Junyo*, plus two cruisers and three destroyers, was some 165 miles southwest of Dutch Harbor. Kakuta's mission was to strike this main U. S. Aleutians base, thus diverting Nimitz's attention to the north and preventing American forces from interfering with landings scheduled later at Kiska and Attu in the outer Aleutian chain. *Ryujo* carried 12 Zeros and 18 Kates and *Junyo* 30 Zeros and 18 Vals. The total of embarked aircraft was a respectable 78.

The weather was typically Aleutian—meaning foggy and bad—even though daylight was almost perpetual at this latitude in June. In a ceiling as low as 700 to 900 feet *Junyo* launched six Vals and 12 Zeros and *Ryujo* three Zeros and nine Kates, a tenth Kate crashing on takeoff. For once even the skilled Japanese pilots could not form up, and so each carrier's planes proceeded independently. *Junyo*'s Zeros found a luckless PBY out of Dutch Harbor and shot it down, but the Vals could not find their target and had to turn back. *Ruyjo*'s Kates and Zeros found a break in the low clouds near the American base and attacked, destroying some oil tanks and strafing some water-bound Catalinas. But even the Japanese pilots considered the results to be "below expectations."

One Zero radioed that it had engine trouble and was lost. Its pilot force-landed on the tundra of an island near Dutch Harbor, but the plane's wheels dug into the mush, and when the plane flipped onto its back, the pilot's neck snapped. The Americans later brought the virtually undamaged Zero to San Diego, repaired and thoroughly tested it. The information obtained greatly aided American fighter pilots—who learned of the Zero's inability to turn in a high-speed dive—as well as the designers at Grumman and Vought, who were perfecting the new F6F Hellcat and F4U Corsair fighters.

On their return the Japanese pilots spotted in Makushin Bay near Dutch Harbor five ships identified as destroyers. Admiral Kakuta ordered a strike against these by carrier planes accompanied by four biplane reconnaissance seaplanes. The weather forced the carrier pilots to turn back, but the hapless biplanes encountered a flight of U. S. Army P-40s operating from a new airfield at Otter Point on Umnak Island. One fell, and another limped back riddled with holes. From the surviving crews Admiral Kakuta received the unwelcome news of the presence of land-plane fighter opposition. Heretofore, he had assumed that the Americans had no airstrip near Dutch Harbor. Kakuta reversed course as planned to reconnoiter Adak and Atka islands, intending to return and strike the Dutch Harbor again next day, June 4.

For his part Rear Admiral Theobald, at sea near Kodiak Island with his planeless Task Force 8, had been caught completely out of position to protect Dutch Harbor. Theobald had not accepted Pearl Harbor's intelligence and had positioned himself off Kodiak so as to protect the Alaska mainland. If near Dutch Harbor he might have found Kakuta's carriers and attacked out of the fog. It is also possible that he might have been spotted by Kakuta's scout planes and attacked from the air. His contribution to the Midway battle added up to a neutral zero.

While Kakuta's carriers were retiring from the first Dutch Harbor strike, Admiral Nagumo's four flattops were speeding toward their launching point northwest of Midway. During the night of June 3–4 the thick, cloudy weather over the Nagumo force began to clear, and by first dim light the overcast had broken into scattered cumulus scudding low overhead between 1,000 and 2,500 feet.

At 4:30 A.M. on June 4 Air Officer Commander Shogo Masuda twirled his green lantern once again. Moments later Lieutenant Shirane's Zero lifted from the *Akagi*'s still-dark flight deck. Nagumo had started launching his first strike of 36 Zeros, 36 Vals, and 36 Kates—in all 108 planes. He had elected not to go all out against Midway. He was holding back aboard the carriers an equal number of his best planes and crews, plus a 12-plane CAP of Zeros. If the seven scouting planes he was also sending out should find enemy warships, he wanted plenty of reserve striking power to deal with them. Already on the hangar decks crews were rigging long Type 91 torpedoes beneath the Kates.

This time Commander Fuchida was not leading the strike. Having undergone an emergency appendectomy aboard the *Akagi* en route, he was recuperating. Leading the pack was Lieutenant Joichi Tomonaga, the *Hiryu*'s aggressive air group commander. Like Tomonaga, many of the pilots flying the Midway strike were new to carrier combat though veterans of war in China.

In Fuchida's opinion Nagumo already had made a bad mistake. To search for a possible American fleet lurking near Midway, he had dispatched a single-phase search system, which relied principally on float planes for reconnaissance. This system sent one plane into each of seven sectors of a fan-shaped area ahead of the striking force. He could have used a two-phase search with two planes in each sector and in Fuchida's view should have done so. Catapult trouble delayed the takeoff of the plane from cruiser *Tone*, whose sector included Point Luck, where Frank Jack Fletcher's three carriers still were loitering undetected. The plane eventually sighted the *Yorktown* but not in time to affect the battle decisively.

At 5:34 A.M., when Lieutenant Tomonaga's strike force had been airborne for an hour, a PBY search plane out of Midway spotted Nagumo and radioed a message heard both on the island and aboard the *Yorktown* and *Enterprise*—"ENEMY CARRIERS." A few minutes later another plane spotted Tomonaga's approaching strike 50 miles out from their launch point and radioed, "MANY PLANES HEADING MIDWAY, BEARING 320 DEGREES, DISTANCE 150." Now both the Midway defenders and Admiral Fletcher knew the approximate position of the enemy. When Nimitz was informed he smiled and said, "This will clear up all the doubters." Turning to Commander Edwin T. Layton, his I. O. (Intelligence Officer), he remarked, "You were only five miles, five degrees and five minutes off," referring to Layton's predictions as to Nagumo's speed and course.

On Midway the Marines, sailors, and Army airmen began preparing all planes for immediate takeoff. Admiral Spruance with *Enterprise* and *Hornet* began racing with the wind on a converging course to close the range to Nagumo's still unsuspecting fleet. Throughout the day on June 4 the American carriers had a light wind at their sterns. This meant they had to turn away from the enemy into the wind to launch and recover. Admiral Nagumo in contrast had the wind to his bow and could launch and recover while closing Midway. Fletcher, in *Yorktown*, delayed to recover some Dauntlesses searching to the north, then put about and followed at best speed.

Combat began around 6:30 A.M. about 30 miles north and west of Midway. Twelve Marine Corps fighters, seven F2A Buffalos and five F4F Wildcats under Major Floyd Parks dove full throttle through the tight, disciplined V-of-Vs of Tomonaga's approaching planes. They concentrated on the Kate-level bombers, shooting down two and damaging others. All of Lieutenant Heijiro Abe's 17 surviving Kates from the *Soryu* returned with bullet holes, five being damaged beyond repair. Three others had to ditch en route home because of battle damage. Had the inexperienced American pilots been content to make this one pass, get in their lick, and dive away, most might have lived. But they pulled out to swing around and found Lieutenant Masaharu Suganami's Zero escort swarming onto their tails. This was Suganami's second encounter with U. S. Marines; his first had been while strafing Ewa Field on December 7.

The sharpshooting, well-trained Japanese got the range with their .30-caliber nose guns, then blasted Wildcats and Buffalos from the sky with their wing-mounted 20-mm. cannon, the plane of Major Parks among them. Major Kirk Armistead, leading another dozen Buffalos, fared no better. His planes tried to climb above the Japanese formation as it neared its release point off Midway, failed, bored in anyway, and got the same rough treatment. A Zero from the *Soryu* chased one Buffalo across the island, caught up with it as if it had been tethered, then dropped it into the lagoon. Only one Zero fell in aerial combat, though another Zero pilot suffered a fatal wound and succumbed after returning to his carrier. Nine Zeros were damaged, two beyond repair, but of the 25 Buffalos and Wildcats only six landed more or less intact and only two were immediately flyable. Eleven Marine pilots survived.

Those who landed safely all told similar stories. Finding Zeros on their tails and unable to shake them, they dove at speeds up to 400 knots to get away. Major Armistead dove out vertically after a Zero had followed him through a violent split S. He eased from his plunge at 3,000 feet and managed to flatten out at 500. "It seems useless," he reported afterward, "to even try to make more than one pass." Captain Marion E. Carl, one of the few to claim a Zero, also escaped after a headlong dive. A disgusted and angry Captain Philip R. White reported, "The F2A-3 [Buffalo] is *not* a combat airplane. The Japanese Zero . . . can run circles around the F2A-3." Perhaps with pardonable exaggeration he recorded his estimate of the top speed of the Zero as "better than 450 miles per hour." And he concluded, "It is my belief that any commander that orders pilots out for combat in an F2A-3 should consider the pilot as lost before leaving the ground." He too had escaped after a wild power dive and violent pullout at 3,000 feet.

Lieutenant Tomonaga's Vals and Kates did considerable damage to Midway's ground installations, while losing two Kates, a Val, and a strafing Zero to antiaircraft. On Sand Island, the seaplane base, they burned four oil tanks and demolished the hangar and dispensary. Perhaps to the joy of some Marines they also destroyed the brig. On Eastern Island, site of the airfield, they wrecked the power house and hit the CP of Major William W. Benson, killing him and wounding many of his sector command staff.

Yet Tomonaga's ten-minute attack had not damaged Eastern Island's runways or beach defenses on either island. The lieutenant himself realized this from the viciousness of the antiaircraft fire. He had lost about 11 planes* and had at least as many more badly damaged and struggling to keep up with the returning formation. At 7:00 A.M. he therefore radioed to the *Akagi*, "THERE IS NEED FOR A SECOND ATTACK WAVE."

Prior to Tomonaga's arrival Colonel Harold D. Shannon, Midway's air commander, had dispatched the last of his bombers as soon as his radar had picked up the enemy 93 miles out. Four Army B-26s and six Navy TBF Avengers equipped with torpedoes had already scrambled at 6:00 A.M. Sixteen high-flying B-17s had taken off earlier. Major Lofton R. Henderson led out 16 SBD Dauntlesses, followed by Major Benjamin W. Norris, who commanded 11 of the older SB2U Vindicators, the latter making their first and only appearance in the Pacific war. Some of the planes spotted the approaching Japanese aircraft and evaded them. All, including the B-17s when redirected by radio, headed directly for Nagumo's carrier fleet. No protecting fighters accompanied them.

The fast B-26s and Avengers—the latter also making their first appearance in the war—arrived at about 7:05 A.M. and attacked bravely into a storm of AA fire and a combat air patrol of 12 planes. This CAP was soon reinforced as the Japanese carriers sliced off additional Zeros. Three attackers fell at once as they slowed to drop speed, the remaining seven released their fish, but the *Akagi* turned two full circles and evaded the slow-moving Mark 13s. These could make only 33 knots in the water, about the same as a destroyer. Just two B-26s and a badly shot-up Avenger managed to shake the Zeros and limp back to Midway. Nagumo's only losses were two AA gunners on *Akagi* felled by strafing from a B-26 that had roared right over the ship, barely missing the bridge.

The attackers had, nevertheless, forced Admiral Nagumo to make another of his several mistakes. Up to this point he had been reserving his second strike and his best pilots. But Tomonaga's message, reinforced by the arrival of the torpedo planes, led him to conclude that he must launch

---

* Admiral Nagumo's report lists six planes lost in its text. Detailed reports from each carrier, however, record seven Kates, two Vals, and two Zeros lost.

another strike at Midway. Hence he ordered at 7:15, three minutes after the torpedo planes had departed: "PLANES IN SECOND ATTACK WAVE STAND BY. . . . RE-EQUIP YOURSELVES WITH BOMBS." This meant that the torpedo-armed Kates now on deck would have to be stricken below and rearmed with Type 80 land bombs—a process that could take nearly an hour. At once the hard-working deck crews began pushing Kates onto the swift-moving after elevator of the *Akagi.*

During a lull that now set in, between 7:15 and the beginning of the next attack from Midway's planes, Nagumo was jolted by a message from the cruiser *Tone*'s float plane—the one that catapult troubles had delayed. At 7:28 A.M. its pilot radioed, "SIGHT WHAT APPEARS TO BE 10 ENEMY SURFACE SHIPS, IN POSITION BEARING 10 DEGREES DISTANCE 240 MILES FROM MIDWAY. COURSE 150 DEGREES, SPEED OVER 20 KNOTS." This was the first indication—and that not a firm one, since the pilot had used the phrase "appears to be"—that an enemy task force might be lying in ambush. Also the position given was within range of Nagumo's ships.

Now the Japanese admiral was in a real quandary. His Kates had been struck below for rearming and many Zeros earmarked for the attack force were aloft reinforcing the CAP. Also Lieutenant Tomonaga's flight soon would be returning, short of fuel and with many planes battle-damaged. What should he do? He could launch his Val dive bombers at once with little or no escort to attack the enemy ships. But the pilot had reported no enemy carrier. If none was present he might be better advised to hit Midway again before dealing with possibly a planeless task force north of Midway.

For about 16 minutes Nagumo and his staff thought over the situation while his task force sought to resume its normal cruising disposition. Then he abruptly sent his force another message at 7:45: "PREPARE TO CARRY OUT ATTACKS ON ENEMY FLEET UNITS. LEAVE TORPEDOES ON THOSE ATTACK PLANES WHICH HAVE NOT AS YET BEEN CHANGED TO BOMBS." Two minutes later, annoyed that the *Tone*'s pilot had not reported more fully, he sent a message asking him to "ASCERTAIN SHIP TYPES AND MAINTAIN CONTACT."

But Nagumo's time for uninterrupted decision-making had ended. Roaring in at 20,000 feet were Lieutenant Colonel Walter Sweeney's B-17s from Midway. *Chikuma* began firing at them at 7:48. Bombing in treys, pairs, and singles over the next quarter hour the big Flying Fortresses missed *Soryu* with a stick of 600-pounders, then straddled the *Hiryu.* Zeros that had been circling at low altitude began climbing frantically as bombs fell near the *Akagi.* But they managed to attack only two of the B-17s and to damage only one. The Zeros found the big planes too high and too fast to catch. On the other hand the Flying Fortresses had scored no hits.

At 8:00 A.M., while the B-17s still were making their last runs, look-outs on the *Akagi* sighted Major Lofton Henderson's 16 Dauntlesses racing in. Henderson's men had little flying training on the SBD—some as little as a week, with no bombing practice—so the major tried a glide bomb run with planes in trail from 4,000 feet. This led him squarely into the midst of the Zero CAP, which shot him down before he could drop his bombs. Not one of the pilots following did better than score a near miss.

Twenty minutes later, at about 8:20 A.M., Major Norris with his slower Vindicators showed up, breaking out of the low cloud cover near the battleship *Haruna*. Norris could see the carriers in the distance, and realizing that he could never get through the Zeros to them, he had his men dive-bomb the battle wagon. Two missiles rattled the *Haruna*'s stern with very near misses but caused no serious damage. Norris lost two of his crews.

In the midst of this terrific uproar the *Tone* reconnaissance pilot belatedly reported at 8:20 A.M., "THE ENEMY IS ACCOMPANIED BY WHAT APPEARS TO BE A CARRIER." It had taken the pilot (or his observer) 52 minutes to discern the distinctive shape of a flattop. The reason probably was because he stayed very low, just off the horizon, and could not make out the *Yorktown*'s distinctive shape. Nevertheless, his belatedly amplified report confirmed that a major American task force was within range and that it had at least one carrier in company.

But the roar of the *Akagi*'s guns, the violent maneuvers of the ship, and false reports at one point that the *Hiryu* had been hit all had distracted Nagumo's attention from his tactical problem. He was angered at 8:50 when the *Tone* pilot, low on fuel, reported, "I AM NOW HOMEWARD BOUND." He responded curtly, "POSTPONE YOUR HOMING."

By 8:55 Nagumo, accepting the advice of Commander Genda, finally had decided on his future course of action. The bulk of Lieutenant Tomonaga's returning air crew by now were orbiting the task force, waiting to land. He would delay launching an immediate strike on the American task force, take Tomonaga and his airmen aboard, and rearm and refuel all planes. After that he would launch a "grand scale" air blow at the American carrier and its escort. His Kate torpedo planes, his staff told him, including those returned from Midway, could be ready in 90 minutes, at about 10:30. The Zeros, refueled, could easily make it to the enemy fleet and back. The decision made, he radioed all ships, "PROCEED NORTHWARD AFTER TAKING ON YOUR PLANES. WE PLAN TO CONTACT AND DESTROY THE ENEMY TASK FORCE." In the next 23 minutes all airborne Vals, Kates, and Zeros of the Midway force landed, and at 9:18 A.M. all ships heeled sharply to port out of the wind, heading northward at full speed.

Nagumo's real trouble and the true source of perhaps inevitable errors was his lack of adequate plane strength. With another carrier group—say, Carrier Group 5 from the *Shokaku* and *Zuikaku*—he could easily have gotten away a strike force while recovering his own planes. He might have done so had he possessed *Zuiho*, *Ryujo*, and *Junyo* or even *Zuikaku* alone with a pick-up air group. But he did not have these ships, and so

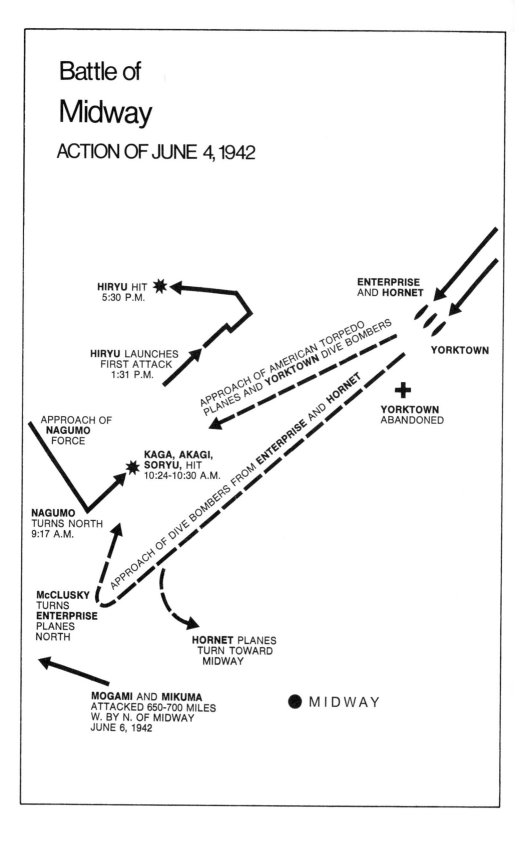

Battle of
Midway
ACTION OF JUNE 4, 1942

HIRYU HIT
5:30 P.M.

HIRYU LAUNCHES
FIRST ATTACK
1:31 P.M.

ENTERPRISE
AND HORNET

YORKTOWN

APPROACH OF AMERICAN TORPEDO
PLANES AND YORKTOWN DIVE BOMBERS

YORKTOWN
ABANDONED

APPROACH OF
NAGUMO
FORCE

KAGA, AKAGI,
SORYU, HIT
10:24-10:30 A.M.

APPROACH OF DIVE BOMBERS FROM ENTERPRISE AND HORNET

NAGUMO
TURNS NORTH
9:17 A.M.

McCLUSKY
TURNS
ENTERPRISE
PLANES
NORTH

HORNET PLANES
TURN TOWARD
MIDWAY

MOGAMI AND MIKUMA
ATTACKED 650-700 MILES
W. BY N. OF MIDWAY
JUNE 6, 1942

● MIDWAY

Yamamoto's decision to disperse the carriers already was having a decisive impact on the battle's outcome.

In the meantime, while the Midway planes were gallantly and futilely expending themselves, Admiral Spruance with *Enterprise* and *Hornet* was racing south to get within easy range for his short-legged Wildcat fighters and Devastator torpedo planes. Fletcher in *Yorktown* was following after recovery of his scout bombers.

Finally, about 7:00 A.M., growing uneasy lest he lose the advantage of surprise, Spruance ordered his *Enterprise* and *Hornet* planes launched although the distance to the enemy was still great for the Devastators and Wildcats. The *Enterprise* launched 14 Devastators of Torpedo 6, 33 Dauntlesses of Scouting and Bombing 6, and ten Wildcat fighters. *Hornet* dispatched almost an identical force of 15 Devastators, 35 Dauntlesses, and ten Wildcats, all from Air Group 8. Admiral Fletcher aboard *Yorktown* kept a squadron of Dauntlesses aboard and spotted for takeoff just in case the enemy was sneaking down another carrier force from the north. He remembered the Coral Sea, where the *Shoho* had operated independently. Consequently, he launched an hour after the other carriers 12 Devastators, 17 Dauntlesses, and six escorting Wildcats.

At it turned out, Spruance's staff had made a grievous blunder in predicting "Point Option," that spot in the ocean where planes and enemy ships should converge. It had assumed that the Japanese would hold a steady course and speed toward Midway. As already seen, however, the First Air Fleet had been slowed by manuevering to avoid the Midway attackers, and for reasons still inexplicable not one American pilot had bothered to radio to Midway a position report before going in. As a result, only the American torpedo planes flew directly to their target.

Perhaps because of long peacetime experience in exercises, perhaps because they were so acutely conscious of the fuel limitations of their awkward Devastators, Lieutenant Commanders John C. Waldron of *Hornet*'s Torpedo 8 and Eugene E. Lindsey of *Enterprise*'s Torpedo 6 decided that the Japanese would not make Point Option. Both selected a course farther to the westward and so. contacted the enemy. All of *Yorktown*'s planes flew a similar course toward a more realistically calculated Point Option. Lem Massey's torpedo planes took the lead, and the Dauntless pilots followed the Devastators below. Badly thrown off were the *Enterprise* and *Hornet* dive-bomber squadrons. Commander Stanhope C. Ring led *Hornet*'s Dauntlesses and fighters to Point Option, found nothing, and made a bad guess. He decided that the Japanese were closer to Midway and turned southeast toward the island. He sighted nothing and lost three of his SBDs and all ten of his F4F-4s when they ran short of fuel and had to ditch. After flying past Point Option and running low on fuel, Lieutenant Commander Wade McClusky, leading the *Enterprise* dive bombers, made a better guess and turned northwest, doubling back on Nagumo's projected course. Nagumo's course change might still have thrown him off, but he fortunately sighted a Japanese destroyer and followed its bearing directly to the enemy fleet. He arrived at almost the same minute as the *Yorktown*'s dive bombers.

John Waldron's Torpedo 8 from *Hornet* arrived first. At 9:18, just as the *Akagi* was steadying on its new northward course at 28 knots, lookouts on the *Chikuma* sighted the Devastators low off the water ten miles distant. Waldron had been a Navy pilot since 1927 and knew well enough that without a fighter escort his chances were slim. But he led his squadron in anyway in what will stand forever as one of the bravest acts of American naval history. The first Zeros attacked while the 100-knot Devastators still were eight miles away. Some Zero pilots dove from the rear to zoom upward, loop, and plunge down again for another pass. With but one single-mount .30-caliber free gun in their rear seats, unable to maneuver with their big torpedoes, the Devastators were helpless. One by one they tumbled blazing into the water, hitting with crushing impact, each splash generating frantic Banzais from the watching crews topside on the Japanese cruiser and destroyer screen. Flying near the rear of the formation was Ensign George (Tex) Gay. After seeing every other plane fall, Gay might have been pardoned for aborting the attack. But he closed the *Akagi*, dropped his torpedo, and was shot down by a Zero on the other side of the flagship. Clambering from the wreck, he found a seat cushion and a raft and remained in the water for a survivor's view of the rest of the battle.

Coming in a half hour later was Eugene Lindsey's Torpedo 6 from *Enterprise*, followed after some minutes by Lem Massey's Torpedo 3 from *Yorktown*. The Zeros dealt almost as handily with Lindsey's Devastators as they had with those of Torpedo 8. Few managed aimed drops, the carriers evaded the slow-running Mark 13s, and only two shot-up planes survived. The Zeros had a harder time with Massey's planes because they carried twin-mount guns in their rear seats. Also they had some help at first from two of Commander Jimmy Thach's Wildcats from Fighting 3, the only planes to offer direct support to the TBDs. But after the two fighters had been driven to cloud cover and more Zeros arrived, Massey's Devastators also began to suffer heavily. Only four of the *Yorktown*'s fourteen survived. Of 41 attacking American carrier torpedo planes, not one scored a hit, and all but six were shot down.

Though they could not protect the TBDs, Jimmy Thach and two of his squadron mates managed to demonstrate that the Wildcat, properly handled, could survive in combat with a Zero. Thach, with four planes on high cover, had intended to dive to help Massey's squadron, but a gaggle of Zeros attacked from the rear and shot down one of his planes. Thach and his two surviving companions then began using a defensive tactic known later as the "Thach weave." As the Zeros dove on the Wildcats, the Americans turned sharply toward each other, giving the Japanese pilots difficult deflection shots and allowing each man as he swerved around to shoot from head on at the Zero on another's tail. Thach, a marksman who knew how to "lead" his target, claimed two Zeros with short bursts from 400 feet as the Zeros climbed ahead, stalled, and began their famous "snap-around" turns. Another he picked off in a head-on shot. He and his men survived, but they dared not break out of their "weave" until the Zeros had given up.

Thach left the battle convinced of the soundness of the two-pair, four-plane formation—the famous "Rotte" or "finger four"—that would soon become standard American Navy and Army air-to-air combat doctrine for the rest of the war. The Wildcat pilots, he was convinced, would do best by flying in two pairs. When attacking the enemy each wingman would protect his leader, and if jumped by the much more maneuverable Zeros, each pair would "weave" sharply toward the other. But Thach was not satisfied with the Wildcat. The new folding-wing F4F-4, though more could be stowed on a carrier, permitting larger fighter squadrons, seemed to be somewhat slower and more sluggish than the F4F-3. It was grossly inferior to the Zero in climb, speed at low altitude, acceleration, and turning radius.

Together with the torpedo planes, Thach had occupied the Nagumo force and virtually all of its embarked Zeros for about an hour. But except for a few Zeros shot down—Thach and his two companions claimed five among them and had seen a Devastator rear-seat man drop another—the First Air Fleet was virtually unscratched.

By about 10:20 A.M. Nagumo needed only a few minutes' respite to land his fighters, rearm and refuel enough of them to furnish an escort, and then send his nearly ready Vals and Kates on that full-strength strike against the American task force. *Kaga* already had her after deck jammed with planes ready for takeoff. *Akagi* was bringing up planes while continuing to launch replenished Zeros for CAP. The *Hiryu*, whose air group had suffered the most losses in the Midway attack, was busy striking below damaged planes and bringing up rearmed ones on her elevators. She had pulled well to the north of the other carriers in evading the torpedo planes and could hardly be seen through the smoke. Until literally this moment the First Air Fleet had enjoyed fabulously good luck since the beginning of the war. Not one bomb or torpedo had yet struck home. But this fortune now was about to desert it for six terrible and decisive minutes.

10. Midway: Climax and Pursuit

Commander Wade McClusky from the *Enterprise*, approaching from the southwest, had sighted the Nagumo force at about 10:05 A.M. from 30 miles out. He now had only 30 Dauntlesses, three planes having aborted because of engine trouble. At about the same moment from considerably to the east Commander Max Leslie and his 17 Dauntlesses from *Yorktown* also sighted Nagumo. Neither American formation knew of the presence of the other until their attacks had begun. Not a single Japanese fighter was in sight at their altitudes, about 19,000 feet. Every Zero was on or near the deck, orbiting or going after Lem Massey's torpedo planes now on their run-ins.

By this time *Kaga* was west of the *Akagi* and *Soryu*. *Hiryu* was farther north and out of sight of the other carriers. McClusky saw her, but none of the American pilots picked her as a target, and in his phase of the battle she escaped attack entirely. McClusky's planes were dangerously low on fuel, having been in the air a full hour longer than Leslie's. But on sighting the enemy, McClusky's only thought was to score hits.

Lookouts on the enemy carriers were caught napping; not a single puff of antiaircraft had as yet blossomed in the sky. Probably the torpedo planes had drawn their binoculars away from high altitudes. Snapping on his radio, McClusky reported his sighting to the *Enterprise*. Then, as remembered by Lieutenant Clarence E. Dickinson, he called to Lieutenant Gallaher, commanding Scouting 6, and Lieutenant R. H. "Dick" Best, leading Bombing 6: "EARL GALLAHER, YOU TAKE THE CARRIER ON THE LEFT AND, BEST, YOU TAKE THE CARRIER ON THE RIGHT. EARL, YOU FOLLOW ME DOWN." Trailed by Scouting 6 and two divisions of Bombing 6 that somehow had misunderstood the instructions, McClusky started diving at 10:20 A.M. on the *Kaga* on the left of the formation. Best, seeing him go, led his remaining five planes on toward the *Akagi*, the carrier on the right, though he had not heard McClusky's order.

McClusky plummeted at 280 knots to 1,800 feet, releasing a bomb that missed. Lieutenant Dick Jaccard and Ensign William Pittman missed, too, but Gallaher's 1,000-pounder crashed into the fore part of the *Kaga* just forward of the bridge. It exploded with tremendous violence, blasting apart a small refueling cart that drenched the bridge with flaming gasoline, killing every man there, Captain Jisaku Okada included. The next three bombs hit, too, smashing the flight deck to splinters.

Diving ninth in line was Lieutenant Clarence Dickinson. He could identify his target as of the *Kaga* class, "and she was enormous." He aimed at "the big red disk with its band of white up on the bow" and thought that his 500-pounder and two 100-pounders struck amid planes parked forward. They may have, too, because by now the *Kaga* was such a roaring conflagration of blazing gasoline and exploding munitions that more bombs may have struck than the four the Japanese later recorded.

Lieutenant Commander Leslie, approaching from the southeast with the *Yorktown* SBDs, picked out a ship he thought was of the *Akagi* class but which probably was the *Soryu*. He dove at 10:25. Three of his pilots scored in as many minutes, though Bombing 3 suffered once more from windshield and gunsight fogging in the humid, lower air. One pilot placed his bomb on the flight deck in front of the forward elevator. The next two landed missiles on either side of the amidships elevator. The three blasts knocked overside a Zero taking off, wrecked the deck, and spread flames to gasoline tanks, munitions storage rooms, and 18 torpedo-armed Kates spotted aft ready for launch. Induced explosions began in only five minutes, and in 15 more the ship was so completely aflame that Captain Ryusaku Yanagimoto ordered abandon ship. Destroyers *Hamakaze* and *Isokaze* moved alongside to take off survivors.

Leslie's last four pilots, who could see into the flaming bowels of the *Soryu* through gaps torn in the flight deck by the 1,000-pounders, concluded that the carrier was no longer a worthwhile target. Two near missed the *Isokaze* and two others a nearby battleship.

While McClusky and Leslie had been diving, Lieutenant Best and his first division of Bombing 6 had continued on to the *Akagi*, which had about 40 planes spotted on its after deck. As recorded by radio monitors on the *Enterprise*, on seeing McClusky tip over, Best had called to his pilots, "FIRST DIVISION . . . STAY WITH ME AND COME ON OVER. DON'T LET THIS CARRIER ESCAPE." Followed by four of his men and possibly a plane or two of his third division, he plunged at the *Akagi* at 10:26. Best's bomb near missed, landing about 30 feet abeam of the bridge, doing little harm other than to drench exposed personnel with hundreds of gallons of sea water. But Lieutenant Edward J. Kroeger, diving next, hit the flattop near the elevator amidships, ripping open the flight deck and spreading flame and blast to planes in the hangar and on deck. Ensign F. T. Weber, diving third, landed a bomb on the extreme end of the flight deck, knocking off a chunk but otherwise doing little damage.

Although the other pilots missed, Kroeger's hit proved to be enough to doom the *Akagi*. With gasoline hoses entwined about and with a full complement of bombers and torpedo planes gassed and armed, his bomb touched off in moments uncontrollable fires. Commander Fuchida, who had come topside to watch the action from the bridge, has recorded his impressions:

> Looking about, I was horrified at the destruction that had been wrought in a matter of seconds. There was a huge hole in the flight deck just behind the amidships elevator. The elevator itself, twisted like molten glass, was drooping into the hangar. Deck plates reeled upward in grotesque configurations. Planes stood tail up, belching livid flame and jet-black smoke. Reluctant tears streamed down my cheeks as I watched the fires spread. . . .

Water pressure on fire mains failed; there was no way to check the flames. By 10:29, only four minutes after Kroeger's bomb had struck, induced explosions from torpedo warheads on blazing Kates began.

Best's initiative in flying on to attack the *Akagi* had paid off handsomely. The bombing accuracy of the three American squadrons had not been spectacular—only nine certain hits from 47 planes—but the pilots had wrecked three different targets. Only the *Hiryu* was speeding away unmolested to the northeast. Good intelligence and good tactics had enabled the Americans to throw the first punch at their enemy and to catch him at his most vulnerable moment with their most effective weapons, the Dauntless dive bombers. Sheer good fortune had placed McClusky and Leslie over the target at the same moment and had led them to choose separate targets. In the circumstances, with no fighter opposition and negligible antiaircraft, the pilots could hardly fail to hit, and they had not.

Retirement from the scene was easy for Leslie's SBDs from the *Yorktown*. The pilots pulled out to the northeast just above the water and sped off through gaps in the screen of ships about the burning *Soryu*. Just one enemy plane attacked, that not a Zero but a Dave reconnaissance float plane that soon fell behind.

For McClusky's *Enterprise* pilots retirement was a nightmare. They pulled out of their dives to the west, flying right through the Zero CAP that had been hunting down Massey's torpedo planes. Lieutenant Joe Penland, with four pilots of his second division of Bombing 6, had the unwelcome company of four Zeros for some 20 miles. The fast, agile Japanese fighters would dive, climb away steeply several thousand feet, then dive again for another firing pass. The five Dauntlesses stuck tightly together, turning in a fashion similar to Thach's "weave," their rear-seat men keeping up such a concentrated fire that the Zeros seemed reluctant to close. None of the five was shot down directly, but four planes, including Penland's, had to ditch when out of fuel.

Of Bombing 6's Third Division, only Lieutenant E. L. Anderson made it home in airplane 6-B-16. The other four planes went into the water. Anderson's rugged Dauntless was hit in the prop, elevators, elevator torque tube, wings, in the fuselage at frame 17, and its radio antenna was shot away. A bullet lodged in rear-seat gunner Stuart J. Mason's parachute, others in the radio. Mason was wounded in the face and legs, but he managed to repair the radio and enable Lieutenant Anderson to use his ZB homing equipment to locate the *Enterprise*. A 7.7-mm. machine-gun bullet had penetrated the left main gas tank, but the tank had sealed itself successfully. A 20-mm. cannon hit probably would have torn a hole so large the fuel would have leaked out—which may have been one reason the other four planes ditched.

On his retirement Lieutenant Dickinson was most concerned about three Zeros he had seen take off from the *Kaga* as she was being bombed. Two flew directly under him and did not attack; the third spotted him but made only one pass, pulling away when his gunner, Radioman Joseph F. De Luca, fired on it. Moments later Dickinson sighted another Zero crossing his course. It was stalking an SBD of Scouting 6 ahead. It was in good range of Dickinson's two fixed .50-caliber guns, but the young pilot hesitated. "If I miss him he'll be alive and awfully mad at me." Then he fired ten to 20 rounds from each gun, and the Zero abruptly reeled to the left and into the water. It did not burn, leading Dickinson to conclude that he had hit the pilot.

De Luca, hearing the forward guns, called on the intercom, "Do you think we got him, Mr. Dickinson? Did you get him?"

"Yes, De Luca, I think I did."

"That's good, Mr. Dickinson."

"Can you see any more back there? I'll take care of the front. You take care of the rear. For Christ's sake keep a good lookout."

"Sure, Mr. Dickinson. I'm looking out mighty good."

Dickinson's next problem was his fuel situation. The long flight and detour before finding the Japanese fleet had depleted fuel well below the safety margin in all of the planes of Bombing 6 and Scouting 6. Only one or two crashed near the enemy, who picked up one pilot and his gunner, but others began dropping out soon after leaving the vicinity. In all, 18 planes from the two squadrons failed to return. Rescuers picked up only six pilots and five gunners.

Dickinson was one of the last to ditch. Twenty miles from the *Enterprise* his engine began to sputter, and ten miles out he had to set down, skipping across the water, wheels still retracted, at 80 miles per hour. Unhurt except for a blow on the cheek from his tubular, three-power telescopic gunsight, Dickinson scrambled out with De Luca, and both jumped into the water. They watched silently as Dauntless 6-S-10, just a month out of the Douglas factory, bubbled under nose first.

"Nice swimming, De Luca."

"Feels fine. I'm glad we're back, Mr. Dickinson. Just enough gasoline."

"Gasoline! De Luca, I prayed that plane back the last twenty miles."

Dickinson had ditched alongside a destroyer that picked them up in a matter of minutes. At least four pilots were not so lucky. Other crews saw them ditch and get into their life rafts, but rescuers found no trace of them.

Back aboard the burning, exploding *Akagi*, Admiral Nagumo soon discovered that he could no longer control his fleet; *Akagi*'s power and communications had failed. At 10:43 A.M. a Zero parked to the starboard of the bridge caught fire and spread flames to the structure. Minutes later destroyer *Nowaki* came alongside to take off the headquarters staff. Nagumo had to leave by a line attached to the bridge; flames barred descent by ladder. The admiral then transferred to the light cruiser *Nagara*.

While Nagumo was shifting his command Rear Admiral Hiroaki, aboard the cruiser *Tone*, assumed tactical command of the First Air Fleet. At 10:50 he radioed to Rear Admiral Tamon Yamaguchi aboard the *Hiryu*, "ATTACK THE ENEMY CARRIERS," to receive the reply by blinker, "ALL OUR PLANES ARE TAKING OFF NOW FOR THE PURPOSE OF DESTROYING THE ENEMY CARRIERS." At the same time Yamaguchi radioed to Admiral Yamamoto aboard the fleet flagship *Yamato*, "FIRES ARE RAGING ABOARD THE KAGA, SORYU, AND AKAGI RESULTING FROM ATTACKS CARRIED OUT BY ENEMY LAND-BASED AND CARRIER-BASED ATTACK PLANES. WE PLAN TO HAVE THE HIRYU ENGAGE THE ENEMY CARRRIERS. IN THE MEANTIME, WE ARE TEMPORARILY RETIRING TO THE NORTH. . . ."

This message had literally the impact of a thunderbolt on Yamamoto. Until this moment he seems not to have realized how irreplaceable his fleet carriers were or how drastically their loss would cripple Japan's war effort. Even now he failed to issue what could have been a saving order—to have the *Hiryu* flee west at full speed to escape what the message implied were superior enemy forces based on Midway and carriers.

Admiral Yamaguchi, aboard the *Hiryu*, had no intention of retiring. Earlier, before the attack, he had urged Admiral Nagumo to launch an immediate strike. Now, at 10:58 A.M. he began launching the 18 Val dive bombers and five Zeros he had ready on his flight deck. Below, his torpedo planes still were frantically rearming. He also maintained a northeasterly course, directly toward the position of the American fleet being continuously reported by cruiser *Chikuma*'s Number 5 scout plane.

By this time *Akagi*, *Kaga*, and *Soryu* all were derelicts. None could land a plane or maintain headway with the fleet. *Soryu* sank at 7:13 in the evening, taking down 718 of her crew. *Kaga* went down following an internal explosion a few minutes later, after losing about 800 officers and men. The *Akagi* burned all day and night to succumb to a Japanese destroyer torpedo the following morning. Considering the damage, her loss of life was relatively light—only 221 officers and men.

Pilot losses from all Japanese carriers may have been as high as 100, though most were transferred from the carriers soon after their ships were hit. The Zero pilots on CAP suffered the most heavily; many had been shot down in the American attack, others were lost in ditching. Few seem to have landed aboard the *Hiryu* even though their own carriers could not take them aboard.

Eleven A.M. on June 4, two minutes after *Hiryu* launched, saw carrier

Yorktown in the process of dispatching ten SBDs to scout west and north. The pilots had orders to fly out 250 miles and look for additional carriers. Admiral Fletcher vividly recalled his experience in the Coral Sea and still suspected that a fifth Japanese carrier was about. *Yorktown*'s seven remaining Dauntlesses were below in the hangar, fully gassed, and armed with 1,000-pound bombs. Twelve Wildcats had just flown off on CAP to protect the ship. Some 20 miles to the southeast Admiral Spruance with *Enterprise* and *Hornet* was operating separately, and all three flattops were "sweating out" the return of their air groups.

At 11:59 A.M., while *Yorktown* deck crews were refueling Jimmy Thach's fighters just returned from their escort mission, Radarman Vane Bennett picked up on the scope a force not registering on the IFF (Identification Friend or Foe) with which the *Yorktown* now was equipped. Captain Elliott Buckmaster at once ordered plane refueling stopped, all gasoline lines and tanks drained and filled with carbon-dioxide gas at 20 pounds pressure, and an auxiliary gasoline tank given the deep six off the stern. Crewmen dogged and secured all watertight doors between compartments. Buckmaster, the skipper whose ship had been hit in the Coral Sea, was taking the sort of precautions his Japanese counterparts had totally neglected.

When Commander Leslie's gas-shy SBDs returned from their strike, they were ordered to orbit out of harm's way. Fighters in the air dashed west to intercept the enemy, and although they experienced the usual difficulty of coordination with the ship's air controller, they nevertheless did contact the incoming force of 18 Vals with a small Zero escort from the *Hiryu*. Wildcats from the *Hornet* and *Enterprise* also piled into the action. Told by aides that the enemy was about to attack, Admiral Frank Jack Fletcher, bent over and studying a chart, rejoined, "Well, I have my tin hat on. I can't do anything else now!"

The Vals and Zeros suffered very heavily, and only seven of the dive bombers managed to get through. Yet they gave the Americans a lesson in dive-bombing. They scored three hits on the *Yorktown* and pulled out of their dives at 500 feet, much lower than the 2,500 to 1,500-foot average of the Americans.

One bomb, tumbling in flight, hit the *Yorktown* just abaft the Number 2 elevator on the starboard side, exploding on contact and ripping a hole ten feet by ten feet in the flight deck. It set afire three gassed planes in the hangar, but Lieutenant A. C. Emerson, the hangar deck officer, released the sprinkler system and extinguished the flames. Another 550-pounder penetrated deep into the ship's stack, snuffing out fires and cutting speed to six knots. The third bomb passed through the No. 1 elevator and on through the hangar deck to explode in a rag-storage space. There it started a fire adjacent to the gasoline storage and the magazines. The *Yorktown* could not launch or recover planes until the hole in the flight deck was patched, but it had been infinitely better prepared to receive battle damage than any of the Japanese carriers. By 1:50 P.M. the crew had all fires under control, the deck had been patched, and steam pressure built up again. Fueling of Thach's fighters had just begun once more when at 53 miles' range the radar picked up another incoming flight.

This one consisted of ten Kates and six Zeros, all of the remaining operational aircraft that the *Hiryu* could launch. Again the American fighters managed an interception from ten to 14 miles out, at least three of the Kates fell, but two of the big, fast torpedoes bored into the port side of the *Yorktown* at frames 90 and 75. Steam pressure dropped immediately, electric power failed throughout the ship, the rudder jammed at 15 degrees left, and the big flattop slowed to a stop, then began listing heavily. When the list reached 26 degrees, Captain Buckmaster, after conferring with Admiral Fletcher, decided not to risk further the lives of the crew. If the ship capsized hundreds would be lost. With the edge of the hangar deck already dipping into a fortunately calm sea, Buckmaster ordered "Abandon Ship!" But this tough and well-serviced flattop refused to sink. Of itself the list stopped increasing, and the *Yorktown* floated throughout the night with a fire still smoldering in the rag compartment.

The *Hiryu*'s attack groups had crippled the *Yorktown* but had suffered heavy losses. Three Zeros and 13 Vals had failed to return from the first attack, and five Kates and three Zeros fell in the second attack, one of the Kates being that of Lieutenant Tomonaga, who had led the Midway strike. Counting repaired planes made operational, *Hiryu* had left only six Zeros, five Vals, and four Kates. Nevertheless, an undaunted Admiral Yamaguchi resolutely began to prepare for still another strike. He believed that his planes had attacked and disabled two American carriers, an understandable mistake since the *Yorktown* during the torpedo-plane attack showed no sign of previous damage. He therefore wanted to finish off the third carrier—prisoners and reconnaissance planes had reported three by now—in a twilight attack.

In the meantime the *Yorktown*'s search mission had borne fruit. At about 2:30 P.M. Lieutenant Samuel "Red" Adams turned in a superb contact report. He had picked up the *Hiryu* and its escort, noting that the force consisted of a carrier, two battleships, three cruisers, and four destroyers. He also gave its course and position accurately, enabling Admiral Spruance's staff to calculate a precise "Point Option" for another attack.

At 3:30 P.M., while many of the *Yorktown*'s crew still were in the water awaiting rescue, the *Enterprise* launched another strike of 24 Dauntlesses. Ten of these were from the *Yorktown*'s strike force that had landed aboard the Big E after their own ship had been hit. Scouting 6 led, followed by Bombing 6, and then the *Yorktown*'s Bombing 3. Lieutenant Earl Gallaher, skipper of Scouting 6, acted as Air Group Commander, Wade McClusky having been wounded in the first attack. A half hour later the *Hornet* also launched, sending out 16 more SBDs toward "Point Option."

When Gallaher sighted the *Hiryu* at 4:45 P.M. he caught her in much the same condition that the *Akagi, Kaga,* and *Soryu* had been in during the morning. She was preparing to launch a third strike of the remaining Vals and Kates. Gasoline hoses lay threaded about, and perhaps because they were tired, the crews had carelessly failed to mop up pools of oil and gasoline.

But the *Hiryu* never had a chance to launch. At 5:01 P.M. the cruiser *Chikuma* spotted an enemy plane directly over the carrier and diving. This was Gallaher leading Scouting 6. Gallaher had tipped over as four Zeros on CAP dove in and followed the Dauntlesses down. Most of the pilots picked the carrier, two the battleship *Haruna* as a target. Gallaher's bomb missed as the *Hiryu* turned sharply away from the direction of the dive. But Lieutenant Dick Jaccard, third man down, scored near the bow. Three more hits on the bow followed in quick succession, ripping apart the forward third of the flight deck and slamming the No. 1 elevator against the bridge. Flames boiled up from gasoline and ammunition set afire in the yawning gap and swiftly worked their way aft through parked planes and along gasoline hoses.

By the time the *Hornet's* SBDs arrived 20 minutes later the *Hiryu* was burning throughout her length. They passed her by as a target and dove on other ships. Several missed the *Tone* at 5:20, according to Japanese records, and nine the *Chikuma* at 5:32.

The dive-bombing from the *Enterprise* and *Hornet* planes had been ragged. The pilots had hit no ship other than the *Hiryu*. Pilot fatigue doubtless had something to do with it, since most of the pilots had flown the tiring morning missions. But so had vigorous resistance from an aggressive Zero CAP that shot down three Dauntlesses and badly damaged three more.

During his dive on the *Hiryu* Lieutenant DeWitt W. Shumway, commanding Bombing 3, had been followed by a Zero that forced him to drop his bomb at 4,000 feet. On pullout two more fighters jumped him, riddling his plane's fuselage and engine, tearing open the right main gas tank with 20-mm. explosive shells, and shooting up the left stabilizer and elevator. Somehow Shumway managed to get the badly damaged Dauntless home. Ensign B. R. Cooner, flying airplane 3-B-15, had to spiral all the way down to evade three Zeros that jumped him at the top of his dive. The Japanese pilots would get the range with their 7.7-mm. nose guns, then fire short bursts with their 20-mm. cannon. Fragments hit Cooner in the leg and seriously wounded his gunner, who nevertheless claimed one of the Zeros. On return Cooner found scattered bullet holes in the aft section of his fuselage and in the tail and 20-mm. hits in the radio and in the life raft, leaving the latter in shreds.

Nevertheless, the Zeros had been too few to save the *Hiryu*. Admiral Nagumo had lost his last flattop. The *Hiryu* continued at fleet speed for some hours until smoke and heat forced her engine rooms to shut down near midnight. Then the crew abandoned ship. Captain Tomeo Kaku and Rear Admiral Tamon Yamaguchi, commander of Carrier Division 2, remained aboard. With them 416 crewmen went down with the ship. One small group of engine-room personnel—34 in all—survived in a whaleboat to be picked up and made prisoners by the U. S. Navy.

Not the least of Japan's losses at Midway was Yamaguchi, a brilliant, aggressive commander. Scuttlebutt in the Japanese Navy had had him tapped to succeed Admiral Yamamoto as Commander-in-Chief, Combined Fleet.

While the main show was on near Midway, the second act of Rear Admiral Kakuji Kakuta's diversionary sideshow in the Aleutians was coming to an inconclusive end. At 4:00 P.M. on June 4, while the *Enterprise* planes were stalking the *Hiryu,* Kakuta launched another strike at Dutch Harbor composed of three Zeros and six Kates from the *Ryujo* and six Zeros and 11 Vals from the *Junyo.* The planes did considerable damage to oil tanks and other installations, but on their way back they flew near the new Army Air Force fighter base at Otter Point on Umnak Island, where a squadron of P-40s jumped them. The Army pilots lost two of their number but shot down a Zero and four Vals.

In the meantime, five B-17s and B-26s had found and attacked the *Junyo* and *Ryujo.* They scored only near misses and lost two planes to antiaircraft and Zeros. But they brought home to Kakuta the danger of operating so close to an enemy land air base. Kakuta was glad enough, therefore, to receive an order from Admiral Yamamoto to leave the Aleutians and to rendezvous with the main Japanese force near Midway. But he found the implications of the order disturbing. What could have happened at Midway to require his presence?

At first Yamamoto, hundreds of miles from the scene, had not realized the full extent of the damage to the *Kaga, Akagi,* and *Soryu.* But by noon on June 4 he had learned that all three were "inoperational." Hence his message to Kakuta. He also ordered Admiral Kondo, commanding the supporting Second Fleet with light carrier *Zuiho,* to make full speed and join Nagumo. At long last Yamamoto was doing what he should have at the outset—mass his forces, including his four remaining carriers, *Junyo, Ryujo, Zuiho,* and *Hosho.*

By 5:55 P.M. Yamamoto had learned that "BOMBS HIT HIRYU, CAUSING FIRES." Now he knew that all four of his big fleet carriers were out of action. Nevertheless, at 7:15 P.M. he ordered his surface units to "PURSUE THE [ENEMY] . . . AND AT THE SAME TIME TO OCCUPY AF [MIDWAY]." The Midway invasion still was "go" so far as Yamamoto was concerned, at least for the time being. Kondo's force was already steaming northeast at full speed to join Nagumo's and on joining both would rush west to attack the enemy by night.

On the American side Yamamoto's counterpart at sea was now Admiral Raymond A. Spruance. Admiral Fletcher, with the *Yorktown* inoperational, had relinquished command to him. On recovering the *Enter-*

prise and *Hornet* SBDs after their successful attack on the *Hiryu,* Spruance decided that he had no business staying in the vicinity and risking a night surface engagement with battleships. He recalled very well how often this had happened in peacetime maneuvers with the *Saratoga* and *Lexington.* He therefore put his flattops about and sailed east for part of the night of June 4–5, then put about and steamed west toward Point Luck north of Midway. As he explained it to Admiral Nimitz after the battle:

I did not feel justified in risking a night encounter with possibly superior enemy forces, but on the other hand, I did not want to be too far away from Midway the next morning. I wished to have a position from which either to follow up retreating enemy forces or to break up a landing attack on Midway.

Like Fletcher, he also believed that a fifth enemy carrier might be nearby, "possibly with [the enemy's] Occupation Force or else to the northeastward. . . ."

In retrospect, Admiral Spruance's coolheaded decision stands as a tactical masterpiece. Had Admiral Yamamoto persisted in his desire to seek a night surface engagement and had Spruance steamed west in the conviction that his enemy was fleeing, he might well have encountered Nobutake Kondo's powerful force of surface ships speeding northwest to join Nagumo's defeated squadrons. Then, as Navy historian Samuel Eliot Morison puts it in his analysis of Midway, "Yamamoto would have been handed the fleet action he so ardently desired on a silver platter." But Spruance had foiled Yamamoto's strategy, and apparently shortly after midnight between June 4 and 5, the Japanese admiralissimo changed his mind. First, he cancelled a bombardment of Midway scheduled by Admiral Kurita's four heavy cruisers, the *Kumano, Suzuya, Mikuma,* and *Mogami.* Then at 2:55 A.M. on June 5 he ordered the entire fleet to put about and return home. The invasion of Midway was off. When one of his staff protested, "But how can we apologize to His Majesty for this defeat?" Yamamoto curtly replied, "Leave that to me."

As dawn broke on Friday, June 5, Admiral Spruance found his Task Force 16 steaming westward into an area of bad flying weather. As the ships cruised on through the morning he set a course to the northwest of Midway, roughly in the opposite direction to Admiral Nagumo's approach. He knew from reports from submarine *Tambor* and from Midway that enemy ships could be found 90 miles to the west of the island, but he' wanted to stay after a force to the northwest that had been reported to contain a crippled carrier—the *Hiryu*—and two battleships.

Finally, at 5:00 P.M. Spruance ordered his Dauntlesses launched. Thirty-two from the *Enterprise* and 26 from the *Hornet* flew out as far as 315 miles but failed to find the *Hiryu* that had sunk. On their return they ran across the destroyer *Tanikaze* and attacked. Every plane missed! This, as Admiral Nimitz noted later, was in striking contrast to the Japanese performance against destroyer *Sims* in the Coral Sea. Moreover, the

Tanikaze managed to bring down one of the Dauntlesses that attacked her. Spruance's pilots redeemed themselves, however, by landing successfully aboard their carriers after dark.

Planes from Midway did better—though not by much—thanks to the prior work of submarine *Tambor*.* At about 2:15 A.M. on June 5, the *Tambor* had sighted Admiral Kurita's Midway Island bombardment force of four *Mogami*-class cruisers plus a destroyer escort steaming toward the island. These big, powerful ships displaced better than 15,000 tons each and were armed with ten eight-inch guns apiece. Shadowing them, *Tambor* watched them put about as they received Yamamoto's order to call off their scheduled bombardment. Then, as they doubled back, lookouts aboard the cruisers sighted the submarine. Kurita ordered an emergency turn, the three lead ships executed, but the *Mogami,* last in line, failed to get the word and piled into the port quarter of the *Mikuma*. Both ships suffered severe damage, *Mogami* so much to her bow as to limit her speed to 16 knots. *Tambor* then lost the trail but reported her find by radio.

After daybreak six Midway-based Dauntlesses and six Vindicators went after the damaged Japanese. Six pilots near missed, but the plane of Captain Richard E. Fleming, USMC, crashed into the after turret of the *Mikuma*. Either by accident or choice Fleming had become a Kamikaze. His hit was important, too, for it slowed the *Mikuma.*

On June 6 Admiral Spruance still was steaming west with the *Enterprise* and *Hornet*. At daybreak he launched a search that showed nothing to the northwest for 200 miles but picked up to the southwest the damaged *Mogami* and *Mikuma*. The huge bulk of the cruisers convinced some pilots that at least one was a battleship or battle cruiser. The *Enterprise* hurled one strike at the ships and the *Hornet* two. The pilots had no fighter opposition and not too much antiaircraft after the first bombs struck. *Mogami* took two half-ton hits in the first attack and three more in the second, but though a shambles topside she managed to limp away at ten knots, eventually to make Truk. The *Mikuma* suffered a more dire fate. *Enterprise* pilots claimed five hits on her, stopping her dead in the water, and *Hornet* pilots in a final attack hit destroyer *Arashio* with a bomb that killed many of the cruiser's survivors. *Mikuma* stayed afloat long enough to allow American photographic planes to take some of the most spectacular photos of the war, then sank during the night.

Again the bombing accuracy was by no means superior, partly because by this time the pilots were near exhaustion. Seeing the enemy, however, had perked up most of the *Enterprise* air crew, to judge by their comments heard and recorded by radio monitors at Midway.

From *Enterprise* to attack group:

TARGET MAY BE BATTLESHIP. . . . ATTACK!

---

* The day previous, submarine *Nautilus* had bounced a torpedo that failed to explode from one of Nagumo's crippled carriers.

From *Enterprise* Air Group Commander to ship:

I HAVE THE ENEMY IN SIGHT. I AM GOING TO ATTACK. I AM GOING DOWN.

From unidentified to unidentified:

WE ARE RIGHT BEHIND YOU. GET GOING!

ENTERING DIVE. OUR OBJECTIVE IS THE REAR SHIP. STEP ON IT! ARE WE GOING TO ATTACK OR NOT?

THEY'RE ALL BURNING!

LOOK AT THAT SONOFABITCH BURN!
HIT THE SONOFABITCH AGAIN!

THAT SCARED HELL OUT OF ME. I THOUGHT WE WEREN'T GOING TO PULL OUT.

YOUR BOMB REALLY HIT THEM ON THE FANTAIL. BOY, THAT'S SWELL!

THESE JAPS ARE EASY AS SHOOTING DUCKS IN A RAIN BARREL.

GEE, I WISH I HAD JUST ONE MORE BOMB!

TOJO, YOU SONOFABITCH, SEND OUT THE REST AND WE'LL GET THOSE TOO.

ONE SHIP OF THE FOUR IS MOVING NORTHWARD. ONE CA [HEAVY CRUISER] IS BURNING AND ONE BB [BATTLESHIP] IS BURNING FIERCELY. APPARENTLY THE BB IS ASKING FOR HELP FOR HER ENTIRE PERSONNEL.

From *Enterprise* to attack group:

WELL DONE! WELL DONE!

Though convinced that they had done in a battleship and a cruiser, the *Hornet* and *Enterprise* pilots were nevertheless extremely unhappy about the effects of their instantaneously fused 1,000-pound bombs. The bombs had caused havoc topside, but they had not reached the vitals of their targets. Delay-fuse bombs, the pilots were convinced, would have put both ships on the bottom in short order. On the other hand, they agreed that the instantaneous fuse was "ideal" for smashing up the flight deck of an enemy carrier and stopping launching operations.

By nightfall on June 6 Admiral Spruance was convinced that his best course was to abandon further pursuit. His pilots could fly no more; they needed rest. Also, only four of his destroyers had enough fuel to stay with his two carriers. Already he was 400 miles to the west of Midway, and any further advance would bring him within range of Japanese search planes operating from Wake. He therefore put his ships about and steamed eastward to a rendezvous with fleet oilers *Cimarron* and *Guadalupe*.

Up to this point the Midway battle had been without qualification a sweeping American victory. According to Mitsuo Fuchida, fifty-six Japanese planes had been shot down in combat and some 280 more lost aboard the carriers. Four Japanese carriers and a heavy cruiser had been sunk. Another cruiser and two destroyers had been damaged. Personnel losses stood at 2,150 from the carriers and about a thousand more on the cruisers and destroyers. *Yorktown,* though crippled and listing heavily, was still afloat and on June 6 was under tow by minesweeper *Vireo.* Captain Buckmaster had a skeleton salvage crew aboard cutting away top weight to restore her stability and correct her list, while a Black Gang labored to relight her boilers. A ring of destroyers was circling the ship Indian fashion 2,000 yards out, "pinging" with their sonar to detect any lurking submarines.

But stalking the *Yorktown* was submarine I-168, commanded by Lieutenant Commander Yahachi Tanabe. Admiral Yamamoto had dispatched him to the scene for the specific purpose of getting the *Yorktown.* Somehow Tanabe managed to slip his boat undetected under the destroyers and fire a spread of four torpedoes. One missed, two hit the carrier and one the destroyer *Hammann* moored alongside. The destroyer broke in half and sank in minutes with heavy loss of life; the *Yorktown* floated until the next morning, then capsized and sank. This disaster brought total American losses at Midway to 547 sailors and Marines, of whom 350 were killed. Though the torpedoes had struck on the opposite side of the two previous hits, the accumulated damage was just too much for *Yorktown*'s strained bulkheads. By himself, in one of the most brilliant individual submarine exploits of the Pacific war, Commander Tanabe salvaged something for Japan from what was otherwise a total disaster.

Perhaps recalling their overexuberant reaction to the Battle of the Coral Sea, U. S. Navy officials reacted with initial caution to the results of Midway. But after reports made clear that three carriers had almost certainly been sunk and after capture of prisoners confirmed the additional losses of the *Hiryu* and the *Mikuma,* jubilation took over, both in Navy circles and in the American press. Clearly, a great victory had been won.

Tokyo radio also proclaimed a victory, but in terms much more subdued than in its reporting on the Coral Sea. Two American carriers had been sunk, it said (which is what the Imperial Navy then believed), 120 American planes had been destroyed (an understatement—the true total was about 150), and Kiska and Attu in the outer Aleutians had been occupied. It confessed to Japanese losses of one carrier sunk and another and a cruiser damaged. Inside Navy circles the densest gloom prevailed. Commander Fuchida, who had been injured escaping from the *Akagi,* was brought to the Yokosuka naval base aboard a hospital ship, then disembarked after nightfall with other Midway wounded and taken to a hospital on a covered stretcher. There he was kept in a private room in complete isolation. Not even the nurses and corpsmen were allowed to see him. But nothing the Navy leaders could do could resurrect the *Kaga* and *Akagi,* pride of the fleet, or the smaller but equally useful *Soryu* and *Hiryu.*

Following closely on the Coral Sea engagement, the Battle of Midway established beyond doubt the primacy of the aircraft carrier. As the after-action report of Admiral Spruance put it, "ships unsupported by aircraft carriers are easy prey."

In all navies carriers were in desperately short supply after Midway. Japan now had only two regular fleet carriers, *Shokaku* and *Zuikaku,* backed up by one medium-sized converted carrier, the *Junyo,* and three CVLs. *Hiyo,* sister to the *Junyo,* was completing. The United States had in the Pacific the *Saratoga, Hornet,* and *Enterprise* and in the Atlantic the *Wasp* and *Ranger.* Since the *Ranger* was considered to be too slow and was not equipped to handle a balanced air group, this gave the United States, in effect, only four capital ships. Four bombs or torpedoes in the right place could deprive the U. S. Navy of its carrier air power.

The magnitude of their victory did not lull the American navy leaders into complacency. Instead they were quick to criticize their own perform-ance and to seize upon Midway's many lessons in the still new art of carrier task-force operations. Both Frank Jack Fletcher and Ray Spruance reported their conviction to Admiral Nimitz that in a carrier duel the side getting in the first blow was likely to win. Both were therefore distressed by the weakness of American reconnaissance. PBYs had made prompt initial contact with the enemy, and radio communication on a common ship-and-shore station channel had been good. But follow-up contact with the enemy fleet had been poor, and none of the American torpedo-plane squadron leaders had radioed the position of the enemy before attacking. Neither Spruance nor Fletcher said so, but they probably shuddered in-wardly in recalling how the *Hornet*'s planes had missed the Japanese carriers. They knew that only the bravery and dogged persistence of Wade McClusky had carried the *Enterprise* dive bombers to their targets.

The battle had again demonstrated the vulnerability of a carrier to gasoline fire, though this time at the enemy's expense. In his after-action report Captain Elliott Buckmaster of the *Yorktown* singled out for praise Machinist Oscar W. Myers, USN. It was Myers, he wrote, who had con-ceived of and installed a carbon dioxide purging system for the ship's gasoline lines and also a CO_2 blanket for the gasoline-tank compartments. The battle lesson was clear. When properly disciplined, buttoned up, and prepared to receive battle damage a carrier should be a tough customer.

Admiral Nimitz accepted these conclusions and added some of his own in his "Lessons and Conclusions from the Action" sent to Admiral King in Washington. Noting the inadequate performance of the Wildcat vis-à-vis the Zero, he added that it might be necessary to further increase fighter strength aboard a flattop, up already from 18 to 27 planes thanks to the folding wing of the new F4F-4.

Nimitz was satisfied with the *Yorktown*'s performance and with the protection furnished by its cruiser and destroyer screen. Had the carrier not been slowed by the earlier bomb hit in the funnel, he noted, it might have dodged the torpedoes that brought it dead in the water. Nor did

Nimitz criticize Captain Buckmaster for ordering abandon ship. He praised both Spruance and Fletcher for showing "sound judgment and decision in correctly interpreting the many confused situations that came up during the action." All hands, he concluded, had performed at "the highest order."

Although a study was begun and a factual report prepared, nobody on the Japanese side was inclined to make immediate official post-mortems. Commander Minoru Genda summarized his feelings by remarking tersely, "It's no use talking about what-might-have-beens now." Even Japanese Prime Minister Hideki Tojo, an Army man, was considerate. On being briefed in closest secret he had only three comments. No one was to blame the Navy, raw materials to make good the losses would be made immediately available, and the facts of the disaster should be kept strictly secret.

It was clear that Admiral Yamamoto's program (and everyone else's) for extension of Japan's conquests in the Pacific had come at least to a temporary end. A week after Midway Imperial General Headquarters suspended the plan to take the New Hebrides, New Caledonia, Fiji, and Samoa originally set for July. Breach of America's lifeline to Australia now was out of the question. The loss of four fleet carriers had temporarily paralyzed the naval leadership. "Victory disease" had given place overnight to almost a state of catalepsy.

11.   The Eastern Solomons

Victory at Midway emboldened the Joint Chiefs in Washington. By July 1942 the Pacific already had been divided into two sectors—a Southwest Pacific Area, encompassing Australia and New Guinea, and a Pacific Ocean Area, including the rest of the Pacific and the Solomons Islands. General Douglas MacArthur, hero of the defense of Bataan and Corregidor, commanded the former; Admiral Nimitz, architect of victory at Midway, commanded the latter. The Solomons were placed just inside Nimitz's bailiwick, and he had available Major General A. A. Vandegrift's First Marine Division equipped and trained for amphibious landings.

On July 2 the Joint Chiefs of Staff authorized Operation "Watchtower." The First Marine Division would land across beaches to seize Tulagi Island and take Lunga Point on Guadalcanal, hopefully before the enemy could make operational an airfield that was under construction. By July 10, 1942, Nimitz had his orders to attack, and a race against time began.

To cover the landing Nimitz assigned his most experienced carrier admiral, Frank Jack Fletcher, who had performed acceptably both in the Coral Sea and at Midway. Fletcher had three carriers, for by this time the *Wasp* was in the Pacific, having come racing around the world after twice delivering deckloads of Spitfires to beleaguered Malta in the Mediterranean. *Saratoga* was also on hand, modernized, with eight-inch turrets removed and replaced by paired five-inch antiaircraft. Present also was the veteran *Enterprise* and a new fast battleship, *North Carolina*. No one expected Fletcher to have much trouble, especially since the enemy probably would be taken by surprise. In any event Fletcher's carrier strength should be at least equal to the enemy's.

Dawn on August 7, 1942, found the *Enterprise* steaming off the southern tip of Guadalcanal. *Saratoga* was operating some ten miles distant with her own screen, and on the horizon was the 14,700-ton *Wasp,* distinctive because of her smaller size and relatively thin, high funnel. Aboard flagship *Saratoga* Frank Jack Fletcher was edgy. He knew that his ships would have to stay within Wildcat range of the about-to-be-established beachhead for a considerable time. Enemy search planes from Rabaul could hardly fail to find him; air attack on his ships seemed a certainty.

Of the three carriers only the *Wasp* had a cohesive air group that had flown together for some time. But none of its pilots had combat experience. The air groups of *Enterprise* and *Saratoga* were scratch outfits, mingling some veterans from a collage of prewar air groups with a bulk of recent graduates from operational flight training. The dispatch of three flattops on a single operation had left Admiral Nimitz with just one reserve carrier, *Hornet,* in the entire Pacific. Operation Watchtower admittedly was a gamble, too daring a gamble to suit Fletcher.

Yet this first American amphibious landing since 1898 went easily on opening day. Strafing and bombing runs by *Enterprise, Saratoga,* and *Wasp* planes hardly were necessary. On Guadalcanal the 2,300 men of the 11th and 13th Japanese Construction Battalions, mostly Korean laborers, fled into the jungle as soon as the planes appeared, leaving behind their equipment. On Tulagi and on two adjacent islets, the sailors of the small naval air base detachment put up a stiff fight, holding out in caves and bunkers through the next day. But they, too, had been totally surprised. Strafing Wildcats from the *Wasp's* Fighting Squadron 72 destroyed on the water all seven of their Mavis flying boats and their nine "Rufe" floatplane Zeros. Japanese aerial reconnaissance had bungled incredibly in allowing an invasion force of more than 80 ships, plus three carrier task groups, to slip up to Guadalcanal undetected literally until the moment preinvasion gunfire and bombing began.

In Rabaul news of the American landing, received tersely by radio from Guadalcanal, came as an annoying surprise. It posed a difficult tactical problem for Rear Admiral Sadayoshi Yamada, commanding the 25th Air Flotilla of the 11th Air Fleet, constituting Rabaul's Base Air Force. Immediate counterattacking missions would have to begin. But Guadalcanal was 560 miles from Rabaul, a stiff flight for his Betty medium bombers, barely within the radius of his Zero fighters, and well beyond the range of his Val dive bombers. Nevertheless, he at once cancelled plans for a strike at New Guinea by already gassed-up and bomb-loaded Bettys and dispatched 27, with 18 escorting Zeros, for the beachhead at Guadalcanal.

Yamada's Zero flight leader was Lieutenant Commander Tadashi Nakajima of the crack Tainan Air Group. This fighter outfit had wiped out America's fighter squadrons in the Philippines. Operating from Rabaul and from an advanced base at Lae, New Guinea, it had been giving flying lessons to General MacArthur's P-40 and P-39 Airacobra pilots at Port Moresby. It contained Japan's three leading aces.

Top scorer with 57 planes was Saburo Sakai, a China-experienced veteran with 3,000 hours on fighters. Next was tall, thin, pale, malarious Hiroyoshi Nishizawa, who would surpass Sakai with a claimed hundred kills. Third was Toshio Oka, a personable, friendly rookie who had run up a remarkable score over New Guinea.

Nakajima warned his aces about their critical fuel problem. Their round trip to Guadalcanal of 1,100 miles, he said, would be "the longest fighter operation in history." They must obey orders, keep together, and "above all" not fly recklessly and waste fuel. If anyone ran short he was to land at Buka on Bougainville Island, where Japan had a garrison and was completing an airfield.

The Bettys took off about 8:30 A.M., followed by the Zero pilots, who leaned their mixtures to cruise as economically as possible. Here was the Zero at its unique best, flying a mission of a range double that of any other operational fighter and thrice the distance possible for a Wildcat.

Nearing Savo Island off Guadalcanal's northwest tip, the Zeros split. One group of nine darted ahead to attack patrolling Wildcats in a fierce battle in which Hiroyoshi Nishizawa, holding his fire until at point-blank range, downed five *Saratoga* pilots from Fighting 5. He might have done still better had he not encountered a pair applying Jimmy Thach's "weave." As he attacked the lead fighter of a pair, the wingman drove in from the side, forcing Nishizawa to break and head for home, raging at his close call.

The other nine planes, which included a section led by Saburo Sakai, stayed with the Bettys, watched them drop and near miss the warships and transports below, and began to escort them home. Over the center of Florida Island four Wildcats, led by Lieutenant Vincent P. De Poix, jumped them, made a diving pass, then zoomed to attack from below. Sakai and the other Zero pilots then swarmed them, but though riddled, all four Wildcats managed to escape into a towering cumulus.

A few minutes later, while the Japanese formation was now 35 miles north of Savo Island, heading for Rabaul at 180 knots, six Wildcats led by Lieutenant Raleigh E. Rhodes attacked from either side. Sakai and his fellow pilots drew three into dogfights, but the other trio attacked unimpeded to claim three Bettys. Sakai shot down a skilled American pilot after the hardest dogfight he had experienced; the other two fell to the other Japanese pilots. Shortly after, Sakai and a wingman jumped eight planes he took to be Wildcats but which turned out to be a flight of SBD Dauntlesses of Bombing 6 led by Lieutenant Carl Horenburger who were looking for targets near Tulagi. Closing from astern, Sakai hit the vane of a bomb on one plane and the elevator of another. But with a devastating concentration of .30-caliber fire, the eight gunners shattered Sakai's windscreen and wounded Japan's leading ace in the scalp, face, and eye. Watching Sakai's Zero plunging vertically toward the sea, the gunners concluded that they had finished him. Sakai managed to pull out, and in one of the truly epic flights of World War II he flew his battered Zero back to Rabaul, though repeatedly blacking out en route. His wounds sent him to Japan for treatment, but even the attentions of a specialist failed to restore sight to his injured eye. On his first mission to Guadalcanal Lieutenant Nakajima had lost an ace.

More tragic than the fate of Sakai was the plight of nine Vals that arrived at the beachhead after the Bettys. For them the flight to Guadalcanal was a one-way mission. They dove on destroyer *Mugford* and hit an after mount but were intercepted by *Enterprise* and *Saratoga* Wildcats. Six fell to the fighters; the other three ran out of fuel and splashed trying to make the Buka emergency strip.

For the American combat pilots D-day at Guadalcanal was dismal enough. Eight Wildcats and an SBD had been shot down against the loss of only two of Commander Nakajima's Zeros. But nine Vals had been lost, five Bettys had also fallen, and worst of all Saburo Sakai was through for the Guadalcanal campaign. Except for the hit on *Mugford,* all bombing attacks had failed.

For the next day, August 8, Base Air Force Chief Yamada planned an all-out air strike on the beachhead. He dispatched all 23 of his remaining operational Bettys, this time carrying torpedoes, plus his remaining nine Vals and a strong escort of Zeros. Because their planes flew low they evaded American radar detection until almost over Savo Island. Most patrolling Wildcats missed them, though six shot down four Bettys and a Zero. The remaining Bettys deployed to attack the American transports that put up a ferocious barrage of AA fire. No fewer than 13 Bettys smashed blazing into the water. A Zero—either fatally damaged or flown by a suicidally minded pilot—crashed transport *George Fox Elliot* to start a fire that proved fatal. Destroyer *Jarvis* took a torpedo hit but began to retire slowly from the anchorage by evening. These successes of Yamada's airmen had been at a cost entirely prohibitive to themselves. Eighteen of the 23 Bettys were lost with two Zeros.

Nevertheless, Rear Admiral Richmond Kelly Turner, commanding the amphibious forces, did not get his transports fully unloaded before having to withdraw. Just after midnight on D-day plus one, August 9, a Japanese cruiser force badly defeated his own covering force of cruisers in the Battle of Savo Island, sinking four and stripping away all heavy gunnery-ship protection. Also, Admiral Fletcher had withdrawn his flat-tops from the operation on the afternoon of D-day, running south for 12 hours before requesting permission to withdraw. Fletcher justified his decision by citing a decline in Wildcat fighter-plane strength from 99 to 78 due to combat and operational reasons. He also claimed to be concerned about the fuel situation in his destroyers. Fletcher had entered battle determined to accept no risks; he left it with the same determination.

Even as Fletcher's carriers were steaming away lights were burning in Admiral Nagano's Naval Staff Headquarters in Tokyo. By August 13 both Nagano and Army planners had decided to commit ground troops to the recapture of Tulagi and the airfield at Lunga Point on Guadalcanal. The Americans were hurriedly readying the airstrip, soon to be named Henderson Field after the fallen Marine Corps dive-bomber leader at Midway.

For once Admiral Yamamoto was in hearty agreement with Nagano. To protect the landing troops he would dispatch from Japan most of his Combined Fleet. He would risk in battle his remaining pair of large carriers, four fast battleships, and a powerful force of cruisers and destroyers. He himself would steam to Truk in the Caroline Islands to command this Operation "KA" personally from his flagship *Yamato*.

As August 23 dawned another major Pacific carrier battle clearly was in the making. Approaching the northern Solomons from Truk was the Combined Fleet, split into several separate groups in Yamamoto's favorite tactic. Leading was Vice Admiral Kondo's advance force. It consisted of a main body of five heavy cruisers with escort and a support group made up of seaplane carrier *Chitose* with a destroyer escort. Behind it steamed a vanguard group under Rear Admiral Hiroaki Abe consisting of fast battleships *Hiei* and *Kirishima* with cruiser and destroyer escort. Following was Vice Admiral Chuichi Nagumo's carrier group, consisting of the big flattops *Shokaku* and *Zuikaku*. Despite the fiasco at Midway, Nagumo somehow had remained Japan's leading carrier admiral.

The prize feature of Yamamoto's Operation KA was a special diversionary group under Rear Admiral Tadaichi Hara. This consisted of light carrier *Ryujo* with cruiser *Tone* and a pair of destroyers for escort. Yamamoto's gambit would have the *Ryujo* detach itself from Nagumo's carrier group and steam ahead to launch an air strike. Then—hopefully—the American carriers assumed to be patrolling in the area would launch all of their planes against this "bait" flattop. This would give Nagumo's two big carriers a chance to launch full deckloads of Kates and Vals without danger of retaliation. Like the American commanders, Yamamoto had come to realize that he who struck first in a carrier duel was the likely winner.

As a finale to Operation KA Rear Admiral Raizo Tanaka embarked in light cruiser *Jintsu* was to escort to Guadalcanal with his ship and seven destroyers a force of five transports carrying the Ichiki Detachment and the 5th Yokosuka Special Naval Landing Force. If all went well the 800 sailors of the 5th Yokosuka Force and the 700 infantry of the 2nd echelon of the Ichiki force would land unopposed after the destruction of the three big American carriers still operational and of all Marine planes on Guadalcanal. Seizure of Henderson Field would follow soon after.

As Yamamoto had anticipated, the commencement of Operation KA had lured his enemies to sea. August 23 found Fletcher steaming eastward of Guadalcanal near the Stewart Islands in *Saratoga* accompanied by the *Enterprise* and *Wasp* task groups. Fletcher was as anxious as Yamamoto to throw the first punch, and when a Catalina patrol plane found Admiral Kondo's advance force late in the day at extreme range the nervous American admiral promptly launched a strike of 31 Dauntlesses and six new TBF-1 Avengers. The Air Group skipper was a veteran dive-bomber pilot, Commander H. D. (Don) Felt. Felt's air crewmen failed to locate

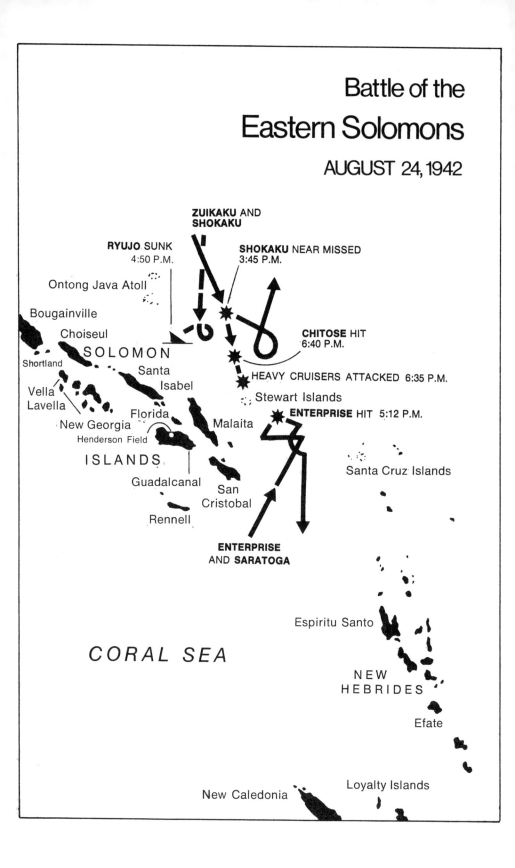

Battle of the
Eastern Solomons
AUGUST 24, 1942

Kondo, who had temporarily reversed course after being sighted, and all planes landed at dusk on Guadalcanal to spend the night.

In the meantime Fletcher had made his first serious mistake. On learning from Nimitz's staff at Pearl Harbor that Intelligence had placed all of Japan's carriers north of Truk, and on hearing from another PBY that Kondo had reversed course, Fletcher detached *Wasp* south to a refueling rendezvous, even though her destroyers were not yet short of bunker oil. It would be, he now believed, several days before his enemy showed up, a conviction reinforced when his *Saratoga* planes found nothing and flew on to Guadalcanal.

Dawn on August 24 found all Japanese forces still heading south. Already *Ryujo* had detached herself from big sisters *Shokaku* and *Zuikaku* to race at high speed toward Guadalcanal. The 30-odd Zero and Kate pilots embarked on the CVL probably had few qualms and were looking forward only to their projected strike on the enemy's airfield. But Rear Admiral Hara, commanding from cruiser *Tone,* can hardly have failed to recall the fate of CVL *Shoho* under remarkably similar circumstances in the Battle of the Coral Sea.

As Admiral Yamamoto had anticipated—perhaps had hoped—a Catalina flying a long-range search spotted *Ryujo* at 9:05 A.M. and radioed this information back to its base. When its message finally reached Fletcher aboard the *Saratoga,* Frank Jack refused to be impressed. He was thoroughly disgusted with the Catalina pilots for triggering the wild-goose chase of the day before. Now he was awaiting the return of his planes already en route from Guadalcanal.

At 11:28 A.M. another PBY found Hara's little flattop just as the *Saratoga* was steadying into a southerly wind to take aboard her Dauntlesses and Avengers. "Reluctantly," as he admitted in his after-action report, Fletcher now ordered carrier *Enterprise* to launch at 1:15 P.M. a search-and-strike mission. This was composed of 23 Dauntlesses and Avengers with all planes armed with 500-pound bombs and flying in pairs. Frank Jack had sent all of his planes after the *Shoho* in the Coral Sea battle, and he strongly suspected that Yamamoto was trying to bait him. He therefore set the *Saratoga*'s plane handling crews at once to rearming her returned planes and spotting them aft for launch. Even though the pilots had had very little sleep on Guadalcanal and were tired from their morning flight home, he wanted a strike ready to go if the *Enterprise* scouts turned up something.

Shortly after her planes had left, *Enterprise*'s radar picked up at about a hundred miles a flight of planes, obviously enemy, flying on a course and bearing which suggested that Guadalcanal was their objective. These planes—15 Zeros and eight Kates—were, indeed, from the *Ryujo*. Fletcher now had to assume that his enemy was close, that enemy search planes might have spotted him already, and that the morning contact reports from the PBYs, which until now he had questioned, were correct. At 1:45 P.M.

he ordered Don Felt aloft again with 29 Dauntlesses from Scouting and Bombing 3 and eight TBF Avengers from a reconstituted Torpedo 8 to fly to Point Option, *Ryujo*'s predicted coordinates. Fletcher held back a few planes from the *Enterprise* and the other half of Torpedo 8's Avengers, but this reserve power was relatively feeble. Though desperately anxious to avoid doing so, Fletcher had "shot his wad" in a strike against "bait" carrier *Ryujo* and in the search mission from the *Enterprise*. He had 51 Dauntlesses and 15 Avengers in the air, and besides a CAP of Wildcats, only 14 Dauntlesses and 12 Avengers were aboard his carriers. Now he sorely needed *Wasp* and its well-trained Air Group 72.

In the meantime Admiral Nagumo, with the *Shokaku* and *Zuikaku*, was having his own problems. He had no direct contact with reconnaissance flying boats operating from Rabaul—two of which Fletcher's CAP already had shot down—and he had to rely on his slow cruiser float planes to find the enemy. A Jake from the *Chikuma* finally got off a report just before a Wildcat downed it, but this was not until 2:05 P.M., an hour after the *Enterprise* had launched its scouts and *Saratoga* Commander Felt's strike group. Even then a hesitant Nagumo waited another full hour before dispatching his first strike from his big carriers.

While Nagumo was hesitating Don Felt was droning on toward the *Ryujo*. This strike was much different from all earlier ones of the war. With their big R-2600 Wright engines the heavily laden Avengers could fly faster than the Dauntlesses and range as far. Hence, Felt's strike could hold in one formation, climbing gradually, in approaching its enemy, estimated to be 216 miles distant. At 3:48 P.M. Felt intercepted a radio report from an *Enterprise* scout that erroneously put the *Ryujo* some 60 miles east of the previously reported position, but after altering course and failing to make contact, the experienced Felt turned back to the west. His radio receiver had just failed—but not his transmitter—when at 4:06 P.M. from about 14,000 feet he sighted the *Ryujo*. He also noted and correctly identified the long, lean *Tone* with all four of its eight-inch twin turrets mounted forward and two escorting destroyers. Turning north so as to approach from the northeast, Felt snapped on his radio to bark his orders. Lieutenant Commander L. J. "Bullet Lou" Kirn with Scouting 3 would dive first, followed by the first two divisions of Lieutenant Commander DeWitt Shumway's Bombing 3. Shumway's last division and two torpedo planes from Torpedo 8 would attack the *Tone*. The other Avengers, Lieutenant Bruce L. Harwood commanding, would strike the *Ryujo* after the dive bombers had begun their attacks.

As his planes neared their tip-over point, Felt noted that the *Ryujo*, which had turned south into the wind, was launching several Kate torpedo planes, probably because its Zeros already were airborne.

First man down was Lou Kirn, followed by 14 pilots of Scouting 3 and six more of Bombing 3. Felt, circling above, believed that every plane had missed. Only two bombs landed close enough to the *Ryujo* to appear to cause damage and set the ship to smoking. Ensign W. B. Behr, who dove third in the Bombing 3 group and who watched most of the other pilots drop, believed that his mates had underestimated *Ryujo*'s wind drift. He noted that as the carrier maintained a constant sharp turn to port throughout the attack, it skidded to starboard, causing the planes attacking from downwind to overshoot just enough to miss. If Captain Tadao Kato, the *Ryujo*'s skipper, had been consciously trying to produce this result, he deserves credit for superb ship handling.

On seeing the waterspouts rise one after another, Felt again triggered his transmitter, ordering Lieutenant Harold S. Bottomley and his seven pilots of Bombing 3 to abort their attack on the *Tone* and shift to the carrier. This they did, even though the first planes already had started their dives.

Without waiting, Felt then plunged himself, dropped, and hit just to the left and abaft of the center of the *Ryujo*, according to his rearward-facing radioman. Felt did not see Bottomley's planes dive, but three of them hit also, turning the *Ryujo* into a furnace below the flight deck.

Thrice smoke from the carrier frustrated the run-ins of Lieutenant Harwood's Avenger torpedo planes, but on their fourth try it cleared enough to make a good approach possible. The planes, numbering five, split, with two coming in from the *Ryujo's* port bow and three from the starboard to execute a well-delivered "anvil" attack. Though AA fire was brisk and both Zeros and Kates harried them, the pilots raced in at 200 knots, twice the speed possible for the old Devastators, to drop their tin fish from 200 feet at 800 to 900 yards' range. At least one torpedo appeared to hit, further adding to the woes of the little flattop. The other two Torpedo 8 pilots dropped at *Tone* as ordered and missed her.

In forming up afterward the *Saratoga* pilots found somewhat to their amazement that not a plane was missing, either to the antiaircraft, which had been heavy but inaccurate, or to the Zero and Kate combat air patrol. By contrast the Japanese gunners claimed 14 planes destroyed, a Wildcat, eight Dauntlesses and five Avengers. But they were mistaken, the victims of the overoptimism usual to combat.

Despite the poor bombing score, the *Saratoga* attack group had finished *Ryujo*, ending the remarkable career of the veteran 10,600-ton CVL. Hopelessly ablaze, it floated until 8:00 P.M. that night. Casualties were fairly heavy, being seven officers and 113 men killed and 138 other personnel wounded, mostly with burns. Of her air group, five planes fell to Marine fighters at Guadalcanal; the remaining planes airborne had to fly to the unfinished grass strip on Buka Island. Two battle-damaged planes crashed attempting landings. As Yamamoto had anticipated, using *Ryujo* as a sacrificial pawn had cost him the carrier and part of her air group but had diverted from *Shokaku* and *Zuikaku* most of Fletcher's planes.

Had two of *Enterprise*'s search pilots been a little more accurate—or perhaps a bit luckier—Yamamoto's strategy might not have worked. Flying at 1,500 feet, Lieutenant Ray Davis and Ensign R. C. Shaw, both in Dauntlesses armed with 500-pound bombs, spotted at about 3:45 P.M. Nagumo's force well east of the *Ryujo*'s position. The pair were about to dive on a light cruiser when they sighted the *Shokaku* and *Zuikaku* cruising at the rear of the formation. Climbing away and circling, Davis and Shaw reached 14,000 feet, apparently unseen by lookouts; then they dove from upwind at the *Shokaku*. Both pilots released at about 2,000 feet and near missed. Davis's bomb, according to his gunner, landed not more than five feet from the starboard side of the carrier aft, Shaw's about 20 feet off the *Shokaku*'s starboard quarter. Since both bombs had 1/100th-second delay fuses, concussion and splinters caused the carrier "some damage" and killed six men but did not, apparently, hinder the fighting capabilities of Captain Masafumi Arima's ship.

Had either Shaw or Davis placed his bomb aft on *Shokaku*'s flight deck the result could have been fatal. Shaw's gunner, H. I. Jones, counted eight planes parked amidships and 12 more spotted aft. If these planes, presumably ready for launch and armed, had caught fire, *Shokaku* might have suffered *Ryujo*'s fate. Another nod in the Japanese favor from the gods of war came in the failure of Davis's messages reporting *Shokaku*'s position to get through. *Enterprise*'s radio monitors caught only a fragment sent after the attack, and Admiral Fletcher did not learn of the presence of the two big fleet carriers until after Davis's return.

Otherwise, fortune smiled on Davis and Shaw. The two pilots counted a CAP of seven or eight Zeros circling the carriers, but only one made a firing pass, and it flew into the antiaircraft fire of an escorting destroyer and crashed. To the American pilots the plentiful flak thrown up appeared to resemble silver dimes tossed in batches into the air. "It looked like the end of broom straws coming up."

None of the other *Enterprise* scouts had rubbed their rabbits' feet this day. Two found and bombed a heavy cruiser of Kondo's force. Both missed when the ship turned abruptly to starboard, skidded around, and reversed course.

Both the *Shokaku* and *Zuikaku* had launched their strikes at 3:37 P.M., just before the arrival of Davis and Shaw. It probably was a second strike being spotted on deck that Shaw's gunner, Jones, had sighted when diving 18 minutes later. For their first strike the two carriers launched about 18 Vals, nine Kates, and 12, perhaps 18, Zeros. These planes headed directly for Fletcher's task force. (One after-action report states that *Zuikaku* sent up siz Zeros and nine Vals; no mention is made of Kates. No figures are given for the *Shokaku*.)

At 4:32 P.M. *Enterprise*'s XCAM radar picked up Nagumo's strike 88 nautical miles to the northwest. From the characteristics of the signal the operators estimated the altitude of the enemy planes at 12,000 feet. Moments later the signal faded out as the Japanese pilots flew into a "null." At 4:49 the radar again picked up the enemy flight on the same bearing and at the same calculated altitude. There no longer could be any doubt: a big enemy attack group was coming, and the Big E was going to catch it. Both she and *Saratoga* began launching every available fighter, followed by all the remaining Dauntlesses and TBFs which were hastily targeted against the *Ryujo*, the Americans still being ignorant of the presence within range of the *Shokaku* and *Zuikaku*. *Saratoga* launched her last F4F-4 at 5:06 P.M. and *Enterprise* her last Avenger just as the Japanese arrived overhead. Between them the two carriers had aloft 53 fighters from Fighting 5 and Fighting 6.

First to sight and "tallyho!" the Japanese formation was Lieutenant Albert O. Vorse, leading a four-plane section made up of himself, Ensign Richard L. Loesch, his wingman, Machinist H. M. Sumrall, a veteran enlisted pilot, and Ensign Francis R. Register. From 35 miles out from the *Enterprise,* flying below 10,000 feet, Vorse spotted the enemy well above him at 18,000. Immediately, he slammed his throttle to the firewall and began climbing, noting that the Vals were in nine-plane divisions with covering Zeros above and below.

Well before reaching the dive bombers, Vorse and his men found Zeros diving at their tails. Machinist Sumrall turned into one, diving, and when the Zero missed and passed overhead, he swung back on course as the enemy plane pulled up sharply in front in a favorite Zero tactic. Sumrall fired, the Zero flamed, and, burning intermittently fell toward the sea. Ensign Register got one at 18,000 feet while still climbing and followed it down to 6,000 feet, where its pilot bailed out—without a parachute. Climbing back up, Register engaged a clipped-wing Zero and set it afire. Vorse blazed another, assisted by Ensign Loesch, who, as a good wingman should, had stayed with his leader through the entire fight.

The four Americans had done well, discovering that at 18,000 feet a Wildcat could equal a Zero in speed and climb by virtue of the two-stage supercharging in its Wasp R-1830 engine. But none had closed a Val.

At 4:59 P.M., when about 25 miles from the *Enterprise,* the Japanese formation appeared to the American radarmen to split as the Vals and their escorts broke formation and moved around to the north. Evidently they hoped to throw off the CAP by altering course, which they assumed that the Americans had plotted and had radioed to the pilots. If so, the tactic was not fully successful, for when the Japanese were 14 miles from the ship an unidentified pilot reported Vals at 16,000 feet, triggering a rapid series of "tallyhos."

At once the single radio channel jammed. It was being used both by the planes and by the *Enterprise*'s two fighter-direction officers, Lieutenant Commander Leonard J. Dow and Lieutenant Henry A. Rowe. As Dow complained later, many transmissions were "nonessential," such as "Shift to high blower," "Look at that one go down!" and "Bill, where are you?" Dow and Rowe tried to shush the excited pilots but soon completely lost control of the circuit. They could neither understand nor be understood in the jumble of simultaneous transmissions. Also, static was bad and ordinary reception poor all day.

Despite the number of American fighters airborne, distressingly few intercepted the Vals before they began their dives. Lieutenant Hayden M. Jensen, leading a three-plane section from *Saratoga*'s Fighting 5, managed to catch the second nine-plane division of Vals about 15 miles from and to the east of the *Enterprise*. Jensen claimed three and Lieutenant Carlton B. Starkes and Ensign J. M. Kleinman four more before the Zeros tied them up. Jensen then dove out to safety, finding, as had many pilots before him, that a Zero could not catch him in a high-speed, corkscrewing dive. Kleinman damaged a clipped-wing Zero, and Starkes flamed another riding the tail of a Wildcat.

Equally successful was Machinist Donald E. Runyon, leading Aviation Pilot Howard S. Packard, and Ensigns Beverly W. Reid and Joseph D. Shoemaker. Utilizing an altitude advantage few other fighter sections had managed to gain, Runyon dove from out of the sun at 20,000 feet on a division of Vals at 18,000 feet. The first he dispatched in an attack from above and behind in textbook form. Climbing and diving again, he dispatched a second, then dropped a Zero that had made an overhead pass at him and missed. The third Val he downed by climbing up from underneath for a belly shot.

Packard, like Runyon a veteran flyer and good shot, damaged two Vals but modestly claimed no more than a "probable." The aggressive young Shoemaker stayed with the Vals through their pushover, noting that they "S"-turned before diving on the *Enterprise*. He chased a Val down through the Big E's antiaircraft fire until he overran it.

At 5:10 P.M., about a minute before the first dive on *Enterprise* began, Machinist D. C. Barnes, leading a four-plane section composed of himself, Ensign Robert A. M. Dibb, Gunner C. E. Brewer, and Ensign D. M. Johnson, spotted some Vals flying in three three-plane sections in line formation just as they began to dive on *Enterprise*. Dibb set a Val afire; Brewer claimed two more and got a Zero, attacking the enemy planes all the way down through the AA fire. Johnson bagged a Val just as it released its bomb and on landing discovered that the Japanese rear-seat gunner had done a pretty thorough job on his Wildcat. Its left aileron connecting rod was shot away, a bullet had left a neat hole in the propeller, the radio antennae had been shot off, and several holes had been punched in the wings and fuselage. Machinist Barnes failed to return, the others surmising that the *Enterprise*'s own AA may have claimed him.

Many more than half of the 53 Wildcat pilots in the air managed to attack either Vals or Zeros, but most not until after the Japanese flyers had started for home. Veterans of earlier engagements questioned whether this crop of Zero pilots were as well trained as Japan's initial team had been. Many overshot in steep diving attacks and then pulled up when still in range of the Wildcat's six powerful .50s. Others tried to outdive the F4F-4s instead of resorting to the exceptional climb angle of the Zero to get away.

Aboard *Enterprise* the radar operators had tracked the Japanese planes in, reporting at 5:11 P.M. over the flattop's loudspeakers the disquieting news, "The enemy planes are directly overhead now!" Finally, a 20-mm. gunner spotted a glint from a wing and began firing. Others immediately joined him, banging away with more of the accurate and useful Oerlikons, the hard-to-traverse 1.1-inch quadruple pompoms, and the 5-inch 38s. On the bridge Captain Arthur C. Davis noted that the Vals dove at precise seven-second intervals and that the pilots seemed to be skilled and "absolutely determined." The first plane came down at about 5:12 P.M., the last just four minutes later. A dozen or maybe more (nobody obtained an accurate count) dove at 70 degrees from the east on the port quarter of the *Enterprise*, which heeled sharply to starboard at 30 knots. The Japanese pilots released with precision between 1,500 to 2,000 feet—and they did not miss.

At 5:14 the first of three bombs to score struck the forward edge of the carrier's after elevator. Crashing through the thin plating, it passed on through the hangar deck to explode well below in crew quarters on the third deck. It traveled 42 feet before its delay fuse touched off a high order of detonation. A jarring blast killed 30 men, wounded twice as many more, and tore apart berthing spaces, bunks, lockers, and compartments. Fragments ripped downward through the ship, holing the hull and flooding two compartments. The hangar deck bulged above the blast but did not rupture, and the inevitable fires proved both small and containable. In this area the crew had chipped paint from the bulkheads to reduce the fire hazard. Before the attack Machinist W. E. Fluitt had directed the securing, draining, venting, and flooding with CO_2 gas the gasoline system of the carrier. Fragments from this and later hits severed avgas (aviation gas) lines, but none caught fire.

The second bomb hit very close to the point of impact of the first, only 30 seconds later. It landed 11 feet from the starboard edge of the flight deck, penetrated, and exploded with a terrific blast and terrible loss of life just three feet above the deck of a five-inch gun gallery. The blast bulged the flight deck but tore only a 12-inch hole. Forty-one men of the 53 of the gun battery died, including Lieutenant Williamson. Men close to the blast were ripped to bits; others were blasted stark-naked, seared, and frozen in their working attitudes. It also torched about 40 ready powder bags for the five-inch gun, causing a short but fierce blaze that produced a welcome spectacle for Val pilots still diving on the ship.

The third bomb hit the flight deck just aft of the amidships elevator. Its delay fuse evidently was defective, for it exploded instantly on contact with the three inches of teakwood planking and evidently with only a low order of detonation. Splinters from the bomb and deck peppered the island and pierced into the hangar but ignited only one small fire. Also, the hole in the deck was only ten feet in diameter, small enough to permit easy patching.

In addition to the three hits, at least three more bombs near missed close enough to rupture hull plating and cause minor flooding. Others tossed huge waterspouts over the ship, clearly attesting to the skill of the Val pilots, who had bombed much more accurately than their American counterparts even though they had faced far stronger fighter and anti-aircraft opposition.

Aboard the *Enterprise* 74 crewmen had been killed outright and 95 more wounded. "It is doubtful," Captain Davis wrote, "that bombs explod-ing anywhere else in the ship could have caused such a large number of casualties." Both hits aft had been in areas of necessarily high personnel concentration. Davis concluded grimly, "There could hardly have been a more serious test for an aircraft carrier."

One of the Val divisions picked out *North Carolina*, a new 35,000-ton fast battleship, and found her no easy mark. She worked up her full speed of 27 knots, put up a tremendous volume of antiaircraft fire, and the best the jounced-about Vals could manage were three near misses. The Val pilots saw the *Saratoga* steaming about 10,000 yards astern of the *North Carolina*, but none attacked her. Some of the Japanese pilots diving on *Enterprise*, however, thought that they had hit a second carrier and so reported to Nagumo.

Not a single Kate torpedo plane made a run against an American ship. The Kates may have gotten lost and failed to find their targets, but another explanation came after the battle when Ensign George W. Brooks reported the action of his four-plane Wildcat section. After chasing down several vectors given to him by the *Enterprise* controllers and finding nothing, Brooks sighted just 50 feet off the water a mixed flight of Kates and Vals 60 miles from the *Enterprise*. Since this was after the attack on the ship, it is possible that some returning Val pilots had encountered the Kates and were trying to lead them in to attack. Either that, or the Kates may have been flying a search.

Brooks and his men attacked, the enemy planes scattered, and many reversed course away from the *Enterprise*. A running fight followed at wave-top level, with the Wildcat pilots finding to their surprise that the Kate was almost as fast as the F4F-4 on the deck, about 200 knots. Brooks claimed one and Ensign Harry A. March, Jr., another.

Four Vals retiring from battle had the misfortune to encounter the Dauntlesses of Scouting and Bombing 3 returning from their strike on *Ryujo*. Bullet Lou Kirn saw them and ordered his 18 planes to alter course to meet them head on and from below. When the Vals closed the Daunt-lesses nosed up and fired; then the rear-seat gunners blazed away with twin .30s as the Vals passed overhead. Three dipped smoking. Several pilots wheeled from formation after them to finish them off. Ensign Aldy Hansen of Bombing 3 dropped one with a neat high side port attack at low altitude. His Val smoked intensely and cartwheeled into the sea. Others claimed the other three.

No complete Japanese record of planes lost from *Shokaku* and *Zuikaku* has survived, but the latter ship listed eight Vals and three Zeros shot down and a Zero and a Val ditched, their pilots recovered. American after-action claims of 70 kills may be discounted as much too high, but probably less than half of the Zeros and Vals made their carriers. American fighter losses totaled three pilots and four Wildcats from the *Saratoga* and two Wildcats, flown by enlisted Machinists D. C. Barnes and B. W. Reid, from the *Enterprise*.

While the Japanese were launching their four-minute blitz on the *Enterprise*, 13 Dauntlesses and 12 Avengers from her and from the *Saratoga* were trying vainly to rendezvous as a single attack force to launch the second strike on *Ryujo*. None of the pilots knew of the presence or whereabouts of the *Shokaku* and *Zuikaku*, and none thought, either, of trying to follow the Japanese planes home.

Lieutenant Commander Max Leslie was supposed to lead them in a TBF-1, but as he circled the task force twice the *North Carolina* fired on him and damaged his plane with her first salvo of five-inch. Leslie congratulated her, but then had to swerve away from a Val which his turret gunner took under fire and claimed as shot down. Thus preoccupied, Leslie failed to find any of his command and proceeded alone by himself at high cruising speed, 165 knots.

The 11 *Enterprise* Dauntlesses found nothing in their assigned target area, which they reached after dark. They then flew on to Guadalcanal, where they became an involuntary but most welcome addition to the Guadalcanal air force. Five *Saratoga* Avengers had better luck—though not by much. They picked up Admiral Kondo's cruiser force, formed a line abreast, and attacked from the enemy's port bow. None hit, and two pilots had to ditch at San Cristobal Island.

Only two pilots managed to augment the enemy's woes. These were Lieutenant Robert M. Elder and Ensign Robert T. Gordon, flying SBDs from the *Saratoga*. They found Captain Seigo Sasaki's seaplane carrier *Chitose,* which they somehow mistook for battleship *Mutsu,* and bracketed her with very close misses with thousand-pounders. The heavy bombs exploding on contact set ship and embarked seaplanes afire, tore open the engine room, and started progressive flooding that ultimately gave the *Chitose* a 30-degree list and almost capsized her until Captain Sasaki shifted fuel to opposite tanks to correct the list.

By himself Max Leslie cruised over an open ocean, briefly mistook Roncador Reef for a squadron of ships moving at high speed, and continued until his fuel became critical. Then he returned to the *Saratoga,* utilizing his ZB homing equipment. He was the last pilot to land aboard, at 11:33 P.M.

Enterprise had added to its reputation of being a lucky ship. It had taken her crew only about an hour to control all fires and to patch her deck with sheet metal, enabling her at 6:49 P.M. to resume flight operations again. Even so, she came uncomfortably near repeating the experience of the *Lexington* in the otherwise closely similar Battle of the Coral Sea.

Shortly after resuming flight operations and while a second strike from *Shokaku* and *Zuikaku* was looking unsuccessfully for her and the *Sara*, a steering engine electric motor "grounded" as the result of battle damage. The Big E's rudder suddenly jammed 20 degrees right, forcing her to steam in circles until the fault could be remedied. The Japanese second strike, consisting of six Zeros, some Kates, and 18 Vals, first headed directly for the *Enterprise* but then altered course to the south and swung around her some 50 miles to the west before heading for their home decks empty-handed. The *Enterprise*'s radar tracked the planes, but nobody on her or on *Sara* was inclined to attract their attention by sending a Wildcat patrol after them. Had the Japanese Kate pilots found the *Enterprise* when she was unable to maneuver they might have finished her with an "anvil" torpedo attack.

In purely tactical terms the Battle of the Eastern Solomons had been a defeat for Yamamoto. He had lost a light carrier and a considerable number of planes, while Fletcher had suffered only damage to the *Enterprise* and 17 planes lost from all causes, including water landings and barrier crashes. Yamamoto's strategy had worked, but his air crews had failed to deliver a victory.

On the American side there could be little cause for rejoicing. Bombing by the Dauntless crews had been very inaccurate, partly the result of little opportunity to stay in practice. Also, radar interception and especially vectoring of defending Wildcats had literally broken down as a result of the massive overload thrown upon the single radio circuit. Finally, reconnaissance had been unsatisfactory. Because the *Enterprise* scouts had experienced trouble in keeping their voice radios attuned to the correct frequency, Nagumo's two big flattops had remained undetected. The Japanese had gotten off their punch while remaining free of major attack themselves. Good damage control in the *Enterprise* and a most generous portion of good luck had combined to give Fletcher a victory.

At battle's end Yamamoto still had more carriers than the Americans, but that was all. Six Japanese flattops had now been sunk against only two American. In terms of embarked planes at sea, the odds in the Pacific war were just about even.

12. Santa Cruz

The Battle of the Eastern Solomons ended on August 24, 1942, with Admiral Yamamoto still cruising near Truk in Combined Fleet flagship *Yamato*. With the battle wagon was CVE *Taiyo,* a ship that would have made less expensive bait than the *Ryujo.* At first Yamamoto refused to recognize that his forces had been defeated, for his returning pilots had recorded heavy damage to two U. S. carriers and to sundry other ships. He therefore ordered *Zuikaku* and *Shokaku* to resume the search for the enemy. But his disillusionment began on the 25th when Marine Dauntless pilots from Guadalcanal damaged light cruiser *Jintsu* and set afire transport *Kinryu Maru* carrying the Guadalcanal occupation forces. Yamamoto ordered his big carriers to retire north of the Solomons.

For his part Frank Jack Fletcher had hauled out fast on the night of August 24 with *Saratoga* and damaged *Enterprise* for a fueling rendezvous deep in the Coral Sea. The next day *Wasp* cruised eastward of Guadalcanal, but her Dauntless scouts flown out to 200 miles failed to locate Nagumo.

In the next two months, until late October, Zeros and Bettys from Rabaul continued to suffer heavy losses trying to attack Guadalcanal. Ground attacks launched by troops infiltrated by sea failed also. Alerted by radar that could pick up a high-level flight at 125 miles, or by a brave Aussie coast watcher hidden on some one of the northern Solomons, U. S. Marine Wildcats would climb to 20,000 feet or higher as the Japanese approached. Then they would dive on the Betty formation in overhead attacks, counting on their six .50s to set fire to the massive unprotected fuel tanks located in the wing roots of each Betty. Zeros they avoided unless compelled to fight.

Japanese bombing afflicted Henderson Field only lightly. The widely dispersed Wildcats, Dauntlesses, and U. S. Army Airacobras on the ground made poor targets, and the Japanese did little strafing. Consequently, American carriers had no need to operate within air range of Rabaul. They patrolled farther south in the Coral Sea, amid, as it unhappily turned out, a concentration of Japanese submarines Yamamoto had posted there to sink them. This region American sailors came to call "torpedo junction."

On August 30 the *Saratoga* was steaming in the same 60-by-150-mile rectangle of water in which she had been operating for some time. Submarine I-26 sighted her and from outside her destroyer screen fired six torpedoes at long range. Captain DeWitt C. Ramsey spotted a destroyer's warning flag at 7:46 A.M. and immediately put over the ship's rudder. One hit caused little structural damage, but inflowing salt water shorted out part of the *Sara*'s complex electric drive system. Once again she made course for Bremerton, missing a critical phase of the Guadalcanal campaign.

Two weeks later, on September 15, submarines I-15 and I-19 ambushed the force featuring the *Wasp, Hornet*, and the new fast battleship *North Carolina. Wasp* caught it at about 2:45 P.M., Greenwich plus 12 time, just as she was steadying on her base course after completing launch and recovery of some patrol planes. A lookout suddenly yelled, "Torpedo wake!" Ensign C. G. Darr, USNR, on the bridge, looked and saw only 300 to 400 feet away three torpedoes racing toward the *Wasp* at an angle of 30 to 45 degrees from the bow. Turning to Rear Admiral Leigh Noyes, he pointed and said, "These have got us." Noyes said nothing, and both men braced their feet for the impact.

In quick succession two, perhaps all three, of the fish slammed into the ship forward of the bridge on the starboard side. Everywhere men fell sprawling, though Noyes and Darr somehow kept their feet. Two minutes later another explosion came, evidently an induced gasoline blast, and a burst of flames enveloped the bridge. Instinctively Darr flung up an arm to protect his face and received his only injury, a burn on the back of the hand. Then he ran down to the flight deck to help fight rapidly spreading fires. Noyes was not injured then, but a severe induced explosion at 3:05 P.M. sent incandescent gasses again billowing past the bridge, burning his shirt, hair, and ears.

The torpedoes had struck *Wasp* at the worst possible moment, while she was moving slowly and while her gasoline pumping system was operating. The torpedoes did not start fatal flooding; damage control quickly corrected a 10- to 15-degree list. But the torpedo explosions forward set the forward half of the hangar deck ablaze. A fire curtain dropped across the hangar amidships temporarily contained the flames. When Air Group Commander Wallace M. Beakley inspected the forward half of the hangar deck moments after the hits, he found it already an inferno, with three depth-charge-armed SBDs burning fiercely and blazing Wildcat wings stored overhead dripping molten metal on the deck. Water pressure already had failed throughout the ship, and it was apparent to Beakley that gasoline from the ship's fuel lines and tanks was feeding the conflagration. Within ten minutes ammunition had begun to cook off at the forward 5-inch and 1.1-inch mounts, and the depth charges under the Dauntlesses had begun to explode. *Wasp* was almost as badly off as the *Hiryu* had been at Midway.

Captain Forrest P. Sherman backed his ship to keep the flames from washing back through the fire curtain and along the flight deck to envelop the hundreds of men who now began to congregate at the stern. But this maneuver jeopardized others forward as smoke and hot gasses blew over them. Assembled on the forecastle at the bow were about 150 survivors collected by Lieutenant B. J. Semmes, Jr., the Assistant Gunnery Officer. Finally, the heat and flames became so bad that the men could stay aboard the *Wasp* no longer. Looking at the blazing gasoline on the water surrounding the bow, they hesitated, then a badly burned seaman dove overside and the rest followed. All but six had on kapok life jackets. Lieutenant Semmes dove last, ". . . disproving the theory that [by diving while wearing a jacket] you break your back." He came up amid flames, ducked his face under, and swam clear as the ship backed away from him.

At about 3:20 P.M., 35 minutes after the hits, Captain Sherman concluded that the fires were totally out of control, that to battle them further would not only be useless but lengthen an already long casualty roster. He ordered "Abandon Ship!" Engine-room personnel were surprised, conditions not being too bad in their area, but when they emerged and saw the inferno forward they understood the reason for Sherman's order. The men went overside down hoses and lines slung over the stern, very orderly, without panic. Most had on their life jackets as ordered.

By dusk all known survivors from *Wasp* had been recovered, and destroyer *Lansdowne* was ordered to sink the listing, burning wreck with torpedoes. Of *Wasp*'s complement of 2,247 officers and men, 193 were killed and 366 wounded, nearly all by burns. An additional fatality was war correspondent Jack Singer of International News Service. *Hornet* recovered all but one of *Wasp*'s 26 airborne planes; 45 others were lost with the ship.

About a half hour after her sister sub had tagged *Wasp,* submarine I-15 fired a spread of torpedoes at *Hornet.* This spread missed, but at 2:52 P.M. a torpedo hit *North Carolina* and two minutes later another destroyer *O'Brien.* One fish could not sink the battle wagon, though it tore a wound 32 by 18 feet just below the armor belt. But like *Saratoga* the *North Carolina* had to go stateside for repair and a refit. Destroyer *O'Brien,* its bow mangled, limped to Espiritu Santo but later broke in two while trying to steam to the West Coast. Two other destroyers, *Lansdowne* and *Mustin,* reported that torpedoes had passed under their keels without exploding. Submarines I-15 and I-19 got away.

The disaster left Admiral Nimitz with just one operational carrier in the Pacific. *Enterprise* was still undergoing a crash refit at Pearl Harbor, and *Saratoga* was limping toward that base at a dangerously slow 13 knots. Henderson Field on Guadalcanal remained, a priceless unsinkable flattop, immune to torpedoes and nearly so to bombs. The entire Guadalcanal campaign now revolved about its 3,500-foot steel-planked surface and a dirt strip a mile away called "Fighter One."

Seconded by the Imperial High Command in Tokyo, Admiral Yamamoto began planning another offensive to be launched in late October. He proposed transporting to Guadalcanal by destroyers the entire Japanese Army 2nd Division, plus the Aoba Detachment of regimental strength. Naval air reinforcements from Java and Singapore would rebuild the depleted Base Air Force at Rabaul. Then the flyers would destroy American air power at Henderson Field and protect shipments of troops and heavy artillery to Guadalcanal. Admiral Nagumo would hover protectively north of Guadalcanal with *Shokaku* and *Zuikaku*, reinforced by *Zuiho*, *Hiyo*, and *Junyo* now available with fresh air groups. If all went well Henderson Field would be seized by the fresh ground troops and the campaign ended.

With their superb efficiency Admiral Nimitz's cryptographers learned the essentials of Yamamoto's operational orders. Again Nimitz was able to anticipate his antagonist's moves, and on October 16 the hastily repaired *Enterprise* departed Pearl Harbor in company with fast battle wagon *South Dakota* and a cruiser-destroyer escort. She now carried eight more 20-mm. AA guns and new quadruple 40-mm. Bofors AA mounts in place of her 1.1-inch quads.

South of Oahu *Enterprise* landed aboard Air Group 10. This new outfit had been training as a unit for about three months. Its veteran flight leaders and squadron commanders led lieutenant jg's and ensigns not long out of advanced flight school. Though without combat experience the new men were—as the Big E's Landing Officer Robin Lindsey later recalled— "red hot and ready to go." As soon as the deck crews had tied down or struck below the planes, the *Enterprise* steadied on a southwesterly course for the Solomons.

On October 23 the Big E joined the redoubtable *Hornet* north of Espiritu Santo, where under Rear Admiral Thomas C. Kinkaid the pair became Task Force 61. Frank Jack Fletcher was out of the campaign; he had been injured when the *Saratoga* was torpedoed. Kinkaid had ambitious orders: He was to sweep north of the Santa Cruz Islands and seek battle with the enemy.

A near clash developed on October 25 as the Japanese on Guadalcanal were implementing their big push. A Catalina from tender *Curtiss* spotted one of Yamamoto's carrier forces 360 miles from Task Force 61. Both *Hornet* and *Enterprise* sped north, and late in the afternoon the Big E launched a strike group of 11 Wildcats fitted with a newly designed underwing drop tank and 12 Dauntlesses and six Avengers. No contact developed, and the pilots returned for night landings for which they had not been trained. When a deck crash delayed operations, six TBFs had to ditch. One pilot was lost, a Wildcat jockey who vanished only 20 miles from the *Enterprise*.

The force that the *Curtiss* plane had sighted probably was Admiral Nagumo's Carrier Division 1, consisting of *Shokaku*, *Zuikaku*, and the light carrier *Zuiho*, escorted by a heavy cruiser and eight destroyers.

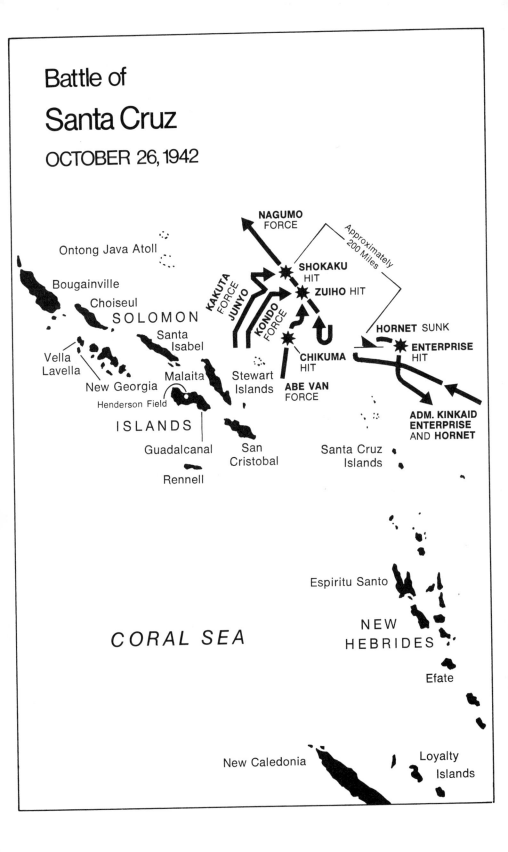

Battle of
Santa Cruz
OCTOBER 26, 1942

Ontong Java Atoll

Bougainville

Choiseul

S O L O M O N

Santa
Isabel

Vella
Lavella

Malaita

New Georgia

Henderson Field

I S L A N D S

Guadalcanal

Rennell

San
Cristobal

Stewart
Islands

KAKUTA FORCE

JUNYO

KONDO FORCE

ABE VAN FORCE

NAGUMO FORCE

Approximately 200 Miles

SHOKAKU HIT

ZUIHO HIT

CHIKUMA HIT

HORNET SUNK

ENTERPRISE HIT

ADM. KINKAID ENTERPRISE AND **HORNET**

Santa Cruz
Islands

Espiritu Santo

**N E W
H E B R I D E S**

Efate

CORAL SEA

New Caledonia

Loyalty
Islands

Operating as an advance force and also under Nagumo's overall command were two surface squadrons under Vice Admiral Hiroaki Abe.

Steaming by herself 120 miles westward as Carrier Division 2 under Rear Admiral Kakuji Kakuta was *Junyo*, the flattop converted from a liner. She had with her only two destroyers, but almost within sight from her deck was a second advance force under Vice Admiral Kondo.

This time Admiral Yamamoto was not offering a carrier as bait. *Junyo's* was no decoy mission. Rather, Yamamoto was trying out a tactical concept devised by Commander Minoru Genda of operating two carrier forces separated by more than 100 miles, thrice visual sighting distance from the air in normal weather. This allowed each force to attack the same target but separated them so widely as to make almost impossible simultaneous enemy attacks on both. *Junyo* should have been accompanied by sister ship *Hiyo,* but on October 22 an engine-room fire had sent *Hiyo* to Truk for repairs and her air group to Rabaul. *Hiyo's* absence considerably reduced overall Japanese air strength, although *Junyo's* 24 Zeros, 21 Vals, and ten Kates greatly augmented Nagumo's three-carrier punch of 63 Zeros, 47 Vals, and 47 Kates and made the Japanese tally 212 planes.

Admiral Kinkaid thus was ordered into battle outnumbered in the air. His flagship *Enterprise* and the *Hornet* could muster but 70 Wildcats, 72 Dauntlesses, and 27 Avengers, 169 aircraft in all. Only in dive bombers were the Americans superior, and that by only a trifle.

The dawn of October 26 disclosed Admiral Kinkaid still headed northwest on an aggressive course as ordered, but he was uneasy and had every reason to be so. Across the *Enterprise* and *Hornet* at 2,000 feet drifted scattered cumulus clouds adequate to conceal ugly Val dive bombers and swift Kate torpedo planes. These clouds linked intermittent rain squalls that blanked out radar. The sea was dead calm with a slight swell; the light wind of six to ten knots was blowing toward the oncoming Nagumo and away from Kinkaid. This meant that the American flattops would have to put about to launch and recover planes, forcing them to stay in roughly the same locale all day. The Japanese had enjoyed this considerable advantage—a tremendous help to their reconnaissance and strike forces by boosting their effective range—in every engagement since Pearl Harbor.

The American carriers were in their now standard defensive formation. In the center of a circle about 4,000 yards in diameter the *Enterprise* steamed with battleship *South Dakota,* heavy cruiser *Portland,* antiaircraft cruiser *San Juan,* and eight destroyers. *Hornet,* ten miles to the southeast, had as consorts in a similar formation heavy cruisers *Northampton* and *Pensacola,* antiaircraft light cruisers *San Diego* and *Juneau,* and six destroyers.

At 6:00 A.M.* the *Enterprise* sounded General Quarters and launched an armed search of 16 SBDs flying in pairs. Earlier, a PBY had found

* Times given in this account are those utilized in the American task force.

Nagumo's three carriers of Carrier Division 1, but a communications SNAFU* had delayed its report, and Admiral Kinkaid had elected to fly his own reconnaissance. Eighty-five miles from the Big E two search pilots, Lieutenant Vivian W. Welch and his wingman, Lieutenant (jg) Bruce A. McGraw, spotted a scout on an opposite course. This was a *Shokaku* plane, one of eight Kates and 16 seaplanes searching for the Americans. Welch and McGraw left the Kate alone, which in turn ignored them. Like the other SBD pilots, they had 500-pound bombs along and wanted to expend them on an enemy ship.

At 7:17 A.M. Welch and McGraw found Admiral Abe's advance surface force but flew on past to continue searching and radio home their find. Welch still was transmitting about 7:30 when a Japanese pilot found the *Hornet* and reported, "Large enemy unit sighted, one carrier, five other vessels." The rival carrier forces were now about 185 nautical miles apart, close enough for strikes.

Welch's skipper, Lieutenant Commander James R. "Bucky" Lee, boss of the Big E's Scouting 10, was the first to sight Nagumo's carriers. He found them at 7:50, reported, and then found himself being bounced by eight Zeros of the CAP. Neither Lee nor his wingman, Ensign William E. Johnson, managed to break free and dive, but turning sharply toward each other in the "Thach weave," they not only managed to survive but to destroy three Zeros, a remarkable performance for two SBDs.

On the flight decks of *Zuikaku, Shokaku,* and *Zuiho* Admiral Nagumo had warmed up, armed, and ready to go a strike of 67 planes. This consisted of 22 Vals from *Shokaku,* 18 Kates from *Zuikaku* under Lieutenant Jiichiro Imajuku, and an exceptionally strong escort of 27 Zeros, 18 from *Shokaku* and nine from *Zuiho* under Lieutenant Commander Hideki Shinzo. Commanding the strike overall was the Val squadron leader Lieutenant Commander Mamoru Seki. The first Zeros took off at 8:18 A.M., about 22 minutes before *Hornet* began launching her own strike. The last planes, Kates, had just flown off when trouble arrived.

The trouble was in the form of two search SBDs flown by Lieutenant Stockton Birney Strong, a U. S. Naval Academy regular of the class of 1937, and his wingman, Ensign Charles B. Irvine, nicknamed "Skinhead" because of his short haircut. Mindful of Commander Lee's order given before takeoff that all scouts should rendezvous and attack if one pair found the enemy carriers, Strong and Irvine had abandoned their search on overhearing Lee's transmission and had flown 80 miles to find the *Shokaku* and *Zuiho.* Birney Strong, a veteran of 800 flying hours and the attack on the Marshalls, maneuvered into position unseen by the Zero CAP, aided inadvertently by other scouts that had tangled with the Zeros, and dove on *Zuiho* at 8:40 A.M. with Irvine following.

_____

* SNAFU—"Situation normal all fouled up." Communications snafus occurred repeatedly throughout the war when PBYs reported back to headquarters ashore instead of directly to the carrier task forces.

Caught completely by surprise, even though the accompanying *Shokaku* now had operating radar, Captain Sueo Obyashi's little carrier had no opportunity to maneuver or fire a shot before a 500-pound bomb struck. It blew a 30-foot hole in *Zuiho's* flight deck aft, started fires that burned over an hour, and stopped radio communications. *Zuiho* stayed in formation with the *Shokaku* but was unable to land planes. It did contribute planes to Nagumo's second strike, already being readied on the other two carriers. Strong and Irvine had a nasty running flight for 45 miles with irate Zeros in getting away, but their gunners, Clarence H. Garlow and Elgie P. Williams, put up a stiff battle with their twin .30s and claimed a Zero apiece.

Of other *Enterprise* scouts only one pair managed to elude the Zeros and dive. They claimed a hit on a gunnery ship, probably destroyer *Akatsuki*, disabling her No. 1 boiler room and starboard engines. Surprisingly, all 16 of the scouts returned to the *Enterprise,* though some were badly shot up.

Meanwhile, both *Hornet* and *Enterprise* had been launching. Lieutenant Commander William J. "Gus" Widhelm led out 15 Dauntlesses from the *Hornet* at about 8:40, trailed by six Avengers. An eight-Wildcat escort joined, and the Dauntlesses and Avengers in separate formations set out immediately for the enemy. *Enterprise* followed with a strike of all her remaining planes, eight Wildcats, nine Avengers, and just three Dauntlesses, led by Air Group 10's skipper, Commander Richard K. Gaines. The *Hornet* completed the American launch of 73 planes by dispatching at 9:15 A.M. a second strike of nine more Wildcats, nine Dauntlesses, and seven bomb-armed Avengers led by Commander Walter F. Rodee, skipper of Air Group 8.

None of the American formations joined up, and the Avengers flew low and the Dauntlesses high, splitting and weakening the fighter escort. With an estimated 227 miles to go on the basis of the contact reports, both Gaines and Rodee believed that fuel would be critical for the Dauntlesses, and neither wanted to expend gasoline by assembling a single formation. This meant that the American planes were strung out for miles as they flew northwest toward the enemy.

Up to this point Dame Fortune had favored the Americans. Already Nagumo had a flight deck disabled. Also, he believed, erroneously, that Kinkaid had only one flattop that his pilot had wrongly identified as the *Saratoga.* But for Nagumo fate now took a much more favorable turn.

About 60 miles out from the *Enterprise* the Japanese and American strike formations began to pass each other. Lieutenant Commander Shinzo let the first group, Widhelm's, go by, failing to recognize the planes as enemy. But from up sun Lieutenant Moriyasu Hidaka's nine Zeros from *Zuiho* ambushed the Big E's Avenger flight that was climbing slowly at 120 knots at 6,000 feet. They blasted down three in seconds with their 20-mm. guns and damaged another so badly that it had to return. Then they tangled with four escorting Wildcats, chopping down three and damaging the other. Lieutenant Commander Jimmy Flatley, leading the other four fighters that had been banking away from the attack, finally spotted Hidaka and flashed in to divert a Zero maneuvering to attack the five surviving Avengers from below. He missed a deflection shot from a diving turn, smoked the Zero with a second run, pulled up, dove again, and plopped it into the sea with a high-side pass. But at a decidedly reasonable price Hidaka's pilots had reduced the *Enterprise* torpedo-plane strength and had deprived the U. S. Navy of an experienced squadron leader, Lieutenant Commander Jack Collett.* In so doing, however, the Zeros depleted their fuel and had to return, leaving Commander Shinzo to assume entire responsibility for escort with his 18 Zeros from *Shokaku*.

Probably because both friendly and enemy aircraft had mingled on their radar scopes, neither the *Hornet* nor the *Enterprise* identified Commander Seki's oncoming strike until it was 45 miles out. *Enterprise* had initial charge of fighter direction, and it proved even less effective than in the Eastern Solomons battle. The air controller had positioned the 38 defending Wildcats much too low, and with wing tanks the stubby fighters could climb only about 1,200 feet per minute. Thus all but four failed to intercept Seki's Vals coming in overhead. Also, the controllers gave "relative" bearings from the direction of the ship, thereby confusing those pilots who could not see the *Enterprise*. They did not know where to look or go when the controllers radioed, "Bogey ahead 20 miles" and "Hey, Rube, look for bogies, look for Hawks on port quarter." Where was the "port quarter"? Directions should have been given, of course, in true compass bearings.

One four-plane flight of *Hornet* planes led by Lieutenant Edward W. Hessel caught some of the Vals at 17,000 feet 20 miles out and claimed one or two with a single pass. Three *Enterprise* pilots caught up with the Vals in their dives, Lieutenant Albert D. Pollock claiming one and Ensign Steve G. Nona another. But most of the 22 Vals and Lieutenant Imajuku's 18 Kates reached attack position unmolested to begin a beautifully coordinated simultaneous dive-bombing and torpedo attack. Listeners on the bridge of flagship *Shokaku* heard "Mamu" Seki, Japan's most experienced air-group leader, report at 9:55, "Enemy aircraft carrier in sight," then: "All planes go in!"

Below on the *Hornet* Captain Charles P. Mason knew by about 10:00 A.M. that his ship, in commission just 371 days, was going to catch it. Lucky *Enterprise*, steaming about ten miles away, had entered a rain squall at 9:57 in which she stayed concealed until 10:20, escaping attack. *Hornet's* lookouts counted off 12 Kates and about 15 Vals as the carrier began twisting and squirming at 28 knots. At 10:08 her loudspeakers barked, "Stand by for dive-bombing attack!"

* Collett and his gunners were lost. Japanese destroyers rescued two of the fighter pilots.

At 10:12 Seki's first two Vals came screeching down through a rising cloud of red balls of flak. Their bombs missed and cast water over the ship. The next plane, bearing a squadron commander's markings, which appeared to be afire to some observers and undamaged to others, plummeted vertically into the ship, glancing from the stack and smashing through the flight deck. One of its hundred-pound bombs exploded, but its 550-pounder did not, having failed to arm. Blazing gasoline doused the signal-bridge crew and started a fire in No. 2 ready room that burned for two hours.

Two minutes later, while other Vals still were hurtling down, two Kates from Lieutenant Imajuku's torpedo-plane squadron raced in from starboard about 20 seconds apart. Their tin fish ripped twin holes 15 by 30 feet in *Hornet*'s tender hull and opened to the sea both firerooms and the forward engine room. Power and propulsion quickly failed, and the ship coasted to a stop. Bereft of pressure on the fire mains, the crew continued fighting the fires with buckets of dry foamite.

Moments after the torpedoes hit, three more Vals crashed 550-pounders into the *Hornet*. One missile killed 12 Marines at a gun battery; the other pair penetrated to the fourth deck, ripping apart storerooms, the chief petty officers' quarters, and the forward messing area. The last bomb decimated a repair party, slaying 30 men, but it failed to start a serious fire because this space had no paint.

Hornet took her final blow of this first attack at 10:17. A Kate, afire with weapon already dropped, deliberately crashed the now drifting ship. It struck the port forward five-inch gun gallery, exploded just outboard of the No. 1 elevator shaft, killed three or four crewmen, and started a dangerous, hot fire. The Kate's engine wound up in the junior officers' bunk room on the second deck, while the fuselage and the two crewmen tumbled into the elevator pit. On searching the wreck for items of intelligence value, the *Hornet*'s crew found a nautical chart of Costa Rica.

The end of eight minutes of firing at about 10:20 found the *Hornet* badly hurt. Her damage had cost the Japanese 25 planes by Japanese count, including Mamoru Seki's, mostly Vals and Kates and mostly to AA fire. But hits by two torpedoes, three bombs, and two planes from 49 aircraft dispatched had left the ship burning from midships to bow with small fires, dead in the water and listing seven to eight degrees. Medics were succoring the many injured, burned, and wounded. One very young signalman asked his chief, Commander O. H. Dodson, the communications officer, "Sir, am I being brave enough?" A pharmacist mate was treating him for severe burns of his head, neck, arms, and hands. His flashproof clothing had saved his life.

Captain Mason had no intention of abandoning his ship. About 800 crewmen were fighting the fires, and destroyers *Morris* and *Russell* soon bumped alongside to pass aboard fire hoses. But *Hornet* was finished as a fighting ship. *Enterprise* would have to service every airborne plane, and these numbered more than she could handle.

Ignorant of the fate of their seagoing home were the flyers of the *Hornet's* air group. Ten minutes after the attack on her had ended, the *Hornet's* 15 SBDs of the first strike found themselves directly over heavy cruisers *Tone* and *Chikuma.* Flight leader Gus Widhelm, skipper of Scouting 8, passed them up. Twenty miles farther north and west he spotted battleships *Hiei* and *Kirishima* and nine Zeros that tangled with his four-plane Wildcat escort, led by a fiery veteran, Lieutenant Commander H. G. "Mike" Sanchez, commander of Fighting 72, *Wasp's* old squadron. Sanchez lost two planes, and other Zeros arrived to begin firing runs on Widhelm's rugged Dauntlesses.

Widhelm's squadron, a mixed outfit from Scouting and Bombing 8, stayed in tight formation, wings almost overlapping. His gunner, Radioman George Stokely, acted as fire-control director, calling out the direction of oncoming attackers to Widhelm, enabling Gus to weave the formation just enough to give his pilots deflection shots at Zeros passing ahead without hampering the gunners. The vulnerable Zeros found this hard to take and several flamed, but as the Japanese carriers came in view a Zero bullet severed Widhelm's oil line, forcing him after a few minutes more to jettison his bomb and dive away to ditch when his engine "froze" and stopped. He and Stokely were lucky; a PBY found them in their little yellow life raft three days after the battle. The Zero CAP shot down two other Dauntlesses, and Lieutenant White turned back after a Zero bullet had passed through his arm and shoulder. He managed to land aboard the *Enterprise* despite his wound and a useless aileron.

Now led by Lieutenant James E. "Moe" Vose, the 11 survivors deployed into line and with Zeros still trailing after them dove at 10:50 A.M. on the larger of the two carriers below. This was the *Shokaku* with Admiral Nagumo aboard. The accompanying *Zuiho* they ignored because it was smaller—Vose identified it as a "converted carrier"—and because it still was smoking from the scout's earlier hit. Captain Tameteru Nomoto's *Zuikaku* was out of sight well to the east, having become separated from the others. Vose dove first and afterward reported, "I claim four direct hits on this carrier." Lieutenant Bates in one of the last Dauntlesses to dive also thought he saw four hits.

According to Japanese counts, at least three and possibly as many as six 1/100th-second fused thousand-pounders burst just under *Shokaku's* flight deck amidships, tumbling great chunks through the air, starting fierce fires that gutted the hangar deck, wrecked all communications, stopped flight operations, and reduced the carrier's speed. Fortunately for Nagumo, *Shokaku* had no planes aboard to burn and explode; otherwise she would have been lost. She and *Zuikaku* had launched their second strikes at 9:00 A.M., clearing decks and hangers. But now the Japanese, too, were short of flight decks on which to recover planes. *Zuikaku* and *Junyo* would have to land every plane in the air.

As it turned out, the bravery and professionalism of Widhelm, Vose, and the other Dauntless pilots from *Hornet* mitigated a day of combat that otherwise was turning disastrous for Kinkaid and Task Force 16. These were the only pilots of the entire striking force to find the primary target, the enemy flattops. *Hornet's* torpedo planes, its entire second strike under Commander Rodee, and the *Enterprise* group all failed to sight and attack the carriers for reasons that almost defy explanation. Apparently, these strike units flew too far to the westward, thus missing the carriers that were more directly north. But this error would not have mattered had they heard Widhelm's report giving the position of the carriers, which he had voice-broadcast several times. A radio problem that had first surfaced in the Battle of the Eastern Solomons had again plagued the Americans. Either Widhelm's radio or those of the other planes had drifted off the precise frequency required by the sensitive voice transmitter, with the result that only the *Hornet* and perhaps a third of the pilots had heard him. No flight leader had picked up his report. An angry Widhelm reported caustically after his rescue:

It is criminal on the part of the Bureau of Engineering not to have equipped all planes with crystal control radios. . . . The present radio equipment cannot be set exactly on frequency in war waters, and unless it is, all future attacks will be doomed to similar failure. The set is too complicated for aircraft operation. The rear-seat gunner has plenty on his hands without fiddling with all of the radio dials in flight. . . . If radio equipment is so complicated that it cannot be operated by personnel that fight, it should be thrown out and changed immediately.

Ironically, by using crystal radio equipment and crews well drilled in dot-dash transmission and reception, the Japanese had no difficulty. They communicated easily both plane-to-plane and plane-to-ship in the battle.

The other flight leaders found Nagumo's advance force of battleships and cruisers, searched beyond without success, and then returned to attack the surface ships. Some flew box searches but turned west rather than north, thus missing Nagumo's carriers.

The six *Hornet* torpedo planes launched at heavy cruiser *Suzuya* with results that hardly spoke well for the Mark 13 torpedo. One hung up and failed to release, two ran erratically, and although the crews claimed to see the other three explode, one on the starboard side and two on the port side of *Suzuya,* these sightings either were products of youthful imagination or "prematures" triggered by the tricky Mark 6 magnetic exploder. The exploder often would activate the warhead just short of a ship's hull and result in a toss-up of water that gave every appearance of being hit.*

The five *Enterprise* torpedo planes also attacked a ship they thought was a cruiser, but the ship's only damage came from a vicious strafing attack delivered simultaneously by Jimmy Flatley and his flight of four Wildcats. The three *Enterprise* Dauntlesses dove on *Kirishima,* and although

* In the South Pacific a large ship's magnetic field usually was stronger vertically than horizontally, thus triggering the premature explosion even when the exploder did not malfunction.

they claimed to see two hits, these must have been no better than near misses, because the battleship reported no damage.

The second strike from the *Hornet* also failed to find the enemy carriers. At 10:40 A.M. nine Dauntlesses led by Lieutenant J. J. Lynch dove on heavy cruiser *Chikuma*, unopposed except for antiaircraft. Lynch dropped first and hit the bridge, knocking six-foot-tall Captain Keizo Komura sprawling, injuring him, and killing all but twelve of the bridge watch. The other eight planes followed Lynch down and scored three more hits and two very near misses in a fine display of bombing. Their instantaneously fused thousand-pounders tore apart the ship's main battery control post and the torpedo tubes, started a fire amidships, and wrecked the forward engine room. Had these big missiles been fitted with delay fuses the *Chikuma* might have sunk. But as in the case of the *Mogami* at Midway, she managed to limp away to Truk, escorted by a pair of destroyers. She sailed right past Widhelm and Stokely in their rubber boat, the pair noting her damage with gratification.

Lieutenant W. F. Powell's nine Avengers watched Lynch attack the *Chikuma* but elected to fly on to the end of their search vector to find the carriers. They saw nothing to the northwest and so turned west and then flew back to attack the cruiser *Tone*. Each plane carried four 500-pound bombs instead of a torpedo, and all pilots but one dropped in salvo from high altitude. Powell believed that his men scored five hits, as did an escorting fighter pilot, but Japanese sources cite only one 50-meter miss.

With the exception of Widhelm's and Vose's determined and skilled attacks and the remarkably successful search flight from *Enterprise*, the two American air groups had done badly. The failure to team up at the outset probably was a mistake. They had let themselves be surprised by Zeros en route to the target. They had been given a target bearing which should have been good enough to find the enemy carriers. Had either the *Enterprise* or *Hornet* Dauntlesses found *Zuikaku* the chances would have been good that Nagumo would have had a third damaged carrier.

13. "Then There Was One"

On October 26, 1942, at 10:30 A.M., the *Enterprise,* now clear of the rain squall in which she had taken refuge, swung into the wind to land planes. These were Wildcats and Dauntlesses from her own and crippled *Hornet'*s CAP and Inner Air Patrols and SBDs of Commander Bucky Lee's valiant scouting group. In her flag plot Admiral Kinkaid was planning another strike of nine dive bombers to be led by Lieutenant Commander James A. Thomas, skipper of Bombing 10. Thomas was due to fly off at 11:00 A.M., as soon as the maintenance crews could refuel and rearm the planes.

This mission never left the Big E's deck, nor did all of the orbiting planes land. Approaching the *Enterprise* was Lieutenant Commander Shigeharu Murata. He personally led 12 Kates from *Shokaku.* Ahead of him was Lieutenant Sadamu Takahashi with 20 Vals from *Zuikaku* and 16 Zeros flying cover. A half hour behind Murata under separate command were 30 planes from *Junyo.* Lieutenant Maseo Yamaguchi from this carrier was leading 18 Vals and Pearl Harbor attacker Lieutenant Yoshio Shiga 12 Zeros in very close escort. Virtually all of the Japanese were to vent their fury on *Enterprise;* just one straying Val plunged at *Hornet* and barely missed.

Once again radar warning came dangerously late to the Americans, the blips of the attackers having mingled with those of Bucky Lee's returning Dauntlesses on the Big E's screen. Again, too, the CAP was positioned too low, and only two Wildcats intercepted Lieutenant Takahashi's Vals. Lieutenant Albert D. Pollock, flight leader of "Red 2," recalled, "Our fighters never had a chance. They were below and behind the attack." Lookouts aboard the *Enterprise* spotted the lead Val only when the plane was far down its controlled, shrieking plunge. In the next four minutes, between 11:15 and 11:19 A.M., all of Takahashi's Vals had dived to score two hits and a very close miss, by Japanese standards mediocre bombing.

The probable reason was that for the first time in the war Japan's airmen got a truly tremendous AA reception from a U. S. task force. The 40-mm. quad mounts on *Enterprise* and *South Dakota* pumped out shells rapidly and accurately, reaching high enough to rip some Vals apart before they could release. Hitherto, the best American weapons, the 20-mm. guns, had been unable to shoot a Val to pieces before it reached its release point. Probably half the Vals fell, either to antiaircraft or to Wildcats of the CAP during retirement.

Notwithstanding, the Japanese pilots had displayed their customary absolute determination worthy of the Pearl Harbor and Midway veterans most of them were. The first bomb to hit scored well forward, smashing through the *Enterprise*'s flight deck to explode just off the ship's clipper bow. Its blast set afire a rearmed SBD parked near the bow and hurled another overside. Fragments punched 160 small holes in the ship's hull between water line and forecastle deck.

The second bomb, also a 550-pounder, hit *Enterprise* almost at the center line of the flight deck about ten feet aft of the forward elevator. This missile broke in two, half exploding at hangar deck level, inflicting casualties, the other half penetrating to the third deck to massacre Repair Party Two. It also made a mess of the ship's junior officers' staterooms, smashing bulkheads and raising hob with the ship's watertight integrity on the second and third decks. From an operational standpoint its most serious effect was to jam the forward elevator in the "up" position.

A third bomb near missed starboard and aft close enough to dish in the hull plating three inches, open a seam, and flood two empty fuel tanks. The Big E was still fully operational, and its new skipper, Captain Osborne B. Hardison, was impressed with his veteran crew.

Sixteen minutes later, at 11:35 A.M., Murata appeared with his 12 Kates. He had the misfortune while still ten miles out to encounter four Wildcats led by Lieutenant Stanley W. "Swede" Vejtasa. This young Navy regular from Circle, Montana, had switched from dive bombers to fighters after the Marshalls raid. Vejtasa already had caught and claimed two Vals retiring after their dives, and after climbing to 13,000 feet he had led his flight outward along the vector of the Japanese attack. About ten miles from *Enterprise* he heard Ensign Hank Leder sing out, "Tallyho, nine o'clock down." Below were Murata's Kates coming in fast at 250 knots. Vejtasa dove steeply, rapidly building up speed in his heavy little fighter, followed by Leder and Lieutenants S. G. Ruehlow and Dave Harris. He and Harris torched two Kates and scattered the others. Pulling up and recovering, Vejtasa then followed a three-plane element into thin cloud cover drifting at 2,000 feet. What happened he recorded as follows:

I followed very close a three-plane section and blew up the number-two man with two short bursts. I then fired at the leader and shot the rudder off before the plane caught fire. The third plane started a shallow turn and caught on fire after I fired a rather long burst into it. These attacks were no-deflection runs from directly astern in a heavy cloud. I observed no return fire from the planes.

Breaking from the cloud, "Swede" then spied a Kate above him and tried a low side attack, ". . . but I missed him badly." Antiaircraft opened up, Vejtasa pulled away, and the Kate, going much too fast to drop its torpedo, slammed deliberately into the bow of destroyer *Smith* in a suicide crash. Backing around, Vejtasa spotted another Kate leaving the battle, emptied his last few rounds of ammunition into it, and followed it for five miles as it sank lower and lower to geyser into the sea. He had become an ace in a hurry, claiming seven enemy planes in one patrol. One of his victims may have been Shigeharu Murata, for the commander did not return, and his last transmission heard aboard the *Junyo* had been "All planes go in!"

Despite Vejtasa's efforts, several of Murata's Kates managed to close the *Enterprise* and launch torpedoes. Captain Hardison ordered hard right rudder to dodge a fish, then left full rudder to avoid colliding with the burning *Smith* of the screen. This brought *Enterprise* parallel to a torpedo running from ahead. Gunners downed the Kate that had dropped this one, and Hardison and the bridge crew could see the faces of the two Japanese flyers clinging to the wreck as the Big E tore past at 28 knots. Hardison foiled the last five attackers by keeping the ship's stern toward them. The Kates had to fly around the ship at less than a thousand yards in range of the 20-mm. batteries to get an attack angle. Heavy AA fire dropped three close aboard and forced another to pull up sharply into a climbing turn just off the stern. The plane stalled, dropped its fish in a desperation release, and crashed. The lone remaining Kate managed an aimed drop from astern at an angle of 20 degrees, but the torpedo missed as Hardison skillfully conned *Enterprise* right to parallel its track.

Hardison and Kinkaid with him on the bridge scarcely had time to catch their breaths when Lieutenant Yamaguchi appeared leading *Junyo's* 18 Vals. Yamaguchi had failed to spot *Enterprise* in flying through scattered squalls and had ordered his pilots to "Take attack preparation formation," followed by "Attack target, cruisers." *Junyo's* radio monitors had picked up his message, and he was hastily told, "There are other carriers. Search the area." The monitors had earlier intercepted American radio messages at 10:27 A.M. that had convinced Admiral Kakuta his enemies had more than one flattop. Yamaguchi countermanded his orders, broke off his approach, flew a box search, found *Enterprise* just as she had begun to swing into the wind to resume recovering planes, and commenced a 45-degree glide attack through low cloud and rain. His radioed "Enemy carrier in sight. . . . All planes go in" was heard aboard *Junyo* with rejoicing.

This able deed cost Yamaguchi his life. The Big E's 40-mm. gunners hit him during his shallow dive, and Lieutenant J. J. Lynch, circling the *Enterprise* after returning from his successful attack on *Chikuma,* watched Yamaguchi's Val and the three following plunge into the sea, caught in a literally murderous stream of 40- and 20-mm. bullets. At least eight of the 18 Vals fell to the AA, some catching fire, spinning out of control, and releasing bombs as much as 500 yards wide of the carrier. Only one bomb hit the *Enterprise,* glancing from the side of the heeling, turning ship to burst about 15 feet underwater. The pressure dished in the side plating and flooded three voids but otherwise did no harm.

Not all of the Vals dove on the *Enterprise*. One pilot planted a 550-pound bomb squarely atop the No. 1 turret of battleship *South Dakota*, jamming it in train, killing one man and wounding about 50 others, including Captain Thomas L. Gatch, the skipper. Another smacked a bomb with a defective fuse right through the light antiaircraft cruiser *San Juan*. It failed to explode and did no damage other than to drill a hole from main deck through double bottom. Destroyer *Smith*, the "can" crashed by the Kate, was much more badly hurt, with 28 killed and 21 wounded.

While the Japanese Vals and Kates had been attacking, several vicious dogfights had developed between Lieutenant Notomi's 16 Zeros from *Zuikaku* and Lieutenant Shiga's 12 from *Junyo* and the Wildcats of the CAP. *Enterprise's* VF-10 pilots claimed 17 Vals, Kates, and Zeros against the loss of seven of their own Wildcats and four pilots. *Hornet's* VF-72 claimed 15 Vals, five Kates, and eight Zeros against the loss of ten planes —some ditching when out of fuel—and five pilots. These American claims were probably too high, though Japanese losses were extraordinarily heavy. Only six *Junyo* Zeros returned in formation, and only nine were serviceable after the battle, including one stray from *Zuikaku* that landed aboard. Lost were all three Japanese Kate squadron leaders and two of the three Val leaders. Lieutenant Takahashi of *Zuikaku* survived after ditching his battle-damaged Val. Other losses included air group skipper "Mamu" Seki, hit apparently by AA fire just after giving his attack order, and Lieutenant Shoei Yamada, another Pearl Harbor veteran and leader of *Shokaku's* second Val attack unit.

Many American pilots exhausted their ammunition and had to watch in frustration as Vals and Kates sped away after their attacks. Others were so low on fuel they dared not slam forward their throttles and mix it up with the enemy. Four such were Jimmy Flatley and his three Wildcat pilots returning from escorting *Enterprise's* torpedo planes. On arriving near the *Enterprise* and requesting permission to "pancake" (land aboard), they were waved off to orbit clear of the combat area, anxiously watching gas gauges flickering near empty. While thus engaged at about 12:35, three Zeros, led by *Junyo's* fighter squadron commander Lieutenant Yoshio Shiga, jumped them. Shiga dove on Flatley, who turned sharply toward his wingman, employing the "Thach weave" and forcing the Japanese veteran to break off his run. Shiga pulled up steeply into the wing-over for which his Zero was famous, dove again, and once more found himself endangered by the wingman. After five minutes, unable to get in a good shot, Shiga angrily broke off and returned to the *Junyo*. On reporting the incident in his after-action report, Flatley wrote, "We avoided their attacks without employing more than 50 percent power, and if the attacks had persisted, we would have shot down the enemy VF [fighters]."

Perhaps by design but more probably by accident, the Japanese managed to coordinate their air strikes on the *Enterprise* with a submarine attack. At 11:02 A.M. destroyer *Porter* had stopped to recover a TBF crew that had ditched. So engaged she was a "sitting duck" for submarine I-21 that fired two torpedoes. Lieutenant Harold Wells, standing at the rail amidships and watching the rescue, was one of the first to see the fish. One, he instantly realized, was going to miss the ship forward, but the other would strike squarely beneath his feet. He raced to the other rail, looked back, and saw several shipmates fly into the air as the torpedo struck and exploded. With both engine and firerooms flooded, the *Porter* was doomed. Her crew, less 15 of the "black gang" killed by the explosion, had to abandon ship.

Good luck at 11:55 A.M. averted a worse loss. Heavy cruiser *Portland* felt three heavy shocks just as lookouts reported torpedo wakes. A submarine, either I-21 or a sister, had launched a spread from so close that the fish had failed to arm. Had these exploded *Portland* probably would have joined *Porter* in Davy Jones's Locker.

By 12:35 P.M. the *Enterprise* had ceased firing and was able once more to turn into the wind. She had to land planes immediately, for the air literally was swarming with Wildcats, Dauntlesses, and big-bellied Avengers from Air Groups 10 and 8, many desperately short of fuel.

The key man aboard ship now was Lieutenant Robin M. Lindsey, the landing signal officer. He was already a hero. He and Lieutenant James Daniels, his assistant, had jumped into the rear seats of two parked Dauntlesses to fire on Murata's incoming Kates. Now he again proved his resourcefulness and ability to operate under pressure at an absolutely critical time.

With paddles outstretched, standing on his little platform to the side of the flight deck, Lindsey began landing planes on the damaged ship while repair crews were hastily covering the bomb holes forward. He brought in Wildcats with as little as five gallons in their gas tanks—including Jimmy Flatley, who had been airborne four hours and 35 minutes. Then he landed Dauntlesses and finally desperate Avengers. Parked planes soon filled the area forward of the crash barriers. When planes had jammed the flight deck back to the No. 2 elevator, Lindsey received orders to stop landing planes. But as he recalled afterward:

Well, I knew the *Hornet* planes were just about out of gas, and I couldn't see any reason for not landing them and taking a chance. . . . I brought about six more in before they screamed down and said, "That's all, knock it off, brother." I disobeyed orders and continued landing planes even when Number 2 elevator was down. I admit that was a rather stupid trick because somebody might have been killed if one of the planes had missed a wire and gone into the elevator. But the last 14 planes all landed on Number 1 and Number 2 wires with no damage, and I heard later that finally the Air Officer just said, "Leave the kid alone, he's hot."

Lindsey had landed some 95 planes, had saved millions of dollars for his country and doubtless some lives. But a considerable number, mostly

Wildcats and Avengers, had had to ditch. Destroyers recovered most—but not all—of the pilots.

Lindsey's feat accomplished, the *Enterprise* at Admiral Kinkaid's order began hot-footing south out of the battle zone at 1:35 P.M. No strikes could be flown immediately from the jammed flight deck, Kinkaid knew that at least one Japanese carrier still was intact, and submarines had been reported. The only reason for staying would be to fly CAP for damaged *Hornet*, and this Kinkaid opted not to do.

The end of the initial attack had left *Hornet* afire, dead in the water, and nearly helpless. Yet the crew, aided by destroyermen, had all fires controlled by 11:00 A.M. Cruiser *Northampton* finally managed to get the flattop under secure tow by mid-afternoon, but towing speed was only three or four knots, insufficient to pull her clear of the battle area by nightfall.

In the meantime, the *Hornet's* "B" Engineering Division had been trying for five hours to raise steam in undamaged boilers No. 1, 2, and 4. Working with hand lanterns, they managed several times to raise steam pressure to 150 pounds, only to have spurts of water in the fuel-oil lines douse the fires under the boilers. Finally, they found an uncontaminated fuel tank and at 3:45 P.M. had 300 pounds of steam on No. 4 boiler. Also, they had improvised a complex arrangement to pipe this steam to the after engine room that had not flooded. At about 4:00 P.M. the ship's generator was being warmed and switches aligned for a start-up. The possibility was at hand of getting electric power through the ship. Then pumps could be operated, the list corrected, and possibly the engine and boiler rooms shored and pumped out.

Twenty minutes later, at 4:20 P.M., nine of carrier *Junyo's* Kates appeared to carry out this ship's second strike. With no CAP to threaten them Lieutenant Yoshiaki Irikiin and his pilots deployed to attack both *Northampton* and *Hornet*. The cruiser cast off the two-inch towing cable and combed the torpedo wakes to escape damage. Antiaircraft downed some Kates, but at 4:23 a single fish bored into the wounded starboard side of the *Hornet* below the island at frame 100. A violent explosion tore open the unflooded after engine room, from which the crew barely escaped, and within a minute the ship's list noticeably steepened. Seventeen minutes later five of *Junyo's* remaining Vals appeared, led by Lieutenant (jg) Shunko Kato, the senior surviving Val pilot. They dove, near missed, and did no more than violently shake the cripple.

When *Hornet's* list had reached 18 degrees Captain Mason decided that to endanger his crew further would be foolhardy. His last hope of saving his ship had vanished with the flooding of the after engine room. Already he had evacuated to destroyers his 108 wounded and 800 others, including all maintenance and air group personnel.

Abandonment still was under way at 4:55 P.M. when six twin-engine high-level bombers appeared, probably Bettys from Rabaul. They dropped a neat, very tight bomb pattern that landed a single hit on the after starboard corner of the flight deck. The bombs caused no known casualties, and abandonment continued in a "quiet and orderly manner." A highlight of the abandonment, one officer recalled, came when 30 sailors paddling a life raft approached a destroyer. In total discord the men were lustily singing, "The Sidewalks of New York."

At 6:02 P.M. four Vals from *Zuikaku* showed up—all the planes the carrier had available—dove on the now abandoned derelict, and scored a hit just forward of the island. By dark all survivors that could be located had been recovered and destroyers *Mustin* and *Anderson* first torpedoed *Hornet* and, when she stubbornly refused to sink, fired hundreds of rounds of five-inch into her that set her ablaze from stem to stern. At 10:30 P.M. a Japanese surface force appeared, sent by Nagumo to dispatch cripples, and after finding that *Hornet* could not be taken in tow, destroyers *Akigumo* and *Makigumo* sank her with four of their "Long Lance" super-torpedoes.

The Battle of the Santa Cruz Islands had cost the Americans dear. *Hornet* was gone, along with 111 of her crew. Damaged *Enterprise*, with 44 killed and 75 wounded, was now the only American carrier operational in the Pacific. *Porter* had sunk and 74 planes had been lost, about 20 or so in combat and 54 more in water landings or aboard sunken *Hornet*. Twenty-three pilots and ten air crew were missing.

The surviving Japanese air crew were jubilant and with considerable reason. They honestly believed that they had sunk two flattops and possibly a third, plus a battleship, three cruisers, and a destroyer. Admiral Nagumo, who had been forced to transfer his flag once more to a destroyer, was wan and drawn after the battle, but he appeared to have tossed off an apathy that had gripped him since the Battle of Midway. At 9:00 A.M. on October 28 Nagumo dispatched a victory message to all hands:

From Commander-in-Chief, 3rd Fleet, to All Forces: "We congratulate the officers and men under our command, and especially the air personnel, on the courage and valor which they have displayed in the recent engagement, which saw the destruction of major American naval units, and the annihilation of the American air force. While offering our condolences for those who gave their lives for the nation, we pray for the speedy recovery of the wounded who participated so courageously in this fierce battle."

Imperial Headquarters in Tokyo accepted initial reports with caution, then with growing warmth. It officially named the engagement the "Battle of the South Pacific" and described it as "a great victory . . . achieved without losing a single vessel." True enough, but the weakness of the final attacks on the *Hornet* illustrated the terrible losses to the Japanese air groups. Japanese planes shot down numbered 69, with few pilots recovered, a loss that took away a sizable proportion of Japan's remaining first-team pilots. Another 23 planes had to ditch because of battle damage or loss of fuel. Some were CAP Zeros that Widhelm and Stokely watched landing alongside destroyers. Burned out *Shokaku,* much more severely damaged

Three of the earliest carriers: HMS *Furious* (top), as she appeared in 1919; USS *Langley* (middle) in 1927; and USS *Saratoga* (bottom) in 1932. *Furious* served in both world wars, launching the world's first successful carrier strike in the First World War. *Langley* was too slow for fleet work, but was sunk in the first months of World War II while ferrying fighters to the Netherlands Indies. *Saratoga's* sister ship and rival was USS *Lexington*. Both were converted from battle cruiser hulls made surplus by the Washington Naval Treaty of 1922.

The National Archives (top)
US Navy, The National Archives (center)
US Navy, The National Archives (bottom)

Fleet Admiral Isoroku Yamamoto, the Commander of Japan's Combined Fleets, architect of the Pearl Harbor attack, studies a chart. Never an optimist about the outcome of a war with America, Yamamoto believed that It was necessary to cripple the US Navy's striking force as much as possible if Japan were to have any chance for victory.

Naval History Collection, Naval Photographic Center, Washington, DC

Vice Admiral Chuichi Nagumo, IJN. As executor of Japan's Pearl Harbor attack and first wartime commander of Japan's fast carrier force, Admiral Nagumo was immediately responsible for the Japanese Navy's greatest tactical triumph (Pearl Harbor) and Its greatest defeat (Battle of Midway).

Naval History Collection, Naval Photographic Center, Washington, DC

Launching planes was largely the same on Japanese and American carriers. Here Japanese carriers launch a Zero fighter (above) and (below) a Nakajima B5N torpedo bomber, or Kate. The Zero is carrying a belly tank to provide greater flight range, and the pilot has left the cockpit canopy open for a faster exit in case of a power failure on takeoff. The Kate is taking off from the *Akagi,* distinguished from her near-sister by portside island structure, and is carrying a deadly Type 91 torpedo.

US Navy, The National Archives

Torpedo plane attack, Pearl Harbor, December 7, 1941, photographed by one of the Japanese attackers. A Kate torpedo plane (center of photo) has just pulled up after dropping its torpedo at the *Oklahoma*, outboard ship of the era, in center of photo). All outboard ships were hit. Had the oil tank farm (upper right of photo) been selected as a target, the entire Pacific Fleet might have been immobilized for many months.

Two views of the Japanese attack on Pearl Harbor. Torpedo tracks (above) can be seen leading to USS *Nevada*, already noticeably listing. Water boils about the *California* (stern to camera and to right of picture). In the background smoke rises from the Army's Hickam Field. Below, *Neosho*, loaded with gasoline but not a target, backs clear from a listing *California*. Behind *Neosho*, *Nevada* has already capsized.

Naval History Collection, Naval Photographic Center, Washington, DC

US Navy, The National Archives

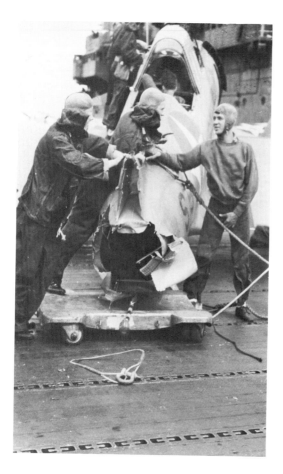

Two photos of USS *Enterprise* in action early in the war, February 1, 1942. An SBD dive bomber (above) has just lost its tail to the first Japanese Kamikaze, which then splashed over the ship's side. Crewmen prepare to send the damaged SBD below on the ship's elevator. *Enterprise* crewmen (right), splattered with antifire foam, man their Cal. 50 machine gun on the catwalk alongside the flight deck.

An *Enterprise* SBD in the "drink," while a plane guard destroyer moves in to rescue the crew. This incident occurred on March 17, 1942, but such "splashes" were common throughout the war and accounted for as many losses in both the Japanese and American carrier forces as they sustained in combat.

Colonel Jimmy Doolittle and his Tokyo raiders pose with Captain Marc Mitscher on USS *Hornet* shortly before takeoff. One of the B-25 Mitchell twin engine bombers used in the attack appears in the background.

D-Day at Guadalcanal found these ordnance men of Air Group Six bombing up an SBD *Dauntless* with a thousand-pounder. The "crutch," or U-shaped cradle to which the bomb will be attached, will be lowered by the pilot to swing the boom clear of the propeller during a dive-bombing attack.

US Navy, The National Archives

Devastator landing on *Enterprise.* A TBD-1 Devastator, tail hook down, is about to snag an arresting gear wire on USS *Enterprise.* The misnamed Devastator, much too slow and short-range to be effective, was replaced in mid-1942 by the fast and effective TBF Avenger.

US Navy, The National Archives

Pounced on during the Battle of the Coral Sea by American dive bombers and torpedo planes, the small but efficient light Japanese carrier *Shoho* is shown under attack by air groups from the *Lexington* and *Yorktown*.

US Navy, The National Archives

On May 8, 1942, during the Battle of the Coral Sea, an explosion of gasoline vapors in the AC motor generator room of the *Lexington* started uncontrollable fires. Few ships have been abandoned as reluctantly as was the *Lexington*. Some "plankowners" (men who had been aboard since her commissioning in December 1927) sat down on the deck and cried. The sea was warm and loss of life not heavy.

US Navy, The National Archives

Four views from the Battle of Midway that began June 4, 1942.

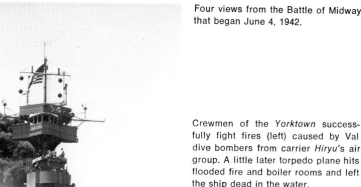

Crewmen of the *Yorktown* successfully fight fires (left) caused by Val dive bombers from carrier *Hiryu*'s air group. A little later torpedo plane hits flooded fire and boiler rooms and left the ship dead in the water.

US Navy, The National Archives

The *Akagi* (bottom) is shown dodging sticks of 600-pound bombs dropped from 20,000 feet by Colonel Walter Sweeney, Jr.'s, Hawaii-based B-17 Flying Fortresses. Bombing runs from this high altitude seldom hit maneuvering ships.

US Air Force, The National Archives

SBDs (above), on June 6, prepare to dive on Japanese heavy cruiser *Mikuma,* already hit and burning.

US Navy, The National Archives

Survivors of her crew (below), driven from their battle stations by fires, can be seen clustering on *Mikuma's* stern. *Mikuma* was soon sunk, joining four other Japanese carriers.

US Navy, The National Archives

At the Battle of Santa Cruz, Oct. 26, 1942, hard-working "plane pushers" of the *Enterprise*'s flight deck crew shove a Wildcat F4F4 fighter clear of the landing ramp on the stern of the ship. Note the arresting wires. Along the catwalk, gunners, who have already repelled an attack, stand by their 20 mm. guns.

Admiral "Wild Bill" Halsey (left) chats with Admiral Chester Nimitz (center) and Cincpac Chief of Staff Rear Admiral Forrest Sherman.

The USS *Tang* on lifeguard duty off Truk fishes yet another carrier pilot from the "drink." By closing perilously near to Truk Lagoon's encircling reef and coast defense batteries, Commander R. H. O'Kane's submarine rescued a record 22 airmen shot down in the second of three carrier strikes on the atoll. Such rescues raised morale enormously among the fliers.

US Navy, The National Archives

Aviation Machinist Kenneth Bratton is lifted from the aft gun turret of his TBF after the first attack on Rabaul by USS *Saratoga's* squadrons in November 1943. Zeros jumped the torpedo planes as they retired from attacks on Japanese cruisers that had gathered in Simpson Harbor to attack the US Navy's transports and supply ships supporting the invasion of Bougainville. Bratton recovered from his wounds.

US Navy, The National Archives

Death of a Kate. A 20 mm. gunner on USS *Yorktown* has sawed the port wing from a Kate torpedo bomber that has just released a torpedo at Captain "Jocko" Clark's carrier on December 4, 1943. A violent turn by the carrier caused the missile to miss.

A lineup of *Essex*-class carriers pose for their picture at a fleet anchorage in the Pacific. Dapple camouflage, added to confuse Japanese pilots and submarine skippers, glistens in a midday sun. *Essex*, the first of her class as CV-9, commissioned on the last day of 1942. She reached Pearl Harbor in mid-1943.

Admiral Marc Mitscher, Task Force 58's commander and boss of the carriers in the Central Pacific, and his Chief of Staff, Captain Arleigh Burke, confer on the flag bridge of USS *Randolph*.

Admiral Ernest J. King, the Chief of Naval Operation, is shown here aboard USS *Indianapolis* with Admiral Chester W. Nimitz (left) and Admiral Raymond A. Spruance (right) on July 18, 1944. King's visit was to check on the progress of the Marianas invasion and to ascertain Nimitz's and Spruance's wishes concerning future operations.

During the Great Marianas Turkey Shoot, the day-long battle between oncoming Japanese squadrons and Hellcat pilots defending Vice Admiral Marc Mitscher's Task Force 58, the Hellcats landed frequently to refuel and rearm. The Hellcats destroyed so many Japanese planes and aircrew that the Japanese Navy was unable to rebuild again its stock of trained carrier air groups.

US Navy, The National Archives

USS *Cowpens*, an *Independence*-class light fleet carrier, plows ahead "somewhere in the Pacific" in 1944 and battles with Japan's island defenders. These smallish flattops, converted from cruisers begun in 1942, could embark about forty planes. They filled a desperate "carrier gap" in the Navy during the last months of 1943 and in the first months of 1944.

US Navy, The National Archives

than in the Coral Sea battle, would require four months to repair, and *Zuiho* also was out of the Guadalcanal campaign. For Japan Santa Cruz was a victory won at nearly intolerable cost.

The lessons of defeat usually are more cogent than those of victory. In his "Comments, Conclusions, and Recommendations" written after the battle, Captain Hardison of the *Enterprise* singled out radar fighter direction as the greatest American weakness. It had worked well in practice, but the complications of battle had broken it down. Needed, he concluded, were full-scale exercises involving at least two attacking air groups and a great number of defending fighters to work out "sound doctrine."

To remedy an obvious American inferiority in scouting and reporting, Hardison recommended concentrating carrier search planes in the narrow 20- to 30-degree sector from which an enemy attack must almost certainly come. Then the bomb-equipped scouts could rendezvous and form the first attack wave. He also urged a tactical innovation not adopted in World War II—to have the Wildcats strafe the enemy carriers at night. Such an attack "would probably cripple the air group, and the resulting fires could easily put the carrier out of action."

Finally, Hardison was convinced of the wisdom of operating two flattops in proximity. As close as five miles, two carriers and their screens could keep in visual communication, yet maneuver independently in the event of a sudden enemy attack. One carrier alone, he believed, would have too few planes left for a strike after launching routine searches, antisubmarine patrols, inner air patrols, and CAP. Two carriers could alternate the duty, freeing one to have a deckload of armed planes ready to go. If carriers were to operate separately so as to prevent the enemy from sighting both, then "it must be a really wide separation on the order of some thirty to fifty miles, and even this will not guarantee it." If done, separation would need to be planned in advance and not improvised after sighting the enemy.

In his recommendations Captain Mason of the sunken *Hornet* displayed the tinge of bitterness felt by the captain who has lost his ship. New carriers, he recommended, should have better protection for their engine rooms. "The key ship of a task force must not be completely disabled by one torpedo." He disagreed sharply with Hardison that carriers should operate together. They should be well separated, and ". . . it is *firmly* believed that each carrier should conduct its own fighter direction at all times." Mason wanted *Hornet*'s crew "maintained intact" until it could be ordered to a new carrier, "preferably to one which could be renamed U. S. S. *Hornet*."

As the defeated admiral Tom Kinkaid probably realized that he was likely to be "beached."* He complained bitterly and with considerable justification about the failure of the PBY search reports to reach him,

---

* Kinkaid was relieved by King on November 28, 1942, but returned later as Commander, Seventh Fleet, "MacArthur's Navy."

noting that until commo improved, "Our carriers will continue to operate at a great disadvantage."

In his "Comments and Conclusions" forwarded to Admiral Ernie King in Washington, Admiral Nimitz at Pearl Harbor found most disturbing the demonstrated Japanese superiority in search and tracking. He agreed with his subordinates that the fighter direction had been "less effective than in previous actions" but noted the lack of opportunity on the part of *Enterprise* and *Hornet* to practice together prior to the battle. He said nothing about the problem of the radio receivers drifting off frequency, perhaps because he knew that VHF (Very High Frequency) radios ultimately would ease the problem. He noted also that "the 1,000-pound AP bomb now is available in the South Pacific [which] should improve our aircraft striking power." He did want placed on all carriers immediately, however, gasoline-powered pumps that could put out 2,000 gallons of water per minute, thus giving the ships a fire-fighting capacity even when their electric pumps were out.

Nimitz stayed out of what had become the major controversy in the Pacific at high-command level—how to operate carriers, whether together or as single-ship task groups. The issue was currently academic. For the next several weeks, until *Saratoga* could be repaired, Nimitz would have only one fleet carrier, the damaged *Enterprise*. The Big E would have to operate alone, by itself constituting American carrier air power in the Pacific.

14. Finale at Guadalcanal

Admiral Yamamoto's jubilation over Santa Cruz quickly faded when he contemplated his problem at Guadalcanal. He believed that he had eliminated the last of the American fleet carriers, but the enemy still held Henderson Field. Repeated attacks by the Sendai Division had been no more successful against the U. S. Marine Corps perimeter than earlier assaults. Dauntlesses flown by Marine and Navy pilots had continued to harass his convoys, sinking light cruiser *Yura* on October 25. Unless the airfield was knocked out, American reinforcement of Guadalcanal would continue, and the 30,000 Japanese troops that had been infiltrated would not get enough supplies.

Yamamoto was therefore gratified when Army and Navy planners in Imperial Headquarters finally agreed in early November to go all-out. From henceforth fancy-Dan infiltration tactics by the troops would be dropped. An entire field army would mount a powerhouse drive from base areas in northern Guadalcanal toward the American perimeter around Henderson Field with 60,000 infantry. Nearly 30,000 more men, 300 artillery pieces, and 30,000 tons of supplies would have to reach the island by mid-December, the time tentatively set for the offensive. To ferry and supply the army would require 150 round trips by transports or 800 by destroyers, "a giant problem in logistics," as Yamamoto recognized.

On November 8 Yamamoto issued his orders. Eleven transports would carry the 38th "Hiroshima" Division to Guadalcanal. Vice Admiral Kondo's surface fleet would operate in support 150 miles north of the island, backed up by the air groups of *Junyo* and *Hiyo.** But the two converted liners would not strike Henderson Field or approach closer than 150 miles to the troublesome "unsinkable flattop." Instead, the Base Air Force at Rabaul would fly softening-up raids, after which the battleships *Hiei* and *Kirishima* would race in at night to smother the field with 14-inch bombardment projectiles. The transports would steam in unmolested the next day to unload.

* *Shokaku* and *Zuiho* had gone to Japan for repairs; *Zuikaku* had returned home to replenish her air group.

Yamamoto's main opponent now was Vice Admiral Bill Halsey, who had taken over as Southwest Pacific Commander just before the Santa Cruz battle. When Halsey arrived back in Nouméa, New Caledonia, on November 9 after a short visit to Guadalcanal, he found that Nimitz's communications intelligence already had unraveled much of Yamamoto's plan. Also, photos and other intelligence data clearly indicated that a big enemy push was imminent. Halsey would have to send everything to sea, including damaged *Enterprise*, if he would stop it.

Working in Nouméa's anchorage to restore the Big E's mangled innards were 59 men from repair ship *Vulcan* and an entire Seabee work battalion. The *Vulcan's* repair officer had estimated three to four weeks to make her combat worthy; now on November 11, with the work about a week along, Halsey was ordering her to sortie with battleships *Washington* and *South Dakota*. Once under way, Captain Hardison refused to let his crew test the supposedly repaired forward elevator. Should it jam in the "down" position his ship could not launch planes. With it up the Big E could launch normally and strike planes above and below with her Number 2 and 3 elevators.

As it turned out, the main chore of stopping Yamamoto's projected battleship bombardment—which might indeed have crippled Henderson Field—fell not upon the *Enterprise*, which could not reach the Guadalcanal area in time, but to a small American cruiser force under Rear Admiral Daniel J. Callaghan. In a terrific night battle the force led by heavy cruiser *San Francisco* stopped the *Hiei* and *Kirishima* from making a firing run on the field at the cost of antiaircraft light cruisers *Atlanta* and *Juneau* sunk, together with four destroyers. *San Francisco* was badly damaged and Admiral Callaghan killed. "Long lance" torpedoes from the Japanese destroyers caused most of the hurt. But Japanese destroyers *Akatsuki* and *Yudachi* also went down, and daybreak found battleship *Hiei*, with steering engines wrecked from some of 85 shell hits, crawling slowly and erratically north of Savo Island off Guadalcanal's east coast, screened by three destroyers. If ever a capital ship was a sitting duck for aircraft, *Hiei* was it!

This same dawn had found carrier *Enterprise* some 280 miles from Henderson Field. Wary of encountering *Hiyo* and *Junyo,* which he knew were at sea, Admiral Kinkaid, still TF 16's commander, launched at first light a 200-mile search. He had no inkling as to the outcome of the vicious night surface action, but in an inspired decision he dispatched eight torpedo-armed Avengers to Guadalcanal. Flight leader Lieutenant Al "Scoofer" Coffin had orders to land at Henderson Field and report to the commanding officer, Bridgadier General Louis Woods.

Arriving near the island at 11:00 A.M., Coffin's TBFs swept wide to the east of Savo Island and in so doing spotted *Hiei* crawling painfully below. Coffin also identified some planes on the horizon as Zeros that most probably were escorting Kates or Vals from *Hiyo* or *Junyo*. Climbing hard to gain altitude for a high-speed run-in, Coffin split his squadron into two four-plane sections to "anvil" the ship. Then from both bows the Avengers dove, running up air speed to 250 knots as the *Hiei* began a slow turn and commenced firing what AA weapons she had left. At Coffin's four-plane flight coming in from port, she ponderously swung her forward main turrets and disgorged four 14-inch shells that whished past to explode miles astern in an even row.

At 150 feet all eight pilots leveled off and throttled back, letting their air-speed indicators sink back toward 180 knots, the maximum that the tender Mark 13s could take. Jiggering sticks and rudders to keep the *Hiei* aligned in their hooded sights, the pilots steadied and at a thousand yards and 170 knots released their fish, feeling their planes billow upward when relieved of their burdens. Then they nosed down to skim the water below the level of depression of the AA, banking sharply when close to fly down the *Hiei*'s 600-foot side. The backward-riding gunners agreed afterward that three columns of water shot up from the ship, one to port and two to starboard. Three more hits on the *Hiei*? Probably not really, though the column at the stern carried up wreckage and forced the *Hiei* to circle aimlessly, steering now completely gone.

For the rest of the day a shuttle of planes bombed and launched torpedoes at *Hiei*. Dauntlesses blew off chunks from her superstructure, starting raging fires. Lieutenant Henry H. "Swede" Larsen of *Hornet*'s old Torpedo 8, now flying from Guadalcanal, attacked with three of his own and two Marine pilots, claiming a torpedo hit amidships. Coffin attacked again and claimed three more. Most of these, perhaps all, must have been prematures or duds, for the Japanese say that only three torpedoes exploded all day. Nevertheless, by dusk *Hiei* clearly was finished; her fires were uncontrollable and 450 of her crew lay dead, including Captain Suzuki. After dark the survivors opened her seacocks and boarded the faithful escorting destroyers that had suffered nothing worse than strafings from Wildcats.

American planes finally had disposed of their first enemy battleship, though by no means gloriously and only with the aid of surface gunfire. This was no fault of the Marine and *Enterprise* airmen. Had their Dauntlesses and Avengers been equipped with Japanese 550-pound delay-fuse bombs and torpedoes with reliable Japanese contact exploders, they would have finished off *Hiei* about as expeditiously as their rivals had disposed of the *Repulse* and *Prince of Wales* on the third day of war.

Though his operation had gone awry, Admiral Yamamoto's new strategy can hardly be faulted to this point. It made sense to knock out Henderson Field with battleships and then to follow up with the reinforcement landing. But the bombardment had failed, and so had Kondo's efforts to save *Hiei*. Yamamoto might be pardoned for assuming that his codes were secure and that the Americans had not learned of the plan in advance, but he cannot be pardoned for continuing an operation that was clearly failing. But this he did by allowing Rear Admiral Raizo Tanaka to continue toward Guadalcanal with the 11 troop-laden transports carrying the Hiroshima Division on the afternoon of November 13. Tanaka was better attuned to reality; he had smelled trouble from the beginning. But orders were orders, and he carried them through with his customary tenacity.

For Tanaka to reach Guadalcanal safely Henderson Field still had to be neutralized. Told by Admiral Kondo to accomplish this that night (November 13–14) was Vice Admiral Gunichi Mikawa. Mikawa took two heavy cruisers, a light cruiser, and four destroyers and bombarded Henderson Field shortly after midnight. The force failed to hit the bomber strip and did surprisingly little damage to the Wildcats along their fighter runway, even though it expended almost a thousand shells. Only two F4Fs had to be written off, though 15 more were holed by fragments. Nor could Mikawa get far enough away by morning to escape retribution. Daybreak found him only 140 miles northwest of Guadalcanal, close enough to receive at 8:00 A.M. a most unwelcome visit from six Avengers and seven Dauntlesses from Henderson Field. The Avengers, flown by three Marine and three Navy pilots, "anviled" heavy cruiser *Kinugasa* and claimed four torpedo hits. One or more must have exploded against her hull because she began to list and to burn fiercely though still making way.

In the meantime, the *Enterprise* once more had gotten into the act. At dawn Admiral Kinkaid had again ordered a reconnaissance, and this time he struck pay dirt. Two search planes found Mikawa's cruisers just as a strike of 17 Dauntlesses was leaving the deck. The two search pilots dove at 9:15 A.M. on damaged *Kinugasa* and registered two hits. Their 500-pounders restarted fires that ultimately doomed the ship. At 9:50 A.M. Lieutenant Commander Bucky Lee arrived with the 17 Dauntlesses. Passing up the foundering *Kinugasa,* Lee sent five SBDs after the heavy cruisers in the group, seven others after the light cruisers, and himself led five planes in a search for possible enemy carriers to the north. Finding none, he returned and dove on light cruiser *Isuzu.* One bomb opened the ship's engine and firerooms but failed to sink her, and another of Lee's pilots near missed heavy cruiser *Chokai* to inflict light damage. On returning south to land on Henderson Field, the pilots watched *Kinugasa* roll onto her beams ends, tilt up, and sink. Bubbles of air, debris, oil, and smoke rose from her grave until the planes flew out of sight.

Though he had not so intended, Mikawa's cruiser force had effectively acted through most of the morning to decoy both Henderson Field and *Enterprise* planes, luring them from Admiral Tanaka's transports that by noon were just north of New Georgia Island and within easy range of Henderson Field. Tanaka, who had left the Shortlands at 1:30 P.M. the day before, had begun to hope that he would not be molested. As Commander Tadashi Yamamoto, the skipper of destroyer *Hayashio,* recalled later for an American questioner, "We were very happy, for we thought that . . . [Mikawa's] bombardment had succeeded in destroying your planes the night before."

That the commander (who was no relation to Admiral Yamamoto) had little reason to be happy became clear at 11:50 A.M. when a mixed bag of *Enterprise* and Marine planes from Guadalcanal showed up and dove. Seventeen more followed at 12:45, plunging from 12,000 feet and blasting one of the transports in two. Some four-engine B-17 Flying Fortresses from Espiritu Santo appeared next, dropped in ponderous formation, and got at least one hit. Their rear gunners gave some defending Zeros from either *Hiyo* and *Junyo* or Buka a bad time, claiming six. A few minutes later "Scoofer" Coffin used up the last seven torpedoes on Guadalcanal in a well-executed attack that sank transports *Canberra Maru* and *Niagara Maru,* ships that previously had suffered bomb damage.

By late afternoon just four transports were left of the original 11. One had turned back; all of the others had sunk, the escorting destroyers rescuing about half of their embarked troops. The Zeros, both these from the carriers and from Buka, had failed miserably to protect their charges. They had effectively intercepted only one flight of Dauntlesses, seven SBDs from Bombing 10 led by Commander Jim Thomas, shooting down three and damaging others. Navy-Marine losses for the day totaled six Dauntlesses and two Wildcats. Japanese losses included six *Junyo* Zeros and three pilots.

Carrier *Enterprise* had contributed mightily to what had been Japan's worst day of the war, excepting only Midway. Save for 18 Wildcats for CAP she had sent against the enemy every plane aboard before racing south at 2:00 P.M. into a protective weather front. For the next several days her Air Group 10 was destined to "enjoy" the mud and malaria of Guadalcanal's Henderson Field. *Enterprise*'s work on November 14 had shown Admirals Halsey and Nimitz how greatly the air punch of a land base could be enhanced by a carrier able to feed in fresh planes and air crews.

The destruction of Yamamoto's convoy totalling 77,608 tons of shipping, together with about half of the troops of the Hiroshima Division, ended whatever chance the Japanese might have had to regain Guadalcanal. *Enterprise*'s escorts, battleships *Washington* and *South Dakota,* underscored the American triumph by sinking on the night of November 14–15 *Hiei*'s sister battleship *Kirishima* in another wild gunnery action. Three days of naval combat, between November 13 and 15, rightly named the Battle of Guadalcanal, had been decisive. For once a rough and ready Halsey comment told a simple truth: "We've got the bastards licked!"

It took until mid-December, however, for the lesson of the battle to register fully in both Tokyo and at Rabaul. There was, as one participating Japanese naval officer recalls, ". . . bitter discussion in both the central and local commands on the disposition of Guadalcanal." At year's end Imperial Headquarters finally bit the bullet, and on January 4, 1943—

fortunately by courier and not by radio—Rabaul received the word to withdraw all surviving Japanese troops on Guadalcanal. Evacuation began on February 1, and in just three runs Japanese destroyers pulled out without loss the 11,000 survivors of more than 30,000 that had landed.

The end of the Guadalcanal campaign in February 1943 brought to a close the opening phase of World War II. The same month saw American and British forces driving into Tunisia to clear North Africa. In Russia the last remnants of Hitler's 6th Army surrendered to conclude the Fuehrer's disastrous Stalingrad campaign, surely the decisive engagement of World War II. President Roosevelt called this period "the turning point," and Prime Minister Winston Churchill, exercising his inimitable ability to turn a phrase, called it "the end of the beginning."

In his heart of hearts Admiral Yamamoto probably would have agreed. To his old friend and Naval Academy classmate, Admiral Mitsumi Shimizu, the commander of Japan's submarine forces, he wrote, "Guadalcanal was a very fierce battle. I do not know what to do next. . . . At this moment I would like to borrow some knowledge from a wise man."

15. New Georgia and Points North

As intended, the American seizure of Guadalcanal had wrested the strategic initiative from Yamamoto and the Tokyo high command. It was highly desirable for the U. S. Navy to retain that initiative by launching more attacks and keeping the Japanese off balance. But where could the most damaging blow be struck without overtaxing still limited resources of ships, supplies, planes, and men?

One possibility was to stand pat in the South Pacific, mounting an attack from Pearl Harbor westward across the Central Pacific. This would amount to updating and reactivating the prewar War Plan Orange. The Marshall Islands might be taken first, followed by an atoll-to-atoll advance to the Philippines and the China coast. From there, Japan's oil supply from the refineries of Borneo, Indonesia, and Burma could be cut and an oil embargo reimposed by force. The days remaining of Japanese martial glory then would be numbered by the barrels of Japan's oil reserves.

This "everything in the Central Pacific" option was very attractive. An attack in this theater only would confer many advantages. However, there is no evidence that either Admiral King in Washington or Admiral Nimitz at Pearl Harbor even considered halting the South Pacific advance after Guadalcanal. The clinching reason was the lack of available carrier air strength. New fleet carriers to supplement the *Enterprise* and *Saratoga* would not be available until mid-1943. A Central Pacific offensive demanded at the very least parity with Japan in carrier strength—and even this optimistic calculation assumed that planes from escort carriers would support the landings, escort convoys, and ferry replacement aircraft for the big flattops. But a South Pacific attack would not require extensive use of carrier air. Most landings either in New Guinea or in the Upper Solomons could be covered by planes from land bases, a thing impossible in the Central Pacific, where targets were out of reach of any planes other than long-range Army B-24s equipped with so-called "Tokyo tanks."

The U. S. Joint Chiefs of Staff in Washington envisaged for the Pacific a four-pronged offensive. Targets would be the Aleutians, the Central Pacific, the South Pacific (Solomons), and the Southwest Pacific

159

(New Guinea). The theater commanders could begin their offensives immediately, but Nimitz in the Central Pacific would have to wait six months or more for new carriers and air groups, new amphibious ships, and amphibious-trained fighting men.

Wisely, the Joint Chiefs did not tell the various theater commanders just where to attack. In the Aleutians the targets turned out to be Kiska and Attu. Outermost Attu was seized first, in May 1943. Rear Admiral Tom Kinkaid did so expeditiously and with air support only from escort carrier planes. The outflanked Japanese at Kiska, closer to the Alaska mainland, then withdrew in July 1943 to end the campaign.

In the South and Southwest Pacific Admiral Bull Halsey as Sopac commander and General MacArthur agreed to a joint plan of attack code-named "Elkton." Its purpose was to neutralize Rabaul and put Mac-Arthur's Sixth Army in position to leap-frog along the northern New Guinea coast toward the Philippines. MacArthur would take the small ports of Lae and Salamaua on the Huon Gulf first. Their fall would flank Rabaul and Japanese bases on New Britain Island and set the stage for an advance farther west. In the meantime, Admiral Halsey would strike northwest up the Solomons chain in quest of airfield sites from which to bring Fortress Rabaul under aerial siege with short-range fighters and dive bombers. When finally brought under intensive, daily, air bombing Rabaul's naval base and four active airfields would quickly become useless.

Any staff officer with a pair of dividers could see that Bougainville Island had to be Halsey's goal. Airfields in central Bougainville—say, at Empress Augusta Bay—would be 200 miles from Rabaul's Simpson Harbor, within range of a Dauntless. But New Georgia covered Bougainville and would have to be taken first, hopefully in the spring of 1943.

Mountainous, 45-mile-long New Georgia already contained an airstrip cleared by the Japanese from a coconut plantation at Munda Point. They also had built another at Vila-Stanmore Plantation on nearby Kolombangara Island across the Kula Gulf from New Georgia's north shore. Two more airfields a hundred miles farther northwest at tiny Ballale Island and on Bougainville's southern tip at Kahili completed Japan's chain of airstrips.

Yamamoto and Imperial Headquarters in Toyko also recognized New Georgia's importance and gave it first priority in their defensive plans. Before the evacuation of Guadalcanal the "Tokyo Express"—a shuttle of destroyers—was at work, ferrying in the first of about 7,000 men to defend New Georgia and a cluster of adjacent islets. More, eventually 10,000 in all, were arriving at Kolombangara. But with four Army divisions and a Marine division on hand and available for use, Halsey could match these numbers twice or thrice over.

Nevertheless, the New Georgia operation was inordinately slow in getting started. From a desired date of April 1 the New Georgia landings slipped to the end of June 1943. MacArthur's attack on Lae and Salamaua also fell behind schedule. The net effect was to give Yamamoto and the Japanese command at Rabaul a respite of many weeks.

Even so, Yamamoto did not take advantage of Halsey's and Mac-Arthur's delay in the most effective way. This would have been to use carriers *Zuikaku, Junyo, Hiyo,* and *Zuiho* to strike at Kelly Turner's thin-sided transports anchored at their New Hebrides and New Caledonia bases. Instead, he ordered his carrier planes to Rabaul. From thence he planned to attack Halsey's and MacArthur's forward bases (where few big ships were) in a series of raids he grandiloquently termed his "I" Operation. An assemblage of 96 Zeros, 65 Vals, and a few Kates would join Admiral Kusaka's Base Air Force at Rabaul in striking first at Guadalcanal, staging through Solomons airfields, and then at three airfield-port complexes in New Guinea.

"I" Operation began with a huge raid on Guadalcanal and Tulagi on April 7, 1943. The attackers inflicted only minor damage considering the scale of the effort, sinking a destroyer, a tanker, a corvette, and two medium cargo ships. About 25 Allied fighters fell to Yamamoto's Zeros in exchange for 39 Japanese losses.

The significance of the strikes lay not in what was actually achieved but in what Yamamoto and Base Air Force commander Kusaka believed that they had accomplished—namely, the destruction of 175 planes, a cruiser, two destroyers, and no fewer than 25 transports. The loss of transports seemed to Yamamoto and Kusaka especially significant. Believing the MacArthur–Halsey "Elkton" attack team to be short of troop lift, they ended the "I" Operation after this single punch. Yamamoto's Combined Fleet planes returned to their carriers.

To inspire his "I" Operation attackers and to improve what in his opinion was a less than satisfactory state of morale and interstaff co-operation at Rabaul, Yamamoto had flown down to Rabaul from Truk shortly before the strike on April 7. Service cap held high over his head in a characteristic gesture, he had stood in the early dawn watching his fliers take off for Guadalcanal. In the next few days he attended a series of conferences between his Combined Fleet staff officers and those of Admiral Kusaka's Base Air Force staff group. This done, he intended to inspect the new airfields at Bougainville's southern tip.

His flight from Rabaul to southern Bougainville did not seem particularly dangerous. It was being flown daily by transport planes without incident. So it was without much concern that Yamamoto finished his conferences while his aides using the Japanese Navy's high-security code, the one the Americans called JN25, set up his Solomons inspection tour. Within hours after Yamamoto's precise-to-the-minute itinerary had been radioed to subordinate commands Admiral Nimitz had the news from intercepts made at Pearl Harbor. The same information came in via the Aleutians to Navy headquarters in Washington. It seemed that the admiral would leave Rabaul at exactly 6:00 A.M. local time, April 18, 1943, his destination being the Ballale airstrip a few miles off Bougainville's southern-most point.

When Captain E. T. Layton, Fleet Intelligence Officer, told Admiral Nimitz of the Yamamoto itinerary, the Texas-born fleet commander had some terse questions: Could Yamamoto be replaced as Japan's supreme Navy commander by a better man? Answer: No. Would his loss be a shattering blow to the morale of the Japanese Navy and Japan's public? Yes. Then shoot him down. In Washington, D.C., Secretary of the Navy Frank Knox asked similar questions and got similar answers. Curiously, neither in Washington nor at Pearl Harbor did anyone seem to have been greatly concerned about a key point: Would shooting down Yamamoto reveal to the Japanese that their naval code had been compromised? Nor was the easy assumption questioned that Yamamoto was Japan's best possible fleet commander, and this despite his obvious lack of success in planning operations from Midway on.

Upon receiving the Yamamoto assignment, Halsey's staff bucked the task to Rear Admiral Marc Mitscher, ex-commander of the *Hornet*. Mitscher's job now was Commander Air, Solomons—Com Airsols for short. He immediately rallied his air officers at his Guadalcanal bunker to confer on how to "get Yamamoto." After a long conference Mitscher accepted the obvious course: Shoot down the admiral's plane where it made landfall at the Bougainville coast en route to Ballale airfield. The actual triggermen would have to be Army pilots, not Navy or Marine. The brute of an F4U Corsair fighter now in use would have been fine for the job except for a lack of range. Only the Army's twin-engine P-38 Lightning fighters of the 339th Squadron could make it when fitted with extra-large drop tanks rigged alongside either Allison engine. Young Major John Mitchell, C. O. of the 339th Fighter Squadron, would command the mission. He would personally lead a 14-plane escort flying cover for four "killer" planes that would actually destroy Yamamoto's plane (expected to be a Betty bomber). An aggressive young pilot would lead the four "shooters," Captain Thomas G. Lanphier. Flying wing on Lanphier would be Lieutenant Rex Barber, who had tried solo to intercept the Pearl Harbor attackers in an obsolescent P-36.

In spite of the skill of Mitchell and his pilots, the chances of inter-cepting Yamamoto's plane did not look bright. A slight navigational error or a hundred other contingencies could cause the P-38s to miss contact. When the planes left Guadalcanal's steel-planked fighter strip on the early morning of the 18th, prospects dimmed further. A Lightning from Lan-phier's shooter section blew a tire on a broken fragment of Marston matting and veered off the runway. A few minutes later another of the shooters pulled alongside Mitchell, indicating by sign language that his 310-gallon drop tanks would not feed fuel. Without using his radio Mitchell signaled the pilot to turn back and waved two of the escort group to close up on Lanphier and Barber. Now 16 Lightnings flew a steady 200 mph on an arcing, 250-mile course toward the intercept point just south of Bougainville's Empress Augusta Bay. To avoid radar in the Japanese-held Upper Solomons they hugged the water, the twin props of the fighters leaving a broad wake behind the formation on the dead-calm, indigo sea.

The planes had just begun their climb to attack altitude from a checkpoint 40 miles off Empress Augusta Bay when keen-eyed Lieutenant Doug Canning of the escort group suddenly broke radio silence. "Bogies," he called, "eleven o'clock." Then softly: "High." Mitchell looked and counted them off, six Zeros of a fighter escort and—a surprise—two Bettys, not one. No way of telling which Betty held Yamamoto; both would have to go down. The time was 9:34 A.M., April 18, 1943.

By his own schedule, Yamamoto was 16 minutes early. But not by the American. Mitscher's staff at Guadalcanal had anticipated that the dead-calm weather would leave the Bettys without the normal head wind to slow them up. Yamamoto rode the lead plane, dressed in informal khaki, but with white gloves and his sword between his knees. He had taken the co-pilot seat and was watching Bougainville's 10,000-foot spine of peaks come into view. Three staff officers, all pilots, rode in the rear of his plane, Betty No. 323 of the 705th Air Group. In the second Betty close behind Rear Admiral Matome Ugaki, Yamamoto's chief of staff, and several other officers followed their commander-in-chief. The pilots of the new planes, whose brown-green camouflaged paint shimmered in a bright sun as if waxed, were veteran warrant officers Hayashi and Kotani. Yamamoto's pilot, Hayashi, was formation navigator. Above and behind the Bettys the Zero escorts in two Vs of three cruised watchfully.

What happened next was brief, deadly, and to this day shrouded with ambiguities. When Lanphier and Barber closed the formation, the Betty pilots saw the big Lightnings coming. Hayashi instantly dove Yamamoto's plane, turning inland low over the jungle to evade the Americans, or, failing that, to keep them from firing under-the-belly shots from their .50-caliber and 20-mm. guns. Ugaki's pilot dove also but flew ahead briefly before banking seaward. Spurred by Mitchell's radio call to Lanphier, "All right, Tom. Go get him. He's all yours," the four shooters dove. Soon the rear pair lagged as Lieutenant Besby Holmes violently rocked his Lightning, trying to shake off a sticky wing tank. As his wingman, Lieutenant Ray Hine, covered him, he broke off the attack and paralleled the coastline still rocking his P-38. Lanphier, followed by Barber, closed the bombers. Zeros dove at them, forcing Lanphier to pull up vertically through the fighters, guns blazing. Then he rolled upside down, looking frantically for the Bettys. Barber pressed ahead, overshot the bombers, and as he banked to lose speed he lost sight of them. He did not see the left and right break of the Yamamoto and Ugaki planes. Spotting the left-hand plane—Yamamoto's probably—he again closed, fired, knocked pieces from its tail and overshot once more as its pilot banked away in an almost stalling turn. Tracers flashed past Barber's head as the Zero escort closed, forcing him to turn toward the sea.

Meanwhile Lanphier, high above, caught a flitting shadow just above the jungle that he rightly took for a Betty. He dove, riddled the plane ("I was no gunner, but I did know enough to fly behind a guy and spray him"), then watched as a wing broke off and a blazing plane hit the trees. High above with his escort section Mitchell saw the smoke of this kill rise up.

This was Yamamoto's plane. As it hit, the admiral was catapulted from the co-pilot seat and, still clutching his sword with his white gloves, was slammed to the jungle floor, dead. Flames spreading from the plane burned his body, but the features were quite recognizable.

From his Betty a horrified Admiral Ugaki had seen Yamamoto's plane drop into the trees and burn. His own plane had not long to live, either. As it passed over the ocean shore Barber, who had turned that way too, attacked, splattering the interior of the machine with bullets. Men crumpled about Ugaki. Escorting Zeros then dove at Barber's Lightning, but Besby Holmes, free at last of his recalcitrant tank, dove in with Hine, shooting down two Zeros and probably a third. Barber continued his attack, swerving off only a few feet away as the Betty broke in two just aft of the wing, stalled, and slapped into the ocean close offshore.

Rather incredibly Ugaki, one other staff officer, and pilot Kotani survived the crash. Of the Lightnings, Ray Hine's plane had disappeared, probably the victim of a sharpshooting Zero pilot. No one saw Hine crash, but he did not return. The rest of the Lightnings made it back.

The raucous celebration that followed at Guadalcanal contrasted vividly with the gloom that now descended on Rabaul. After a search had found Yamamoto's wrecked plane, the admiral's remains were reverently collected, cremated with sad ceremony, and dispatched to Japan. A grieving Admiral Ugaki pronounced the Navy's epitaph on its fallen leader: "To us Isoroku Yamamoto was a god [Kami]."

He was so treated during the state funeral held June 5, 1943, in Tokyo. A million Japanese watched as his funerary urn was borne in pomp past the Imperial Palace grounds to the Tamabuchi cemetery. The urn was placed beside that other great naval hero, Admiral Togo, under whom Yamamoto had served as a young officer. Only 12 other Japanese, including Togo, had been so honored with a state funeral.

Fortunately for the planners of his death, another Japanese reaction failed to win acceptance at Imperial Navy headquarters. Several staff officers sent urgent messages from Truk and Rabaul insisting that the attack on the Bettys had been carefully planned and that code JN25 must have been compromised. But Tokyo communications experts preferred to believe that the untimely arrival of the P-38s off Bougainville must have been a coincidence. Code JN25 was unbreakable, they asserted.

When deciphered, these Japanese exchanges over code security created a considerable uproar in American naval-intelligence circles. So did the jolting discovery that it had become fashionable in the South Pacific to pass rumors that codebreaking had triggered the Yamamoto mission. When Mitchell, Lanphier, Barber, and Holmes were summoned to Nouméa, they were lectured sternly on the necessity of keeping their mouths shut, congratulated, and forthwith remanded to stateside duty—for the duration in the case of Mitchell and Lanphier. However, the security uproar soon died down at least in the South Pacific. Everyone was too busy with the New Georgia attack to prolong the concern.

The New Georgia attack plan called for a preliminary American lodgment on Rendova, a small island east and within artillery range of the Munda airstrip. This done, regimental combat teams from the 43rd and 38th Divisions would cross to New Georgia, seize a beachhead, and take Munda. MacArthur's simultaneous offensive in New Guinea—the other half of Operation "Elkton"—would hopefully draw away Rabaul's bombers, seen as the only serious threat to the landing. Nothing happened on D-day to upset the optimists on Halsey's staff, though as expected Kusaka did his best to punish the venture from the air. Transport *McCawley,* hit by a torpedo, was the only serious naval loss. In the days and weeks that followed, Kusaka's Base Air Force continued to attack the American beachhead with raids that mostly were merely annoying. More serious was the failure of U. S. ground forces under Major General John H. Hester to overrun quickly the Munda Point area so that Seabees could build two air bases. As Halsey later summarized it: "Our original plan called for 15,000 men to wipe out 9,000 Japs on New Georgia; by the time the island was secured, we had sent in more than 50,000. When I look back on Elkton the smoke of charred reputations still makes me cough."

If the road to Tokyo via the Solomons Islands was to be a succession of New Georgias, the Japanese would have good reason to believe that the Americans might either tire of war and make peace or perhaps become Japanese citizens. The next island up the chain was Kolombangara, and its garrison, reinforced by New Georgia evacuees, therefore sharpened its bayonets and prepared to make Halsey's men pay dearly in another prolonged campaign.

But the Kolombangara Japanese were not attacked; they were bypassed. Halsey's men landed on Vella Lavella Island about halfway between New Georgia and Bougainville and took it at small cost. The large Japanese 17th Army Kolombangara garrison, stranded and useless, had to be evacuated by barge and destroyer. MacArthur adopted a similar strategy on New Guinea by skipping past Lae to land at Salamaua. Then he struck successively along the north coastline, always landing to the rear of the next Japanese concentration. By mid-October of 1943 MacArthur's staff was preparing to land at Saidor, deep in the Japanese rear; Halsey's was readying a landing on Bougainville, not in the heavily defended southern portion but at Empress Augusta Bay halfway up the western coast where only a handful of defenders guarded the landing beaches.

Throughout the entire period from February to October 1943 Halsey had operated his carriers defensively, mostly keeping them close to Nouméa. His supercaution seemed out of character to those who remembered the "Wild Bill" of 1942. Halsey had reason for his caution. He had only the *Saratoga* and *Enterprise* for much of the time, and the Big E's tender hull condition and questionable watertight integrity due to bomb damage were worrisome. She badly needed a drydocking and a thorough-going overhaul. Halsey also had to be concerned about the possibility of a surprise attack on his bases. Hence, whenever the Japanese carrier force sortied from Truk, as it occasionally did, Halsey would order the *Saratoga* to weigh anchor at once from Nouméa and *Enterprise* from Espiritu Santo.

Help from an unexpected quarter finally allowed the Big E to get her drydocking and overhaul. Much concerned over the loss of the *Hornet* at Santa Cruz, Admiral Sir Dudley Pound, Britain's First Sea Lord, had re-quested information concerning American naval dispositions in the Pacific and noted that the lack of fleet carriers raised ". . . issues of gravest im-portance concerning the ultimate command of the sea." The message infuriated Admiral King, a man whom no intimate ever accused of being pro-British, but it had the useful result of initiating negotiations that cul-minated in H. M. S. *Victorious* being sent to Halsey's command. Although the British flattop could carry fewer planes than the *Enterprise*—45 fighters and torpedo bombers plus spares—she was a tough ship with a war-wise crew. Her embarked squadrons were experienced; fighters from her 882 Squadron had shot down several Vichy French rivals during the North African invasion.

Before the *Victorious* could sail, however, she had first to re-equip with planes entirely of American manufacture. Only her F4F squadron (Martlets in British nomenclature) could be serviced from U. S. aircraft-parts stores and that incompletely due to differences in radio, oxygen, and other avionic equipment. She had to disembark her Fulmar fighters and Albacore torpedo planes. What with receiving new planes and training her pilots on them, it was March 1943 before Captain L. D. Mackintosh, R.N., could get his ship via Norfolk and Panama to Pearl Harbor, and it was May 17, 1943, before he conned the *Victorious* into the Great Road at Nouméa. That same day *Enterprise* entered Drydock No. 2 at Pearl Harbor to begin the first phase of her upkeep.

Almost before Captain Mackintosh and his crew had a chance to admire the greenness of New Caledonia's mountains, they sortied again the next day as part of Task Force 14 under Rear Admiral D. C. Ramsey. The British carrier followed the *Saratoga* as formation guide, and fast battleships *North Carolina, Massachusetts,* and *Indiana,* with destroyers and AA cruiser *San Juan* formed a protective screen. To her British pilots *Victorious* was "Orange Base" in voice radio code, a jargon they had mastered in Pearl Harbor exercises. In a last-minute message Admiral Ramsey had admonished them and the *Sara* pilots: "Do not let fear of breaking radio silence permit the force to be surprised due to lack of in-formation." The mission was a simple "Seek out and destroy enemy forces." Japan's carriers had put to sea from Truk, and Ramsey's flattops were to go to "Point George" in the Coral Sea southward of Guadalcanal to await developments.

The two carriers ran west to their assigned position, alternating in flying fighters, antisubmarine, and search patrols. The first day *Saratoga* lost a TBF on takeoff, and two days later a *Victorious* fighter went overside. The air crews were rescued by plane guard destroyers. On May 22 fleet course was set for return to Nouméa, and Admiral Ramsey took the opportunity to schedule exercises during which the *Victorious* air group launched a practice strike at their own carrier as battleships *Indiana* and *North Carolina* covered on either flank. On the 24th the British carrier entered the Bulari Passage to the Great Road, but the *Saratoga* stayed out three more days. Though the enemy had not shown his hand, the emergency sortie was an unqualified success; the *Sara* and *Victorious* had worked well together. In mutual visits that now followed at Nouméa, British visitors quickly discovered the location of *Saratoga*'s "Gedunk" (ice-cream parlor), and the Americans found—at least the officers—that the British carrier was not "dry." Both discoveries were reported to be pleasant.

After a short training cruise in mid-June, during which the two carriers landed each other's planes, Admiral Ramsey's Task Force 14 became Support Group C of TF 36 for the New Georgia operation. Its role was basically defensive, to loiter southward of the Upper Solomons at "Point Dog," a spot suitable for intercepting Japan's carriers should they try to intervene. This was out of carrier-plane radius of New Georgia and even of Guadalcanal. Several times Admiral Ramsey received orders to sweep northward, but each time Halsey stopped him 500 miles or more from the reported location of the enemy.

That the carriers were made, in Admiral George C. Dyer's words, the "reluctant dragons" of the New Georgia assault was because Halsey's staff was determined to keep them out of range of Betty torpedo planes from Rabaul. The main interest in what otherwise was almost a peacetime cruise was Admiral Ramsey's experiment in shuffling the air groups of the carriers. He decided to try out a tactic many had recommended and to concentrate fighters on the *Victorious* and bombers and torpedo planes on the *Saratoga*. In consequence 16 Tarpons (British TBFs) joined Dauntlesses and Avengers on *Saratoga* for searches, practice strikes, and inner and outer air patrols, while 24 Wildcats joined 38 Martlets in flying CAP from the *Victorious*. How this would have worked in combat Ramsey had no opportunity to find out.

The "Vic," as her crew called the *Victorious*, had one deficiency that Captain Mackintosh could do little about; this was her wretched habitability in tropical waters. Her steel flight deck and box-type, fully enclosed armored hangar soaked up and trapped the heat and made her a near furnace below decks. When after having steamed over 12,000 miles in 28 days at sea the *Victorious* returned with the *Saratoga* to Nouméa, her crew had few regrets. It had fewer still when in a few days the "Vic" was detached to return to Pearl Harbor on the first leg of a journey home. Only the "tigers" aboard had regretted the lack of action.

When the *Victorious* entered Pearl Harbor on August 12, 1943, the British sailors noted a ship in harbor that they had seen earlier at Norfolk. This was the brand-new U. S. S. *Essex*, namesake of her class of 27,500-ton flattops. The first of the war-built carriers had joined the Pacific Fleet.

16.   The New Fast Carriers

The arrival of the *Essex* in Pearl Harbor on May 31, 1943, had been a great relief to Admiral Nimitz. Now he would have something better than baby flattops for his Central Pacific Fifth Fleet, though it would be some time before *Essex* truly was battleworthy.

In fact, Nimitz was the wartime victim of a mistaken peacetime policy. From 1936 through Pearl Harbor Day the U. S. Navy had given the construction of battleships a higher priority than flattops. The result was that between the commissioning of the *Hornet* on October 20, 1941, and of the *Essex* on the last day of 1942 not a single fleet carrier had been completed. Also, after the first three ships successors to the *Essex* would follow slowly. None of the next four could possibly reach Nimitz before the winter of 1943–44.

Fortunately for Nimitz, stopgaps for fleet carrier work were nearing readiness. Beginning in 1940 the giant Camden, New Jersey, yard of the New York Shipbuilding Company had received contracts to build 19 identical light cruisers. These were of the 10,000-ton *Columbia* class, of which the Navy intended to commission 30. On January 10, 1942, a surprising message abruptly arrived from the Navy Department: Complete the U. S. S. *Amsterdam* as a fast carrier. Jarred by the blow at Pearl Harbor, the Bureau of Ships had decided to go again the route of converting a gunnery ship into a flattop. Orders for similar conversion of other cruisers building in the yard followed until by July nine had been selected. In the process the ships lost their cruiser names (for cities) in conformity with the usual practice of naming carriers for famous battles or celebrated ships of the old Navy. *Amsterdam* thus became the U. S. S. *Independence,* CV (later CVL) 22.

Completing the *Independence* as a carrier meant not merely slapping a flight deck atop her. Barbettes, ammunition hoists, and other gear required for a six-inch main battery had to be pulled out and heavy bulkheads added athwart the ship to wall off gasoline storage tanks. With a flight deck this made the ship dangerously top-heavy, and so blisters or bulges were added on either side to broaden her beam and improve stability. To offset

169

the weight of the small island built on the starboard side, concrete was poured into the blister installed to port. The ship's knife-edge cruiser bow made it necessary to lop off the flight deck at 544 feet, 50 feet short of the stem. Four ugly-looking square funnels dispersed stack gases on either side of the stern, giving her an appearance somewhat similar to the *Ranger,* which was not too much larger.

When complete the *Independence* displaced about 11,000 tons, was 610 feet overall in length, and with her cruiser engines and boilers could made a speed of 32 knots, only a knot slower than big sister *Essex.* The other eight ships that followed were almost identical.

Just the same, the *Independence* CVLs were makeshifts when compared to the *Essex*-class ships. With a flight deck 854 feet in length and with a hangar 650 feet long, the 27,100-ton *Essex* could normally carry 85 planes; this was double the *Independence*'s top capacity of about 40. Fitted as a flagship, the *Essex* had room to house an admiral, his staff, and the extra communications required by a task force or even a fleet commander. Three hydraulic elevators, one of the deck-edge type mounted amidships, greatly facilitated plane handling and launch, for a plane could take off or land while the deck-edge elevator was down. By contrast the *Independence* had room only for her own captain and had just two centerline lifts. Both ships had bow catapults, the *Essex* two and the *Independence* one.

With her larger displacement the *Essex* was a much better sea boat than the *Independence,* being steadier in a rough sea than any other carrier afloat except the venerable *Saratoga.* Working and living spaces were commodious, and considering the fact that she was a man-o'-war, the *Essex* was virtually a luxury liner when compared to the much more cramped *Independence.* Her armament was heavy. She carried twelve five-inch guns, of which eight were paired in twin mounts fore and aft of the large, starboard-side island. The *Independence,* in contrast, could carry only two, one each on bow and stern. Both ships also mounted many of the efficient 40-mm. Bofors and 20-mm. Oerlikon light AA weapons scattered along catwalks along either side of the length of the flight deck.

Both carrier types shared wartime lessons. Gasoline storage in both the *Essex* and *Independence* employed a built-in inert gas protective system in which CO_2 gas was continuously released into the tanks as avgas was gulped by the engines of the embarked air groups. The menace of blazing hundred-octane fuel that had done in the *Lexington* and *Wasp* was thus greatly reduced. Room was provided everywhere in the new ships for fire-extinguishing equipment, much of it being the foam type that had proved especially effective in smothering gasoline fires in open spaces. Diesel generators and "handy billy" self-powered pumps offered ready means of furnishing water pressure on hoses even if the main power plant failed. Nimitz's recommendations after the Battle of Santa Cruz had evidently been taken to heart in the Bureau of Ships. Men were available in lavish numbers to man hoses or guns as the occasion demanded. *Essex* could accommodate 360 officers and 3,088 enlisted men; *Independence* about 1,569 officers and men.

Total horsepower from an eight-boiler steam plant in both ships worked out to 150,000 shaft horsepower for the *Essex* and 100,000 for the *Independence*. Otherwise the ships were similar, each mounting four drive shafts and four propellers. In the *Essex* steam lines could be cross-connected so that each of the four firerooms could supply power to the turbines. The sort of desperate improvisation attempted by the Black Gang of the late *Hornet* would not be needed in the *Essex* should the ship suffer two or more flooded firerooms.

In fine in the *Essex*-class carriers the United States Navy had ships so well built that some would still be serving more than 30 years later. The *Independence*-class ships proved to be amazingly successful conversions, and, most important, they came into service very quickly, filling a vital need at a crucial time.

As the *Essex*- and *Independence*-class flattops began to commission rapidly in 1943,* a shortage of trained crewmen quickly developed. Sometimes literally hundreds of enlisted men reported aboard direct from "boot" training at Chicago's Great Lakes Naval Training Station on the morning their ship commissioned. Some of the carriers put to sea with 70 percent of the seamen and half of the officers totally without prior sea experience, some having never before been aboard an oceangoing vessel. "Old Salts" from sunken or other ships became pearls beyond price to the new captains and "execs."

This was often unnerving for the older men. All too typical was the experience of Lou Mitnich, an experienced fireman first class, when he was ordered to report to the Camden Yard, where the *Belleau Wood,* third of the *Independence* CVLs, was nearing completion. Expecting some leave after his transfer from heavy cruiser *Tuscaloosa,* he reported to the personnel officer of the yard, but, as he reports:

I rushed in a chit for leave, but the officer, after looking through some papers, said, "You're just the man we are looking for. B division has been waiting weeks for a fireman like you." I retired wearily . . . and prepared to hit the sack. . . . After breakfast [the next morning] I met the chiefs and some of the boys and was ready to get my first glimpse of the *Belleau Wood.* . . . Suddenly somebody yelled, "That's her!" You could have knocked me over with a feather. All the time I had thought the *Belleau Wood* was one of the big *Essex*-class carriers, but there she was, a little ugly flattop and with a starboard list to boot. For a moment I wished I'd joined the Army.

Even the commissioning ceremonies of the new carriers were kept businesslike and brief, so urgent was the need to have them. The commissioning ceremony of the U. S. S. *Princeton,* the second ship of the CVL

* For a list of war-built U. S. carriers and their dates of commissioning, see Appendix.

class, was held on the flight deck at 1:50 P.M. on February 23, 1943. The Philadelphia Navy Yard band played the National Anthem, the new skipper, Captain George R. Henderson, made a brief speech, and Chief Boatswain R. C. Hawk piped his boatswain's mates and set the watch. Dr. Harold W. Dodds, president of Princeton University, added a nice touch by presenting the ship a silver punch bowl, and a representative of the New York Princeton University Club presented a Currier & Ives print of the old gunboat *Princeton,* the new ship's namesake. Key men among the ship's company watching were survivors from the old *Lexington, Yorktown, Wasp,* and *Hornet,* ships whose names would be repeated in the new *Essex* class.

Commissioning did not mean that a new ship was ready for battle— far from it. Repair work to correct construction faults could keep a new carrier alongside a navy-yard pier for precious days or even weeks and sometimes even require drydocking.

Serious trouble turned up on the *Princeton* in the form of leaks in the avgas tanks that for some time defied the best efforts of the Philadelphia Yard experts to isolate and correct them. Not until May 17, 1943, 82 days after commissioning, were the tanks finally pumped free of test fluid and the ship released for remaining shakedown cruises. The *Essex* turned up a "less than satisfactory" ventilation system that vexed even technical specialists from the Bureau of Ships. The ship also had a trash burner that turned out to be a masterpiece of bad design and workmanship. Navy writer Scot Mac Donald has recorded the frustration of Captain Donald B. Duncan, *Essex*'s skipper, over the offending equipment:

Requested to comment on the adequacy and operation of the trash burner . . . , Captain Duncan started off quietly enough. "It is most unsatisfactory," he said. Then he warmed to his subject. "It is doubtful if it could be worse. It is in the very center of the office spaces. There is no satisfactory place for collection of trash waiting to be burned. . . . The heat from the trash burned when it is operating (which is not often because it is usually broken down) is such as to make the surrounding spaces almost untenable. The design of the trash burner is poor. Its construction is worse. The ship had not been in commission a month before it practically fell apart. The brick work fell down, the door fell off, and it suffered other casualties too numerous to mention."

Mac Donald concludes laconically, "The trash burner was redesigned."

Some few carriers had very little trouble. CVL-25, the *Cowpens,* passed from commissioning to battleworthiness in only four months with but a single mishap and that no fault in her construction or design.

Airplanes and new carriers first merged during short day-long cruises in Chesapeake Bay. Hundreds of critical spectators swarmed topside to watch the first landings, heedless of warnings from veteran sailors that snapped arresting cables, pulled tail hooks, or bounding airplanes could be as fatal to bystanders as to plane handlers and pilots. Seldom were the kibitzers disappointed during a day of flight operations, though they quickly learned that mishaps sometimes meant mustering for funerals conducted by the chaplain. The majority of deck crashes were of the "barrier" type, occurring when a plane would miss the arresting wires and pile into a web of rope and cable set up forward of the landing area. Though often fatal to the plane, a barrier crash seldom killed or seriously injured either the pilot or his gunner. Also, more often than not the pilots and air crewmen of planes plunging over the side managed to get out and be rescued. The worst sort of landing accident occurred when a plane leaped the barrier to pile into planes being spotted forward.

Most of the new flattops carried in their air groups the familiar combination of Wildcat, Dauntless, and Avenger aircraft that had become standard at the beginning of the Guadalcanal campaign. A few received new types of planes, designs that hopefully would provide better performance.

VF-9 on the *Essex* and VF-5 on the *Yorktown,* the carrier named for the ship lost at Midway, received Grumman's F6F Hellcat fighter. Designed in part to take into account test data derived from a captured Zero and bearing a superficial resemblance to the F4F Wildcat, the Hellcat was a larger, heavier, faster plane fitted with the new Pratt and Whitney R-2800 Double Wasp engine rated at 2,000 hp. The plane could match the turn rate of its smaller brother (though not the Zero) and had characteristics especially important for carrier work. It was dependable mechanically, had a rugged airframe, a wide, stout landing gear that folded up into the wing, good forward visibility in takeoffs and landings, and docile low-speed handling characteristics. Tests showed that it was easy to maintain and handle on a carrier and that the climb rate and speed derived from its extra power gave it a performance that would enable even a green pilot to deal with a Zero. Armament was six of the reliable .50-caliber machine guns with a much greater ammunition supply than carried in the Wildcat. The range of a Hellcat with belly tank was the greatest of any U. S. carrier-type plane. When carrying a thousand-pound bomb it could double also as a fighter-bomber.

The *Yorktown*'s bomber squadron, VB-6,* was much less fortunate than its fighter outfit. Newly assigned to this squadron in June 1943 was the new Curtiss SB2C Helldiver, soon to be labeled—not lovingly—as the "Big-Tailed Beast." The "Beast" was fast and could carry nearly double the bomb load of the smaller and slower SBD, but it was unstable longitudinally in flight and prone to shed its wings when dived "clean" (without dive brakes opened). In its initial carrier landings aboard the *Yorktown* the "Beast" ran up a formidable tally of tail-hook failures, tail-wheel collapse, and structural damage when landed "hard" on the flight deck. In total disgust Captain J. J. "Jocko" Clark, himself a veteran test pilot, submitted a seven-page list of defects and demanded that the offend-

---

* In 1943 scouting and bombing squadrons were consolidated and given a VB number. VS-6 and VB-6 became just VB-6.

ing machines be replaced with Dauntlesses. This was done after shakedown. Clark also recommended that the entire production program for the Curtiss plane be canceled. This the Bureau of Aeronautics elected not to do, even though it was well aware of the difficult teething problems of the plane. Several plants in the United States and one in Canada were already tooled up for its production. The result was a hasty modification program to strengthen the offending tail wheel along with the plane's structure generally, combined with tinkering with the control system to improve longitudinal control. The *Bunker Hill's* Air Group 17 then drew "the duty" of trying to tame the "Beast."

Gradually, Air Group 17 managed to work out the problems of the SB2C until the plane finally was ruled acceptable for carriers, though marginally so. But it was, nevertheless, mid-1944 before Helldivers were in the fleet in appreciable numbers. Until then the dive-bomber squadrons made use of the latest version of the Dauntless, the SBD-5, despite its lower top speed and lack of folding wings.

Air Group 17 failed completely, however, to qualify the big F4U Corsair fighter for carrier operations. Although this plane had better performance than the Hellcat and the Marines had begun using it early in 1943 from Guadalcanal with success, the first models proved unsuitable for carrier landings. Problems were many, but perhaps the worst was the stiffness of the landing-gear oleo. The plane tended to bounce too high on hitting the flight deck, leading to missed arrestings, barrier crashes, nose-ups, and a decision by Bu Air not to deploy the plane on flattops until the problem had been corrected. Air Group 17 kept Corsairs until the *Bunker Hill* reached Pearl Harbor and then exchanged the Corsair squadron for one flying Hellcats. O. K. for land use, VF-17 and its Corsairs went to Guadalcanal and New Georgia.

The *Bunker Hill's* arrival at Pearl on October 2, 1943, brought the roster of new carriers in the fleet to nine, four CVs and five CVLs. But the build-up through summer had been slow. Not until late July had the *Independence* and then the new *Yorktown* joined the *Essex,* and only as late as August 9 did Admiral Nimitz enjoy a real bonanza when the new CV *Lexington* arrived in company with CVLs *Princeton* and *Belleau Wood* after a fast trip from the Canal Zone. Another month passed before CVLs *Cowpens* and *Monterey* became the seventh and eighth fleet carriers to arrive in 1943. On July 14, however, Admiral Nimitz had felt able to order the battered *Enterprise* to set course for the Strait of Juan de Fuca to undergo a thorough refit at the Bremerton Navy Yard. A new era was about to dawn for U. S. seaborne air power.

In Japan surface-ship construction continued to overshadow that of carriers even after the war's outbreak. Since seven of the huge *Yamato*-class 18-inch gun battleships had been authorized, battleship enthusiasts quite obviously had continued to dominate staff planning sessions.

It took the thunderbolt of Midway to force the Japanese to the realization that the nation must concentrate, immediately, on all-out carrier production. Because of a lag in Japanese carrier construction programs, no fleet carrier would complete in 1943 and only one, the *Taiho*, in 1944. On June 30, 1942, therefore, in Navy Secret Document No. 191, Chief of Staff Nagano authorized 20 new carriers, six of the *Taiho* class and 14 of the *Unyru* class, closely similar to the successful design of the *Hiryu*. The trouble was that only four of the new ships could possibly commission before 1945. By that time, the naval staff knew, the United States was bound to have more than a dozen *Essex*-class ships in service.

The only practical immediate step that Nagano could take was to authorize more conversions. Fast seaplane tenders *Chitose* and *Chiyoda* could quickly be given flight decks and converted into CVLs. Together with the *Ryuho,* already converting, that would give the Combined Fleet three ships similar to the *Zuiho,* enough to form a Third Carrier Division. Three liners—*Argentina Maru, Brazil Maru,* and the former German ship *Scharnhorst*—could be removed from service as transports and converted into CVEs, escort carriers. There was *Shinano,* warship No. 110, the third battleship of the *Yamato* class, that had been laid down with a sister ship, *Kii,* and had been building slowly, as shortages of armor plate and design changes slowed progress. She could be converted into a very large carrier, although the chances of completing her before the end of 1944 were not good. So also could a new heavy cruiser building, *Ibuki,* set to be launched in May 1943. All of these conversions Nagumo eventually authorized.

A final decision, strange and difficult to understand, but indicative of the Naval Staff's desire to have carrier air power quickly, was one that in 1943 removed from service battleships *Ise* and *Hyuga.* Both had their after 14-inch gun turrets removed and replaced with abbreviated flight decks and hangars. Eleven dive bombers could be accommodated and catapulted from the ships. The planes would not come back aboard; rather, they would either ditch or fly to the nearest land base after returning from their missions. Both of these hermaphrodites completed in December 1943.

Counting newly authorized fleet carriers and conversions, the Japanese post-Midway building program came to 33 ships—35 if *Ise* and *Hyuga* be counted.* This was a most impressive number and comparable to American and British building programs. The trouble was that Japan lacked the resources to carry out its program even though construction of all major warships larger than a light cruiser was stopped. In the end Japan managed to acquire in late 1942, 1943, and the first half of 1944 only one fleet carrier, the fine armored-deck *Taiho* of 30,000 tons, perhaps the most advanced flattop completed by any belligerent, and the converted CVLs *Ryuho, Chitose,* and *Chiyoda.* In a like period the United States would commission nine CVLs and ten CVs. What Admiral Yamamoto had feared before the war's outbreak was about to happen. With its much greater

* See Appendix for a list of Japanese carriers projected or built during World War II.

resources the United States was about to overwhelm Japan in a flood of carrier-borne naval air power.

Nevertheless, Japan still enjoyed one significant advantage over the United States. She had a vast network of island air bases scattered through the waters through which the U. S. Navy must pass. If she could get enough planes she had a chance to blunt U. S. offensives with land-based bombers, using these islands as "unsinkable flattops." Combined Fleet Commander Koga could operate in much the same way that Halsey had been exploiting Guadalcanal, using his carriers only to back-stop an island air defense.

This logic was also apparent to Nagano and the Naval General Staff. After careful study the staff concluded that 5,876 planes in operational squadrons was the air strength that the Navy must maintain to hold the island barrier through 1944. For 1945 they calculated that 14,548 planes had to be the Table of Organization strength of the combat squadrons. Since the total of planes built had to exceed greatly the squadron strength, the staff requested on August 11, 1943, that the Navy's technical bureaus must supply 30,200 planes for fiscal year 1944. That meant doubling existing plans that had been based on the estimated maximum number of planes that Japan's industry could build. Somehow, plane production capacity would have to be doubled.*

An even more critical problem was the training of enough flight crews. As a short-term solution two months were lopped from training programs. Training for nonspecialist mechanics was cut to five months, about enough to allow new men to perform first-echelon maintenance. They could pour in gas and oil and change spark plugs and that was about all. Proper maintenance of aircraft would require no fewer than 222,000 ground crew at the end of 1944, far beyond Japan's capacity to train properly.

What Japan's expansion plans really amounted to were to build as many planes and train as many ground and air crews as possible. To achieve maximum plane production it would have been desirable to continue building the proven Zeros, Vals, and Kates with little or no change. But that was not possible, for it would have meant a fatal trade-off of quantity for quality.

Jiro Horikoshi, the designer of the Zero, had realized before hostilities began that his famous warplane soon would become obsolete. As early as September 1939 he began designing a new interceptor fighter, the Mitsubishi J2M "Raiden" (Thunderbolt), a plane that the Americans ultimately were to nickname "Jack." To get the best possible speed and climb Horikoshi selected as a power plant the 1,430-hp Mitsubishi Kasei engine and designed around it a short, rounded, chubby airframe with a closely fitted cowl. He pushed to the limit of the state of the aerodynamic arts to provide a laminar-flow wing to give the plane a top speed of close to 360 mph at 17,000 feet

---

* Actual aircraft production fell far short of these figures. Calendar-year production in 1943 was 7,681 combat and 1,795 training aircraft. Production in 1944 was 10,369 combat and 2,354 training planes.

altitude, a performance only slightly less than the considerably more powerful Grumman Hellcat.

The Raiden got into the air two months ahead of the Hellcat on March 20, 1942, but in contrast to the American fighter was plagued with assorted difficulties. Horikoshi had done his basic design work well, for the plane was stable and flew gracefully, but test pilots complained of distorted vision through its sloping windscreen. They also found that they could not retract the landing gear at speeds above 100 knots. But the main difficulty, never fully solved, was in the severe vibration of the Kasei engine. The Imperial Navy accepted the Raiden for quantity production in October 1942, but output was so low that only 14 aircraft were in service by March 1943, the month in which the first Hellcat squadrons went into service on U. S. carriers. Between July 1943 and July 1944, crucial months of the Pacific war, Mitsubishi produced only 141 Raiden, not enough to re-equip Admiral Koga's fighter squadrons.

Fortunately for Japan, Horikoshi's Zero had considerably more "stretch" in its airframe than most fighter designs. In March 1944 Mitsubishi began producing the Zero Model 52 with stronger wings to permit dives to 460 mph. Little armor was added, but fire extinguishers in the wing tanks somewhat reduced flammability. More power in the basic engine pushed speed to a respectable 351 mph at 20,000 feet. The Model 52 Zero still was slower than either the Hellcat or Corsair.

In building new bombers the Japanese Navy did rather better than with fighters. Development of a replacement for the torpedo-carrying Kate was already under way when the war began in the form of Nakajima designer Kenichi Matsumura's B6N Tenzan ("Heavenly Mountain"), called by the Americans "Jill." In appearance it was closely similar to Kate, though with slimmer and finer lines, and much faster when fitted with either the approximately 1,850-hp Nakajima Mamoru or Mitsubishi Kasei 25 radial engines. Its top speed was close to 300 mph at 17,000 feet. Like the Curtiss SB2C "Beast," the Jill had tail-hook problems when first tried on carriers in 1942, but by 1943 the plane was in mass production, replacing the Kate.

Against Wildcat opposition the Jill might have been quite effective with its good speed at low altitude, but the advent of the faster Hellcat placed designer Matsumura's torpedo bomber, which had no armor or self-sealing tanks, in the same relative position of inferiority that the Kate had been.

This was less true, however, of Val's replacement, the Yokosuka D4Y, well named the Suisei (Comet), though called prosaically "Judy" by its foes. When fitted with either the Aichi Atsuta liquid-cooled engine (a Japanese copy built under license of Germany's Daimler-Benz 601A that powered the Messerschmitt fighters) or a Mitsubishi Kinsei radial, Judy was by far the world's fastest dive bomber. Its speed of nearly 360 miles per hour when "clean" nearly equaled that of the 375-mph Hellcat and was much superior to Curtiss's "Beast." But the Judy also suffered for want of armor and self-sealing tanks, and the Atsuta engine never attained the reliability demanded for long overwater flights. Judy thus did not replace but supplemented the sturdy and reliable Val that stayed in production with it until VJ-Day in 1945.

In general it may be said that the quality of Japanese carrier planes remained high throughout the Pacific War. Had her naval leaders been willing to sacrifice some speed and performance to include armor and self-sealing tanks, then Japan's American foes would have enjoyed at best only a marginal superiority in fighting capability.

In terms of pilot quality Japan had a clear superiority over the United States at the outset of the war. This superiority, most vividly apparent in the quality of Japanese as against American dive-bombing, had vanished with the Battle of Santa Cruz. By early 1943 both sides were becoming dependent on pilots who had begun their training either just before or during the war. In this area, as in the case of warship production, America enjoyed an enormous advantage.

The U. S. Navy's pilot training program, based on the aviation cadet (Avcad) system introduced in the mid-1930s, sufficed with modification to supply an adequate number of pilots. Added were preflight centers with a capacity of 9,350 trainees and many new primary and basic flying schools. A typical cadet went through primary training flying the Boeing-Stearman N2S biplane and then through intermediate training in the 450-hp Vultee SNV Valiant—usually called the "Vibrator." He then went to advanced flight school at Pensacola or Corpus Christi and finished up with carrier qualification, perhaps aboard either the *Wolverine* or *Sable,* converted excursion steamers with flight decks that operated on Lake Michigan. In terms of actual flying time his 500 or so hours were not far short of what U. S. naval aviators had received in peacetime.

In contrast, Japan's naval flying training program can only be described as inadequate. The Naval Staff in Tokyo was slow to realize the enormous quantity of pilots that would be needed and hence slow to expand training facilities. When the full impact struck during the Guadalcanal campaign in late 1942 it was already too late. About all that the staff could do was to hastily recruit new pilots and load up existing facilities, such as the Kasumigaura airfield complex near Tokyo, Japan's equivalent to Pensacola. In some cases classes were simply doubled or tripled in numbers of men; in others men with only basic or even primary schooling were assigned directly to operational squadrons to complete their advanced and operational training. "We didn't have enough time," recalls Saburo Sakai, the ace who by 1943 had recovered from his wounds and was assigned to operational training.

We couldn't watch for individual errors and take the long hours necessary to weed the faults out of the trainees. Hardly a day passed when the fire engine and ambulances did not race down the runways, sirens shrieking. . . .

About all that Sakai and his fellow instructors could do was to teach the new men the elements of aerobatics and to shoot. Long before most were truly combat-ready they had to be sent to depleted squadrons at Rabaul and elsewhere.

Nor could Japan keep pace with other sorts of training necessary to naval air warfare. In 1941 and 1942 the U. S. Navy enlisted great numbers of car-tinkering kids to fill large maintenance and ordnance schools. Two at Chicago and Jacksonville, Florida, had a capacity of 10,500 trainees. Air stations at Norfolk, Pensacola, San Diego, Alameda, and Seattle added 4,600 more. The Japanese had nowhere near this training capacity and had trouble in finding young men with technical backgrounds. The inevitable result was poor maintenance work and a much higher out-of-commission rate for Japanese naval aircraft than for American. The best specialists went to the carriers but at the cost of poorer maintenance at air stations. By mid-1943 Japan was short of both pilots and technicians. She clearly had lost the "training war."

17. "Makee Learn"

Newly formed U. S. carrier air groups operating in the Central Pacific often had along a rear admiral slated for an air command. He was aboard the force flagship as an observer without command responsibility. This process was dubbed "makee learn." As the new fast carriers gathered at Pearl Harbor during the summer of 1943 even the most experienced commanders were also—in a sense—in the "makee learn" process. Carrier operations in the South Pacific had been sometimes good, sometimes mediocre. The need was to bring all carrier task-force operations to a uniform standard of excellence. At his regular morning conferences Admiral Nimitz placed carrier training on his daily agenda of items for discussion. He also ordered Vice Admiral John H. Towers, now his principal assistant for naval air matters, to suggest improvements.

If any naval officer could be considered "Mr. Naval Aviation" it had to be Georgia-born Jack Towers. Towers was one of the first officers assigned to aviation duty; he had test-flown the stick-and-wire hydroplanes of Glen Curtiss, had commanded the Navy's pioneer aviation camp at Annapolis, had been the Assistant Director of Naval Aviation during the First World War. In the 1920s and 1930s he had commanded the *Langley* and *Saratoga,* and he had served a tour as Chief of the Bureau of Aeronautics. Towers was the natural leader of those officers whose interest was entirely in naval air. Yet he understood, too, the viewpoint of the "gun club" that had devoted years of study to the use of 14- and 16-inch rifles in battle. It was to a well-rounded man that Nimitz now wisely turned to review procedures for using the fleet carriers in the forthcoming mid-Pacific offensive.

On August 16, 1943, Admiral Towers convened a meeting in his Commander Air, Pacific, office. Present were three rear admirals in charge of the Pacific Fleet's carrier divisions, the captains of every fleet carrier, and several ComAirPac staff officers. Towers asked each of the 15 officers present for his ideas concerning administrative and combat organization of carrier groups and their tactical employment.

All spoke, beginning with Rear Admiral Alfred E. Montgomery, commanding Carrier Division 2. He thought that the administrative and combat organizations of carrier groups should be unified. Others interjected that this was impractical, and the discussion became general. Towers let it drift, adding his own comments where appropriate. All of the conferees realized that two or more carriers would operate in a circular formation. But how many exactly? Two carriers? Three? Or what Towers declared was the maximum number, four? Few were agreed on how to use the *Independence*-class light carriers. Some wanted them to operate in separate groups, others in combination with the *Essex*-class fleet carriers. Captain J. J. "Jocko" Clark, *Yorktown*'s skipper, probably expressed the majority view when he opted for a carrier group composed of a CVL with two CVs.

Admiral Towers raised the issue of speedy launch of air groups. The Hellcats and Helldivers were larger and harder to manhandle; the launch of deckloads was correspondingly being slowed. Would it be feasible to launch a single attack group from several carriers simultaneously? "Worth trying" was the conclusion, only *Essex*'s skipper, Captain Donald B. Duncan, dissenting.

Duncan received plenty of support, however, when he insisted that 90 planes were too many for an *Essex*-class ship to carry. The number could be embarked, but hangar and flight decks then became too cluttered for flexible operations. Duncan favored a 78-plane arrangement. Without accepting Duncan's exact number the conference agreed. Tacked onto this conclusion was another—that the light carriers should embark only Hellcat fighters and Avenger torpedo-bombers. Dauntless and Helldiver dive bombers would be a large carrier monopoly because they had trouble getting off a CVL deck unless catapulted.

Admiral Towers raised a final problem. Carrier strikes in the Central Pacific would be more difficult to organize than in the South Pacific. Because Central Pacific atolls were mutually self-supporting, the fast carrier groups would have to strike several island airfields simultaneously. If Admiral Koga's carriers intervened, the groups would have to deal with them, too.

The Towers conference helped to clarify issues, but "makee learn" by battle was better. One "for real" combat strike would be worth days of speculation. Realizing this, and after conferring with Towers, Admiral Nimitz ordered the new carriers to assault the isolated target, Marcus Atoll, that Wild Bill Halsey had hit early in the war. Now, Rear Admiral Charles A. Pownall, CarDiv 3's new commander, who had been serving as Commander, Fleet Air Wing, San Diego, would clobber it with a team composed of his flagship *Yorktown,* plus *Essex* and *Independence*. These ships had the best-trained air groups. Nothing fancy would be tried—just approach, strike, and return to Pearl.

Nimitz was as anxious to test Admiral Pownall as his airmen. Pownall had transferred to aviation following duty as a destroyer skipper in 1923. Since then he had held many aviation assignments, his last carrier duty being as skipper of the *Enterprise* in 1938. His seniority (Annapolis, Class of 1910) and experience gave him a strong claim for the command opportunity. Also, he was personable, got along well with the "gun club," and was regarded as a good administrator. But he was cautious and inclined to be a worrier. It was typical of him to become mightily upset when one of his carriers out from Pearl crossed its own track eight times in a day. Recalling the fate of the *Wasp,* Pownall considered such an action to be taking too many chances with Japan's submarines.

If Pownall was obviously no Bill Halsey, would he be a Ray Spruance, who also was cautious? More specifically could he replace Spruance, who had left his carrier command and was now in charge of all Central Pacific naval forces as Commander, Fifth Fleet? Nimitz had to find out.

Pownall's Task Force 15 rendezvoused north of Kauai Island in the Hawaiian group on the morning of August 23, 1943. With Pownall as an observer was Rear Admiral Alfred E. Montgomery, who was occupying the flag quarters of *Essex.* Montgomery, who had commanded task groups in the South Pacific, was not entirely on "makee learn" status. He had helped to plan the strike and had loaned some of his staff to the newly arrived Pownall to help carry it out. Also, if anything happened to Pownall, he would take over.*

The attack plan called for Task Force 15 to head northwesterly past Marcus, then to turn south to hit the island from the northern flank. If all went well the Marcus air detachment, supposedly good-sized, would be wiped out by the first of a series of strikes.

Though Pownall and Montgomery had differed as to the details of the strikes, both agreed that Marcus should be hit no later than an hour after dawn. Pownall, however, had wanted to use a night-trained Avenger squadron from the *Independence* to ambush the field before first light. The black-painted bombers then would guide in strafing Hellcats and Dauntlesses. Pownall was concerned that a night-ranging Zero might by skill or luck find *Yorktown* and strafe its plane-laden deck if he waited until daylight to launch. Montgomery had favored a more conventional strike arriving at first light. Montgomery's plan was adopted, but Pownall managed to get agreement to stepping up the takeoff time by 15 minutes, from 4:30 to 4:15 A.M. local time. Planes would launch in total darkness. First to attack would be six Avengers loaded with incendiary and high-explosive bombs to light up the targets.

Yorktown's planes led off the attacks by all three carriers. The blacked-out takeoff (actually beginning at 4:22 A.M. on August 31) was "hairy." Guided only by hooded stern lights on destroyers ahead, Commander Jimmy Flatley of Air Group 5 led 16 Hellcats and 29 other planes off the deck. Except for an Avenger flight that later attacked independently, all planes successfully formed up, following the lead torpedo planes that

---

* Nimitz apparently had elected to step outside the ranks of his combat-experienced carrier commanders in selecting Pownall, who was senior to most of them, including Montgomery. For a thorough discussion of command relationships, see Clark G. Reynolds, *The Fast Carriers* (1968).

identified Marcus at 18 miles with their new airborne radar. Surprise was complete; seven grounded Bettys and a partly dismantled Nell were erased in the first strafing and bombing runs. After that Flatley's fighters concentrated on the 15-mm. and 25-mm. AA batteries, silencing them entirely with guns disabled or crews dead by mid-afternoon. The strikes gave the airfield, the AA defenses, ships, the radio station, barracks, and sundry other installations a considerable beating.

They were not without loss, though no enemy planes got off the ground. Three Hellcats and an Avenger fell to the flak, all from *Yorktown*'s Air Group 5. The Avenger crew, Lieutenant J. W. Condit and Machinists Kahlbert and Marshall, was picked up by a Japanese submarine. Condit was held secretly in a special Japanese Navy camp for POWs deemed worthy of "special treatment"—meaning beatings—in order to exact information about U. S. carrier forces. Some critics held that Condit's loss, plus two downed Hellcats and a ditching by a third, made the strike not worth the cost. This view, however, overlooked the many very valuable lessons that combat had brought and were embodied in the after-action reports filed by the *Yorktown, Essex,* and *Independence* skippers.

Both Pownall and Montgomery reported that operating three carriers in a single circular formation apt for AA defense had been an unqualified success, and this despite light wind conditions that had forced the carriers to steam at the unusually high speed of 30 knots to launch armed planes. The predawn takeoff also had succeeded. As Pownall wrote to Admiral Nimitz, "It was a beautiful piece of work on the part of the pilots, getting into the air and on their way in the dark without loss."

Other lessons concerned mainly the combat test of new equipment. The new four-channel VHF voice radio sets had proved to be remarkably interference-free. Air Group Commanders Jimmy Flatley and John Raby had had no difficulty in conversing with their ships, their men, and with each other up to hundred-mile distances. Comments about other equipment included everything from condemnation of the AN-M123 delayed-action bomb fuse ("Unsafe! Don't use.") to praise of the Dead Reckoning Tracer equipment in the carrier Combat Information Centers (CICs) as the only certain way to maintain bearings and determine distance accurately to targets from the constantly maneuvering task force. Finally, though his ship flew only one strike at Marcus, all other flights being patrols, Captain George R. Fairlamb had high praise for *Independence*'s catapult. The CVL had been able to use the powerful hydraulic device to fling planes into the air without the necessity for the 30-knot speeds that *Essex* and *Yorktown* had had to use.

Armed with these and literally dozens of other valuable items of information, it was with some complacency that Admiral Pownall brought TF-15 back to Pearl Harbor, arriving in the first week of September. Pownall did find it expedient to explain to Admiral Nimitz why he had broken off his attacks in mid-afternoon after only four had been flown. "We would have continued," he wrote in a letter to Nimitz (information copy to Admiral Towers), "but the pilots were getting tired, landings were getting ragged, and one [pilot] pulled a boner by giving his plane the gun after landing, missing the crash barrier and planes parked ahead by inches."

At Pearl Harbor planning already was far advanced for the long-awaited drive across the Central Pacific by Admiral Nimitz's command. Nimitz was to use his Fifth Fleet and attached amphibious forces to carry out, in effect, the prewar Orange and Rainbow war plans for Japan's defeat. Already, the Joint Chiefs of Staff in Washington had directed Nimitz to seize Tarawa and Makin atolls in the Gilbert Islands by mid-November 1943. After that, early in 1944, the Marshall Islands would be seized. Advances farther westward would follow.

Nimitz needed an air base in the Gilberts mainly for photographing the more heavily defended Marshalls. Also, land-based planes based there could help to "pound down" the Marshall airstrips while one or more of the Marshall atolls underwent seizure.

That Nimitz would try to seize the Gilberts had long been anticipated in Tokyo. Strategists in Imperial Headquarters could appreciate as well as the Joint Chiefs the reasons for an American advance through the Mandated Islands. Also, an ill-advised commando raid launched from submarines in 1942 had seized Makin for a brief period, causing Admiral Nagano at Navy headquarters to decide to reinforce both it and Betio Island in Tarawa Atoll as points expected to be attacked. To Betio's airstrip, therefore, came from Kizaru training center in Japan the Tarawa detachment of the 755th Air Group equipped with Betty bombers. Air crews of this outfit had been specially trained in techniques of long-range search and in night aerial torpedo attack. Fighters also arrived for local defense, and to Makin went four Mavis flying boats to fly distant reconnaissance from its sheltered lagoon. Wake Island north of the Marshalls likewise received reinforcements.

From communications intelligence Nimitz's staff at Pearl Harbor was aware in a general way of the nature of these reinforcements. A logical step would therefore be to clobber Tarawa and Makin as soon as possible. Also, a decision would have to be made very soon as to the beaches across which amphibious landings would be made. Urgently needed were low-level oblique aerial photographs.

To this end Admiral Pownall put to sea again in mid-September. This time he flew his flag in CV-16, the new *Lexington*. As guide ship for the now familiar circular formation the Lady Lex led light carriers *Princeton* and *Belleau Wood*. All three ships and their escort fueled from oiler *Guadeloupe* on September 15 and 16 while Pownall paced *Lexington*'s bridge, then headed for the launch point.

Pownall expected little trouble from the Betio airfield at Tarawa, assuming that his planes could smother it, but the Marshalls were close by with plenty more of the 755th's night-flying Bettys. En route Pownall decided also to annihilate the four flying boats at Makin and to overfly and photograph Abemama Atoll southwest of Tarawa. The ever-nervous American admiral suspected it might harbor an airfield as yet undiscovered by American submarine and air search. He wanted no unpleasant surprises.

The core of the attack, to be made September 18–19, was to be the planes of *Lexington*'s Air Group 16. A half moon and brilliantly glowing stars oriented Commander Leonard B. Southerland's airmen in their take-offs from a blackened deck. Their departure time of 3:31 A.M. had been carefully chosen to enable them to arrive over Tarawa at 5:15 A.M., an hour before sunrise. This they did, but the predawn blackness still covering Betio kept them from attacking until the predawn light grew strong enough to allow them to pick out assigned targets. Against a fully alerted and manned light flak that holed 40 of 83 attacking *Lexington* planes, the pilots dove to destroy nine of the 18 twin-engine bombers of the Tarawa-based squadron of Captain Sakae Yamashita's 755th Air Group. A four-plane flight to Makin found and burned three of the Mavis flying boats and wrecked the other. The sweep to Abemama Atoll proved Pownall's fears to be groundless, turning up no airfield and drawing no fire from the handful of Japanese present but costing the admiral a Dauntless photo plane that failed to return to the *Lexington*.

Six more attacks followed this day and the next, burning many structures on Betio and Makin islands but doing slight harm to the dug-in artillery, automatic weapons, and searchlights of the seaward defenses. From the standpoint of morale the raids merely steeled the resolve of the Japanese to fight to the last.

Nevertheless, Admiral Nimitz received what he most needed. Low-level oblique photos of the Betio beaches were rushed to the Marine Corps amphibious planners working on the details of the landing plan for Tarawa. A reel of 35-mm. movie film taken from the rear seat of an SBD by war correspondent Senick of Movietone News was forwarded directly to Nimitz. In his report to Admiral Pownall, Captain Felix B. Stump, *Lexington*'s skipper, asserted that "Air Group 16 proved itself definitely ready for combat." His only negative comment was that 89 planes aboard his ship were too many. A maximum load should be no more than 36 Hellcats, 30 Dauntlesses, and 19 Avengers.

Admiral Pownall reported himself pleased that his carriers had maneuvered well as a unit. It still took too long to launch and recover planes, and he admitted that the predawn strike had gotten off too soon. Moon-light less bright than expected had not permitted predawn attacks. Fear of being ambushed by night still worried him greatly, though the Japanese had not attacked. Four night fighters aboard each carrier were a necessity, he concluded.

Now that the southern flank of the Marshalls had been hit, Admiral Nimitz decided to strike Wake Island on the northern flank. Wake could not be easily reinforced, being 600 miles north and slightly west of Kwajalein. Hence, it made an ideal training target—not too tough but far from easy. Hopefully, the Japanese high command might interpret a strike as preparation for an amphibious landing. If so, it might pull defenders from Tarawa and the Marshalls (the real targets) to Wake.

Wake was a small, triangular-shaped atoll, containing an airfield with three runways forming an overlapping "A." Two islets off either leg of the triangle—namely, Peale and Wilkes—contained storage buildings, oil tanks, seacoast defense guns (some of them five-inchers captured from the U. S. Marines), and plenty of AA. The gunners would give the incoming American pilots a bumpy ride.

Nimitz had six carriers, three CVs and three CVLs. In overall command this time would be Rear Admiral Montgomery as Commander Task Force 14. Other flag officers would command each of the three smaller task groups into which TF-14 would subdivide. *Essex* and *Yorktown* would form one, *Lexington* and CVL *Cowpens* another, and CVLs *Independence* and *Belleau Wood* a third. Montgomery would coordinate their movements from the *Essex*.

This six-carrier task force was the largest yet assembled by the U. S. Navy in the Pacific war. It was not, however, as potent as Admiral Nagumo's Pearl Harbor striking force. In numbers of planes embarked and especially in experienced air crew, Nagumo's had been superior by a wide margin. Except for a few South Pacific veterans, the *Cowpens* pilots were completely green.

Montgomery's plan called for TF-14 to sortie from Pearl on September 29, 1943, rendezvous and steam in one formation toward Wake, top off with oil, close the atoll, and then divide into the three separate task groups just before launching on the morning of October 5. Light carriers *Independence* and *Belleau Wood* from 50 miles northeast of Wake would fly patrols over cruisers assigned to bombard it and if necessary vector other Hellcats to shoot down Japanese planes flying up from the Marshalls. Their Avengers would range out to all points of the compass for 200 miles in a precautionary search for surface ships. *Essex, Yorktown, Lexington,* and *Cowpens* in two groups would simultaneously launch a four-ship strike, trying out the tactic proposed in Admiral Towers' conference. Because radio intercepts had indicated that Wake's air strength had been augmented, 48 Hellcats (12 from each ship) and 24 Avengers would hit the airfield a half hour before sunrise at 6:15 A.M. The more vulnerable Dauntlesses and more Hellcats and Avengers would follow. Repeat attacks would continue all day and into the next if remaining targets warranted.

Such was Montgomery's complicated plan, and except for an initial foul-up in assembling the four-ship strike formation it was completed almost to the letter. Montgomery had not counted on obtaining surprise, and from their air-search radar the Japanese picked up the attackers 50 miles out and scrambled 33 Zeros. A fierce air battle taught the Americans anew to respect the climb, acceleration, and especially the nimbleness of the Zero. On the other hand the attackers brought to Japanese attention the disquieting message that the big Hellcat, even when flown by inexperienced pilots, was a far more dangerous foe than the sluggish Wildcat.

Lieutenant Commander Philip H. Torrey, Jr., commanding Fighting 9 from *Essex,* found himself alone over Wake at 7,000 feet. In the gathering light he noticed a Zero above and to port, diving in with wing cannons winking. Turning his Hellcat and climbing to port himself, Torrey got in a good burst, sending the Zero into a spin as he passed it by. Torrey then stalled and spun into the seven-tenths cloud cover hanging in tropical fashion low over Wake. As he recovered two more Zeros dove in, forcing him to scissor in and out of clouds cat-and-mouse style until he lost them.

Nine thousand feet above, seven *Essex* fighters were deploying to dive and strafe Wake's airfield. From above, two Zeros bounced them. Two pilots new to combat, Lieutenants Mayo A. Hadden, Jr., and J. S. Kitchen, immediately broke from the formation and turned into the Zeros. Two more Zeros—possibly the planes that had attacked Torrey—made a firing run from above and behind but missed. As they shot past Hadden and Kitchen both fired at the rearmost plane, sending the Zero tumbling into the sea offshore of Wake. Hadden was watching, fascinated by the sight, when he was again jumped from above and behind. He turned into his opponent, but the Zero turned faster and gave the Hellcat a full burst with cannon and 7.7-mm. machine guns. Five 20-mm. rounds holed the oil tank, inflicted sundry other damage, and wounded Hadden. Twisting to starboard, the *Essex* pilot reached the safety of a cloud. Wingman Kitchen rejoined him and escorted him back to the carrier, where he landed with but a gallon and a half of oil remaining for his R-2800 engine.

Strikes continued on October 5 and into the next day, and so did losses. Air Group 25 from *Cowpens* became the hard-luck outfit. The first mission cost two Hellcat pilots, cause unknown, but perhaps to the vicious light AA the defenders hurled up. Another fighter, damaged, had to force-land on the *Lexington.* Strikes on the 6th cost AG-25 three more F6Fs, two in combat and one operationally. Air Group skipper Mark A. Grant was one, shot down while on a strafing run over Peale Island. Lieutenant Harold J. Kicker ditched off Wake's Peacock Point, swam from his sinking Hellcat, waved to his squadron mates, and was not seen again. Total losses to Air Group 25, including deck crashes, totaled eight planes, as many as AG-5 suffered on the larger *Yorktown.* Total combat losses were 13 and operational losses 14, not excessively heavy considering that Task Force 14 had launched 738 sorties.

Pilot losses would have been five more than the 12 suffered had it not been for U. S. S. *Shark.* Commander Eugene B. McKinney's submarine had been stationed ten miles off Wake for the purpose of picking up downed airmen. Its rescues were the first of a long series of similar successes on missions that came to be known as "lifeguarding."

Shark's rescue attempts began poorly. Lacking VHF voice radio equipment, the submarine could not listen in on aircraft frequencies over which were broadcast the locations of pilots lost offshore. McKinney saw planes fall in the distance, guessed that some were American, but otherwise had no information. McKinney therefore decided to close Wake on the surface, the better to act when and if a rescue request came through. He had not proceeded far, however, when a Zero strafed the sub, fatally wounding Lieutenant Willis E. Maxson III, who was on the *Shark*'s exposed bridge.

Squally weather hampered McKinney's efforts the next day, but the *Shark* closed Wake and finally received a report of two airmen down near the beach. Ignoring shelling from a coast defense gun, McKinney ran the sub awash with bow and conning tower out of water and picked up Lieutenant Commander Grant, *Cowpens'* AGC, and Ensign Orson T. Head, one of Grant's pilots. *Shark* then threaded its way out to sea, ducked two bombs dropped by a pair of planes that the bridge watch had reported as friendly, and escaped. A wide search of the area about Wake netted four more surviviors, three pilots and an air crewman. McKinney went home to plead vociferously for VHF radios and for fighter cover for lifeguard subs.

McKinney and his crew were proud of their pioneering mission, but some of the airmen, stung by their losses, were less happy. Commander Charles L. Crommelin, boss of *Yorktown*'s Air Group 5, thought submarines were too slow to get to downed men in time. He suggested using PT boats or even destroyers as lifeguards. Admiral Nimitz read Crommelin's report, considered it, but left lifeguarding—with improvements suggested by McKinney—to the submarines. He still had too few destroyers to release these ships for rescue work during a strike.

Admiral Montgomery was less critical of *Shark*'s lifeguarding than his airmen, observing that the rescue of six of eleven men down off Wake was "remarkable . . . under the circumstances." But he approved also of using PT boats as well as submarines for rescue. He seconded his pilots in praising the VHF radios, noting that their better voice modulation made aircraft commo vastly more comprehensible. He approved with enthusiasm the circular antiaircraft screen (which type of formation Admiral Nimitz had personally innovated in the prewar years), and he lauded the deck catapult. He wanted two on each CV and CVL to facilitate launchings. The relatively high number of operational losses disturbed Montgomery, especially three that had occurred after dark. Better night training was needed, he declared, and he concluded: "In general it may be said that all carrier training is still short of what is desired."

Whether his carrier airmen were short of training or no, Admiral Nimitz declared an end to the "makee learn" raids when Task Force 14 returned to Pearl. The Tarawa attack was coming, and it was time to prepare the carriers for it. But the gods of war intervened. There was trouble—at Rabaul.

18. Rabaul Interlude

While Nimitz's fast carriers were hammering Marcus, Tarawa, and Wake, Admiral Mineichi Koga at his Truk headquarters was attempting to divine his antagonist's next move. As a disciple of the late Yamamoto, Japan's new Combined Fleet commander also believed implicitly in the strategy of winning the One Big Battle. He knew that the odds were building against him with every new American warship commissioned. He wanted, therefore, a decisive victory as soon as possible.

Koga knew that Nimitz would have to support a Central Pacific offensive with carriers. This would give Japan an opportunity. And he became convinced after the Wake attack of October 5–6 that this small atoll was an imminent target. He therefore assembled his available carriers—*Shokaku, Zuikaku,* and *Zuiho*—and sailed to Eniwetok Atoll, entering on October 17. There, he waited for a week for Nimitz to show his hand. When nothing developed, Koga steamed back to Truk, arriving on October 26.

On return the Japanese fleet admiral set in motion an offensive planned earlier, the "RO" operation. This he had patterned after Yamamoto's earlier air strikes on Guadalcanal and South Pacific targets. As in Yamamoto's "I" Operation, the Combined Fleet carriers would dispatch their air groups to Rabaul, and from there the planes would make a massed attack to shatter Admiral Halsey's advance up the Solomons toward Bougainville. Koga had taken at face value the wildly exaggerated reports of ships sunk in the "I" Operation and hoped that Operation "RO"'s results would be still better. Besides, as a disciple of Yamamoto he believed in repeating what the Master had done. Koga therefore ordered to Rabaul all available carrier planes of his First Air Fleet. These arrived on November 1, 1943, and when combined with the 200 planes of Admiral Kusaka's Rabaul Base Force, the total plane strength of about 373 for Operation "RO" exceeded that for Yamamoto's "I" Operation. Koga and Vice Admiral Tomoshige Samejima, Rabaul's overall naval commander, both hoped to give Halsey's carrier-shy Third Fleet a bloody nose.

"Wild Bill" naturally had other ideas. With eastern New Guinea secured and Vella Lavella taken August–September 1943, Halsey prepared to attack large, mountainous Bougainville Island, landing not where the Japanese expected him, on southern Bougainville, but at isolated Empress Augusta Bay, halfway up Bougainville's eastern coast. Halsey was confident that his Seabees could quickly build fighter and bomber strips within easy fighter radius of Rabaul before Japanese troops garrisoned in the south could march overland and defeat his purpose. A preliminary landing in the Treasury Islands off Bougainville's southern tip would add a fighter strip between Vella Lavella and Cape Torokina. Halsey's target date for beginning the operation was November 1, 1943, exactly coincident with commencement by Koga of the "RO" operation.

Several naval battles in the "Slot" northward of New Georgia had left Halsey short of cruisers and destroyers. He was down to a force composed of four new light cruisers and two destroyer divisions under Rear Admiral A. S. "Tip" Merrill. Because of this, and because it was a good idea anyway, Halsey asked Admiral Nimitz to lend him two carrier task forces for the Empress Augusta Bay–Treasuries landings. Nimitz, anxious to conserve ships for the Gilberts landings coming up later in November, released only two ships, the big old heavyweight *Saratoga* and CVL *Princeton*. Then, after pondering Halsey's needs, Nimitz added another carrier group composed of the *Essex*, CVL *Independence*, and the new *Bunker Hill*, a ship that had arrived at Pearl on October 2, too late to participate in the final "makee learn" raid on Wake. Rear Admiral Ted Sherman commanded the *Sara–Princeton* pair and Rear Admiral Al Montgomery the *Essex, Bunker Hill, Independence* combine. Nimitz's hesitation meant that Montgomery's task force would arrive in South Pacific waters several days after Sherman's—which would have important consequences.

The 3rd Division Marines landed on schedule at Cape Torokina on Empress Augusta Bay on November 1. Opposition from some 300 defenders was slight. The Marines quickly seized a perimeter, and Seabees hacked down trees and bulldozed aside mud to improvise a fighter strip at the Cape. Sites farther inland were surveyed for a pair of strips long enough to handle bombers. At sea off the beachhead Rear Admiral Tip Merrill employed excellent night surface fighting techniques to thrust aside a Japanese cruiser-destroyer force sent down from Rabaul to attack the Marine transports. This Battle of Empress Augusta Bay, fought on November 2, cost the Japanese damage to two heavy cruisers and the loss of a light cruiser. For the moment Halsey's beachhead was safe, but, as it turned out, only for the moment. More Japanese warships soon arrived at Rabaul's Simpson Harbor, more than Merrill's lone cruiser-destroyer force could handle.

On receiving word of the landing, Admiral Koga alerted more planes, bombers of the 12th Air Fleet, to join the carrier planes at or en route to Rabaul. To strengthen the surface forces under Vice Admiral Samejima he sent to Rabaul Vice Admiral Takeo Kurita's cruisers and destroyers of his Second Fleet. These ships would attack Halsey's beachhead pursuant to Samejima's orders while the planes carried out heavy air strikes.

Koga saw no point in sending his carriers south of Truk; they now were planeless. Remembering Guadalcanal, he did not wish to bring his battleships within range of land-based air either from the Solomons or New Guinea. The cruisers and destroyers, aided by the planes at Rabaul, should suffice.

Again it was American cryptography that gave Nimitz and Halsey warning of the southward move of Koga's planes and ships. Halsey now knew that he might have more enemy strength than he could handle. He dared not hesitate; he must seize the initiative and blunt enemy strength.

Saratoga and *Princeton*, organized as Task Force 38, had been fueling near the Rennell Islands southwest of Guadalcanal. During the Empress Augusta landing they had attacked airfields on northern Bougainville. Now, on November 4, they were given a mission that struck some crewmen as "suicide." They were to run north again and strike Rabaul with every plane they could fly off. The purpose: Get those cruisers lying in Rabaul Harbor! Hit and disable as many as you can.

There was no time for formal planning. Halsey at Nouméa radioed Ted Sherman to take his carriers and escorting AA light cruisers *San Juan* and *San Diego* to a point 230 miles southeast of Rabaul; there they would launch the next day. To get there in time required a run at 27 knots, but rain squalls and bad visibility promised welcome cover from Rabaul's snoopers. One launch would be it. The planes would attack, return, and the carriers would hightail it south.

At 8:57 A.M. on November 5, into a seven-knot breeze (for once American carriers would have the wind blowing toward them), *Sara* and *Independence* launched 52 Hellcats, 22 Dauntlesses, and 23 Avengers armed with torpedoes. Overhead, AirSols fighters from New Georgia were orbiting on CAP. The attack had gotten away only 14 hours after Admiral Sherman had received his orders.

Key man of the mission was Lieutenant Commander J. C. "Jumping Joe" Clifton, leader of *Sara*'s Fighting Squadron 12. It would be up to Clifton and his men flying cover to keep defending Zeros from the Dauntlesses and Avengers making the attack. Clifton's plan, as approved by Air Group Commander Howard H. Caldwell, was to keep his force of 16 Hellcats only 800 to 1,000 feet over the bombers. A like number of fighters led by his "exec," Lieutenant Commander R. G. Dose, would take station 3,000 feet higher. Still farther up a high cover of 16 VF-23 Hellcats from *Independence* under Commander Henry L. Miller would be prepared to dive on intruders. Two Hellcats, one each from VF-12 and VF-23, would cover Commander Caldwell's Avenger, from which the air-group leader would both select targets and photograph the action. All fighters had orders to stick close to the bombers, ignoring small groups of Zeros, until the Dauntlesses broke formation and began their dives.

The attack went right by the book. The bomber formation, covered closely by the Hellcats, flew up St. George Channel, then swung left in a huge three-quarter circle, holding their formation despite intensive flak pouring up from below. Fifty-nine defending Zeros alerted by radar held off, expecting Caldwell's Americans to break formation when the AA bursts began. When they did not the Japanese pilots were already too late to catch the leading Dauntlesses and Avengers. As ordered, Clifton's 16 close-in Hellcat pilots eyed the Zeros, resisting the temptation to chase the treys and sixes of the Japanese three-plane formations, still the standard Zero element.

At the order of Lieutenant Commander James H. Newell, VB-12's skipper, the Dauntless pilots split, breaking into sections to plunge at the seven cruisers in the harbor below. One CA was fueling; others were under way at low speeds, trying to clear their anchorage areas on various headings, aiming for Blanche Bay, Rabaul's outer harbor. Peeling off at 14,500 feet, the SBD-5s dove, ignoring the most intense flak that even the Midway veterans had ever seen, watching their targets grow larger and larger in their telescopic sights until release altitude—2,500 to 1,500 feet—was reached. They had no trouble with windscreens fogging; hot-air defrosters kept canopies clear. They did not worry too much about Zeros while diving; they knew that the fighters dove too fast to stay on the tail of an SBD coming down with dive brakes open. Only the last section was attacked. Lieutenant E. F. Cox claimed a Zero with his fixed twin .50s when it appeared in his sights while trying to attack the Dauntless diving just ahead.

Pulling out from their dives, the pilots banked, skidded, and jinked through what seemed like a forest of masts to head out over Blanche Bay into St. George Channel intent on retiring in the same direction from which they had come. Every pilot pulled as much manifold pressure from his Cyclone engine as he dared. Behind them smoke and spray from hits and near misses slowly dispersed. The pilots claimed one to five hits on all of the Second Fleet cruisers save *Suzuya*, which had reached Blanche Bay and evaded attack.

On orders from Lieutenant Commander Robert F. Farrington of VT-12, the Avengers had dropped beneath the Dauntlesses in a high-speed glide. Then they deployed into sections, singling out assigned targets and slowing to 150 knots to drop their still-tender Mark 13 torpedoes. Some sections weaved through scattered low clouds hanging tropical fashion at 1,000 to 2,000 feet partially to conceal their approach. The plan was for them to drop just after the Dauntlesses pulled out of their dives. Each torpedo carried a 600-pound Torpex warhead and was set to run at six feet. The fish were deadly enough—if they would go off.

No Zeros interrupted as Farrington's pilots launched from 200 to

300 feet, mostly at Admiral Kurita's heavy cruisers. The pilots claimed explosions against the sides of four targets and reported seven more fish aiming "hot and true" for their marks. But one Mark 13 tumbled, another turned 90 degrees right, and a third hung up in Avenger T-14's bomb bay. Farrington's men thought that they had had a good run; not a single plane had fallen to the light AA though several had been holed. High overhead, Commander Caldwell circled while Photographer's Mate First Class P. T. Barnett took still and motion pictures.

The Zero pilots, fooled by their enemies when coming in, had no intention of letting them get away unmolested. They dove, closed, and concentrated on single retiring Avengers and Dauntlesses when they could find them. Lieutenant (jg) Arthur L. Teall's SBD soon splashed, crew lost, the only VB-12 plane shot down. In other planes the rear-seat men exchanged fire with the Zeros, claiming two shot down at the price of two gunners killed in the exchanges and eight wounded. The Avengers were hard hit; four fell to Zeros that pursued them well out into the St. George Channel.

It would have been much worse had not Jumping Joe Clifton's fighters kept most of the Zeros busy. Breaking into four-plane sections, the standard Navy formation, the Hellcats weaved above the bombers, ready to pounce when a Zero tried a firing run. Clifton himself led two four-plane flights over the first six Dauntlesses to pull out of their dives. Four or five Zeros dove in to attack the protecting fighters, only to find themselves scissored and attacked from the flank. Jumping Joe and his wingman, Dale D. Klahn, hit one, and when a second Zero made a run on Klahn, Clifton hit it in the cockpit in a nice deflection shot. The plane crashed into the channel. Clifton's squadron claimed 11 Zeros destroyed and 14 probables against the loss of four of their own Hellcats.

The hardest fight of the day fell to Air Group Commander Caldwell and his two protecting fighters. As they left the scene eight Zeros engaged them in a violent fight, with Caldwell and the Hellcats constantly weaving and the Zeros making repeated runs. The Japanese pilots attacked Caldwell's Avenger again and again, hitting it repeatedly with 7.7-mm. and 20-mm. fire, killing photographer Barnett and wounding the two gunners in the plane. One of the escort pilots, Lieutenant H. M. Crockett, was also wounded and the flaps of his Hellcat shot out of commission. Nevertheless, all of the planes got home. Ensign Carlton Roberts made an emergency landing at the Barakoma fighter strip still building on Vella Lavella. Howard Caldwell, the "old man," proved himself to be the skilled pilot he was by landing his Avenger on the *Saratoga* though he had only one wheel and no landing flaps. He was proud of his escorts and reported three of the Zeros shot down. One he claimed himself. Fighter commander Clifton in his after-action report summarized the air battle thus:

Over Rabaul . . . the F6F proved to be far and away the best fighter in the air. . . . The F6F was definitely faster at sea level than the Zeke [Zero]. The

F6F did not have the maneuverability or climb advantage, but again the Thach weave plus the rugged construction and pilot protection offset these. . . . The F6F's superior diving speed proved a Godsend in places where weaving was impossible.

For his part, air-group skipper Caldwell was cautious—with good reason, as it turned out—concerning the results of the torpedo attack. "The number of certain torpedo hits is unknown to me." In truth only two torpedoes had hit and of these only one exploded. The waterspouts seen by the Avenger's pilots probably were "prematures." The torpedo that scored badly damaged the new light cruiser *Noshiro*.

Just the same, the attack had accomplished its purpose, thanks to Jim Newell's reliable SBDs. Five of the six cruisers attacked, as the pilots had claimed, took either hits or damaging near misses. *Atago* was near missed by three 1,000-pounders that killed 18 men, including her captain standing on the exposed navigation bridge, and wounded 20 more. The *Takao* suffered two hits that opened her hull on the starboard side forward and disabled her No. 3 turret, killing three and seriously injuring 14. Sister *Maya* took a bomb down her trunked funnel that burst in her port engine room and disabled the ship, starting a fire that burned all day. *Chikuma* was near missed without serious damage, but *Mogami*, finally repaired after her damage received at Midway, now received a bomb that injured or killed 20, started a bad fire in the aircraft storage area amidships, and rendered her once more in need of extensive repairs. Newell's pilots, in some of the finest American bombing of the entire Pacific war, also hit light cruisers *Agano*, *Noshiro*, and a destroyer. Admiral Sherman had insisted that his aviators get plenty of practice in attacking moving targets, and his foresight had paid big dividends.

Getting Kurita's 2nd Fleet cruisers beaten up was not a part of Admiral Koga's game plan for Operation "RO." When word reached him at Truk of the damage to Kurita's ships, he was relieved to learn also that the Rabaul command had ordered them withdrawn to Truk, save crippled *Maya*, which could not move, and *Agano*, not part of the 2nd Fleet. They left harbor immediately, by so doing avoiding an attack of 27 of General George C. Kenney's Army Liberators striking Rabaul from New Guinea, and at 4:00 P.M. they began steaming for Truk. Four of the heavy cruisers had to continue to Japan for repairs.

Since it had been reinforced by carrier planes, Admiral Kusaka's Base Air Fleet should have been able to take revenge on *Saratoga* and *Princeton*. But the Japanese had been caught unprepared to launch a strike, and when 12 Kate torpedo planes finally got off, *Sara* and *Princeton* already were well south. The Kates could find only a small convoy composed of a PT boat, an LCI "Elsie Item" gunship, and an LCT (Landing Craft, Tank). Though with remarkably fine accuracy they put torpedoes through the LCT and the PT boat, neither fish exploded, and two Kates fell to the automatic weapons of the little ships. Aware of the need to claim a counterbalancing victory to offset American boasts about the attack on Rabaul, Imperial Headquarters propagandists escalated this miserable score into a carrier blown up and sunk, a "medium" carrier set afire and later sunk, three heavy and light cruisers sunk, and, as an afterthought, a destroyer as well. This became "The First Air Battle of Bougainville"— if the truth were considered, hardly an auspicious beginning for Operation "RO."

Bougainville was now safe from Japanese surface attack, but a jubilant Halsey had no intention of leaving Rabaul alone. A quick follow-up strike was deemed desirable. Montgomery's Task Group 50.3 of *Essex*, *Bunker Hill*, and *Independence* arrived at Espiritu Santo as *Saratoga* and *Princeton* were pulling away from their attack. But it was impossible for Halsey to order the groups to rendezvous and strike again immediately because of a shortage of cruisers and destroyers for escort. The delay did, however, give Halsey's staff more time to plan.

This time Halsey planned a one-two punch launched by both carrier groups. Montgomery's carriers, with an escort of nine destroyers only, no cruisers, would launch from a point in the Solomons Sea about 70 miles off Cape Torokina. Sherman's TF-38, still with its two AA light cruisers, would launch from a point near the Green Islands. Rabaul would thus get hit from the east and southeast.

Saratoga and *Princeton* launched at 8:30 A.M. on Armistice Day, November 11. The planes had to fly through thick cloud cover to reach Simpson Harbor at Rabaul, a cover that Japanese radar penetrated. This time 68 Zeros scrambled from Rabaul's Lakunai, Vunakanau, and Tobera airfields to intercept, while ships in harbor darted quickly for covering rain squalls. Dauntlesses and Avengers attacked, missed heavy cruisers *Maya* and *Chokai* hidden by the rain in the inner harbor, but not the new light cruiser *Agano* in the outer harbor. A torpedo shattered the 6,000-ton ship's stern and flooded the after engine room.

Thirty-five minutes later Montgomery's airmen came in, the *Essex* air group first, then the *Bunker Hill*'s, and finally the planes from the *Independence*. *Bunker Hill*'s pilots of VB-17, led by Lieutenant Commander James "Moe" Vose, the veteran of the Battle of Santa Cruz, were anxious to test their Curtiss SB2C "Beasts" in combat. Covered by weaving Hellcats of VF-18 overhead, they approached Simpson Harbor from the northeast, the 23 big-tailed planes flying over squalls covering Crater Peninsula and Rabaul Town. About them Zeros looped and rolled and tried a new weapon, a phosphorous bomb that sent streamers of smoke across the flight paths of the Helldivers. Finally, through their radio earphones the pilots could hear the voice of their air-group commander, M. P. "Bags" Bagdanovich, a former Navy football great of the Class of '28. "This is Bags. There is a cruiser down there and a couple more up ahead. O.K., Moe, take it away!" Moe Vose quickly assigned targets, then: "Let's go, Helldivers!" Down the "Beasts" went in their first combat attack, the Hellcats diving down with them. The torpedo-carrying Avengers had already dropped toward the deck in high-speed glides.

In the few minutes that followed, no one, not even Bags Bagdanovich, who stayed topside in his TBF, could tell who hit what. One section attacked a ship some pilots took to be a heavy cruiser and others a three-stack light cruiser. Each thought that they had sunk their targets, but according to the Japanese their victims were destroyer *Suzunami,* sunk near the harbor entrance by bombs, and destroyer *Naganami,* hit by a torpedo. It may have been Lieutenant Bob Friesz who hit the *Suzunami* after releasing at the dangerously low altitude of only 800 feet.

On the retirement of the planes Zeros stitched 7.7-mm. holes in some, and an Army P-38 covering a simultaneous attack by Fifth Air Force planes took a shot at Bagdanovich, triggering some choice invective over the VHF circuit. Six planes fell to the AA or Zeros. Several "Beasts" came home badly shot up, indicating that the temperamental plane was tough and could take it.

When the planes returned to their carriers Admiral Sherman decided to cancel his second strike. The weather, the aerologists said, was abominable over the target, with squalls and thunderheads. Montgomery did not cancel, even when the oscilloscopes of the SK radars on his ships picked up enemy planes at 119 miles and closing. The best way to get rid of the avgas and bombs aboard the planes was to fly them off. At 1:25 P.M., 12 minutes later, fighters began to roll on the decks of the three carriers.

Despite a lack of cruisers Montgomery had cause to be confident in his AA protection. He was employing an improved circular cruising formation that kept his three carriers in close proximity and massed the AA fire. Also, he had—or thought he had—an augmented CAP of fighters controlled by FDOs in *Essex* and *Independence.* He also had available over his ships 33 fighters from land bases, Commander John T. Blackburn's VF-17, equipped with F4U Corsairs, and a division from VF-23 flying Hellcats. These pilots were carrier-qualified and had landed aboard the carriers to refuel and rearm earlier that day.

The strike that Montgomery's radars had picked up was from Rabaul and consisted of 35 Zeros, 20 Vals, and 14 torpedo-carrying Kates. The pilots knew where they were going; a reconnaissance plane had spotted TG 50.3 at 10:55 A.M. They were also Japan's best, all the Val and Kate air crews being from carrier squadrons.

Some 40 miles out from the task force, a young pilot on CAP spotted the incoming Japanese, and instead of giving the traditional "Tallyho!" and reporting their course and altitude, he hollered an informal "Jesus Christ! There are millions of them! Let's go to work." He and the CAP did, but mostly on the Zero escort and not on the following Vals and Kates. The Vals had an almost free ride to their tip-over point 16,000 feet above the American ships that until a very few minutes before had been refueling and arming planes. Veterans of the Santa Cruz battle aboard the ships took one look at the Vals screeching down and assumed what they later called the "Holiday Crouch," dropping on their right sides prone on the deck and drawing up their knees to protect against blast or concussion, with right hand behind the neck, left over the eyes. On *Bunker Hill,* seemingly the principal target, gunners poured a fusilade of 20- and 40-mm. tracer balls skyward.

Bombs fell close, very close, five near misses showering the *Bunker Hill* with water and tearing open with shrapnel the gas tanks of a parked SB2C. Other near misses punctured *Essex*'s hull in several places and wounded eight men. *Independence* took four near misses, and in a near miracle, a 40-mm. round detonated in the air a fifth bomb dropping at the carrier.

The fighter-directors should have prevented the "free ride" of the Vals. But fighter direction had not been well-handled. The FDOs had failed to contact fighters launched for the second Rabaul strike to vector them against the attack. *Essex*'s FDO had sent 16 patrolling fighters 30 miles out from the task force to intercept what turned out to be 12 friendly Hellcats. Many Hellcat pilots, lacking instructions, simply headed for the AA fire to look for enemy planes. Ensign C. T. Watts, who had barely cleared the deck of the *Bunker Hill* when the Vals started down, saw one as he was retracting his wheels. He hastily charged his .50s and, only seconds after he had taken off, scored his first "kill" by dropping the Val in flames.

As the Japanese attackers continued to dribble in in treys and pairs, John Blackburn's Corsairs made their greatest contribution to the defense. His VF-17 had originally operated from the *Bunker Hill* before the Navy decided that the Corsair was unfit for carrier work. Then he and his "Skull and Crossbones" squadron had gone to the Solomons for duty from land bases. Now, he went after some late-arriving Vals, a few Bettys from Rabaul, and the 14 oncoming Kates. Blackburn, at the head of his own section, tackled some Zeros. He smoked one, followed it into a cloud, then had to break off when his windscreen fogged up. Lieutenants J. M. Kleinman and Mac Burriss dropped a Betty and then a Kate making a run on a carrier. Burriss dropped another Kate, while Kleinman, spotting eight more low off the water, dove to attack. He overshot, did a quick wing-over, got on the tail of the leader, and shot him down within the screening ring of destroyers of the task force. A 40-mm. shell from one of the ships blew up his instrument panel and wounded him in the face. Two F6Fs, mistaking the unusual configuration of his Corsair for enemy, attacked head on and hit his wing. Without instruments, wounded, Kleinman managed to reach the Barakoma strip, navigating by the sun.

The Hellcats, Corsairs, and the AA shot down all 14 Kates and all but three of the 20 Vals attacking. Lost also were two Zeros, two Judy reconnaissance planes, and several Bettys. Not a bomb or torpedo had hit a ship, but "torpedoed" quite effectively was Admiral Koga's Operation "RO."

The Japanese admiralissimo realized that he would have to withdraw his carrier planes if his three carriers—*Shokaku, Zuikaku,* and *Zuiho*—were to have even a cadre of experienced pilots. On November 12 he called off the "RO" operation, and on the 13th 52 surviving carrier planes flew back to Truk. The carrier air groups had lost 43 of 82 Zeros, 38 of 45 dive bombers, and 34 of 40 torpedo planes. All six Judy reconnaissance planes had vanished. What was worse, 86 of 192 highly trained air crew had been killed or were missing in action.

Even so, Koga was reluctant to admit that Rabaul no longer could serve as an offensive base. He ordered to its defense 27 bombers that had been operating from land bases in the Marshalls. But despite his efforts and those of homeland training squadrons to keep Rabaul stocked, the air defenses of the New Britain bastion eroded steadily. With the completion of the airfields on Bougainville, AirSols fighters, including Tommy Blackburn's Corsairs, could escort light and medium bombers over Rabaul in daily attacks. In so doing they and Marine Corps squadrons also flying the F4U proved the plane to be one of the best air-superiority fighters of World War II. It was marginally superior to the Hellcat in straightaway speed, acceleration, and climb at low altitude. To Navy and Marine planes from Bougainville and other Solomons airfields and to General Kenney's Fifth Air Force planes based on New Guinea, the Japanese Navy and Army lost the equivalent of a whole air force at Rabaul. The personal score of the leading Marine ace, Major Gregory "Pappy" Boyington, went up to a claimed 28 planes before the commander of the VMF-214 "Blacksheep" squadron was shot down into St. George Channel to be picked up by a Japanese submarine and made a POW.

The Rabaul attrition mightily aided Admiral Nimitz's campaign to capture the Marshalls and Gilberts, though few if any Americans realized at the time it would do so. Koga had too few planes now to commit his carriers to the defense of the islands. Without carriers he dared not send surface ships. Rabaul also attracted reinforcements that the elementary dictates of strategy would have seen deployed to the Marshalls. The big show in the Central Pacific would begin with the Japanese Navy unable to put up a strong fight.

19. Tarawa and Makin

From Pearl Harbor the strategic Marshall Islands lie some 2,000 miles east by somewhat south. The Gilberts, the New Zealand dependency seized by Japan, lie about 300 miles south and slightly east of the nearest of the Marshalls. All are atolls surrounded by coral reefs resembling white necklaces strung about deep-blue lagoons. Kwajalein Atoll, which was the center of Japanese administration for the Micronesian populace and headquarters for its Sixth Base Force defenders, surrounds a 66-mile-long lagoon, the world's largest. Like the others, its climate is tropical, ranging from 72 to 98 degrees with a mean annual temperature of 81.

Not many of the islands were large enough or faced the proper direction (into the northwest trade winds) to permit construction of coral airstrips. Nimitz's CincPac planners, in considering their strategy, concluded that the best way to acquire needed airfields quickly would be to take them from the enemy.*

In preparation for his CenPac campaign, Admiral Nimitz had reorganized his Pacific Fleet forces as early as March 1943. His Fifth Fleet now included all ships in the Pacific except those assigned to Halsey's Southwest Pacific force, Frank Jack Fletcher's North Pacific Fleet, and ships under the command of General MacArthur. Command of the entire Fifth Fleet had gone to Ray Spruance; its amphibious component was in the experienced hands of Kelly Turner. Except for major actions that found Spruance at sea in heavy cruiser *Indianapolis,* he stayed mostly ashore, usually burdened with planning.

Following the Rabaul attacks, Nimitz designated all of his Fifth Fleet flattops, six large and five light carriers, as Task Force 50. This he subdivided into four task groups. TG 50.1 was under Pownall, TG 50.2 under Radford, TG 50.3 under Montgomery, and TG 50.4 (formerly TF 38) under Ted Sherman. Logically, if all four were to take part in one opera-

---

* After the war Admiral Nimitz indicated, in an interview with the authors, that had he known how rapidly Seabees could convert coral atolls into airstrips, he might have bypassed some of the atolls rather than mount the massive amphibious assaults needed to take them.

tion, there should be, if not a supreme carrier commander, at least an OTC, Officer in Tactical Command. Predictably, Nimitz selected Charles Pownall. Pownall had been working well with Ray Spruance, and his leadership in the "makee learn" raids had been generally satisfactory.

The role of the carriers, as Nimitz envisaged it, would be a dual one. They had to neutralize enemy airfields and bomb and strafe Betio and Makin islands in the Gilberts, the first objects of invasion. At the same time they had to stand ready to attack Koga's Combined Fleet should it appear. It would not do for TF 50's commander to focus all of his attention on either mission. Nimitz could not know that the danger of Koga's appearance was practically nil following the Rabaul raids.

Nimitz did not elect to keep his fast carrier groups together. Instead, he gave each a definite mission that kept them well separated. The Carrier Interceptor Group (TG 50.1), commanded by Pownall himself, took station between Makin, the northernmost Gilbert atoll, and Mili Atoll, closest of the defended Marshalls. Pownall had the *Yorktown* as flagship, plus the *Lexington* and CVL *Cowpens*. His specific mission was to neutralize those southern Marshalls airstrips from which attacks might be hurled at Kelly Turner's amphibious forces.

Not far distant, but closer to Makin, was the Northern Carrier Group (TG 50.2) under Rear Admiral Arthur W. Radford. With the *Enterprise* as his flagship and accompanied by light carriers *Belleau Wood* and *Monterey,* it was Radford's job to work over Makin's defenses and—if need be—to join with Pownall in repelling an advance by Koga's Combined Fleet from the north or west.

Rear Admiral Ted Sherman's TG 50.4, the *Saratoga* and consort *Princeton,* designated the Relief Carrier Group, was to sail almost due north from Espiritu Santo in the South Pacific as the operation was beginning to strike Nauru Island. This drowned volcanic peak boasted an airfield, and it was close enough to Tarawa Atoll (380 miles) to be a threat to the beachhead unless thoroughly worked over. Sherman was to do so, then close the Gilberts at best speed and cover approaching invasion forces. In his spare time he was to keep his search planes looking for Koga.

Rear Admiral Alfred Montgomery had the fourth component, the Southern Carrier Group (TG 50.3), containing the same trio of ships that had battered Rabaul: *Essex, Bunker Hill,* and CVL *Independence.* Now protected by a screen of four cruisers sent from Pearl, Montgomery's flattops were to fly bombing strikes in direct support of the landings at Tarawa and Abemama, the latter the undefended atoll in the southern Gilberts.

This plan for use of the carriers was obviously a good one if Koga stayed at Truk and if supporting the landings were the only criterion. But it had a certain resemblance to Admiral Yamamoto's plan at the Battle of Midway: It scattered the carriers across a wide expanse of ocean. The Relief and Southern Groups were too widely separated for easy mutual support, and so were the Interceptor and Northern groups. The danger was that Nimitz's forces might suffer defeat in detail, as Yamamoto's had at Midway. Combined, TG 50 vastly outnumbered in ships and planes Koga's carrier strength; dispersed, none of the four TGs enjoyed a numerical superiority. It is perhaps just as well that Koga's carrier air groups already had been defeated at Rabaul.

Off Guadalcanal in 1942 Frank Jack Fletcher had pulled out his fleet carriers shortly after the beginning of the operation. Kelly Turner saw to it that this could not happen in the Gilbert invasion, even though the amphibious forces had five escort carriers to furnish air support and antisubmarine patrols. The big flattops would stay close until Betio and Makin had fallen and the transports had unloaded. Hopefully, this would not be long. Marines of the 2nd Division should take Betio at Tarawa Atoll quickly and GIs of the 27th Infantry Division Makin. Each unit vastly outnumbered the defenders on either island.

Had it not been for the Wake raid the Japanese might have been easily able to predict that Makin and Betio would be initial targets of invasion and to reinforce both islands. But the Wake attack had convinced many Japanese staff officers that the Americans might approach the Marshalls from the north rather than from the south. A secret directive to Wake's defenders predicted "Air attacks against our perimeter will be more frequent in the future."

In truth, warnings were about all that Truk headquarters dared send the defenders of Wake, the Gilberts, and the Marshalls. The draining away of planes from these islands to support Rabaul had been a bad mistake. On D-day, November 20, 1943, for example, the now well-established air base at Mili Atoll that Frank Jack Fletcher had raided early in 1942 had available only a handful of miscellaneous aircraft. Ten Kate torpedo bombers normally present had been flown to Rabaul. Other bases in the islands were hardly better off. Against the local defenders each of Pownall's groups held a lopsided advantage.

Because Koga chose not to come out and fight, the Gilberts operation was something of an anticlimax for his antagonists. Ted Sherman's two carriers had little trouble in blasting inoperational Nauru's airfield. Similarly, beginning on November 19 and continuing for five straight days, Pownall's flyers hammered Mili's runway, keeping it out of commission until November 25, five days after the beginnings of the landings. The pilots found only a few aircraft at Mili, apparently transients, but the attacks prevented reinforcing aircraft from landing. At Jaluit Atoll Pownall's Hellcats shot up five flying boats and a half-dozen Jake and Pete float planes to end whatever threat this seaplane base might have posed.

Pownall did *not* attack the important inner Marshalls airfields at Wotje, Maloelap, and Kwajalein atolls that were known to harbor Betty and Nell bombers that could reach the beachhead. This was not Pownall's fault. Admiral Jack Towers and his ComAirPac staff had pressed hard for a strike on Kwajalein, but they had been overruled. The old curmudgeon, Kelly Turner, had wanted Pownall's carriers to stay near his transports and had his way with Admiral Nimitz. This was a strategic error and would have serious consequences.

Support from the carrier airmen for the Marines and GIs was perhaps more enthusiastically than skillfully given. Radford's pilots from *Enterprise, Belleau Wood,* and *Cowpens* began strikes at 5:20 A.M. on November 19, D-day minus one. They downed the only plane they saw over Makin, an unfortunate Dave biplane, and hammered the enemy antiaircraft into silence. The chief problem turned out to be a low-flying four-tenths cloud cover that interfered with attack runs.

A sample follows of a conversation between an observer in a liaison TBF and an incoming strike of 19 Hellcats, 15 Avengers, and 19 Dauntlesses mostly from the *Enterprise.* Lieutenant Commander John L. Phillips, Jr., and Lieutenant W. H. Fitzpatrick in the Avenger were designated "Viceroy" in VHF radio jargon, and the leader of this particular strike was "Charlie Scarlett."

0804 (8:04 a.m.): Viceroy to Charlie Scarlett: "Smack 'em right at How Hour without losing any time."
Charlie Scarlett to Viceroy: "No military installations in Big Makin [Butaritari islet]."
Viceroy to Charlie Scarlett: "I'll be a bulkhead's uncle! Well, get your men and smack 'em with gusto according to schedule."
Charlie Scarlett to Viceroy (planes following): "We've got a pushover" (order to dive on preassigned targets).
Viceroy to Charlie Scarlett: "Bring your boys into position to strafe two or three miles ahead of Red Beach."

And so it went. The landing that followed was easy, and not all of the VHF conversation was serious. The following exchange was between Viceroy and Clipper 1, a Strike Commander:

Viceroy to Clipper 1: "Any slant-eyed activity over target?"
Clipper 1 to Viceroy: "No activity apparent. . . . It looks like all the girls have skivvy skirts on."
Viceroy to Clipper 1: "Ah, that's too bad."

The impression of Clipper 1 and the attacking pilots that Makin's defenses were not strong proved to be correct. On the island were only 284 tranied naval infantry under Sezio Ishikawa, a junior-grade lieutenant. But the willingness of these Japanese to fight to the last man and an apparent unwillingness to advance rapidly on the part of attacking troops from the 27th Division turned what should have been a grim day's work into a four-day ordeal. A furious Kelly Turner, spending a night ashore, had his tent punctured by bullets, not from Ishikawa's men but from nervous Army sentries. So began a trouble-marred combat career for this former New York National Guard division.

The struggle for Tarawa's Betio Island was as different a sort of battle as could be imagined. The Second Marine Division fought superbly but against 4,500 Japanese defenders very strongly entrenched. Rear Admiral Keiji Shibasaki's Special Naval Landing Force literally had to be blasted out dugout by dugout to secure the island at heavy loss of life to the Marines. Air support helped mightily, but the planes were not accurate enough to take out individual positions. Rockets, though under test, were not yet available. Six days of hard fighting cost the Marines approximately 980 dead and 2,050 wounded.

Despite the terrible cost in Marine lives, Tarawa taught everyone all sorts of combat lessons that would be put to good use later. To Admiral Spruance the use of fast carrier pilots to provide close air support over a period of several days seemed decidedly questionable. It took special training to spot targets on smoking, torn-up, low-lying coral islands. Support work had better be left to CVE pilots with specialized training. Even more questionable was the pinning down of the task groups to within 100 miles of Tarawa and Makin while strikes continued from predawn to dark. A nervous Montgomery had kept his TG 50.3 flattops moving about, making it hard for the pilots who frequently had to use their YE homing gear to get home. Montgomery's caution was justified, too. CVE *Liscome Bay,* too slow to move very far, was blown up by a submarine torpedo off Makin with the loss of 614 lives, including that of Rear Admiral H. M. Mullinix, the CVE group commander. This horrible disaster brought Navy loss of life close to that of Marine.

Admiral Koga's reaction to the landing in the Gilberts was pitifully weak. A plan to rush reinforcing troops from the Ponape garrison on cruisers and destroyers was aborted when the troops reached Kwajalein. The planned counterlanding on Tarawa for which the men were intended was called off. Prospects were not much better for an aerial counterattack. Only 46 planes had been left in the Marshalls after 27 Bettys had gone to Rabaul on November 12. But these few, plus reinforcements that trickled in, were enough to give Admiral Pownall and the other task group commanders some anxious moments.

Montgomery's force drew much of the attention from the Japanese— and all of the damage. Shadowers picked up his TG 50.3 as it steamed at dusk about 15 miles west-southwest of Betio on the night of D-Day, November 20. At about 6:00 P.M., while landing the last support strike flown at Betio, some 16 Bettys of the night-trained 755th Air Group flew up the starboard side of Montgomery's force, then deployed to attack the carrier formation from bow, beam, and quarter. *Bunker Hill* fighters on CAP bounced Captain Sakae Yamashita's airmen in rapidly fading light but too late to prevent the drop of several torpedoes from uncomfortably close in.

From near the stern of *Independence* a geyser of water climbed into the air. The ship shuddered, settled aft, but held place in formation. Amid hissing live steam, wreckage, and salt water flooding into the after fire and engine rooms, 17 men died and 43 suffered injury. The light carrier's propeller shafts, knocked out of alignment, wobbled and pounded, and

Captain R. L. Johnson had to con his ship to the nearest friendly base, Funafuti, 700 miles distant. He made it, but *Independence* needed a navy-yard overhaul at Hunter's Point.

The surviving 755th Group airmen magnified their deed, escalating the single hit on *Independence* into three and three more on either *Essex* or *Bunker Hill.* Nine of the Bettys had fallen, carrying in two of Captain Yamashita's best aviators, Lieutenant Nobuki Miyamae, commanding the First Squadron, and Lieutenant Yoshiaki Akiyama, commanding the Second. In Japan both were lauded as heroes. Akiyama, a black-mustachioed judo champion, had flown in the Chungking attacks of the China war. Miyamae, an Eta Jima graduate of the class of 1936, according to a Navy press release, possessed strongly the Japanese virtue of stoicism. The sailors of injured *Independence* had at least this consolation: They had been attacked by Japan's surviving best.

Attacks launched in the next few days by the 755th and a sister air group failed to score. Indirectly, however, they led to the death of one of America's best, Lieutenant Commander E. H. "Butch" O'Hare. O'Hare's destruction of five Bettys attacking CV-2, old *Lexington*, in early 1942 had only launched his notable career. The 1937 Naval Academy graduate had recently taken part in the raids on Marcus and Wake, and at Wake, flying a Hellcat, he had picked off a Zero and a pair of bombers on the ground. In the Gilberts operation O'Hare was commander of Air Group 6 aboard *Enterprise.* Concerned about snoopers and small flights of bombers stalking his carrier by night, O'Hare had taken it upon himself to team up with Commander John Phillips of VT-6 to see what could be done about shooting them down. The plan was innovative: Phillips would take off in a TBF-1C Avenger equipped with a new-model airborne intercept radar. O'Hare and another pilot, Ensign Warren Skon, both qualified to land at night, would fly wing on Phillips to serve as "gunners." When Phillips spotted an incoming Betty, O'Hare and Skon would stick with him until they spotted it visually, then attack and shoot it down.

On November 26 at about dusk the *Enterprise*'s catapult hurled Phillips into the air. O'Hare and Skon followed in their Hellcats. All three then were vectored by the ship's radar eastward toward a blip presumed to be a flight of Bettys incoming from Roi in the Marshalls. The contact faded and the trio turned back west toward the *Enterprise*. Because his TBF was slower and could not stay with the Hellcats, Phillips fell behind and lost contact. Then, nearly over the task force, he was given a vector toward a bogey reported by the radar controller to be only three miles away and closing. Spotting the exhaust flares from an aircraft ahead, Phillips closed and opened fire with his fixed .50s with his radar reading off a range of only 200 yards. At 50 yards he banked away and his turret gunner opened up, spraying the target with fire. Crossing over and ahead of the now falling Betty, Phillips watched it strike the water and spew flaming gasoline over a wide area.

So far the mission had been a brilliant success. Vectored after two more Bettys, Phillips visually sighted them at 1,500 yards. Following the right-hand machine, he gave chase. O'Hare, still in the area with Ensign Skon, may have seen them too, for he used his radio to ask Phillips to blink the Avenger's lights. Apparently O'Hare was fearful that he would fire on the wrong plane. Phillips complied and alarmed the Betty pilot, who began weaving his plane. O'Hare closed with Skon and both fired without hitting. Aided by the radar, Phillips then followed the Betty through a right turn and shot it down. Again, a long streamer of blazing fuel, signaling victory, lighted the surface of the ocean. But now came tragedy.

A few minutes later Phillips' turret gunner sighted a plane crossing under the tail of the TBF. Quickly aiming, he fired a burst, then lost sight of the plane. Trying to get his three charges together, the FDO aboard *Enterprise* asked the American pilots to snap on their recognition lights. Phillips complied, as did Skon and O'Hare. Skon could see the white turtleback light on the other fighter clearly. All three joined in a loose formation.

Suddenly (to Phillips and his crew) what seemed to be another plane crossed the American formation in O'Hare's direction. The turret gunner put out 30 rounds; the stranger seemed to return the fire, then to pull up and disappear. Skon, who did not see the plane, had been watching O'Hare and saw the gunner's tracers appear to pass between his Hellcat and O'Hare's. O'Hare's plane then went into what appeared to be an out-of-control skid, slid out of formation, and Skon lost sight of it. Noting that the two downed Bettys still were burning on the water, Skon after some difficulty closed Phillips. Neither could raise O'Hare on the radio, and both returned to the *Enterprise*.

It seems possible that O'Hare might have been shot down by an enemy plane, but the probability is that Phillips's gunner either fired on O'Hare or hit him accidentally in firing at another enemy plane. Tracers that appear to pass ahead of a target often are going in. Absolutely no trace of O'Hare's plane was found, not so much as a seat cushion.

Tragic as its outcome was, this bizarre little battle obviously had broken up an attempt by three or more Japanese pilots to attack the *Enterprise*. The battle also proved that night interception of enemy torpedo planes was worthwhile, but not by several planes trying to coordinate attacks in the darkness. Planes without radar were worse than useless.

On the fourth day of fighting ashore, November 23, Makin and Betio were both declared "secure," though Pownall's carriers lingered several days more. Then TF 50 retired from the Gilberts by task groups, the last leaving at the end of November. By this time the air crews had become bone-weary and accident-prone. All hands needed a break from the tensions of combat.

Pownall and his staff had no rest. Anxious to get on with the next step of the offensive, the invasion of the Marshalls, Admiral Nimitz now requested TF 50 to soften up the target by striking at Kwajalein, headquarters of the Sixth Base Force. He also needed low-level oblique photographs of Roi and Kwajalein islands at either end of the large atoll and pictures of Wotje and Maloelap atolls to the eastward, all potential targets. Photo interpreters could combine these into a mosaic that could be used to select beaches for assault landings. In addition to clobbering ships, planes, and installations, Pownall's airmen would take the pictures. Planning for the attack began immediately on Pownall's flagship.

For this mission Pownall left behind most of the carriers that had struck at Rabaul, giving them a chance to integrate replacements for their air groups. He took with him TG 50.1 and 50.3, with himself in command of *Yorktown*, *Lexington*, and *Cowpens*, while Montgomery commanded *Essex*, *Enterprise*, and *Belleau Wood*. The force weighed anchor on December 1, 1943, swung north, then west, and finally due south to approach Kwajalein from the atoll's northern flank. His flattops embarked 193 Hellcats, 104 Dauntlesses, and 89 Avengers. To bolster air defense the fighter complement had been somewhat increased at the expense of numbers of dive bombers.

The Air Plan devised by Pownall for the attack was the product of a cautious nature and defensive-mindedness. In it Pownall specified that the *Cowpens* and *Belleau Wood* air groups should be reserved entirely for defense. In addition the plan withheld nearly a third of the embarked Hellcats on the big carriers for CAP. Commander Ernest M. Snowden, Air Group 16's skipper from the *Lexington*, had urged a fighter sweep over the atoll in advance of bombing strikes, but Pownall had turned him down. The Task Force, he thought, probably would not achieve surprise and probably would be attacked. Therefore, "We will plan for the worst and hope for the breaks." To Pownall that meant keeping plenty of fighters aloft, while those assigned to the attack stayed close to protect the Dauntless and Avenger bombers.

Because he also desired flexibility in his attack plan, Pownall had delegated local tactical command to an airborne skipper, Commander Snowden. Each flattop had been told tentatively where its planes should go, but as Senior Air Strike Coordinator, Snowden would have the responsibility of assigning specific targets by voice radio as the attack progressed. Success would thus depend heavily on what Snowden could see from the cockpit of a TBF while orbiting over a lagoon 66 miles long and—equally important—how well he could communicate with other air-group commanders and squadron leaders.

Separated by 12 miles, the two carrier groups of TF 50 reached their launching positions about 110 miles north of Roi airfield on December 4. Swinging through 24 points of the compass, the carriers headed into a northwest trade wind to launch the first strike. It was 6:30 A.M., and a rose-tinted glow on low-hanging but broken clouds hinted the rising of the sun. By the time the sun was fully up three-quarters of an hour later, the 249 planes had formed up and were well on their way. Minutes later, with the American planes 80 kilometers out, Japanese radar operators stiffened and adjusted their sets as they saw a huge blip appear. Shouts of warning and jangling phones sent Zero pilots racing to their planes. Hardly waiting to give their coughing engines time to start running smoothly, they tore off from Roi airfield with clouds of coral dust swirling behind them. The Zeros numbered 27, enough to give Pownall's incoming flights a good workout but not to halt the attack. Rear Admiral Monzo Akiyama, commanding the 6th Base Force, could have no hope of that.

First planes in for the Zeros to jump were a dozen Hellcats that dove to strafe Roi airfield. To Lieutenant M. C. "Boogie" Hoffman, an old hand who had test-flown the first captured Zero, the field seemed covered with planes with engines turning over. Hoffman and others made a single pass, then began weaving violently as the Zeros swept in from behind on their four-plane sections. Hoffman broke away, finally, but lost his wingman, R. G. Johnson, whose Hellcat slid away, wing tanks aflame. His was the only Hellcat loss of the 12, but Roi had not been effectively strafed or even bombed.

On seeing the commotion below, Commander Snowden had tried to assign other fighters to strafe the field but found that he could not contact the Hellcat leader from the *Essex*, whose VHF set had failed. He finally managed to get seven Dauntlesses and seven Hellcats to attack the field, and they did well to burn 13 Zeros and three Bettys and damage ten more of each type. Lost in air-to-air combat, according to Japanese sources, had been 19 Zeros and six Bettys. But the three runways of the field were completely intact, and plenty of Bettys and Zeros were hidden under camouflage in log and sand revetments.

The great bulk of the American planes attacked shipping with results that were very poor considering the number of bombs dropped. As the after-action report of the *Essex* noted, its pilots had not practiced on moving targets for three months, and their skills had rusted. Nor had the trouble-ridden Mark 13 torpedoes from the Avengers worked well. Cameras newly mounted on the planes and aimed backward revealed that far too many turned right, porpoised, ran erratically, hit the bottom of the lagoon, or were simply duds. Explosions that resembled hits must have been prematures. Light cruisers *Isuzu* and *Nagara* were damaged, the former possibly by a Mark 13, but neither sank. Eight merchant ships were hit also and four sank; some probably fell victim to Mark 13s.

If American bombing was bad, then Japanese AA gunnery must be accounted as worse. The attacking pilots described it as generally "on" in altitude and "off" in deflection. *Essex* lost no planes and *Enterprise* but one. *Lexington* was missing a pair and the *Yorktown* two more. But only three pilots were dead or missing.

When the aircraft returned and Pownall heard that many enemy planes on Roi appeared still to be intact, he pondered the implications. Then he made up his mind. Both carrier groups would retire, abandoning a planned second strike on Kwajalein Atoll. Instead, in passing they would hit Wotje, the northernmost of the Marshall atolls. Against Maloelap, site of another airfield in range of Task Force 50, they would send nothing. The aviators protested, but Pownall was firm. The risks did not warrant staying longer, he believed.

As the Wotje strike was getting away at noon on December 4, bogies appeared on the radar screens of TF 50. These came from 15 Kate torpedo planes flown off from Roi and Maloelap. The first group of three attacked *Lexington* in Pownall's own task group. None scored, and *Lexington*'s five-inch gunners employing Mark 32 proximity fuses downed all three. The single fish dropped ran 150 yards astern of the carrier. Some forty minutes later four more Kates turned up, aiming for Captain J. J. "Jocko" Clark's *Yorktown,* Pownall's flagship. Cruiser *San Francisco's* lookouts were the first to spot these planes racing in just off the water under the radar. Its gunners dropped one, and the carrier's 20-mm. gunners sawed the wing from another. A third, hit by both ships, crashed in flames, while the fourth turned away. *San Francisco's* lookouts reported torpedoes dropped, but Clark had turned into the attacking planes and quite possibly saved *Yorktown* from a damaging hit.

The planes assigned to the Wotje strike, forming up over the task group, had ignored the shooting below to head for the target. *Yorktown* planes destroyed a Betty taking off from Wotje's runway and burned four planes on the ground. Lost, according to Japanese records, were three Kates and a pair of flying boats.

The evening of December 4 promised a lively show, courtesy of Bettys from Roi, Maloelap, and possibly Wotje. To make matters worse a full moon came up that shone so brightly that the various ships of the task force were visible to each other without the aid of binoculars. The Betty pilots attacking at night would scarcely need the brilliant, slow-falling parachute flares that had been a feature of every Japanese night air attack since the beginning of the war.

At about 6:50 P.M., forty minutes after sunset, bogies appeared on the radar screens. A scout plane first dropped a string of white lights to mark the course of TG 50 as it plowed along at 25 knots on course 045. Then came flares—but not as many as usual, leading American observers to think that the moonlight negated the need for them or that some Bettys had radar, which they did. Coming in was a big strike, 15 planes in one group, 22 in another, from Roi's airfield that had by no means been made inoperational by the morning's single strike.

As the planes closed Admiral Montgomery ordered his carriers not to fire; only screening cruisers and destroyers shot at the enemy, using full radar control. By keeping his flattops silent Montgomery hoped that despite the moonlight they might be indistinguishable from other large ships. Pownall adopted an opposite policy, ordering all ships to shoot without restriction. He believed that the high silhouettes of the carriers would be readily visible to the Japanese pilots. He would rely on the classic combination of fire and maneuver to frustrate the attack.

This he did in masterful fashion, preventing the Bettys from attacking from either bow to "anvil" the force. He kept antiaircraft cruiser *Oakland* six miles out from the screen in the direction of the attack, hoping that the ship's terrific fire power from twelve five-inch 38s would distract Betty pilots as they maneuvered to find their targets and seek attack angles.

Pownall almost got away with it, as for hours Bettys turned away from the VT-fused five-inch fire or missed with their fish the constantly turning ships. At 11:23 P.M., however, a Betty slipped in and, apparently taking advantage of four bright parachute flames, dropped a torpedo that hit Captain Felix B. Stump's *Lexington* in the stern aft of the propellers. Spray geysered high and the carrier nosed forward, then settled back. Water gushed into the steering engine room, shorting out electrical equipment. The rudder jammed 20 degrees left, leaving the carrier circling at high speed. It took 20 minutes for the hard-working chiefs of the engineering watch to bring the rudder back to zero degrees. Steering with her four propellers, the *Lexington* continued on a retirement course at 21 knots. Nine sailors were dead and 35 were wounded, mostly in the ship's engineering department. Shortly thereafter, the moon set and the Bettys vanished from the scopes. Aboard Jocko Clark's *Yorktown* the quartermaster expressed everyone's heartfelt relief by inscribing at 1:27 A.M. at Jocko's orders, "The moon set—Thank God." The rest of the retirement to Pearl was uneventful.

The Kwajalein raid cost Pownall his job as OTC of the fast carriers. Nimitz's staff was most displeased with Pownall's lack of aggressiveness and his apparent predeliction for seeing the dangers inherent in a carrier strike rather than the opportunities. A penciled note on the margin of Pownall's terse action report, where in his "Comments and Recommendations" he had explained his reasoning for not ordering a second strike, expressed the staff's general reaction. The handwritten insert read, "All defensive!" Nimitz agreed and began looking about for a more offensive-minded carrier commander.

The officer that Nimitz selected on Jack Towers' recommendation was Marc A. Mitscher, the wizened little veteran pilot who had not held a seagoing command since his captaincy of the old *Hornet* at Midway. Though the failure of that carrier's air group to find the enemy had temporarily clouded "Pete" Mitscher's career, he had more than redeemed himself later by aggressive, brilliant handling of Guadalcanal's shore-based airmen. Mitscher had followed Pownall in the post of Commander Fleet Air, West Coast, with headquarters at San Diego. Now he would follow Pownall again, taking his place in the admiral's quarters of the *Yorktown*.

20.   The Marshalls and Truk

After the relatively unsuccessful Kwajalein raid and the sack of Admiral Pownall, Task Force 50 took a breather at Pearl. The air groups repaired to Ford Island and Kaneohe airfields to sharpen gunnery and bombing skills and integrate new pilots.

The new men, fresh from well-developed operational training squadrons in the United States, listened a bit wide-eyed to the coldly delivered advice of the veterans. "You may have been told that Zeros are easy because we shoot down lots of them and have Hellcats. Don't you believe it, and *don't dogfight them.* If one gets on your tail, you're in trouble. Dive out." But the veterans also said, "They aren't unbeatable; one good burst and they still blow up. But don't get separated from your section. *It's murder to get caught alone.*" In off-duty hours and in the "O" club for officers, all pilots, veteran and neophyte alike, groused about their routines and speculated about the next objective. "Kwajalein? Nah, that's too tough. *Lexington* caught it off there, and we didn't knock out Roi. It'll be Wotje and Taroa [Maloelap Atoll's airfield] first."

At Pearl Harbor, while the airmen talked, Admiral Nimitz was busy reorganizing his fast carriers under his new commander, Pete Mitscher. He redesignated Task Force 50 as Task Force 58 with four task groups. TG 58.1 included *Enterprise, Yorktown,* and *Belleau Wood.* TG 58.2 now contained *Essex* and newly arrived CV *Intrepid* and CVL *Cabot.* TG 58.3 had *Bunker Hill, Cowpens,* and *Monterey.* And TG 58.4 had *Saratoga, Princeton,* and new *Langley.* The loss of *Independence* (repairing at Hunter's Point) and *Lexington* (drydocked at Pearl) had not reduced the carrier strength available to Mitscher.

Where the next attack would come was still a matter for debate. Nimitz knew that to bypass Wotje and Maloelap and land directly at Kwajalein would be risky. Not only was Roi airfield "tough" as the aviators had said, but current doctrine held that a fast carrier force ought not operate for long close to enemy land-based air. Yet the potential rewards were enormous. To go directly to Kwajalein and bypass the outer Marshalls would shorten the war by many weeks, to say nothing of the saving in American lives. What seems to have decided the issue was a photo taken by one of Pownall's planes on the December 4 raid that showed an emergency strip on Kwajalein Island that could be lengthened into a runway long enough for bombers. If Kwajalein and Roi* could be "had" and the bomber strip rapidly extended, then land-based planes could daily neutralize Wotje and Taroa and TF 58 could retire. On being briefed about the strip, Admiral Nimitz agreed to the Kwajalein landing and in consultation with the Joint Chiefs of Staff in Washington set the early date of January 31, 1944, for D-day.

In the Gilberts invasions the fast carriers had played purely a defensive role, shielding Kelly Turner's amphibious forces from attack by sea and air. Mitscher would have none of that for the Kwajalein landing. To him carriers were primarily offensive weapons, and he believed in neutralizing enemy planes by making sure they never left the ground. Command of the air as a prelude to bombing strikes was to Mitscher as sound a principle as command of the sea to an amphibious landing. He would have murmured approval in his barely audible voice had he heard the flamboyant "Jocko" Clark pounding his chart desk in Yorktown's flag plot during Pownall's retirement from Roi and shouting to his staff, "Goddammit, you can't run away from airplanes with ships!"

Mitscher's Air Plan for the preinvasion strikes on Kwajalein contrasted sharply with Pownall's for the December 4 raid. On D-day minus two Mitscher planned to hit Roi, Taroa, and Wotje airfields simultaneously. A fighter sweep would strafe first, bombers would then shatter the fields, and standing fighter patrols would continue to orbit and strafe until every last grounded airplane had been destroyed. Winning absolute control of the air would take two days, he estimated. The nearest enemy bases would then be Eniwetok and Wake islands, too distant for daily strikes even by Bettys. With Japanese air power gone, Task Force 58 need not retire, it could refuel in turn by groups while continuing to support the landings until all of Kwajalein Atoll was secure.

Mitscher's concept of winning air control fitted in perfectly with a bold new strategy of Admiral Nimitz. The fleet would not return to Pearl Harbor after the operation. Rather, it would go to undefended Majuro Atoll in the Marshalls, which would be seized simultaneously with Kwajalein. The 4,000-mile round trip to Pearl Harbor in between operations would then be unnecessary. The saving in fuel alone had sensational implications, and carrier strikes by TF 58 could be mounted with much less time between sorties.

Mitscher assigned one task group to attack Wotje's airstrip, another to deal with Taroa airfield at Maloelap, and a third to strike Kwajalein Island at the southern end of Kwajalein lagoon. To Montgomery's Task Group 58.2 he gave the hot spot, Roi, at the north end of the lagoon.

* Roi would not do as a bomber field. Its runways were too short and could not quickly be lengthened.

Mitscher did not expect to evade Japanese radar and counted on his fighter sweeps to pave the way for his bombers. Few Avengers would carry torpedoes; most would drop strings of 100-pound bombs to crater the coral strips with numerous hits and produce maximum fragmentation damage. Finally, Mitscher's plan was not inflexible; if one task group got into trouble, another could be ordered to its assistance. Mitscher's flagship *Yorktown* was with J. W. Reeves's force assigned to Maloelap. As soon as Reeves had neutralized Taroa, Mitscher intended to order him to help Montgomery at Roi.

The fighter pilots on *Essex, Intrepid,* and *Cabot* were muted as they entered their ready rooms on the early morning of January 29. En route from Pearl they had conducted gunnery exercises, firing at towed sleeves pulled by Avengers, and they had been serious about it. They knew the attack plan and what to expect. Also, Big Brother was watching them. As Fifth Fleet commander, of which TF 58 was a part, Ray Spruance was along in heavy cruiser *Indianapolis,* having joined it to the screen of Montgomery's task group.

Two hours before dawn Montgomery's TG 58.2 turned into the trade wind northward of Roi, and moments later 19 Hellcats of Lieutenant Commander Herbert N. Houck's VF-9 trailed from the blacked-out deck of *Essex.* Plans called for Houck's planes to streak in low to strafe Roi airfield, gunning revetments first, then planes found intact on aprons and runways. They would tangle with Zeros only to defend themselves.

On nearby *Cabot* Lieutenant Commander Robert A. Winston led off 11 more Hellcats from the narrow deck of the CVL. In climbing away "by feel" at 5:44 A.M. Winston could sense no horizon. Relying strictly on instruments, he climbed to 1,000 feet and began looking for a white tuck light on a destroyer five miles from *Cabot* where his squadron was supposed to form up. Winston finally found her (she was showing a red light) and rounded up eight of his boys. He could only hope that the other three had not gone overside on takeoff or spun in from attempted instrument climbs. Then he began climbing on a vector toward Roi, intending to reach 20,000 feet, from which he would furnish high cover. He would have felt better had he known that his three strays had joined VF-9 down below.

Suddenly Winston's radio blared. It was Houck: "There is an eight-tenth cloud layer over the target at six thousand feet. Take one of your divisions under the clouds at five thousand, put one just above the clouds at ten thousand, and send the other to fifteen thousand." Winston did what he was told, breaking up his eight-plane formation, wondering why Houck had risked detection to radio the order. Actually, Houck's order was "good joss." Over Roi on December 4 the Zeros had lurked just under a similar cloud cover to bounce some Dauntlesses diving on ships in the lagoon and on the airfield. This time about 27 Zeros were aloft again, Roi's radar having picked up Winston's incoming sweep.

The first hints of light were just peeping from the eastern horizon as six target-making Avengers lighted Roi airfield with strings of incendiaries. Commander Houck's diving Hellcats arced streams of tracer into revetments alongside the dim triangle of runways. Zeros intercepted, and some Hellcats broke off to fight them, but others made repeated strafing runs, hammering single-engine planes first and then the larger bulks of Betty bombers.

Circling at 5,000 feet, Winston listened to the excited chatter of VF-9's pilots. Suddenly a voice broke in loud and clear: "My plane is on fire and I am going to try to land in the water." This was Lieutenant S. D. Wright from the *Essex*. He landed all right and marked his position with a dye marker but was not seen thereafter.

As he began a wide turn under the clouds, Winston suddenly noticed a string of seven or eight planes headed downwind, as if to commence a bombing run. Thinking them American, he closed behind, only to discern from 200 yards that they were Zeros. Winston depressed his stick trigger and spouted a stream of red tracers at the rearmost enemy. The Zeros broke, and Winston and Ensign Cornelius N. Nooy, who had separated from the other pair of Hellcats, prudently began a defensive "Thach weave," each taking a Zero from the other's tail in a stomach-wrenching turn. On the next weave Winston hit a Zero on Nooy's tail, his tracers splattering along the side of the enemy plane. The Zero dropped off on one wing, pilot apparently dead, to plunge rapidly into the lagoon. Winston and Nooy* weaved several more times, then headed for a prearranged assembly point for *Cabot* fighters that had become orphans.

In the meantime Houck's and Winston's other pilots were having their own battles. Those without wingmen, unable to weave, got thoroughly shot up and were forced to run, using the superior speed of the Hellcat for a getaway, a priceless asset lacking in the old F4F-4 Wildcat. Lieutenant Douglas W. Mulcahy of Winston's second section was an exception—and almost a casualty statistic. Bounced by Zeros attacking from above at 10,000 feet, Mulcahy and his wingman dove for the 6,000-foot cloud layer and became separated. Climbing from the clouds, Mulcahy saw five Zeros on an opposite heading. One broke off onto his tail as he passed, shooting up Mulcahy's Hellcat with a burst of 7.7-mm. slugs. Mulcahy again dove into the clouds. Unwilling to give up and forgetting about Winston's rendezvous orders, the lieutenant climbed to 20,000 feet, found the five Zeros again and recklessly bounced them from above and behind, shooting the left wing from a lagging plane he had selected as a target. To his astonishment the other Zeros held course. So Mulcahy climbed, dove, and tried again but missed when his four enemies broke violently from his line of flight. Concluding that he had used up his luck, Mulcahy broke away at high speed and headed for TG 58.2. His comment on return was "Boy, that was sure a group grope!"

---

* Nooy became the U. S. Navy's sixth-ranking ace, with 18 kills.

At the assembly point Winston rounded up seven planes and started back to Roi to look for trouble. He found it, hitting a Zero and knocking off an aileron. Nooy, still flying on his wing, pursued and set it afire, chopping it spinning into the lagoon. After making another orbit Winston headed back to the *Cabot* and landed. He was overjoyed to find that everyone was back aboard except for one pilot who had successfully ditched his damaged Hellcat alongside a destroyer. His opponents had been first-rate pilots, possibly from 32 that Koga had sent to Roi as reinforcements from his dwindling supply of veteran carrier pilots. Captain M. F. Schoeffel, pleased with the initial combat record of this virgin squadron, recommended awards. Winston's reaction was more narrowly professional, reflecting the broad experience of this combat man who had been piloting fighters since 1935. Singling out Mulcahy, he praised the young pilot and then in the quiet of his own quarters lectured him on the virtues of staying with his wingman. "After reminding him that only fools and Irishmen rush into a brawl at odds of five to one, I recommended him for the Navy Cross for being so careless."

For himself Winston modestly claimed only one kill, but his and Houck's pilots had a combined claim of a dozen "for sure" and five "probables." Strafing had accounted, Houck reported, for 15 to 18 Bettys and Nells and 22 to 24 single-engine planes—Zeros, Kates, and maybe others. That this score probably was close to right was attested to by the weakness of fighter opposition met by the *Essex* SBD Dauntlesses that dive-bombed immediately after the sweep. Later, at 9:30 A.M., eight Hellcats from *Essex* orbited the field to draw nothing more than weak AA fire. Absolute air supremacy had been won. All remaining strikes this day and the next concentrated on preinvasion targets.

At Taroa, 210 miles almost due east of Roi, Rear Admiral J. W. Reeves's TG 58.1 delivered a crushing attack through an overcast and rain squalls that normally would have kept carrier planes on the deck. *Enterprise*, *Yorktown*, and *Belleau Wood* pilots delivered eight strikes, erased 32 Bettys and five single-engine planes on the airfield and thoroughly smashed up base facilities. Hellcats claimed five Zeros and three probables, but this was an underestimate. Thirteen Zeros took off to intercept, ten fell in air-to-air combat, and the other three were destroyed trying to land.

Wotje was an easy target for Rear Admiral S. P. Ginder's TG 58.4 of *Saratoga*, *Princeton*, and *Langley*. The pilots found airborne only a single clipped-wing Zero (Hamp) near the task force and shot it down. The field was empty, and so the pilots smashed up the facilities. Since Admiral Mitscher had planned to have his carrier groups refuel by turns, Ginder then withdrew to a rendezvous with TF 58's fleet oilers after tossing a strike at Maloelap.

Ted Sherman's *Bunker Hill*, *Cowpens*, and *Monterey* launched at Kwajalein Island at the south end of the big atoll simultaneously with the flattops of 58.1 at Roi on the northern end. The only game they could find consisted of eight planes at the seaplane base that they promptly shot up. The pilots then concentrated on buildings, AA batteries, and supply dumps.

The invasion of Kwajalein began on January 31, 1944. Vivid memories of Marine losses at Tarawa induced Spruance to make certain that the preinvasion bombardment by warships was prolonged, intense, and aimed at specific targets. Marines landed at Roi, GIs at Kwajalein. The advance was rapid, losses were much lighter than at Tarawa, and Roi was deemed secure on February 2 and Kwajalein on the 6th, where troops of the 7th Infantry Division advanced more deliberately than had Major General H. M. "Howlin' Mad" Smith's Marines of the 4th Marine Division.

Losses at Kwajalein Atoll were so light that neither the Army nor the Marines had had to commit their reserves, 8,000 strong. These men might have been used to assault Wake, but Nimitz's planners thought that this atoll lay too far to the northward of the Central Pacific advance to make it worth the cost of capture. Selected instead was Eniwetok Atoll, an island group that could be considered either the westernmost of the Marshalls or the easternmost of the Carolines. Site of a future H-bomb test, Eniwetok lay some 360 miles north and west of Kwajalein.

The seizure of Eniwetok between February 19 and 22 was no pushover, but it was not terribly difficult, either. The troops landed on each of the atoll's major islands in turn, completing the conquest by securing Parry Island on February 22. This literally made Japanese islands of the bypassed eastern Marshalls "rear areas," useless coral in the American rear and prison camps for their planeless Japanese garrisons. By contrast, Eniwetok by April 1, 1944, supported a garrison of 11,200 Americans, a fighter strip, and an 8,200-foot bomber runway from which B-24s could range as far as Truk. Mitscher's carriers had supported the Eniwetok assault with two task groups. Admiral Sherman's carrier group erased 15 Bettys. Admiral Ginder's *Saratoga* group took over after Sherman retired to refuel and supported attacking GIs and Marines.

By this time "Pete" Mitscher had become a "character" to the *Yorktown*'s crew. His habit of sitting backward all day while facing the stern in a high chair on the flag bridge, his ever-present long-visored cap covering his bald pate, his wrinkled and seamed face set atop a small wiry figure—all of these characteristics were duly noted and commented on. Taciturn, stubborn, soft-voiced to the point of giving real difficulty for those who had to listen to his instructions, Mitscher was, nevertheless, a pilot's admiral. He listened to the recommendations of his aviators, understood their problems in flying complex, high-speed airplanes, and in a hundred little ways made them aware that he was concerned about their welfare. He took personnel losses badly and was willing to accept real risks to save the lives of his airmen. This was not entirely sentimentality, though Mitscher was sentimental. He knew from long experience in an airplane cockpit how hard it was to take off and land in bad visibility, to hit a target with a 30-degree deflection shot, or to relocate a carrier coolly after returning to a prescribed point option and finding only empty ocean. A man who had flown the NC-1 nearly across the Atlantic in 1919—as Mitscher had—knew more than a little about the navigational problems of an aviator. Good pilots were a valuable commodity to the Navy in 1944. Mitscher knew it and acted accordingly. In return the airmen respected—nay, revered—him.

Mitscher made excellent "copy" for the war correspondents who by this time were aboard his flagship during every carrier mission. He received a sympathetic press, but he did not go out of his way to generate personal publicity. That characteristic he shared with the retiring Ray Spruance.

When overruled by Spruance, as Mitscher sometimes was, he did not sulk. He was too much the professional and too disciplined by his many years in the Navy for that. To him orders were orders. If challenged by Spruance, especially on aviation matters, he would bide his time, confident that experience would prove him right. Usually it did.

Mitscher was an extremely able TF 58 commander. Staff work had improved enormously under his leadership and that of Captain Truman J. Hedding, his chief of staff. Attack plans became clearer, sharper, more concise, logical, and workable. After-action reports improved also. Something in the quiet way Mitscher operated seemed to bring out the best in his subordinates. They would need to do their best, too, for their next mission was to attack Truk.

To black-shoe U. S. sailors the word "Truk" (pronounced properly—if seldom—"Trōōk") brought visions of a formidable bastion bristling with turreted long-range guns. To airmen the word stirred visions of AA batteries too numerous to count and Zeros by the score swarming from airfields hewn from solid rock. To those who had read the Sunday supplements to prewar American newspapers, Truk was a mysterious place in the Central Pacific that Japan had carefully sealed off to preserve its secrets. It stood to reason, therefore, that it was very heavily armed.

To Admiral Nimitz and his CincPac planners Truk was an important island position that the Joint Chiefs of Staff had ordered them to capture. They knew Truk was the advanced headquarters of Admiral Koga and the Combined Fleet. They knew, too, from communications intelligence that superbattleships *Yamato* and *Musashi* usually based there. But they needed more facts about its defenses than what a few cloud-marred aerial photographs had heretofore been able to provide. As late as the beginning of the New Year, 1944, they had little more intelligence than they had possessed early in the war. It would be up to Pete Mitscher and the fast carriers to smash open Truk's closed door, photograph its beaches and defenses, and pinpoint the location of its airfields and batteries.

American illusions about Truk's strength were not shared on Truk proper. Rear Admiral Chuichi Hara, the atoll commander, remarked at war's end that when he heard American broadcasts call his command "the Gibraltar of the Pacific," he feared lest his foes discover how weak Truk's defenses really were. The turreted seacoast rifles were purely mythical. Seacoast guns of modest six- and eight-inch caliber covered four entry passes into Truk Lagoon, of which only one was mined. America's Oahu was far better defended. The AA defense was woeful, composed only of 40 guns without any but visual sighting controls. Rabaul had many more antiaircraft weapons. Truk Atoll was different from the Marshalls, consisting of a coral ring about drowned mountain peaks, and consequently was a much more difficult place to construct airfields. Moen Island had a bomber and a fighter strip, Dublon Island a seaplane base, and Eten and Param islands had strips for fighters and bombers. Even the naval anchorage was modestly developed. The naval station had no drydock for a ship larger than a destroyer. In brief, unless heavily reinforced with aircraft, Truk was a "paper tiger" and not a Gibraltar.

Task Force 58 had not retired to Pearl Harbor after Operation Flintlock, the capture of the Marshalls. Instead it rallied in Majuro Lagoon, restocked planes and pilots from shuttling escort carriers, and prepared for a strike on Truk, target date February 17, 1944. Only three groups would go, Ginder's TG 58.4 being still occupied in supporting Eniwetok's seizure. The other groups departed Majuro on February 12–13 and steamed to the north of Eniwetok. The final approach on Truk would be from the east-northeast, with the initial launching point about 70 miles from Dublon Island in the lagoon.

For all he knew Mitscher would be flying preinvasion strikes. A debate had been going on both in Pearl and in Washington concerning the possibility of canceling the invasion and bypassing Truk to assault immediately the Marianas Islands 590 miles northward. But no final decision had yet been reached. Mitscher hoped, also, to catch Koga's Combined Fleet at anchor, perhaps with a carrier or two present. He realized, however, that it would be more probable that Koga had fled. A Marine Liberator had overflown Truk from high altitude on February 3, obtaining an incomplete photo coverage of the islands and anchorages. It was likely that Koga's lookouts or radar had spotted the plane and that he had taken alarm and withdrawn. This surmise was correct. Koga had left Truk for Japan on February 10 in battleship *Musashi*. Commander Fourth Fleet, Vice Admiral Kobayashi Jin, took over Truk's combined forces as senior officer present. Only a light cruiser and some destroyers remained. But much merchant shipping stayed on in the anchorages, including cargo ships, oilers, and fleet supply ships, as Mitscher had guessed that it would.

No American knew how many planes or even airfields Admiral Jin's defenders possessed. Mitscher's Air Plan guessed "possibly" five airfields (too many; there were four) and 186 planes (too few; there were over 365). But some 200 of the planes on a major airfield, Eten, were transients awaiting ferry pilots to fly them to Rabaul. Only 189 planes, 45 of them seaplanes and flying boats, were specifically assigned to Truk's defense. And according to Japanese sources, of these only 70 or 80 were in "first-class shape." Moreover, air defense orders had to pass through a complex chain of command reminiscent of Oahu's on Pearl Harbor day.

Mitscher intended a strike much heavier than Nagumo's at Pearl Harbor and one more thoroughly organized. He planned to repeat his Roi Island attack pattern, hitting first with a predawn sweep of 75 Hellcat strafers, their targets being illuminated by incendiaries from Avengers. Strikes would then follow at approximately hourly intervals throughout the day, each putting out about 12 fighters, 9 torpedo planes, and 14 dive bombers against airfields, shipping, and naval-base installations. Two days of strikes were planned. Mitscher had no doubts about winning command of the air. He hoped for, but did not count on, achieving tactical surprise.

Mitscher did not get surprise, but thanks to the overly complex air defense setup it didn't really matter. As the carriers closed Truk on February 15, 1944, patrolling Hellcats from *Belleau Wood* shot down a snooping Betty. Shortly thereafter a U. S. plane from a land base blundered and reported the task force. Truk's radio monitoring unit picked up its message, and this, plus the disappearance of the Betty, convinced Admiral Jin that Mitscher was coming. At 3:00 A.M. on February 16 he alerted Truk's defenses.

His action did little good; Mitscher's attack plan worked almost to perfection. Truk's radar picked up the 75 Hellcat strafers while they were still a half hour out on February 17, and 40 fighters, mostly Zeros, rose to meet the attack. Had more air crews reached their planes, the interceptors would have been more numerous. Many did not get the word to sortie. The result was that Jin's Zeros failed to stop the Hellcats, and grounded planes took heavy losses. At Moen's largest airfield ground crews manned machine guns emplaced about its perimeter to try to save about 150 Zeros, "Irving" twin-engine night fighters, new model "Jill" torpedo planes, and sundry other types still on the ground. The Hellcat pilots by Japanese admission torched by strafing 52 Zeros, a Jill, seven Judys, three Irvings, and four Type-100 Headquarters Reconnaissance Planes (Dinahs). At Eten, 110 of the transients were burned and others riddled.

Lieutenant George C. Bullard, "exec" of *Intrepid*'s VF-6, did more than his share of the damage. Bullard, a Naval Academy graduate of the Class of 1938, had run up a score of four enemy planes downed in the Kwajalein and earlier attacks. He made at least 12 passes over Moen's bomber strip, then on retiring to a rendezvous outside the lagoon, he spotted training cruiser *Katori* and led his division in strafing the ship. This proved to be his undoing. Hit in the engine by AA, his Hellcat gave out just beyond Truk's reef. Bullard swam to an island near the lagoon's north entrance. His comrades from the *Intrepid* spotted him several times during the day, unhurt and waving, but Japanese gunners from the North Pass batteries reached him before a rescue attempt could be organized. They took him prisoner, and he went later to Japan.

Bullard's loss was exceptional; just 13 pilots were shot down during the entire two days of strikes. On the other hand, by 1:00 P.M. local time on February 17, half of the defending Zeros were gone, and by 6:00 P.M. just one Zero and five torpedo planes remained serviceable. By Japanese count about 270 planes were destroyed, 200 on the ground.

A most unwilling witness to one strike was Major Gregory (Pappy) Boyington, Marine ace extraordinary. After being plucked, wounded, from a life raft off Rabaul by the Japanese, he had been interrogated at length and loaded into a Betty bomber for a flight to Truk. His eventual destination would be the secret interrogation camp run by the Imperial Navy for POWs holding information of exceptional value.

Boyington's plane had barely stopped rolling before the major and several other prisoners were hustled, blindfolded, to a shallow pit and unceremoniously thrown in. They quickly realized that American planes were attacking Moen airfield—and them. In growing excitement Boyington, peering over the edge of the pit from beneath his blindfold, watched Zeros, Jills, and other planes catch fire and blow apart. Heat "cooked off" their guns, sending 20-mm. slugs glancing about and into the pit. The American ace threw some of them out of his unintended refuge.

During a momentary lull a Zero landed to refuel, its pilot clambering out to stroll across the field wearing a fur flight cap with flaps that pulled down over his ears. Seeing Boyington and his five companion POWs in the pit, he started, then, composing himself, said in English, "I am a Japanese pilot." The uninhibited Boyington, a native of Okanogan, Washington, responded impulsively, "With all the goddamn trouble we got, *ain't* you the cheerful SOB, though!" About then Hellcats dove with .50s stuttering, the Japanese pilot ran, ear coverings flapping, and the captives ducked. Somewhat miraculously Boyington with his companions survived both raid and war.

After the fighter sweep had shattered aerial resistance, *Bunker Hill's* VB-17 again had an opportunity to put its SB2C Helldivers to the test. By this time the planes flew well, though their hydraulic systems were giving the air-group mechanics endless troubles and the planes the reputation of being "plumber's nightmares." They also sometimes lost power on takeoff. Strike 1C at noon on February 17 was fairly typical of those targeted this day and the next against shipping.

On this mission the *Bunker Hill* planes rendezvoused and flew to Truk anchorage. Airborne were ten SB2Cs, nine TBF-1Cs, and four F6F-3s. They found plenty of targets afloat. Led by Lieutenant Commander Geoffrey Norman, the "Beasts" plunged from 10,000 feet through three-tenths cloud cover and vented their spleen on a variety of ships, hitting three with thousand-pounders. One they watched explode and vanish in the lagoon. The Avengers, led by Lieutenant Grady Owens and armed with Mark 13 torpedoes with strengthened firing pins, picked on a ship steaming in tight circles at 27 knots. This was destroyer *Fumitsuki,* whose skipper was employing standard and usually successful evasive action for a Japanese man-o'-war under air attack. Owens's nine planes closed as Hellcat fighters strafed and then dropped their torpedoes in an anvil attack that no maneuver could escape. The Mark 13s generally ran poorly at Truk but not entirely this time. One hit, blew the *Fumitsuki* in half, and sank her in two minutes. Forgetting that they had been sternly admonished by Mitscher to maintain radio discipline, Owens's pilots jammed their VHF circuit with their cheering. Commander R. H. Dale, their air-group skipper, enthusiastically reported in his action report, "Our torpedoes really work. Of the 39 torpedoes dropped by VT-17, there were 17 hits." Reports by other carriers, however, and especially pictures taken by telltale rearward-aimed torpedo cameras, showed that if true, VT-17's record was exceptional. The Mark 13s still ran too deep passing under their targets. The shallow six-foot settings used by the *Bunker Hill* squadron possibly explained its apparently improved record.

Nightfall on February 17 stopped flight operations on all U. S. carriers except one, the *Enterprise,* the only CV with a fully qualified night-trained air group. Its Avengers of VT-10 were about to try radar-directed mast-head-level night bombing, a technique in which it had been thoroughly drilled in training by squadron leader Commander William I. Martin. By careful flying on instruments and aided by well-calibrated airborne radar sets, the pilots were confident that they could drop 500-pound bombs with four to five-second fuses, "skip-bombing" them into the sides of enemy ships, using by night a technique used very effectively by day by General George C. Kenney's 5th Air Force pilots in the South Pacific.

Twelve Avengers of VT-10 attacked, releasing single bombs with amazing results. The pilots claimed a 52 percent hit rate as compared with 22 percent for daylight glide bombing. They thought that they had scored 13 direct hits, seven near misses, and two hits on islets in the lagoon mistaken (understandably) for ships. Photos later showed several of these vessels sunk.

Admiral Spruance personally got into the fight on his flagship for the operation, *New Jersey.* Hoping for a gunnery action with fleeing enemy warships, he led his flagship, sister battleship *Iowa,* and heavy cruisers *Minneapolis* and *New Orleans* and four destroyers in a circuit of Truk Atoll. They scored, too, sinking the training cruiser *Katori,* destroyer *Maikaze,* and two small vessels. CVL *Cowpens* kept them protected during the cruise with a CAP.

As Spruance's task group was rounding the southern end of the huge circular lagoon, Mitscher's carriers were undergoing a humiliating air attack. Very few planes were serviceable on Truk, this being the evening of the first day, the 17th, but a half dozen radar-equipped Jill carrier-type torpedo planes took off for a night attack. At first ships' AA fire kept the

Jills at a distance, but then Mitscher elected to rely on a night fighter from *Yorktown* for defense. The fighter failed to make contact, and with the anti-aircraft silent one of the Jills closed the *Intrepid* in Montgomery's TG 58.2, dropped a model-91 torpedo as the ship was making a 90-degree turn with 15 degrees of rudder at 25 knots, and scored a hit near the stern post rearward of the four propellers. The hit was extremely damaging, killing 11 men, jamming the rudder, and wrecking the crosshead and rams of the steering gear. A 30-foot hole let in enough water to cause the big flattop to settle ten feet at the stern. But by securing one of the four screws and using the other three for steering, the *Intrepid* was able to manage a straight course even with the jammed rudder. Mitscher promptly dispatched her to Majuro, telling off *Cabot,* two cruisers, and a destroyer squadron to keep her company.

With enemy airborne opposition negligible, TF 58's strikes on February 18, the second day, were mainly on shipping and shore facilities. Last hit were some oil tanks, that burned and effectively covered much of the lagoon with smoke and whose destruction had deliberately been postponed until then.

By anyone's standard the Truk raid had been a success. The Combined Fleet had gotten away, but much valuable shipping had been sunk, including a fleet oiler, training cruiser *Katori,* light cruiser *Naka,* and destroyers *Oite, Tachikaze, Fumitsuki,* and *Maikaze.* Sunk also were 26 cargo ships and auxiliaries. Counting small ships, the total score was 13 warships and 34 merchantmen.

To Mitscher the Truk raid was another vindication of his extraordinary attention to the details of carrier warfare. His Air Plan had been so detailed and so good that few changes had been needed. Report after report from air-group commanders and ships' captains noted that neither alterations nor improvements had been made. The Truk raid was demonstrably the best performance to date by the Pacific Fleet's fast carriers and their air groups and the most damaging to the enemy.

Mitscher's raid badly hurt Truk and finished Rabaul. The High Command in Tokyo decided as a result to stop sending air reinforcements and to abandon Rabaul's air defense. On February 20, 1944, 37 Zeros, four Judys, and two Bettys left Rabaul for Truk's battered airfields. The High Command was not ready to abandon Truk, not yet.

In the American High Command it was impossible to delay longer the decision on the next major landing operation. General MacArthur wanted TF 58 to support his New Guinea–Philippines axis of attack; the Joint Chiefs in Washington wanted TF 58 to support the seizure of the Marianas Islands 997 miles north and west of Eniwetok. Truk, the Joint Chiefs had finally concluded, was not worth taking. Urgency finally ended five months of unseemly wrangling, and the Joint Chiefs had their way. Saipan would be seized first, then Tinian, and finally Guam. Mountainous Rota would be clobbered and left to wither in the center of the Marianas group. The Joint Chiefs made it final on March 12, 1944, but agreed that MacArthur's landing at Hollandia on New Guinea should have TF 58's help.

Well before the debate had ended Nimitz had anticipated the final outcome. He knew that he would need photographs of Saipan, Tinian, and Rota, about which little was known of beach and reef conditions. Guam, having been an American possession, had been well surveyed. Also, the precise coordinates of all airfields, including new ones that the Japanese were known to be building, had to be determined. Once again TF 58 would have to take the pictures and while in the process smash up Japanese planes and shipping. A one-day strike was therefore laid on for February 23, 1944.

Since the strike followed so closely the Truk attack, Mitscher had no opportunity to take his flattops back to Majuro. Instead, he refueled and reorganized his ships at sea south and west of Eniwetok. Carriers *Essex, Yorktown,* and *Belleau Wood* became TG 58.2 under Rear Admiral Montgomery, while *Bunker Hill, Monterey,* and *Cowpens* formed TG 58.3 under Ted Sherman. The other carriers went to Majuro after transferring some air crew to the attack groups. Planning had to be improvised en route, but the aviators discovered that Mitscher's staff under Captain Hedding's supervision had nevertheless prepared an incredibly detailed and precise Air Plan, considering the limited amount of information available. Mitscher planned his fighter sweeps over Saipan and adjacent Tinian to be followed by overlapping deckload strikes from the carriers. Over Guam and Rota he sent photo planes covered by sections of fighters. On these islands he planned no major attacks, guessing, correctly, that neither had as yet well-developed airfields.

This time a Betty snooped TF 58 far out on its approach at 1035 hours on February 22. The ships would have to fight their way in. From Tinian 35 Bettys carrying torpedoes took off at 2:30 A.M. on the 23rd, intent on making a predawn attack.

With this many planes clouding the radar screens, Mitscher did not experiment with night fighters. He relied on radar-directed ships' AA fire to repel the Betty attack. Fighter director officers gave the gun crews the bearings of the attackers, the fire-control radar locked on, and the five-inch put up a heavy barrage, mixing timed and VT fused proximity shells. This shot down several Bettys and bothered the others so much that nary a ship, carrier or other, took a hit. Yet there was damage in TF 58. In a freak accident on battleship *Alabama* five-inch Mount 9 fired into Mount 5, killing five bluejackets and wounding 11. Over *Mobile* a five-inch proximity shell fired by another ship triggered, burst, and wounded 13 more. This last incident was regrettable but inevitable with enemy planes coming in skimming the water. Mitscher, though heartily glad that this heavy attack had not damaged one of his ships, was moved to recommend that a "night carrier" be added to his task force. It did not work well, he believed, merely to attach a flight of night fighters to each carrier.

The attack of the Bettys delayed for an hour the takeoff of the 48 Hellcats assigned to the air-superiority fighter sweep. The planes had rather more trouble with the weather—a low, nearly solid overcast—than with defending Zeros, of which few were encountered. On the fields the Hellcats found a considerable number of planes, suggesting that, as at Truk, many must have been transients without regularly assigned pilots.

Yorktown's planes under Lieutenant Commander E. E. Stebbins, the air-group commander, made 35 strafing passes on Saipan's Aslito field and 14 more at Tinian. Planes from other carriers did as well, raising the total of claims by the end of the day to 124 aircraft destroyed on and over Tinian, Saipan, and Guam and 22 probables. This was one time when the pilots considerably understated their damage. According to Japanese sources, losses ran to 101 destroyed on the ground and 67 in the air (a figure that must have included Bettys lost in the night attack) for a total of 168. Shipping had been sparse, the Dauntlesses and Helldivers plunging at and sinking merely a few small craft. To the pilots the Marianas had given evidence of being considered by the Japanese as a rear area, not as one likely to be subject to imminent invasion.

As Mitscher's six carriers steamed eastward after recovering their last strikes, every bluejacket felt a sense of relief at being en route home. "Home" would be only Majuro Atoll in the Marshalls, but at least there would be swimming call and no more nerve-jangling summonses to General Quarters. Losses for the Truk and Marianas operations had been 31 pilots and 25 air crewmen in combat and 13 pilots and 16 rear-seat men in operational accidents. Plane losses had totaled a considerable 85. Yet TF 58's accomplishments had been more than enough to give every man a sense of pride and to establish Marc Andrew Mitscher, veteran flyer, Class of 1910, U. S. Naval Academy, as its man of destiny.

21. The Carolines and Hollandia

While Admiral Nimitz had been seizing the Marshalls, his counterpart in the South Pacific, General MacArthur, had been preparing to leap-frog along the New Guinea coast in a giant stride toward the Philippines. By going directly to Hollandia MacArthur could trap very large Japanese forces and leave their reduction to what had become an American ally—the jungle.

To make the strike, however, MacArthur needed the ministrations of Task Force 58, first to neutralize the western Caroline Islands, then to support his landing at Hollandia. Nimitz was pleased to oblige, in part because the raids on the Carolines fitted in with his own design to advance to the Marianas.

On March 9 Nimitz briefed Admiral Spruance on his wants, and on March 21 Spruance had ready an operations plan to give to Mitscher. Three carrier groups would suffice, Spruance concluded, to batter the Carolines, notably the Palau group that the Japanese had been using as an anchorage for elements of Admiral Koga's Combined Fleet. If Koga could be surprised and "Pearl Harbored"—great. If he sought a carrier clash—well and good, for TF 58 should be able to win.

On March 22 Task Force 58 with 11 carriers* and their escorts departed Majuro and steamed southward. *Lexington* was back, torpedo damage repaired, serving as fleet flagship. Admiral Mitscher selected an approach from southward, hoping to avoid planes from Truk. His radar picked up several, and he realized that he probably had been seen. He had been. Admiral Koga, warned either by planes or by communications intelligence, or both, fled Palau on March 29 with superbattleship *Musashi,* light cruiser *Oyodo,* and destroyers. He did not escape unscathed. Submarine *Tunny* spotted the *Musashi,* got off a spread of torpedoes, and one nicked the 64,000-ton battle wagon in the extreme bow, forcing Koga to send her to Japan for hasty repairs.

Spruance had not deigned to tell Mitscher precisely how to strike TF

* TF 58 was comprised of TG 58.1 (Admiral Reeves) *Enterprise, Belleau Wood,* and *Cowpens*; TG 58.2 (Admiral Montgomery) *Bunker Hill, Hornet, Monterey,* and *Cabot*; and TG 58.3 (Admiral Ginder) *Yorktown, Lexington, Princeton,* and *Langley.*

58's assigned targets. In the new flagship, the *Lexington,* Mitscher's staff therefore worked devotedly during the approach to put the finishing touches on the Air Plan for the Palau strikes. The staff had a new boss. Captain Truman Hedding had been replaced as chief of staff by Captain Arleigh A. "31 Knot" Burke.

The change had not been Mitscher's choice. The little carrier admiral had been perfectly satisfied with the competent Hedding. Burke, strictly a surface line officer, had been as astounded by his new appointment as Hedding had been to have to leave. The impulse for the switch came from Ernie King in Washington, who had decreed to the Bureau of Personnel that all carrier task-force commanders should forthwith have "gun club" chiefs of staff. King wanted better coordination between carriers and screening ships and "more balanced thinking" about air operations. Burke had devised plans to defeat the Japanese at their specialty, night torpedo attack with destroyers, and had won a brilliant victory in a destroyer action off Cape St. George near Rabaul. Hedding had himself selected Burke from a list of candidates offered to Mitscher by BuPers.

Mitscher did not submit gladly to dictation from any source, be it BuPers, King, or whomever. The air was therefore frosty when Burke first climbed the ladder to *Lexington*'s flag bridge. Nor would it thaw for a long time. When Burke greeted Mitscher pleasantly each morning, all he would get in return was a grunt. Fortunately, Burke chose to make the best of it until Mitscher finally thawed. It helped, later, to have Hedding return as assistant chief of staff.

Prior to the submarine fracas, while TF 58 still was more than 300 miles from its launch point, six Bettys from the 761st Air Group that the Japanese called the *Kessen Butai* (Decisive Battle Unit) took off from Palau for a dusk attack. Two suffered engine trouble, but the other four continued. Flying one of the planes was enlisted Flight Petty Officer Sumitaka Sakaguchi. Since his graduation from flight school Sakaguchi had been intensively trained, having been given 400 hours in the 761st specialty, night torpedo attack drill, flying an average of over ten hours daily for five months. His home base was at Tinian in the Marianas, and his strike force had staged via Palau.

With the others Sakaguchi found TF 58 at twilight, then dropped very low to avoid the radar he had been briefed to respect. Sakaguchi lost sight of his flight leader, who on becoming impatient had begun a run-in and was shot down, and after that, lost sight of the carriers he was supposed to attack. Finally, in rapidly growing darkness he made a run at a cruiser in his Model 2 Betty (G4M-2) and was hit by AA that severed the oil line to a Kasei 22 engine. Sakaguchi skillfully trimmed the plane and cut and feathered the propeller of the wounded engine before the motor caught fire, but he had to ditch when he found that the other Kasei could not maintain the Betty's altitude even on full power. He made a good landing, and all crewmen except the tail gunner got safely into the life raft. Two days later an American destroyer picked them up.

The next night, March 29, Japanese torpedo planes tried again. Eight Bettys from the 761st and four from the 751st Group flew into Palau. Their crews were given a pep talk by no less than a vice admiral, and they departed in the late afternoon, less two Bettys that crashed on takeoff, possibly because of a failure of the Model 2's tricky water methanol power-boost system. The ten surviving planes found Task Force 58, were astonished to count 11 CVs and CVLs, and attacked. Flight Petty Officer Akio Matsuzawa lined up on a carrier, possibly *Cabot,* released his torpedo, and was shot down immediately by a destroyer of the screen. Though he was knocked unconscious, his crew saved him, got him into a rubber raft, and all became prisoners the next day, being picked up by a boat from an American heavy cruiser.

The loss of nearly all planes of two strike groups virtually wrote *finis* to the Japanese High Command's hopes that night torpedo attack by long-range land planes could be substituted for carrier air power. Sakaguchi and Matsuzawa had been as well trained as it was possible to be, given the conditions of 1944. They had flown the best plane available, carrying a torpedo much superior to the American Mark 13. Yet neither had scored, and both had been shot down on their first attack missions.

At dawn on March 30 Task Force 58 began Operation "Desecrate One," targets being aircraft, airfields, and shipping in the Palau Group. The usual Hellcat sweep led off, composed of 24 fighters from each of the three task groups. They overflew Peleliu and Angaur Islands, tangling with intercepting Zeros.

Close behind came Torpedo 16's Avengers from *Lexington.* At 8:20 A.M. the planes dived low to strew into the main entrance channel of Palau anchorage 16 Mark 10 moored magnetic mines. Others from *Hornet's* Torpedo 2 and *Bunker Hill's* Torpedo 8 planted in other passages Mark 25 ground magnetic mines, long cylindrical infernal machines of mottled sand color, designed to rest on a shallow bottom. If a ship passed over either type the natural magnetism in its hull would trigger the firing mechanism. This mining operation was the brain child of Admiral Nimitz's Cinc-Pac staff and was intended to trap Japanese ships inside the Palau anchorage. The idea worked, for the Japanese saw the mines being dropped, and 32 ships stayed inside.

The strike planes—Hellcats, Dauntlesses, Helldivers, and Avengers—hit repeatedly at trapped shipping, airfields, and shore installations on March 30 and 31. They found and torpedoed destroyer *Wakatake* at sea, trying to flee, bombed to wreckage repair ship *Akashi,* sank Patrol Boat 31 (an old destroyer), three oilers (ships in short supply), and more than a score of other vessels for a count of 36. Dive and glide bombing had again not been very accurate, but some of the Hellcat fighters had tried skip-bombing, bouncing a bomb with a delay fuse into the side of a ship from a fast, low run. This technique yielded good results, but a lack of delay fuses prevented much use of the method. The Avenger crews found, too, that the five-inch HVAR (high-velocity aircraft rocket) was accurate against land targets, hitting with the impact of a five- or six-inch shell. These had been used first at Kwajalein.

An attempt to use Hellcat night fighters from *Lexington* did not work out well and served to deepen the dislike for these planes held by many carrier captains. Using the night fighters prevented the usual tie-down for the night of planes on the flattops' sterns and tired the already overworked "Airedales," who badly needed a good night's sleep after a full day of flight operations. Yet, potentially, the fast Hellcat night fighter had the speed and punch to stop completely Japanese night torpedo and nuisance raids.

At 5:10 A.M. on March 31 the *Lexington* launched four F6F (N)s to intercept several unidentified bogies. At 7:58 a day-fighting Hellcat from another carrier mistook one of the black-painted machines for enemy and badly shot it up. The pilot ditched safely, but the episode was neither forgiven nor forgotten.

In two days of attacks the American fighter squadrons claimed 93 enemy planes. This was a more than usual exaggeration, though by enemy admission they did completely wipe out the "Tora" ("Tiger") Fighter Squadron's 18 Zeros. The pilots also claimed 36 grounded planes destroyed, of which 13 were Bettys, these kills being mostly confirmed by aerial photos.

On April 1 Task Force 58 shifted position and struck at Woleai, Yap, and Ulithi in the western Carolines. The planes blasted airfields and such shipping as their pilots could find. By day's end, the third straight of strikes, the pilots were tired, which was understandable, considering the intensity of flying. Mitscher's airmen had flown 2,645 sorties, dropped 616 tons of bombs, and loosed 35 torpedoes. Combat losses had come to 11 Hellcats, nine dive bombers—of which six were Helldivers—and five Avengers. Operational losses and deck crashes had claimed 18 more planes, of which unfortunate *Lexington* contributed eight. Far better was the story of aircrew casualties that ran to only eight pilots and ten air crew killed or missing. Lifeguard submarines and cruiser float planes picked up 26 of 44 downed airmen.

In retiring from the Carolines, Task Force 58 doubled back on its original course until it reached "*Enterprise* weather," a bad weather front that snugly enveloped it and allowed tensed-up sailors to relax. Entering Majuro Lagoon on April 6, it began a period of replenishment that lasted only a week.

In New Guinea almost due south of Woleai Atoll, the Japanese Army had long regarded its depot and air-base complex at Hollandia on Humboldt Bay to be a rear area to support the main bulk of the island's Japanese Army defenders well to the east. To soften up this area for a landing would be Admiral Mitscher's job before and during the landing of units from General Walter J. Krueger's Sixth Army on April 22. Naturally, if Admiral Koga's Combined Fleet or any part thereof steamed south to interfere—and Admiral Nimitz this time thought it might—then Mitscher was to "destroy or contain enemy naval forces."

For this purpose Mitscher took three task groups to sea on April 13. Rear Admiral "Jocko" Clark, with TG 58.1 composed of *Hornet, Belleau Wood, Cowpens,* and *Bataan,* would attack Japanese positions west of Hollandia at Wakde, Sawar, and Sarmi. The able Alfred Montgomery, with TG 58.2 containing *Bunker Hill, Yorktown, Monterey,* and *Cabot,* would batter Hollandia's five airfields and support the landings at Humboldt Bay. And Rear Admiral J. W. Reeves, commanding TG 58.3 with *Enterprise, Lexington, Princeton,* and *Langley,* would do likewise and then cover other landings at Tanahmerah Bay. If the Combined Fleet appeared, Vice Admiral "Ching" Lee's battle wagons would finally show what 16-inch naval rifles could do.

Roaring in over Hollandia with guns charged and ready for anything, Hellcats of the fighter sweeps found empty skies. Twenty planes from *Enterprise* and *Princeton* spotted a Japanese Army Sally bomber and slaughtered it, the enemy plane making no attempt to evade or seek cloud cover only 2,000 feet below. Repeated firing passes over the airfields riddled dozens of apparently intact planes that would not burn. They had been degassed. Dozens of others showed canopy and cowling damage that revealed that someone else had been there first. The "someone else" had been General Kenney's Fifth Air Force. B-25s and A-20s had wrecked nearly all of 340 Japanese planes on the airfields in five heavy raids between March 31 and April 16. The damage was so complete and thorough as to attest that except for the danger of Combined Fleet intervention, Task Force 58 had made an unnecessary trip.

Strikes continued for the next three days until April 24, the pilots flying 3,117 sorties, but the 749 tons of bombs dropped probably did a better job of clearing jungle than killing the enemy. Ground troops advanced rapidly, driving the scattered defenders inland, capturing the airfields, and establishing a firm barrier in the rear of the Japanese Army troops to the eastward. The main fighting would come when the trapped forces would try to fight their way through the barrier weeks later.

Aircraft losses were light. Only two Hellcats, two Avengers, and an SB2C "Beast" fell in combat, though 16 other planes were lost operationally, including six more of the "Beasts" that the carrier crews still considered to be a severe maintenance problem. Missing were five pilots and six air crew. One of the operational accidents was to Lieutenant Commander Kenneth F. Musick, *Bunker Hill's* VT-8 skipper. He made a normal takeoff for this first-strike mission, but his Avenger wobbled after leaving the carrier, lost flying speed, the right wing stalled out, and the plane cartwheeled in, snapping off a wing and the engine. The fuselage surfaced right side up, and Musick and his crew managed to get out and into a life raft. Musick, a keen and experienced pilot, was convinced that he had been victimized by the ASD radar installed in a dome on the right wing of his plane. On hitting the slipstream of another plane the Avenger had been bounced about, and the radar nacelle had prevented Musick from regaining control. He was lucky to escape with his life, the incident illustrating perfectly the dangers of military flying in general and carrier flying in particular.

Perhaps to the disappointment of Admiral Mitscher, Koga's Combined Fleet did not seek battle. Nor did Japanese naval aircraft offer much activity besides reconnaissance flights.

On the last night of operations the *Enterprise* night fighters had a chance to prove their worth. The veteran flattop at 6:11 P.M. launched two planes of VF(N) 101, led by the squadron's skipper, Lieutenant Commander R. E. Harmer. The aircraft were improved F4U-2 Corsairs equipped with airborne radar and getting their test aboard carriers. At 7:05 P.M. Harmer was vectored away from his wingman when the air controller identified two contacts, Harmer's being aft of the Big E about 30 miles. After trying several different courses Harmer picked up his target at about two miles and dove from 1,500 to 500 feet. At a half mile Harmer sighted visually a twin-engine plane he could not identify but which his intelligence officers later guessed was a Yokosuka P1Y "Ginga" (Milky Way). Harmer popped the flaps on his fast fighter and slowed to 140 knots, dipping below the plane to approach from below. At 250 yards the Japanese gunner shot at him, so Harmer pulled to the side as the bomber dove for the water. Losing sight of the plane, he located it again on his radar, closed to 200 yards, fired, and set the port engine to burning. He reported:

I then pulled alongside and looked him over. The dorsal gunner was still putting up erratic fire at me and the port engine was still burning, leaving a heavy trail of smoke. I slid back on his tail and gave him another long burst at less than 150 yards. The tail gunner took over and threw inaccurate fire at me. I made one more S turn and closed in again. I had less than 100 feet altitude and had to depress my nose to fire. . . . I fired a short burst just as he struck the water.

Climbing to altitude about 7:30 P.M., Harmer reported to the *Enterprise*'s FDO and was directed to orbit south of the ship. At 7:50 the fighter director gave him another target bearing, and off he went, this time looking for a small formation of planes. Finally, at four miles dead ahead, he spotted a white light with a red one to either side. Closing, he recognized that what he had at first taken to be a star was a Betty or Sally bomber. Sliding behind the leader, he charged his guns and fired, getting off only a few .50-caliber bullets before all guns jammed. Charging them again, he fired once more with the same result. This time the enemy plane dropped its left wing and flashed a row of varicolored lights along the upper surface.

I pulled out to port to recharge my guns, and as I did so passed directly under a blacked-out plane. I looked over my shoulder and saw two others in left echelon on him. In all the formation consisted of six twin-engine bombers, four in left echelon on the leader and one flying right wing on him.

The astounded Harmer picked up the tail plane of the formation and tried his guns again. Only one worked, firing just three rounds before it jammed. Faulty ammunition, apparently, had checked Harmer when he had an entire enemy formation in his sights. After repeated attempts to get his guns to work again, Harmer gave up, called the FDO on his VHF circuit, and asked for a vector to the *Enterprise*. After landing he suggested in his action report a practice that few carrier group commanders chose to adopt:

This operation showed the advantage of having VFN in the air, on patrol, at sunset. It is recommended that under conditions when enemy night attacks are probable that this be standard practice.

April 25 found the TF 58 refueling. The day passed quietly, with a *Cowpens* plane downing a search Betty and destroyer *Conner* depth-charging a submarine to provide the major entertainment. Refueling continued the next day while Mitscher was getting new orders. TF 58 should, Admiral Nimitz had decided, polish off "mighty" Truk as a base by taking another swipe at it and also Ponape and Satawan in the western Carolines. This would keep Admiral Koga off balance and soften up those islands for the coming Marianas campaign.

It was well that Nimitz had decided to hit Truk again, for the bastion had been reinforced. Planes from Rabaul and elsewhere had flown in during March, and aircraft strength on the Moen, Eten and Param airfields had reached 104 planes by April 29.

Before first light on the 29th Mitscher's carriers dispatched their standard fighter sweep. The Truk airfields put up a respectable total of 62 Zeros, which would have meant battle royal had not a low, heavy cloud cover limited visibility and the scope of the fighting. In accord with standard Mitscher practice the Hellcats fiercely strafed the airfields, and bombers following made them targets of day-long overlapping strikes. Total bag was 59 planes shot down and 34 more destroyed on the ground in two days of strikes. Only 12 planes in well-nigh impregnable revetments remained serviceable. This was considerably short of the 150 planes Mitscher's airmen claimed, though the 65 they accounted destroyed in the air was very close to the actual figure.

Damage to installations on shore was light for the 785 tons of bombs dropped. Part of the reason may have been a deterioration of bombing skill toward the end of a long cruise, but the chief culprit seems to have been bomb fusing. The planes had used up most of TF 58's GP bombs at Hollandia and consequently had to drop AP and SAP missiles with delay fuses. These had penetrated too deeply to produce much blast effect. Nor was the bag of shipping considerable. The reason was simply because little was there in Truk lagoon. The pilots sank two small freighters, some patrol craft, and assorted luggers and coastal craft. Destroyer *MacDonough* sank the only major warship found, submarine I-174, caught about 20 miles south of the atoll.

American plane losses were neither light nor heavy. Twenty-six fell to AA and Zeros, and nine more suffered various operational mishaps. Yet of 46 air crew and pilots down, more than half were saved in what Admiral

Mitscher described in his action report as "sensational rescues" by seaplanes and lifeguard submarine *Tang*.

Tang, a boat commanded by Commander R. H. O'Kane, was on her second war patrol when diverted to Truk. Beginning at 10:25 A.M. on the 30th, the pigboat began literally racing from point to point, fully surfaced, picking up downed pilots. Once, reluctant to submerge, O'Kane ordered his deck gun crew to man the four-inch gun and shell Japanese gun emplacements on the southwest end of Ollan Island. He recorded, "Fired twenty rounds of H. E. and common while retiring, quite agreeably amazed at the ability of the 4 inch to stay on the target. Corrected radar range fed continuously to the gun. . . ."

The next day, May 1, found *Tang* again "off our favorite Ollan Island" looking for a float plane from *North Carolina* that had capsized inside the reef in Truk lagoon while attempting a rescue. Another plane landed, tossed a line to the rubber raft of the downed airman and float-plane pilot and was pulling both clear when *Tang* arrived and took them aboard. Later, *Tang* plucked seven more men from three different rafts that another float-plane pilot had loaded on the fuselage and wings of his Kingfisher aircraft. At 6:30 P.M. *Tang* picked up its last pair of passengers to complete a fantastically successful rescue mission. Partly it was luck and partly daring of the Kingfisher pilots, but partly also it was Commander O'Kane's willingness to close Truk's reef and get in close where the downed airmen were that raised the score. *Tang*'s exploits tremendously boosted air-crew morale in TF 58. It furnished solid proof to the airmen that, if shot down, they still had a chance.

After two days of mauling Truk the Mitscher force steamed eastward, dealing blows to Ponape Island and Satawan Atoll. The carriers launched small-scale strikes, but the main burden of attack was left to the "black-shoe Navy" component of TF 58. Against Ponape on May 1 Admiral Lee lined up battle wagons *Iowa, New Jersey, South Dakota, Alabama, Massachusetts,* and *Indiana* for a bombardment run. Little damage of consequence was done, but as a morale booster for the warship crews the operation was useful.

Similarly, cruisers *Louisville, Portland, Wichita, New Orleans, San Francisco, Minneapolis, Boston, Baltimore,* and new *Canberra* teamed up to bombard Satawan on April 30. They sent shoreward 803 rounds of eight-inch and 1,428 of five-inch in a bombardment that probably did little more than give the ship's crew a sense of participation. Just this once they were *not* playing second fiddle to those awkward-looking flattops.

May 2 found all hands in Task Force 58 headed homeward for Majuro feeling perhaps a bit more cocky than they should have. The war was by no means over, and they soon would be sailing into more dangerous waters than those about now isolated Truk. Prophets who had become convinced that Japan's fleet would assume the role of "the fleet in being," not daring to challenge Task Force 58, were going to be proved wrong.

22. Operation A Go

As preservers of Japan's Samurai tradition neither Combined Fleet commander Mineichi Koga nor Admiral Shigetare Shimada, now the Chief of the Naval Staff in Tokyo, had relished the defensive role thrust on them. Both wanted still to someday engage and defeat the American carrier fleet in decisive battle. Then they could regain the initiative and roll back advanced Allied outposts in New Guinea and elsewhere.

As Koga and Shimada saw it, the Midway battle and the Guadalcanal campaign had "eaten up" Japan's first team of pilots. Rabaul's defense had consumed the next team, including the pilots assigned to Japan's fast carriers. Koga had thrown the carrier-qualified pilots of his First Carrier Division onto Rabaul's airfields in November 1943 and the pilots of the Second Carrier Division in January 1944. By the end of February, as a Japanese staff officer cryptically remarked after the war, both divisions had "lost the greater part of their strength." Back to Japan they went to be totally rebuilt. They were given new planes and young pilots just out of flight school.

Fortunately, Admiral Shimada had available for assignment by April 1944 four new carriers, in part making good the Midway losses. These ships were the fine armored-deck *Taiho,* commissioned on March 7, 1944, and rushed through sea trials, and CVLs *Chiyoda* and *Chitose,* converted from fast seaplane carriers and recommissioned on October 31, 1943, and January 1, 1944, respectively. Also ready was CVL *Ryuho,* commissioned in late 1942 but delayed in entering combat service by varied and numerous shakedown problems. Their availability enabled Admiral Koga to reinforce his First Carrier Division of *Shokaku* and *Zuikaku* with *Taiho,* to strengthen his Second Carrier Division of *Junyo* and *Hiyo* with *Ryuho,* and to reconstitute a Third Carrier Division with *Zuiho, Chitose,* and *Chiyoda.* The three carrier divisions were assigned, respectively, the 601st, 652nd, and 653rd Naval Air Groups.

In addition to rebuilding the carrier fleet, Admiral Shimada undertook to strengthen greatly land-based naval air in the Central Pacific. He planned to base on the Marianas and adjacent islands two new air flotillas. The new air fleet was supposed to number 20 air groups containing 1,644 planes, but only about half were in the Marianas, the western Carolines, and the southern Philippines. The other half were in Japan on training status, being not yet operationally ready. Actually present in the Marianas by mid-May 1944 were about 172 aircraft based at three fields on Tinian, two on Saipan, and two at Guam. Plane types included Zero fighters, Betty and Frances (Ginga) twin-engine bombers and Judy dive bombers. Reinforcements could be flown in from Yap, Woleai, and Truk. Rota had a completed airfield on which planes could land, but it was not yet in use by June 1944.

Providing enough new planes to equip both the carriers and the land-based Marianas air fleet proved to be a solvable problem. By the spring of 1944 aircraft production in Japan was peaking at 1,700 per month, good by any standard, including American. Enough new Jills and Judys were coming out to re-equip most of the torpedo and dive-bomber squadrons. The small carriers of the Third Carrier Division received Zero fighter-bombers. These planes had strengthened wings enabling them to dive at speeds up to 460 miles an hour. Beneath the fuselage they carried a 550-pound bomb. The Zero fighter units of all carriers got the latest version, the A6M5, code-named by the Allies the "Zeke 52." This model, 416 pounds heavier than its predecessors, could make 351 mph at 20,000 feet, but neither it nor Judy nor Jill had armor or self-sealing tanks. Zero 52b models furnished to the light carriers of the Third Carrier Division, however, had bulletproof windscreens and an automatic fire-extinguisher system for their fuel tanks.

None of the Japanese planes had a speed advantage over the 375-mph Grumman Hellcat. Though Judy could make 343 mph at the standard approach altitude of 16,000 feet, it could not outrun a Hellcat. Nor could it withstand so much as a single well-aimed burst from the Hellcat's six .50s. Even the bomb-equipped Zeros had to be escorted; otherwise, burdened with their 550-pound bomb, they too would be "Hellcat bait."

In an attack on U. S. carriers, everything would depend on the skill of the Zero fighter-escort pilots. If they could entangle the Hellcats into dogfights, taking advantage of the superior maneuverability of their planes, then the Judys and Jills could use their exceptional speed to slip past the CAP and attack. Similarly, the Zero pilots of the land-based squadrons would have to take on and defeat the Hellcats making the now standard fighter sweep. Otherwise, the fields would be bombed out and all planes destroyed.

But the skill of the new pilots was the great weakness. Captain Mitsuo Fuchida, now a staff officer, was most dissatisfied with the state of training of the carrier pilots. All were deck-qualified; they could land on and take off from a carrier successfully. "But beyond that," he told a postwar interrogator, "they had not had what I would call adequate training." Nor was Fuchida pleased with the proficiency of the land-based air crews. Only their flight leaders were veterans, and of the others half were just out of advanced flight school and the other half were "trainee pilots," men who had undergone only a combined primary-basic flying training program before being put directly into the cockpits of combat planes in operational squadrons.

Of the carrier pilots Norizo Ikeda was typical. Ikeda was a Flight Petty Officer of the 601st Air Group assigned to *Zuikaku*. Though accelerated, his training was more or less conventional. He had gone through a combined primary-basic course at Tsuchiura beginning in October 1942 and advanced training at Omura, where he flew old-model Kates. After that he was attached to the Kanoya Air Group for operational training, also in Kates. In December 1943 with other pilots he joined a newly reconstituted squadron of the 601st at Kanoya and manned the cockpit of a Nakajima-built Jill 12 (Tenzan or "Heavenly Mountain"). With its 1,850-hp Kasei 25 engine, Ikeda found the 300-mph Jill a lot of airplane to handle compared to the much less powerful Kate. His plane, like the newest Zeros, had automatic fire extinguishers in wings and engine spaces but no self-sealing tanks and no armor.

Though Ikeda was supposed to be a torpedo-plane pilot, his operational training had included only one run-in with a dummy torpedo against a small craft. In the Kates he flew many antisubmarine patrols off the coast of Japan that gave him flight time on the plane but did little to bolster his combat skills. In a four-day period in October 1943 he made ten landings and takeoffs on the elderly CVL *Hosho*. On shifting to Jills in the 601st, he was given the opportunity to make another dummy torpedo run, this time against a tug. Though hardly yet the master of his plane, he flew south to Seletar airfield at Singapore in February 1944 with other pilots of his squadron. Only the squadron officers had combat experience, and they flew the lead planes.

Given the circumstances, Ikeda's training at Seletar seems to have been realistic; he was taught to hold close formation and conform entirely to the directions of his flight leader. When the *Zuikaku* arrived at Singapore in May, he made a few landings on her deck—and that was it. His first voyage on the ship was en route to combat. Neither he nor his fellow pilots had had the opportunity to fly a single simulated strike mission from her deck.

Zenkichi Uda and Masaji Oe were noncommissioned Judy pilots attached to the 523rd Air Group at Tinian. Oe had conventional training though no combat experience before joining his squadron. Uda was a special "rapid trainee" (*Sokusei*) who in May 1943 had begun a combined primary-basic course at a new field that had just been opened. With a thousand others he flew the Type 93 "Willow" biplane. On graduation in December 1943 Uda went with 50 comrades directly to the 523rd at Suzuka airfield in Japan and climbed into the cockpit of a 343-mph Judy. He was given a hasty checkout and then began flying training missions.

Surprisingly, though half of the roster of the squadron consisted of "trainee pilots" with no more experience than Uda's, he recalled only three fatal crashes.

Long before either Uda or Oe had fully mastered the Judy, both flew to Tinian in April 1944 with the last group of 45 planes from the 523rd to deploy. Both continued their training, including dive bombing, but neither had a chance to dive on even a sled towed behind a small craft. Mostly they bombed small islands and reefs. Uda had no opportunity to experience the feel of the Judy with the weight of a real bomb attached to the plane. All of his practice missions were with small dummy bombs carried under the wings rather than in the bomb bay. Fly their planes both men could, and that was no mean achievement. But as Captain Fuchida had realized, neither was close to being a really well-trained dive-bomber pilot. Nevertheless, as Uda recalls, all hands of the 523rd were "eager and ready for combat," and none had qualms about his lack of training and experience.

Until March 12, 1944, it still was not certain that Oe, Uda, and their mates would have to bear the initial brunt of the next major American landing. But on that date the Joint Chiefs of Staff cut through conflicting counsel and decreed that Nimitz's forces would next take the Marianas. D-day for landing on Saipan would be June 15, 1944, just a week after the Normandy invasion in Europe. Combat ships numbering 531 would carry 127,571 Marines and GIs to the Marianas, covered by Spruance's entire Fifth Fleet. Mitscher's TF 58 would be on hand in full strength. Spruance would be the overall commander with the authority—if he chose to exercise it—to control the movements of all ships, including the carriers.

With the Marianas in hand, the Joint Chiefs believed, the U. S. would have bases close enough to Japan to commence a strategic air bombardment of the home islands with the new B-29 Superfortresses. After Guam had been taken and the Marianas secured, an invasion of the Philippines would follow, at which point Admiral Nimitz's Central Pacific advance would join that of MacArthur's Southwest Pacific advance from New Guinea.

In the meantime, Admirals Koga and Shimada had been working on attack plans of their own. Their sole chance of winning a naval battle, they knew, would come only after their own forces had been rebuilt and while the Americans were tied up in an amphibious landing that would pin down Mitscher's Task Force 58. If one came soon—preferably in the western Carolines—they would attack with the massed carrier fleet, now called the First Mobile Fleet.

A sudden catastrophe at the end of March 1944 interrupted the planning. Admiral Koga, who had been maintaining his Combined Fleet advanced headquarters on Peleliu, decided to remove to Davao in the southern Philippines, where it would be safer. He and his staff officers left in two flying boats that encountered a tropical storm and crashed. Koga was not among the survivors. For the second time an air crash—this one purely accidental—had taken the life of a Combined Fleet commander.

The result was a hiatus of some 30 days while Admiral Shimada's headquarters staff officers in Tokyo debated both naval strategy and the question of whom to pick as Koga's replacement. In so doing they reaffirmed a preliminary scheme for a decisive fleet battle that Koga had originally drafted. They had it ready by late April and called it Operation "A Go." On its success or failure would rest the outcome of the Pacific war.

Operation A Go was handed to the new Combined Fleet commander, Admiral Soemu Toyoda, on May 3. Similar in its essentials to Koga's previous plan, it called for Japan's carrier fleet to seek decisive battle soon after the next major American landing. Presumably, the American carriers would have suffered severely from attacks by land-based planes and would be tied down close to the beachhead. The Japanese hoped that the landing would take place in the Halmaheras or on one of the western Carolines. But if the Americans invaded the more distant Marianas, that would present a grave fuel problem.

Losses to tankers had greatly reduced the ability of Japan to keep its warships fueled. Oil had to be hauled from refineries at Tarakan, Balikpapan, and Palembang in enough quantity to supply the forward naval anchorages. If massed at one anchorage the fleet would have enough oil to steam out and strike a force attacking in the Carolines. But it would not have enough to steam as far as the Marianas. Hence the first draft of Operation A Go specified that if the Americans invaded Saipan or Guam the fleet should not yet come out. Reluctant to see the earliest opportunity for decisive battle lost, the Naval Staff struggled to find a solution.

One simple answer would have been to trim the size of the fleet. Had Admirals Shimada and Toyoda been willing to send out the nine carriers with an accompanying escort only of cruisers and destroyers—as Nimitz had done at Midway—then all ships could have been filled to the brim with refined bunker oil and have been refueled from accompanying tankers en route. But Shimada and Toyoda wanted nearly every major warship in the Japanese Navy to accompany the flattops. This would augment antiaircraft support but overtax the ability of tankers to supply enough fuel.

Another solution was possible though dangerous. The carriers and the surface warships, now combined and designated the First Mobile Fleet, could all be provided with enough oil if the ships were filled with unrefined Borneo crude. This oil, right from the wells, could be fed directly to firerooms. But it was volatile and highly explosive. With it the massed First Mobile Fleet could reach the Marianas, but its use was so dangerous that Shimada and Toyoda were initially inclined not to authorize it.

Commanding the First Mobile Fleet would be Vice Admiral Jisaburo

Ozawa, fifty-seven-years old, long experienced in use of carriers though not an airman himself. He had relieved Admiral Nagumo at the helm of the Third (Carrier) Fleet in November 1942, following the Battle of Santa Cruz. Historian Morison writes of him, "Altogether, Ozawa was a worthy antagonist to Mitscher." But to complete the irony of this story—and perhaps of this book—Nagumo, on being relieved of his carrier command, had been appointed to head the 4th Fleet based on Saipan. This was an organization existing mostly on paper except for a handful of small local defense and harbor craft stationed in the Marianas.

The Japanese Navy High Command left to Admiral Ozawa the problem of how to dispose the fleet's three carrier divisions. One way would be to adopt the American practice of steaming the carrier groups in separate task groups in close proximity. Another would be to steam in three groups but widely separated. A third would be for one group to steam in advance of the other two as an advanced force to absorb the brunt of enemy attack. Of the three methods Ozawa was inclined to favor the last because it would make the best use of his battleships with their strong AA batteries. If the Americans could be induced to attack an advance force containing the likes of *Musashi, Yamato, Nagato,* and the two surviving *Kongos,* their superiority in planes might be whittled down.

Between May 8 and 11 representatives of all commands met at Saipan to discuss the forthcoming decisive naval battle. Everyone still hoped that the Americans would try for the Carolines—say, Peleliu—but the nagging question of the Marianas kept coming up. The fuel question was reviewed and all agreed that if all ships were to be fueled with refined bunker oil, the First Mobile Fleet could not be dispatched to the Marianas. But after the conference Admiral Toyoda had second thoughts. He agreed that Ozawa should steam his ships directly to the piers off the Borneo oil fields and fill them with unrefined oil. Now if the Americans landed in the Marianas, the entire First Mobile Fleet would steam to the vicinity of Saipan and give battle.

Within two days of the issuance of the A Go order on May 5, Japanese radio intelligence monitors began detecting a sudden increase in American radio traffic in the Marshalls and Hawaii and the observance of "strict air security" over Midway. In short, the radio traffic pattern suggested that Spruance and his Fifth Fleet might soon be on the move again. A carrier strike on Marcus on May 19 by Montgomery's task group and on Wake on May 23 convinced Toyoda that the time was near.

For a brief period Japan's admirals began to hope that A Go would be carried out in the waters they preferred, south of the Carolines. This hope developed when General MacArthur's forces invaded Biak Island off the New Guinea coast near the Vogelkop, the Bird's Head. Admiral Toyoda immediately made plans to send ground-troop reinforcements to Biak, not so much because he thought that the island could be retaken as because he believed that the gambit might lure Spruance to the area.

Two attempts to pull off this scheme, called Operation KON, failed, and the plan was dropped when it became clear that a landing on Saipan was imminent.

What Toyoda called "suicide reconnaissance missions" now served him well. Flights of tremendous range dispatched from Truk on May 30 and June 5 picked up and photographed Mitscher's carriers in Majuro. But another, flown on June 9, disclosed only ten transports and a pair of destroyers in the lagoon. "So," recalled one of Toyoda's staff officers, "it was concluded that the enemy attack was imminent." Once again the Japanese estimate was right. The stage now was set for the decisive battle of World War II in the Pacific.

23. Operation Forager

At noon on June 6 the *Lexington* sortied from Majuro. Following was veteran *Enterprise,* then other carriers. On the port side of the *Lexington*'s bridge adjacent to flag plot was Mitscher. With his long-visored lobster-man's green cap pulled down over his eyes he looked to be about seventy years old, though tanned and wiry. He stared astern of the ship "as fixedly as though he were its figurehead," according to Luce Publications newsman Noel Busch, a newcomer to the *Lexington* and carrier war. Operation "Forager," as the Marianas landing was code-named, was under way.

Below in *Lexington*'s vast, dim hangar deck stood dozens of planes with wings folded, about which lay bits of rope, tool boxes, and dozing mechanics. Pervasive was the smell of oil dripped from Pratt and Whitney and Wright engines, though vigilant chiefs kept swabbies busy wiping it up. A roar and clang announced the arrival of an elevator, dropping to scoop up an armed Dauntless due for ASP, antisubmarine patrol. At this point the squawk box spoke up sharply: "Now hear this! The smoking lamp is out! The gasoline pumping system is in operation." Soon the pounding thunder of the SBD taking off would jar awake the dozers in the hangar below.

Outside Majuro's lagoon, clear of shoal water and breasting a moderate swell, the *Lexington* steadied on a westerly course toward Point Roger, a refueling rendezvous in a narrow space between Marcus and Truk. Hopefully, this area of ocean was beyond the range of Emilys or Bettys searching from either island. Quite a lot of oil would have to be transferred from the tankers, for including the 15 carriers TF 58 now numbered 93 ships. All air groups flew training missions under overcast skies on June 7 and 8, a necessity for new Air Group 1 aboard *Yorktown.* To correspondent Busch, Admiral Mitscher confided that he rather expected search planes from Saipan or Guam to spot him on June 11 or 12. Then his carriers would again have to fight their way in to the Marianas. He seemed to Busch to be "pleased rather than otherwise by this prospect."

Inside the *Lex*'s flag plot Mitscher's hard-working chief of staff, Arleigh Burke, and his assistant chief of staff, Truman Hedding, were not at all pleased. They wanted to get in the first punch and hoped to do so even if scouts found TF 58. They therefore accepted plans "Gus" and "Johnny" that fleet Air Operations Officer W. J. "Gus" Widhelm (of Santa Cruz fame) and his assistant, Lieutenant Commander John Myers, had prepared and named for themselves.

Plan "Johnny" called for the usual fighter sweep over Saipan, Tinian, Guam, and Rota. But it would take place not at daybreak but on the afternoon before while the carriers were 200 miles away. Plan "Gus," coordinated with "Johnny," called for stationing pairs of destroyers 20 miles in advance of the fleet. They were to be used as fighter-direction ships and as rescue vessels for battle-damaged planes returning home. Mitscher explained his intent in a dispatch to Admiral Spruance: "Plan is to try to prevent early coordinated attack on our carriers while planes are on deck fueled and armed. . . . We have over two hundred fighters to protect fleet while Plan Johnny effective."

What made "Johnny" possible was the Hellcat's range. Flying at an economical 160 knots, carrying a 125-gallon drop tank, the big Grumman fighter could reach out more than 450 miles and return. This was ample for the proposed mission, though the planes also carried bombs to slow them down and increase fuel consumption.

June 11 dawned clear, but by midmorning it was certain that once again TF 58 had been located. Voice transmissions from a Betty monitored by Japanese-language specialist Lieutenant Charles A. Sims aboard *Lexington* left no doubt. Noon brought fast combat action. Between 12:11 and 12:52 four snoopers fell to CAP Hellcats, three Emily flying boats and an Irving twin-engine fighter.

Already, Rear Admiral Jocko Clark's TG 58.1, consisting of flagship *Hornet, Yorktown, Belleau Wood,* and *Bataan,* had peeled off to southward for a run-in on Guam. The other three task groups continued west toward Saipan and Tinian. Task Groups 58.2 and 58.3, under Rear Admirals A. E. Montgomery and J. W. Reeves, Jr., respectively, would deal with Saipan and Tinian. TG 58.2 contained *Bunker Hill, Wasp, Cabot,* and *Monterey;* TG 58.3 had *Lexington, Enterprise, San Jacinto,* and *Princeton.* TG 58.4, Rear Admiral W. K. "Keen" Harrill's unit with *Essex* and CVLs *Langley* and *Cowpens,* would attack Tinian and also a northern Marianas island, Pagan. The moment of truth was nearing for Rear Admiral Kakuta commanding the air fleet in the Marianas. Kakuta's inexperienced new pilots would have to fight over their own airfields.

Nearing 1300 hours—1:00 P.M. in layman's language—all 15 carriers of TF 58 turned into a 14-knot breeze. Hellcats started rolling down decks or darting from catapults, both methods of launch being used. The big flattops launched 16 F6F-3s apiece, the CVLs 12. Many Hellcats carried bombs. In all, 208 fighters headed for targets distant 180 to 240 miles, escorted by several pairs of Helldivers carrying life rafts and rescue gear.

Correspondent Busch wondered a bit at the attitude of the pilots.

They regarded their work not as "sacrificial" but as having "occupational risks surmountable by skill and alertness." With a bit of luck a good man could survive a prolonged operation such as Forager.

Enterprise's 16 Hellcats, led by Air Group 10's skipper, Commander William R. Kane, were among the first in action. "We arrived over Saipan at 1430 [2:30 P.M.]," he told an intelligence debriefing officer afterward, "and immediately sighted an Oscar [actually a Zero]. He dove away and headed for his field. I was gaining on him . . . but . . . broke off. I was getting too low and close to enemy AA." Later Kane scored a sure kill: "I got in a burst from dead astern and he [a Zero] crashed, burning." Kane's pilots claimed eight enemy planes shot down, six Zeros, a Betty, and an Emily flying boat at a cost of two planes lost, both pilots rescued.

Tinian's air space was also the scene of the largest air battle of the day. The Zero fighter group based there, warned by radar, scrambled and tangled with 12 Hellcats from VF-31, *Cabot*'s fighter squadron. Led by Lieutenant Doug Mulcahy, two four-plane divisions were at 10,000 feet preparing to dive-bomb the field with depth charges; a third flew cover 2,000 to 3,000 feet above. While they were in this thoroughly vulnerable situation the Japanese Zero unit plunged at them out of clouds above and behind. Spotting the Zeros, a pilot yelled, "Skunks!" All pilots released ordnance and began weaving for their lives.

Between six and eight Zeros jumped Mulcahy and Lieutenant (jg) J. M. Bowie. Each turned sharply into the other, forcing the diving Zeros to pull up and break their three-plane formations. One, in trying to avoid fire from Mulcahy, passed below and tried a wing-over in front of Bowie. Dropping his plane's nose, Bowie fired a short burst and flamed the vulnerable Zero, forcing its pilot to jump. Both pilots then chased a second Zero for a dozen miles, caught up to it even though they had not dropped their belly tanks, and Mulcahy, closing, gave it a short burst at point-blank range from six o'clock above. It sheered off, lurched, and fell in flames.

The *Cabot* pilots claimed 14 Zeros, which probably was an exaggeration, and returned with but slight respect for their inexperienced adversaries. "Even when the enemy had the altitude advantage," their action report boasted, "his attack was broken up by weaving," causing him to "become disorganized and confused."

By the time planes from the *Lexington* and *Wasp* arrived over Saipan and Tinian, a little behind the others, no airborne enemy plane could be seen. All pilots of VF-16 and VF-14 dive-bombed the airfields, noting a particularly fierce volume of AA fire from Saipan's Aslito field. They strafed runways and dispersal areas but found grounded Japanese planes hard to find. The best Lieutenant Bert Morris—better known as "Wayne" Morris, the film actor—could do for his first "kill" was to strafe and set afire a waterbound Emily. He cagily tried afterward to get credit for four kills instead of one, arguing that the flying boat had four engines!

Principal targets for the fighter squadrons from Jocko Clark's TG 58.1 were Orote and Agana airfields on Guam. *Hornet's* 16 pilots of VF-2 found "25-plus" enemy fighters awaiting them and piled in. Squadron Commander W. A. "Bill" Dean claimed four, three Zeros and a J2M "Raiden" (Thunderbolt) recently flown down from Japan.

In shooting down the "Raiden"—Allied code name "Jack"—which may have been the first of its type lost in the Pacific war, Dean used water injection, a new feature of the Double-Wasp engines of some of the F6F-3s. He chased the plane from behind, outclimbed it as its pilot used a normally successful evasion technique, made a diving firing run from six o'clock, and set it afire. It burned, Dean noted, as readily as a Zero. Concluding his report, Dean proudly claimed 23 enemy planes downed by his squadron.

The Hellcats began landing aboard their carriers at about 4:30 P.M. When Gus Widhelm finally totaled their claims a few hours later he noted a respectable 81 aircraft claimed destroyed against the loss of 11 Hellcats and eight fighter pilots. Another ten Japanese planes, mostly scouts and patrol planes, had been destroyed during the day near the task force by CAP. As intended, Plan "Johnny" had brought disaster for Admiral Kakuta. It had eliminated whatever hope he might have had that his Marianas-based planes could seriously harm TF 58 and contribute significantly to A GO. If he were to carry out his assignment of reducing American carrier strength by a third, planes from Truk and Yap would have to do it.

Beginning at daybreak on June 13 and continuing all day, Task Force 58 flew routine softening-up attacks for the Saipan landing set for June 15. A fighter sweep found and downed a Judy and Zero, but that was all. The enemy's weakness was mostly because of the previous day's fighter sweep, but it may also have reflected Kakuta's decision to conserve what few planes he had left.

Japanese antiaircraft scored well. The light AA concentrations about Guam's Agana field and Saipan's Aslito downed several planes. *Hornet* suffered the most, Air Group 2 losing two SB2Cs, a TBF, and two fighters. One of the fighter pilots floating close offshore saved himself by looping the line of his life raft about the periscope of a lifeguard submarine sent to retrieve him. The sub towed him out of range of shore batteries, then surfaced and took him aboard. The feat was no improvisation; it was a procedure dreamed up by Mitscher's staff and explained to the pilots.

One of the heaviest blows of the day was to a Japanese convoy that had cleared Saipan the day before and had almost gotten clear, being some 200 miles northwest of Saipan when attacked. *Essex* and *Cowpens* planes jumped it from masthead height, sank the torpedo boat *Otori,* at least three smaller escorts, and several of the merchant ships and fishing-type boats being escorted. Lost with his Hellcat was Lieutenant Commander Robert H. Price, skipper of Air Group 25 aboard CVL *Cowpens.* After being hit and forced to ditch near the convoy, Price managed to clear his sinking plane and later climb into a life raft dropped by a squadron mate. But a cruiser float plane failed to locate him, and when a special search the next morning also failed, everyone in Task Group 58.4, from Rear Admiral "Keen" Harrill down, considered Price a "goner." Operation Forager's schedule could not be interrupted to mount further searches by the task group even for an air-group commander.

To Combined Fleet commander Toyoda, following radio reports from Saipan, Tinian, and Guam aboard his flagship *Oyodo* at Hashirajima, continuing extremely heavy air attacks on June 11 and 12 had been ominous though not necessarily indicative of an invasion. U. S. carrier groups had customarily attacked for two days. But when attacks continued on the 13th, he considered that American intentions were, "on the whole, clarified." He "temporarily" suspended KON, the operation to retake Biak. It now was obvious that a circle of ocean within flying range of Saipan would surely be the scene of what Toyoda termed "the decisive battle of Operation A."

On June 13 antiaircraft fire still gave the American air groups trouble, downing several planes, including the rocket-firing Avenger of Lieutenant Commander Robert H. Isely, the skipper of *Lexington*'s VT-16. Air combat, however, was practically nil. Virtually every plane on Guam, Tinian, and Saipan had either been destroyed or damaged. Task Groups 58.2 and 58.3 steamed late in the day almost to within sight of Saipan, while moving to the west of the island to support the forthcoming landings. Both carried the ball on the 14th, Dog Day minus one, while Task Groups 58.1 and 58.4 of Admirals Clark and Harrill refueled and then headed northeast for neutralizing strikes on the Bonin Islands, 800 miles south of Tokyo. A lonely Commander Price spent another day in his little yellow raft, wishing that a school of sharks would go away and that a rainstorm would provide him with fresh water to supplement his meager emergency ration. Squalls passed a half mile on either side, but not a raindrop fell in his raft.

June 15, D-day on Saipan, furnished, as Admiral Morison (who was there) recalls, "As cool (83 degrees) and lovely a daybreak as you could expect at sea in the tropics; one that grew into a bright, blue tradewind day. . . ." For the Marines of the 2nd and 4th Marine Divisions, however, June 15 was a nightmare. After touching down at 8:44 A.M., all of the assault battalions came under vicious fire. To secure just the beachhead took three days. Bitter fighting would continue until July 9.

At 6:45 P.M. of D-day, ten minutes before sunset, *Enterprise* catapulted a pair of F4U-2N radar-equipped night fighters. Lieutenant Commander R. E. Harmer was aloft again with Lieutenant (jg) R. F. Holden as his wingman. At 7:05 the pair were vectored toward what the FDO called a "large bogie" only five miles from the carrier. This consisted of ten new Frances bombers escorted by five fighters. Harmer and Holden spotted them, dove, and Harmer made a full deflection high-side pass, pulling out over the bombers, taking a 20-mm. hit. This was from a fighter that Harmer and Holden identified as a Tojo but that was probably a new Jack.

Both then withdrew, reporting afterward that the enemy VF "could just stay with the F4U-2s, the latter using full military power." The pair could not again fight, for the 20-mm. hit had shorted "on" Harmer's formation lights, making him feel extremely conspicuous, not merely to the Japanese flyers but also to itchy-fingered American AA gunners below.

Virtually unimpeded, the Frances bombers deployed out of range of AA, dropped flares and float lights, then attacked. Some went for the *Enterprise* and others for the *Lexington*, ignoring CVL's *San Jacinto* and *Princeton* of the box formation. They met a ferocious radar-directed AA barrage that set four afire and dropped another without burning. One approaching from ahead passed the length of *Lexington*'s flight deck, ". . . burning so furiously," as watching correspondent Busch recorded, "that the heat of the flames made a hot wind in the faces of onlookers. . . ." It missed the flight deck aft by a scant 20 feet and crashed just off the stern. Its torpedo and one other passed along the side of the carrier within ten feet of the hull. Two other torpedoes, dropped from a thousand yards off the port bow, paralleled the *Enterprise* at 50 yards as the flattop dodged violently.

Lexington claimed five bombers and the *Enterprise* claimed two. Exact losses are not known, but Japanese records cite 11 planes downed of three Judys, 11 fighters, and ten Franceses attacking. Only 13 returned to base at Yap. By 10:30 P.M. *Lexington*'s radar screen was clear; no American fleet carrier would again undergo attack until June 19.

Admiral Ozawa had left Tawi Tawi at 9:00 A.M. on June 13 to steam his Mobile Fleet to Guimaras Strait in the Philippines so as to be closer to the scene of combat. Also, American submarines had troubled his ships at the exposed Tawi Tawi anchorage, his airmen had been unable to train, and he had not received needed replacement planes, though some were nearby at Davao.

After fueling his ships and learning of the invasion of Saipan, Ozawa early on June 15 received from Toyoda the order "Move out for Operation A." Toyoda also included an appeal to all hands: "The destiny of our Empire lies in the outcome of this battle. Each member will fight to the end." Toyoda's order was a close paraphrase of Admiral Togo's exhortation to his men given before his great victory over the Russians in the Battle of Tsushima Strait. No Japanese sailor could fail to note the coincidence.

Both Toyoda and Ozawa estimated that it would take a minimum of three days' steaming to get within air striking distance of Saipan. The carriers of the Mobile Fleet could not, therefore, arrive before the early morning of June 19, much too late to defeat the initial American landing. Toyoda hoped, however, to take advantage of this delay to improvise a coordinated attack on the American carriers. He hastily devised Operation "TO GO," which involved shuttling planes from the Hachiman Air Unit in Japan to Iwo Jima and from thence to the Saipan area. These planes would attack the U. S. carriers only, not the transports and gunnery ships of the invasion force, and then fly on to Palau and Truk. On landing they would refuel, rearm, and fly north to strike once more, afterward landing on Guam. Other planes already in the Carolines would stage through Truk or Yap to attack.

Toyoda hoped that TO GO would make good both the loss of Japanese air power in the Marianas and the numerical weakness of planes in Ozawa's force as compared to Task Force 58. But like every other Japanese scheme concocted at this stage of the war, TO GO was simpler to draft and looked better on paper than it turned out to be in execution.

Admirals Spruance and Mitscher had anticipated in the Forager plan that Toyoda would try to stage planes via the Bonins, where Iwo Jima was located. Keen Harrill and Jocko Clark would try to prevent this from happening. To this end Harrill's group was to smash up Iwo and Clark's Chichi Jima. No American, not even a stray merchant seaman, had seen either island for many years, but both were known from radio intelligence to be supporting aerial activities.

The morning of June 14 saw both task groups fueling in preparation for a 600-mile run north. This was done expeditiously; CVL *Cowpens*, for example, took on 313,574 gallons of fuel oil and 47,000 of 100-octane aviation gasoline between 11:09 A.M. and 1:24 P.M. From escort carrier *Copahee*, operating with the tankers for just this purpose, the carriers received new aircraft while returning "flyable duds," planes too worn or damaged to be usable in combat.

At 12:25 P.M. Clark flew to the *Essex* to confer with Harrill, who like himself was a pioneer aviator. According to Clark, Harrill was reluctant to strike at the Bonins, fearing that bad weather might cancel flight operations off Iwo and that in the interim Ozawa might show up near Saipan with the Japanese carrier fleet to be opposed by only two task groups. Harrill finally agreed to go, and the two rear admirals worked out a joint operations plan. The usual fighter sweep, they agreed, could be mounted in the afternoon. Bombing attacks would follow and be renewed the next day, June 16.

Clark and Harrill's main target, tear-drop-shaped Iwo Jima, had about a hundred planes on two airstrips, the one an A-shaped field and the other a single runway a mile north. The base unit was Captain Kanzo Miura's 752nd Air Group composed mostly of Zeros but now reinforced by medium bombers from metropolitan Japan. Miura was a veteran airman, but aside from a few flight leaders, nearly all his pilots were grass-green rookies. Few had fired a shot in combat and not many shots at towed target sleeves.

On June 15 the weather worsened over the American task groups as they moved north. On reaching their launching points at 1:00 P.M., they found seas moderate to rough, with a 15-foot swell. Lookouts atop *Yorktown's* mast could see no farther than seven miles. The carriers pitched and rolled, their decks constantly wet from spray and intermittent rain. Clark and Harrill elected to launch anyway, and at 1:34 P.M. the first Hellcats shot from the catapults. Immediately afterward more of the fighters plus Helldivers and Avengers were readied for a full-scale strike.

Steadying on a course of 262 degrees, the 44 Hellcats headed for Iwo Jima, 135 miles distant, in three separate squadrons. Their mission was to engage airborne enemy fighters and to splatter the airfield with 135-pound fragmentation clusters. Iwo's radar picked them up coming in, and despite their greenness Captain Miura's crews managed to get 37 Zeros into the air to trigger the biggest aerial fracas to date of Operation Forager.

First to reach the island were *Yorktown* Hellcats led by Commander B. M. Strean, skipper of Fighting 1. A melee began with Zeros and Hellcats swirling around and around the island. The Fighting 1 pilots, themselves green, did well, claiming 20 Zeros against Lieutenant Paul M. Henderson and Ensign Jack Hogue lost.

Planes from *Hornet* and *Essex* followed the *Yorktown* pilots into action, with *Hornet* flight leader Lieutenant Lloyd G. Barnard claiming five Zeros. Just two *Hornet* planes had battle damage, though the Japanese pilots missed many opportunities. Four boxed in Lieutenant (jg) Earling W. Zaeske, but he kept them from making firing runs by turning violently to port and starboard while climbing ("I don't know how") to 7,000 feet. At this altitude he turned head on into a Zero that finally attacked him, shot it down, and then dove away to join a pair of Hellcats at 5,000 feet. The *Essex* planes chased and downed three Zeros, raising Japanese losses to an admitted 28 of the 37 airborne. Then the fighters of all squadrons began strafing Iwo's airfield on which they counted 86 planes.

AA fire was light in volume but viciously concentrated and therefore more dangerous than the Zeros. It bounced about the *Essex* Avengers and Helldivers coming in after the fighter sweep and downed four planes, a Hellcat, two Avengers, and an SB2C "Beast."

Pilots from Jocko Clark's carriers, striking Chichi Jima and Haha Jima, found only one short airstrip and no land planes but destroyed on the water at Chichi Jima 21 seaplanes and flying boats. They also sank two small freighters and blasted a hangar and other shore installations. Light flak picked off a Helldiver that plunged right on in. *Yorktown* fighter pilot Lieutenant (jg) John H. Keeler ditched after getting a hit in the engine, but, like every other pilot who water-landed that day and the next, he was lost.

The weather worsened as both Clark's and Harrill's task groups retired south-southeast for the night. By the next morning, June 16, it was so bad as to make an immediate repeat strike impossible. It moderated by noon, and at 12:58 P.M. *Yorktown, Hornet* and CVL *Princeton* began launching, followed 42 minutes later by *Essex* and *Langley* of Harrill's carriers. This time not a single enemy plane was airborne, though more than 60 were counted on the ground. Either Captain Miura had not expected his enemy to fly in such bad weather, or (more likely) the strafing of the day before had damaged all planes. The fighters strafed and three bombing strikes, one from Harrill's group and two from Clark's, cratered and battered the Iwo airfields.

Once again the AA proved troublesome. Ensign James Spivey's Hellcat from *Yorktown* spun in flames into the sea. Most tragic was the loss of the experienced Lieutenant (jg) John R. Ivey of VF-15 of *Essex*. With his wingman, Ensign G. E. Mellon, hurtling behind him, Ivey swept over Iwo's airfield with .50s stuttering to have his plane jolt and rock from the impact of a light AA hit. He pulled up but began to fly erratically and aimlessly. Closing, Ensign Mellon and section leader Lieutenant G. R. Carr, who also had joined, could see that Ivey was suffering from a large wound in the face. Both pilots stayed with him and managed to steer him to the vicinity of the *Essex* but could not induce him either to bail out or to land aboard. Finally, Captain R. A. Ofstie, the carrier's skipper, ordered Mellon and Carr to land aboard, and Ivey flew aimlessly off to disappear from the radar screen. A CAP Hellcat sent to search found a slick of oil and some marker dye on the sea that apparently identified the site of his eventual crash some 30 to 40 miles from the *Essex*.

Admiral Harrill recovered his Iwo strike planes while speeding to the south. Never an enthusiast for the operation, uneasy that Ozawa might suddenly appear, he wanted to join the other task groups of TF 58 as soon as possible. Admiral Clark stayed until late afternoon, anxious—if he could —to knock out Iwo's airfield at least temporarily; then he too headed south.

In terms of American planes shot down, the Iwo and Chichi Jima strikes had been costly, with a dozen lost, but Japanese losses in aircraft must have been nearly a hundred. It is certain, however, that Iwo's airfields were not neutralized. Cratering of the runways by Helldivers did little more harm than had similar attacks on Henderson Field on Guadalcanal. Once filled with earth and packed, planes could land and take off again within at most a few hours. Destruction of several gasoline storage tanks may have caused more lasting damage. Admiral Toyoda's Operation TO GO from metropolitan Japan had been only temporarily set back. Iwo remained a potential threat to the northern flank of TF 58.

As Harrill's and Clark's flattops continued south on June 17, flying CAP, antisubmarine patrol, and long-range searches, Commander Bob Price was spending his sixth day in his life raft. None of the search planes found him, nor did he sight any, though they must have passed quite near. He spent the day trying vainly to improvise and use fishing tackle. Small schools of four- to six-inch perchlike fish stayed in the shade of the raft all day long, but he found it impossible to snag them with a crude hook made from the morphine syrette plug of his first-aid kit. "I still wasn't particularly hungry, but was uncomfortably thirsty at all times though not seriously so. It was annoying, as well as very disheartening, to see sizable rain clouds build up in the mornings and evenings and yet never rain a drop on me." Toward evening he took his daily swig of water from his emergency ration—"about an ounce." But he did not despair or give up. "This, I believe, was due to two [factors]: First, an intense desire to live; and second, the knowledge that every effort would be made to pick me up."

24. Mitscher, Spruance, Ozawa

The first indication to Admiral Mitscher that he faced a carrier battle—the first since the Battle of Santa Cruz in October 1942—came in the form of a message from *Redfin*. This submarine had sighted the First Mobile Fleet of Admiral Ozawa when it left Tawi Tawi on June 13. In the next two days Filipino coast watchers reported Ozawa's progress through the central Philippines. At 6:35 P.M. on June 15 submarine *Flying Fish* sighted the fleet's debouche from San Bernardino Strait into the Philippine Sea. On receiving this report several hours later, Mitscher concluded that Ozawa was probably looking for a fight. Also, from plotting the fleet's passage through Philippine waters Mitscher had calculated its speed of advance and had estimated fairly accurately its earliest possible time of arrival near Saipan. Ozawa's carriers could hardly be in range before the 18th and more likely the 19th. Mitscher should, therefore, have time to refuel the flattops of Reeves and Montgomery and rendezvous all four task groups before Ozawa appeared.

There was, however, a disturbing possibility to be guarded against. By hurrying his refueling, launching from as far out as 500 to 600 miles, and staging his aircraft through Tinian and Guam, Ozawa could strike nearly a day early. Mitscher decided that to prevent this he would have to continue to hammer all airfields in the Marianas daily to keep them inoperational.

To this end *Lexington*'s Air Group 16 attacked Guam's Agana airfield on June 16 to discover that the Japanese AA there had lost no potency. If anything the gunners had improved with practice. They picked off Lieutenant (jg) N. R. Landon and his Avenger crew over Agana Bay. His mates of Torpedo 16 saw the plane reel from formation and fall, then a big splash, an oil slick, debris, and that was all. Lieutenant B. T. Mennis of Bombing 16 landed his shot-up Dauntless on the first friendly deck he could find—it happened to be that of *Bunker Hill*. His canopy was riddled, and the left wing of his SBD-5 had a jagged hole through it. A Hellcat of VF-16 landed aboard the *Lex* with cylinders 3 and 4 knocked out, ignition wires cut, and oil lines severed between cylinders 2 and 4 and 1 and 3.

Yet the Pratt and Whitney Double Wasp kept running, meeting a performance standard the U. S. Navy had required of its radial engines since the early 1930s.

In Strike B *Lexington* air-group skipper Ernie Snowden led four Hellcats in a strafing run over Tinian's airfield at Ushi Point. He was disquieted to see many enemy planes parked on the field, some with cowls and hatches untouched by shrapnel or strafing. Some he identified as "Thunderbolts," Raiden. He and three wingmen claimed nine planes destroyed. The Japanese reported the attacks on Guam and Tinian as very heavy but recorded Tinian's airfield as operational again by 6:00 P.M.

June 17 was refueling day for Reeves and Montgomery, but in the afternoon Mitscher hit Guam once more. This time the defenders radioed to Tokyo, "The airfield is temporarily out of commission." *Lexington*'s pilots understood well enough why they had to strike this important target again, but they resented the loss of Lieutenant Mark Bright and his Hellcat. Many believed that Mitscher should have used TF 58's idle fast battleships to work over Agana's AA defense with shellfire before launching more air attacks.

That Mitscher was wise to continue strikes was plainly demonstrated just as the last American planes were completing their runs on the 17th and returning home to their floating airdromes. From Truk five Jills and an Irving night fighter attacked a group of LSTs, damaging one and forcing its abandonment. From Yap a strong force of 31 Zeros, 17 Judys, and two Frances bombers found at dusk the U. S. escort carrier force maneuvering off Saipan. Radar picked up the incoming strike, but a foul-up in fighter direction caused 46 Wildcats to miss an interception. The Japanese pilots had a clear shot, opposed only by AA. Judy pilot Zenkichi Uda dove first, counting off eight flattops and believing that he was attacking Task Force 58. He did not see the results of his drop. The others followed him down, near missing the *Gambier Bay* and *Coral Sea* and slamming a 550-pounder into *Fanshaw Bay* that exploded in her hangar. Her crew quickly controlled the fires, and this CVE—hardly better than a merchantman with a flat wooden deck, elevator, and arresting gear—steamed for Eniwetok, burying 11 dead en route.

Uda, with four other Judy pilots and some of the Zero jockeys, flew to Guam and landed safely after dark. The others returned to Yap. Uda went out again the next morning before daybreak and was shot down while attacking a ship he took to be a battlewagon. Picked up and made a POW, he was one of a handful of Japanese pilot-participants to survive the Marianas campaign.

That Ozawa was coming circulated from flag plot through the *Lexington*'s wardroom on the 17th and from there all over the ship and Task Force 58. Correspondent Busch noted in his journal, "Indications are that the Japanese fleet consists of two major elements which joined together northeast of the Philippines." He added, "It comprises perhaps nine carriers populated by about 450 planes. . . ." This scuttlebut was "right on," to employ an argot more suited to the Vietnam War than World War II. But all day TBFs equipped with bomb-bay tanks searching out 350 miles found nothing. Mitscher had expected this, but at 2:53 P.M. as a precaution he had detached his seven fast battleships from their carrier screens and formed them into Task Group 58.7 under rough, abrupt "Ching" Lee. Lee's ships took position to the westward of the carriers that had been maintaining a leisurely southwesterly heading all day. The carriers steamed on a roughly north-south line of bearing in the same formation that they would use for the next two days. Harrill's and Clark's group were on the northern flank with Harrill leading Clark, Reeves's with *Lexington* was in the center astern of the battleships, and Montgomery's group was on the south flank.

For his part Admiral Ozawa had spent June 16 rendezvousing his own force. Admiral Ugaki had joined with a battleship force that had been assigned to the now cancelled KON Operation. Two fleet oiler units had steamed up, also, to top off the now united First Mobile Fleet. Refueling began late in the afternoon of the 16th and was not completed until 9:00 P.M. on the 17th. The oilers then peeled off to the northeast to wait until the carrier battle was over and then to refuel the hopefully victorious ships. At this time the First Mobile Fleet was about 770 nautical miles from Saipan.

Ozawa was fully aware that his enemy had him outnumbered in carriers and carrier planes, but he hoped that Kakuta's land-based planes would somehow even the odds. He also had two other advantages. His first was that in a carrier duel he could outrange Admiral Mitscher by approximately a hundred miles. Lacking armor and self-sealing tanks, his planes were lighter than the American, could carry more fuel, and could operate at a combat radius of over 300 nautical miles from their carriers. On the American side only the Hellcat could fly as far. The Helldivers and Avengers and the rugged old Dauntlesses still carried aboard *Enterprise* and *Lexington* could not safely go much beyond 240 miles. Ozawa's second advantage was that the prevailing trade wind was easterly, which meant that his carriers could launch into it while Mitscher's would have to put about. This added considerably to his advantage in range, while insuring that Mitscher would have to stay in about the same place all day, making TF 58 easier to find.

If Ozawa timed his arrival off Saipan skillfully, if his reconnaissance planes could early and accurately pinpoint TF 58's location, then the chances were very good that he could attack from outside the reach of Mitscher and not get hit himself. Ozawa was confident that he could pull it off, provided that Spruance kept TF 58 within a hundred miles of Saipan. He gambled that Spruance, whom he regarded as a conservative and cautious commander, would do exactly that.

Normally, Ozawa might have been tempted to try the usual Japanese sneaky tactics, involving elaborate end runs by CVLs, a roundabout approach from either the south or north by his main body, or a considerable deviation from his course from San Bernardino Strait. The shortage of bunker oil forbade that. He could approach Saipan on only a nearly direct course, bending just enough to avoid land-based air search, then launch, attack, refuel, and return. He rejected also trying a staged attack via Guam because his planes had enough fuel to reach beyond the enemy's range and return. By the early morning of June 18 Ozawa was confident battle would come on the morrow.

The early hours of June 18 brought uncertainty in flag plot aboard *Lexington*. Planes on predawn and dawn searches out to 325 miles had sighted only empty ocean. Was Ozawa still beyond range or had he given up? Had Gus Widhelm lost his thousand-dollar wager made on June 16 that there would be a carrier battle?

Admirals Mitscher and Spruance doubted that Ozawa had turned back, but they were nonetheless annoyed. They dearly wanted to know his whereabouts and, equally important, into how many separate task groups he had divided his forces. On June 15 and 17 submarines had sighted what apparently were three separate ones, and they knew it was Japanese doctrine to employ flank attacks and envelopments. In every engagement since the Coral Sea Japanese carrier forces had been divided, and it seemed logical that Ozawa might try a sneak attack on the Saipan beachhead and the escort carriers with a force of his CVLs. Mitscher and Spruance knew in a general way about Ozawa's oil shortage, but they did not know that it confined him to a direct approach.

On June 17 Spruance had rendezvoused with Task Force 58, his flagship *Indianapolis* joining the cruiser-destroyer screen of Task Group 58.3. He had also—in effect—taken over supervisory command of fleet movements. Mitscher no longer was free to act on his own. The two men were still not on close personal terms. Each was aloof by nature, and shortly after Mitscher had taken over as TF 58 commander they had disagreed sharply on several occasions as to how best to use the task force. There is, however, no evidence to suggest bitterness between the two. Neither was a man who would risk Task Force 58 merely to spite the other.

Tension built up with the rising sun on June 18, a Sunday, but although all carriers had strikes ready on their decks and the pilots stayed in flight gear ready to man planes, church services were held as usual. Correspondent Busch recorded those aboard *Lexington*. Attendance was good, but the hymn of the Protestant service ". . . seemed to be a bit on the sober side: 'Lead kindly light amid the encircling gloom,' and, of course, the one about the perils of the sea." Services over, the loudspeaker crisply barked, "Unrig church!"

Search planes roared from decks all day long. At noon the task forces of Harrill and Clark joined, after which TF 58 steamed west by south. Frequent turns into the wind, however, retarded forward advance, and by dusk at 6:29 P.M. when flight operations ceased, the carriers had made good only 115 miles. Nor, as Admiral Morison notes, had "one American search plane sighted a Japanese ship." They found a Jake seaplane searching and shot it down, but the scouting Avengers turned back 50 to 60 miles short of Ozawa's warship force—which was exactly what this able admiral had carefully calculated they must do.

At 8:30 P.M. Task Force 58 heeled about and began steaming east, back toward Saipan. Spruance had already made his key decision of the battle, one perfectly in keeping with Ozawa's expectations. His goal, he had stated in an order issued earlier in the day, was primarily to protect Saipan's invasion forces. He would therefore steam west by day and east at night, "so as to reduce the possibility of the enemy passing us in the darkness." In other words, Spruance was making defense of a fixed island position rather than the destruction of the enemy carrier fleet his primary objective.

In his searches Ozawa did much better than his enemy. Aboard his big carriers he had reconnaissance planes equipped only for this purpose, something the U. S. Navy had not developed. *Zuikaku,* for example, had aboard Jill 12s (Tenzans), of which two had radar. These planes had a maximum range of 1,644 nautical miles and could search up to 600 miles ahead of their carriers, nearly double the radius of an unmodified Avenger. Ozawa launched seven planes at noon on the 18th out 420 miles to dog-leg and return. Between 3:14 and 4:00 P.M. two of the planes found Task Force 58 steaming in between them. This knowledge, radioed promptly and accurately, enabled Ozawa to fix his plan. He would turn south, keeping 400 nautical miles from his foe, then put about again during the night, close, and attack. Basic to his entire reasoning was the presumption that Spruance would not keep coming and close him but turn back to stay within a hundred nautical miles of Saipan.

Ozawa considered and rejected launching a long-range attack on the American carriers about sunset. The distance would be too great without shuttle-bombing via Guam, and he was uncertain as to the status of the island's airfields. His decision checked an impetuous Rear Admiral Sueo Obayashi, commanding CVLs *Chitose, Chiyoda,* and *Zuiho,* from acting on his own. Twenty-two planes took off before Obayashi received Ozawa's order forbidding attack. But on its receipt he cancelled the strike and recalled them.

Of Ozawa's position and activity, Admiral Spruance was entirely ignorant. Yet at 10:00 P.M. on the 18th, two hours *after* he had turned Task Force 58 eastward, he received intelligence information that should perhaps have made him reconsider. This was a report from a "Huff-Duff" (HFDF —high-frequency direction finder) shore-station fix of an enemy radio transmission. The fix apparently was on Ozawa's fleet after the admiral had broken radio silence to report to Admiral Kakuta on Tinian his successful reconnaissance of the American fleet. Convinced that the transmission probably was from Ozawa's flagship, Mitscher's staff calculated that their adversary was 355 nautical miles away, heading easterly at about the same speed that Task Force 58 was making in the same direction. They also calculated that if TF 58 put about at 1:30 A.M. and began steaming west it could by daybreak on the 19th be within 150 to 200 miles from Ozawa at 5:00 A.M., ideal range for an attack.

Said Captain Arleigh Burke in a postwar interview, "We checked this, we drew it on the charts, we very carefully had other people check it, and finally we sent by TBS [short-range voice radio] to ComFifth Fleet [Spruance] a message which said, 'We propose to come to a westerly course at 0130 in order to commence a treatment on the enemy at 0500. Advise.' "*

Admiral Spruance aboard nearby *Indianapolis* received Mitscher's proposal and discussed it with his staff for more than an hour. He finally decided to reject it, so informing Mitscher 38 minutes after midnight. The Huff-Duff fix, he reasoned, might well be a decoy. A transmission from submarine *Stingray* that apparently had been jammed by the enemy might well be the truer indicator of Ozawa's real position, and *Stingray*'s patrol area was supposed to be 175 miles to the east-southeast of the Huff-Duff fix. Even if the Huff-Duff fix was valid, it might well be from a diversionary force rather than of Ozawa's main body of carriers. Ozawa could be sending a CVL force from due west while curling about to approach with his main body from the south. In any event, Spruance saw no reason to alter his basic strategy. As he explained to Admiral Morison after the war:

We were at the start of a very large and important amphibious operation and we could not gamble and place it in jeopardy. The way Togo waited at Tsushima for the Russian fleet to come to him [reference is to the Battle of Tsushima Strait in the Russo-Japanese War of 1904-05] had always been in my mind. We had somewhat the same situation.

The disappointment in *Lexington*'s flag plot was great. Said Burke, "We were brokenhearted." It seemed to him and to Captain Hedding— probably also to Mitscher—that Spruance, despite his experience at Midway, did not really understand carrier war. By failing to turn back west Spruance was handing to Ozawa the enormous advantage of getting in the first and possibly the only punch of the battle. The morning would see the rival carrier groups about 350 miles apart, a distance at which Ozawa could strike and Mitscher could not. Concluded Burke, "This we did not like. It meant that the enemy could attack us at will at dawn the next morning. We could not attack the enemy."

With orders fixed and its desired course of action blocked, Mitscher's staff stayed up the rest of the night trying to devise various alternative plans. As Captain Burke recalled, the staff had to determine how far east TF 58 could steam and still keep on launching planes. It also decided to keep the flight decks as clear of bombers and Avengers as possible to make room for Hellcats. But most plans went into the wastebasket. There was no way to substitute strategy for a bad tactical position.

At 2:00 A.M. the *Enterprise* launched 14 Avengers of its night-flying-

* The exact wording was very close to Captain Burke's recollection: ". . . Propose coming to course 270 degrees at 0130 in order to commence treatment at 0500. Advise."

trained torpedo squadron on a combined search-attack mission. All planes had radar and they thoroughly covered the west to west-southwest sector, 240° to 270°. But as Burke expected they barely missed Ozawa, who was just beyond their reach by 40 to 50 miles. Had the radar of but one of them registered—by some anomaly of electronics—Ozawa's fleet on its screen and had its pilot gotten through his message, TF 58 could still have reversed course to get within attack range by daybreak.

Although he was accepting battle on disadvantageous terms tactically, out of range of enemy carriers and close to active enemy air bases on Guam, Mitscher had one enormous advantage over Ozawa. He had aboard ship 956 planes as against 473 for his opponent. Moreover, some 475 of the American planes were Hellcats, whereas Ozawa had only 151 Zero fighters.* Escorted by too few fighters, Ozawa's Kates, Judys, Jills, Vals, and bomb-carrying Zero Type 21s would head into a skyful of American defenders. Already, Ozawa had lost 11 carrier planes, the majority in an accident the day the Mobile Fleet left Tawi Tawi. A Jill had jumped the barrier on the new *Taiho* to smash into planes parked ahead. Fire had destroyed the wrecked Jill and five more planes.

This accident highlighted the inexperience of the Japanese torpedo and dive-bomber pilots. About all that the torpedo-plane pilots had been trained to do—perhaps *could* have been trained to do—was to fly their planes, maintain tight formation on their experienced flight leaders, drop ordnance on his signal, and then fly home. The dive-bomber pilots had nowhere nearly enough training in their difficult art. Prior to the Santa Cruz battle, as Captain Masatake Okumiya recalls, it was not uncommon for a flight of nine Vals diving on the maneuvering target ship *Settsu* to score nine hits. But the crews assigned to the A GO operation flying the faster-diving Judys, also attacking in nine-plane formations, "rarely scored more than *one* hit."

At 4:00 A.M. on June 19 Admiral Ozawa steadied his First Mobile Fleet on a course of 50 degrees, slightly north of due east, and increased speed to 20 knots. The ships were in their battle formation ready to attack and to be attacked.

Eighty miles in front, acting as a vanguard, were the three light carriers of the Third Carrier Division, *Chitose*, *Zuiho*, and *Chiyoda*. They were deployed abreast, separated by about seven miles, each surrounded by a powerful screen of surface ships. In command was Rear Admiral

* Plane strength broke down as follows:

Type of aircraft:	Fighters and fighter-bombers	Dive bomber	Torpedo plane	Float plane
Japanese	222	113	95	43
American	475	232	184	65

American aircraft strength figures are from availability reports for June 13. Some planes were lost between the 13th and 19th, but CVEs supplied replacement planes. Availability on the 19th probably was close to the total for the 13th.

Obayashi and aboard was the 653rd Air Group under Commander Masayuki Yamaguchi, an Eta Jima graduate of the class of 1936. Planes embarked were 62 Zeros, of which 45 were Model 21 fighter-bombers and 17 Model 52 fighters, plus nine Jills and 17 Kates. Gunnery ships surrounding the carriers included super battleships *Yamato* and *Musashi*, fast battleships *Haruna* and *Kongo*, four heavy cruisers, new light cruiser *Noshiro*, and a very thin screen of only eight destroyers. Ozawa's intent in deploying his Third Carrier Division into what amounted to three mini-task forces obviously was to provide maximum AA protection. If Spruance did locate him, Ozawa wanted the TF 58 planes to attack the van rather than his main body, in the process losing heavily to the AA.

Under his own immediate command Ozawa had *Taiho, Shokaku,* and *Zuikaku,* now the "big three" of the Imperial Japanese Navy. They comprised the First Carrier Division and embarked the 601st Air Group. The air officer was the veteran Commander Toshio Irisa, and the air-group commander was Lieutenant Commander Akira Tarui, an Eta Jima classmate of Yamaguchi's. The two had as their charges 79 Zeros, seven Vals, 70 Judys, 51 Jills, and nine Judy Type 2 reconnaissance planes. In addition to being air-group commander, Tarui also commanded directly the Jill torpedo planes. The surface ship screen was not large; it included heavy cruisers *Myoko* and *Haguro,* light cruiser *Yahagi,* and only seven destroyers.

Steaming just to the north of Ozawa's task group was Rear Admiral Takaji Jojima's Second Carrier Division. It comprised the converted liners *Junyo* and *Hiyo* plus CVL *Ryuho,* the ship that had been so beset with mechanical problems as to be only now steaming on its first strike mission. Jojima's division embarked 63 Zero fighters, 18 Zero fighter-bombers, 27 Judys, nine Vals, and 18 Jills. The air-group skipper was Lieutenant Commander Joyotaro Iwami. Again, the surface warship screen was light, comprising battleship *Nagato,* cruiser *Mogami,* and only eight destroyers.

At 4:30 A.M., a half hour after changing course and stepping up speed, Ozawa ordered off his first wave of reconnaissance planes to search out nearly 400 miles. At 4:45 from Admiral Kurita's battleships and crusiers of the van force, 16 slow but reliable Jake seaplanes shot from catapults. Their mission was to cover thoroughly a fan-shaped wedge centered on 50 degrees. At 5:15 Ozawa ordered out two more reconnaissance waves, also centered on 50 degrees. The first consisted of 13 Kates from Obayashi's CVLs of the Third Carrier Division; the second of 11 Judys from *Shokaku.* Three seaplanes went out, too. The Kates and Judys were to search out to nearly 600 miles.

Ozawa's reconnaissance effort would have been considered extravagant by Admirals Spruance and Mitscher, but it soon paid off. At 7:34 A.M., an hour after full sunrise, when 160 miles from Saipan on his return leg, one of the Jake pilots spotted game. His binoculars showed what he took to be two carriers, four battleships, and "more than ten" other vessels. He had picked up one of Spruance's northernmost carrier groups, either Harrill's or Clark's. This was what Ozawa confidently had been expecting; he notified his carrier groups and then put about to stay a full 400 miles from the enemy. His vanguard ships, he estimated, were only some 300 miles from the point of contact and his own flagship, *Taiho*, about 380 miles. He had nearly the exact position he wanted; his brilliant admiralship had paid off. With some help from land-based planes from Guam, he hoped to pull off a Midway in reverse.

For nearly an hour Ozawa delayed launching. He expected more of the reconnaissance planes to report in and give him a complete picture of Task Force 58's disposition. On the carriers excitement mounted to fever pitch. About to begin, the crews knew, was A GO, the largest Japanese naval combat mission since Midway, one of decisive importance. Here was the opportunity at last to avenge every humiliating failure since Guadalcanal.

Toshio Sakuraba, an eager flight radioman assigned to a Jill torpedo plane aboard *Zuikaku*, had at least some idea of what he would be in for. He had heard the rumors of the huge size of the American task force and from a gunnery petty officer on the carrier of the deadliness of the enemy's radar-directed gunfire. But he was "rarin' to go," as were all other of the air crew, rookies and experienced men alike.

At 8:30 or shortly before, knowing that his reconnaissance planes had reached the limits of their search areas, Ozawa ordered off his first strike from the big flattops of Carrier Division One. *Taiho* veered into the southeasterly wind, and the first Zero climbed from its deck at 8:45. Nearby, *Zuikaku* and *Shokaku* also were launching, putting into the air a strike greater in numbers than Nagumo's at Midway—48 Zeros, 54 Judys, and 27 Jill torpedo planes. Leading was Akira Tauri in a Jill. Two radar-equipped Jills went also as "tracking planes" to fix and pinpoint the American force.

A hundred miles ahead with the van force Rear Admiral Obayashi had already launched his first strike, the lead Zero taking off at 8:25. From *Chitose*, *Chiyoda*, and *Zuiho* 14 Zero Type 52 fighters had gotten away, followed by 43 Zero Type 21 fighter-bombers. Seven Jill torpedo planes had followed, their pilots "sweating out" a takeoff into a wind a bit too light for safety. All made it, and the entire strike of the Third Carrier Division started for the enemy without waiting for the planes from Ozawa's First Carrier Division. They were headed for the same position, designated the 7i contact,* that had been reported by the Jake recce plane an hour earlier.

Until this moment Ozawa's strategy cannot be faulted. But in failing to coordinate his and Obayashi's strikes he had committed the same blunder his enemies had made at Santa Cruz. Also, he had held back a strike from Admiral Jojima's Second Carrier Division, probably because he wanted to

---

* 7i was the grid position of the contact on the Japanese battle charts.

reserve these planes for additional targets. He now had two groups of planes headed for the enemy that would arrive about an hour apart, giving the Americans the maximum opportunity for interception. He would have been better advised to "go for broke," throw every plane in one mass attack, counting on sheer numbers to overwhelm the extremely strong Hellcat screen.

Ozawa's failure to consolidate his first two strikes also led to an unfortunate accident. The planes of his First Carrier Division, en route to the enemy, through an error flew directly over the carriers of Obayashi's Third Division and their powerful surface-ship escort. Believing that they were under attack from Avengers coming over at 24,000 feet, the AA gunners opened a heavy barrage, downing two planes and damaging eight so badly that they had to return. An extremely good AA performance was a tragedy for Japan.

Dawn had come to the American carriers without joy. As Arleigh Burke later said, "We knew that we were going to have the hell slugged out of us . . . and were making sure that we were ready to take it." Wanting to keep his decks clear for his fighters, Admiral Mitscher deflected a suggestion from Spruance that he attack Guam at first light on the grounds of a shortage of bombs. This probably was a mistake, for it was likely that TF 58 was going to get "slugged" from two directions, by Ozawa's carriers from the west and by land-based planes from Guam. It would have been better to have "postholed" the runways of Agana and Orote fields on Guam at first light and, for good measure, the Rota strip also, though "31 Knot" Burke believed the Japanese had no avgas stockpiled there and therefore could not use the field.

At 5:30 A.M. while Mitscher was launching his dawn search, radar picked up bogies on the screen from Guam's direction. A *Monterey* pilot on CAP found two Judys and downed one. These probably were reconnaissance planes sent out by Admiral Kakuta, who was doing everything in his power to mass planes on Guam. En route from Truk to Guam were 19 planes, all that this bastion had available. Counting these 19, Kakuta had about 50 serviceable planes based on Orote field; all other fields in the Marianas either were out of commission or had no intact planes.

At 5:30 A.M. came more action. A Zero, one of a half dozen on a search-strike mission from Orote, jumped destroyer *Stockham*, which was on radar picket duty out ahead of Admiral Lee's battle wagons of TF 58.7. Attacking from a glide out of low clouds, it caught the "can" by surprise but missed. Destroyer *Yarnall* shot it down.

Forty minutes later, at 6:30 A.M., the radar screens of several ships picked up enemy planes over Guam, 90 miles away. Sent after them was a CAP from *Belleau Wood*'s Fighting 24 led by Lieutenant C. I. Oveland. Oveland's quartet had been airborne since 5:40 A.M. and was scheduled to stay up for four hours, a time many squadron leaders regarded as overfatiguing.

Arriving at 15,500 feet over the island, Oveland noted "considerable" flight activity about Orote field, obviously operational again, and then zigged away when AA bursts puffed ominously 2,000 feet below. Glancing up, he suddenly yelled "Skunks!" and began a steep turn. From above and behind he spotted four Zeros diving on his flight. Pulling completely through their turn, the four Hellcats met the Zeros head on, fired, and two Zeros began smoking and falling. Oveland watched his blazing victim do aileron rolls all the way into the water. Lieutenant (jg) R. C. Tabler's Zero dove straight in. Before the pilots could congratulate themselves, more Zeros began diving on the flight from all directions. This time Oveland slammed his throttle wide open and with engine in low blower dove vertically at more than 400 knots indicated air speed. The four planes, still in formation, then pulled up, climbing at a terrific rate to 15,000 feet once more. Oveland was on his radio hollering for help and telling the TF 58 controllers that the enemy had a "substantial concentration" of aircraft over Orote.

Once again the Zeros attacked, but when one got onto the tail of Lieutenant Tabler, Wingman Ensign E. Holmgaard, playing it strictly by the book, turned sharply into the attacker and with a beautiful, full-deflection shot blasted off half of the Zero's starboard wing. Tabler straightened out, turned into two Zeros, fired, and then dove away from four coming up from behind. Ensign Carl J. Bennett found out how dangerous it was to leave formation when he drifted away and was shot up. He came back with a hole through his prop, four punched in his wings, one through the fin, two through an elevator tab, two more in the fuselage, and one through his canopy. He rated a Purple Heart award, too, for cuts in the back of his head caused by showering plexiglass from the canopy. The other planes stuck together, turning into each attack by the Zeros, claiming several more (ten in all), until the Zeros gave up the deadly game. "There was no evidence," Oveland told the squadron's intelligence officer, Lieutenant G. F. Markham, "of a well-coordinated attack which the great superiority of the enemy in numbers should have encouraged."

When several flights from *Cabot*, *Yorktown*, and *Hornet* showed up, they found no game. The Zeros either had hauled off out of range or landed again on Orote to disappear into well-camouflaged revetments.

Action blazed up again at 8:07 A.M. when TF 58 radars again picked up enemy planes heading into Guam. Three groups of Hellcats took off to engage and beginning at 8:24 A.M. and continuing for an hour sporadic fights took place over and near Guam. The fighter boys claimed a goodly bag—probably considerably inflated—of 30 Zeros and five bombers, but Orote still was very much operational when they heard *Lexington*'s controller, Lieutenant Joe Eggert, give the old circus call for help, "Hey, Rube!" That meant, "Come home at once." TF 58, as Burke had feared, was about to get slugged.

25. The Marianas Turkey Shoot

Lieutenant Eggert's "Hey, Rube!" had been ordered by Admiral Mitscher himself. At 10:03 A.M. at the remarkable distance of 140 miles, battleship *Alabama's* radar had picked up an incoming flight not registering on IFF. She had reported at once to *Lex* over TBS and *Enterprise* confirmed. By 10:05 flagship *Lexington* also had the enemy on a bearing of 260 degrees just south of due west in two groups at 121 and 124 miles, respectively, estimated altitude 20,000 feet. By 10:10 A.M. the fast-working Eggert had CVL *Princeton's* CAP section on the way out, followed closely by Hellcats from *Essex, Hornet, Cowpens,* and *Monterey.* He did not make the mistake of all air controllers in the 1942 engagements, ordering the pilots to stay too low; he had the planes climbing hard to 25,000 feet, well above the enemy. To protect against torpedo planes sweeping in beneath the radar, he counted on his 23 fighters returning from Guam, ordering them to orbit west of Admiral Lee's battle line, thus keeping an antitorpedo screen between the enemy and his own flattops.

At this point the inexperienced Japanese who were from the 653rd Air Group from *Zuiho, Chitose,* and *Chiyoda* played right into Eggert's hands. Instead of diving in fast, making maximum use of the exceptional speed of the Jills and bomb-carrying Zeros, the entire enemy formation began to orbit while the leader gave each element specific instructions. The planes circled for about 15 minutes, giving the intercepting Hellcats time to gain thousands of feet of altitude and tens of miles of distance. Also, language specialist Lieutenant Charles A. Sims aboard the *Lexington* was "listening in" on the briefing of the pilots and promptly relayed the gist of the leader's orders to Fighter Director Eggert.

At about 10:19 all carriers began turning southeast into the wind preparatory to launching a "scramble intercept" of every available Hellcat. Within 15 minutes about 140 had taken off to join 82 others already in the air. All standby Avengers, Helldivers, and Dauntlesses gassed and armed for attacks on enemy naval targets were launched with orders to orbit on the eastern—unengaged—side of Task Force 58. This cleared the decks for continuous recovery and relaunch of CAP. All squadrons obeyed

259

orders, but some strayed too close and diverted Hellcats directed to orbit above the fleet. Mitscher's final order was to all captains to keep their ships on course southeast into the prevailing wind. This bearing took them farther away from the enemy fleet and by day's end dangerously close to the enemy's bases on Guam, but the carriers could and did land and launch at will. By about 10:30 the position of Task Force 58 was approximately 80 miles northwest of Guam.

First to sight enemy planes, now in battle disposition, was Commander Charles W. Brewer leading two sections (eight planes) from *Essex*. Brewer, a veteran aviator from the U. S. Naval Academy's Class of 1934 and commander of Fighting 15, had been airborne about an hour. On seeing the enemy, he recorded the time at 10:35 A.M. and estimated the enemy's altitude at 18,000 feet and distance from the *Essex* at 55 miles. Snapping on his radio, he gave the "Tallyho!" reporting 24 "Rats" (bombers), 16 "Hawks" (fighters), and no "Fish" (torpedo planes). Sixteen Zero fighter-bombers formed the core of the 653rd Air Group's formation, with four Zero fighters on each flank and 16 more 1,000 to 2,000 feet above and behind. All were leaving thick white contrails of condensation.

Brewer's own position was ideal. He crossed over the enemy at 24,000 feet, flipped his Hellcat onto its back and dove with his men following in a textbook overhead run. He picked the lead Zero as his target and from 800 feet began firing, sending a torrent of bullets into the fighter-bomber. Its pilot, possibly because he was tired from his long three-hour flight from his own carrier, did not even "jink" his plane. The powerful .50 slugs literally tore it to pieces in a burst of flame and debris.

Pulling out sharply below the formation, Brewer climbed and attacked another Zero from below, lopping off half a wing. This plane slipped toward the sea, flaming. Climbing above the formation to regain attack position, Brewer noted a Zero diving away. He pursued, getting on its tail, and, closing to 400 feet, fired a burst into its vulnerable wing roots, flaming it. Immediately looking around as a good fighter pilot must, Brewer spotted a fourth Zero diving on him, turned into it, and found himself in a dogfight. With both planes making above 160 knots indicated, Brewer found that he could maneuver with the Zero fighter, get onto its tail, and begin firing short bursts. At each burst the Zero pilot would perform half rolls, full rolls, and wing-overs, but Brewer got hits in the fuselage, wings, and cockpit until the Zero blazed, whirled into a tight spiral, stalled, and crashed into the sea. By now Brewer had lost his altitude, and on climbing back up, he found that the raid had been dispersed.

Ensign Richard E. Fowler, Jr., Brewer's wingman, stayed with his leader through the commander's first two attacks. Then he broke off to knock down a Zero that made a diving turn in front of him. Next he got into a wild fight with three more. He tried a snap, 60-degree deflection shot at one and was disconcerted to see the nimble plane flip over the opposite direction. Then he realized that his burst had sawed ten feet off its wing. The Zero spun, its pilot bailing out, but Fowler saw no chute. Fowler next turned sharply into a Zero approaching from his starboard beam, then circled steeply to get behind it. He fired, and the Zero began skidding uncontrollably right and left. This time his .50s had shot away the plane's vertical stabilizer. He continued shooting until the plane flamed. Fowler's last victim was a Zero that had dropped low. Fowler saw it passing through a small cloud, chased, closed fast, and from 1,500 feet away—too far— began shooting. Nevertheless, hits in the fuselage and cockpit sent it into the ocean.

Flight from *Hornet* and CVLs *Princeton, Cowpens*, and *Monterey* followed Brewer's initial attack and also had good shooting. Commander Bill Dean, leading eight *Hornet* Hellcats of VF-2, passed above Brewer's battle, wheeled back, and dove to join at 10,000 feet. He claimed two Zeros and his men eight more. Said Dean to his intelligence interrogator, "I saw twenty to twenty-five parachutes . . . and many flamers and crashes. There were several dye markers in the water." Lieutenant (jg) Daniel A. Carmichael found at high altitude and chased a lone Jill he "definitely identified," noting that the enemy torpedo plane was "very fast and difficult to catch." "I rode him and he wobbled his wings violently from port to starboard. He finally burst into flames at ten thousand feet." Lieutenant (jg) John T. Wolf, also one of Dean's pilots, correctly identified one Zero —albeit tentatively—as a bomber. This one "dropped his belly tank and *what appeared to be a bomb*." His squadron I.O. (intelligence officer) correctly noted the signficance of this statement and underscored it.

Planes from other carriers arriving just minutes later found pickings slim. Some flew past the fight looking for another enemy formation and turned back 60 to 70 miles out after drawing a blank. By about 10:40, only five minutes after the action began, the Japanese formation's survivors had broken into treys, pairs, and singles. The Japanese recorded their losses as totaling eight of 14 Zero fighters, 32 of 43 Zero fighter-bombers, and two of seven Jills. American losses included *Princeton*'s air-group commander, Lieutenant Commander Ernest Wetherill Wood, Jr., Annapolis '38, and two other pilots. Several F6Fs took severe damage, including one the handling crews shoved overside on landing.

A few Zero bombers got as far as Vice Admiral Lee's battle line operating westward of the carriers. One dove at 10:49 on *South Dakota*, scoring a hit with a 550-pound bomb that killed 27 and wounded 23 of her crew. This missile did little harm to the battleship's fighting capacity, less than the one that had hit her turret in the Santa Cruz battle. Another bomb near missed cruiser *Minneapolis*, causing a few casualties. But that was all. Reports by surviving Japanese pilots of hits on four carriers either were illusion or fancy. No carrier underwent attack, and the lone plane at which *Essex* fired may have been a "friendly." At 10:57 after less than a half hour of perhaps the most violent air combat of the carrier war to date, fighter-director Eggert could report to Captain Burke that the raid had dispersed and that no bogies appeared to be closing.

Eggert had only a ten-minute respite, barely enough time to recall his own fighters over their task groups. Then at 11:07 the *Lexington's* radar intercepted another large enemy flight at 250 degrees, 155 miles from the ship. These planes appeared to be orbiting and crossing each other's formations slowly, a phenomenon explained when Lieutenant Sims again heard transmissions from the Japanese flight leader* as he arranged his squadrons for attack. These were the planes of the 601st Air Group from *Shokaku, Zuikaku,* and *Taiho,* numbering about 109.

Once again the first Hellcats vectored out came from *Essex's* VF-15. Leading was the flattop's air-group skipper, Commander David McCampbell. Followed by nine F6Fs, he had left the *Essex's* deck at 10:37 A.M. too late to catch the first attackers. His directions from the air controller were "VECTOR 245 DEGREES, DISTANCE 80 MILES, LINER."

From two miles away McCampbell spotted a huge enemy bogie 45 miles from the *Essex*, 5,000 feet below, bearing nine o'clock. Commander Tarui's air group was in the same type of formation favored since Pearl Harbor, with all planes, even the fighters, flying in three-plane sections, nine-plane divisions, squadron on squadron. McCampbell estimated the altitude depth at 1,200 to 1,500 feet, with all planes making 180 knots true air speed.

Leaving a four-plane section to orbit as high cover, McCampbell and five of his pilots dove at 11:39 A.M., converting their altitude advantage into speed. McCampbell chose a high-side pass at a Judy formation and, with his trembling air-speed indicator pushing through 350 knots, picked out a Judy halfway back in the formation. He planned to knock it down, dive through the enemy pack, and pull up sharply and shoot down the leader. But as he put it:

These plans became upset when the first plane blew up practically in my face and caused a pull-out above the entire formation. I remember being unable to get to the other side fast enough, feeling as though every rear gunner had his fire directed at me.

McCampbell made it unhit, climbed, dove again, and downed a Judy on the other side. Another pass smoked a third plane, damaging it. Finally, McCampbell closed the leader, who was pushing doggedly on course with a wingman hugging close. McCampbell downed the wingman, who was blocking his fire, passed below, and then pulled up for a run on the leader from below at eight o'clock. He fired and ". . . worked onto his tail and continued to fire until he burned furiously." McCampbell hit another Judy, claiming four shot down and a probable, before his guns ran out of am-

---

* Presumably this was Lieutenant Commander Tarui, who commanded the 601st Air Group's planes in the air from his Jill torpedo plane, much as Commander Fuchida had done in the Pearl Harbor operation.

munition and forced him to break away. Snapping on his radio at 11:46, McCampbell reported the destruction of the enemy leader and added, "I doubt if any of them will get through." None of his victims had attempted evasion. Their fishtailing and weaving from side to side had ". . . only slowed them down and allowed me . . . to make quick, successive runs."

McCampbell's subordinates of VF-15 claimed 16 Zeros and Judys as against one man lost, Ensign G. H. Rader. Four planes suffered battle damage and Ensign J. W. Power a leg wound from 20-mm. fragments. The Hellcats, wrote McCampbell in his after-action report, ". . . withstood terrific punishment from enemy 7.7 and 20-mm." He also recorded the usual: "The F6F can catch a Zeke with high speed, but cannot maneuver with it at low speed."

Six minutes after McCampbell attacked other fighter units had plunged into the melee. These included sections from *Yorktown*'s VF-1 and *Lexington*'s VF-16, plus eight Hellcats from *Princeton*'s VF-27, six from *San Jacinto*'s VF-51, and seven from *Bataan*'s VF-50.

Commander B. M. Strean's *Yorktown* pilots performed exceptionally well. They stayed mostly in pairs even when the Zeros and Judys they attacked became widely scattered. They did not dogfight and claimed 22 enemy planes without loss to themselves. "The action of all pilots," reported Strean, "leaves little to be desired."

The *Lexington* pilots under Commander Snowden also saw hot action. High scorer was Lieutenant (jg) Alex Vraciu (pronounced Vray-see-you), who claimed six Judys of the 20-odd reported downed by VF-16. Vraciu, who completed his flight training in August 1942, already had been credited with 13 victories. In this fight he caught a column of Judys well strung out as they approached TF 58. The first he closed from astern to only 200 feet and literally blew to pieces. He downed a pair next, dropping each by attacking from six o'clock. Sighting no Zeros about but more Judys ahead, Vraciu closed at full throttle to pick off a fourth, again from dead astern at point-blank range. A fifth he downed over a U. S. destroyer, flying through AA fire. His sixth and last he hit after it had begun to dive at a warship below. This one vanished in a great explosion, causing Vraciu to wonder afterward if his bullets had exploded its 550-pound bomb. On climbing back to altitude, he watched a battleship shoot down a Judy, then circled and headed east to find and orbit *Lexington*. On taxiing forward after landing, Vraciu held up six fingers, indicating his kills. When he climbed from his plane he was surprised to find Admiral Mitscher on hand to greet him. Mitscher asked a Navy photographer to snap a picture of himself with the handsome, twenty-five-year-old airman, "not for publication, to keep for myself."

Lieutenant (jg) P. C. Thomas, flying from *Bataan* with six other pilots from VF-50, found that in the hands of a really skilled pilot a Zero still could be tough. With the others following he chased a Zero, closed, but found the enemy plane very hard to hit. The Zero pilot would wait until the last instant before Thomas fired and then would pull up into a right wing-over, causing a miss. He would then dip, as if heading for the water, but only for a second or two before jinking up again and snapping into a tight turn. "It was," Thomas said afterward, "like trying to catch a flea on a hot griddle." The clever Japanese probably would have escaped had not Thomas's mates kept forcing him back onto his original course. Finally, possibly because he was overwrought and exhausted, the enemy pilot flew straight and level a few seconds too long. From 600 feet dead astern Thomas got in a good burst. The hapless Zero exploded violently to end the fight. Thomas had chased the Zero by using full throttle and water injection, estimating his speed advantage on the straightaway at about 20 knots over the Zeke 52.

Admiral Mitscher's interceptor pilots had a bit of luck in dealing with the 601st's Jill torpedo planes. These were flying below and behind the main enemy formation, thus evading McCampbell's attack. At 12:42 radar operators on the *Lexington* noted them 40 miles distant breaking away from the rest of the enemy blip, losing altitude and coming in fast from 265 degrees. *Enterprise* vectored out two divisions from VF-10, but first to intercept was a single pilot, Lieutenant William B. Lamb from *Princeton*'s VF-27. Finding himself alone with 12 Jills and with only one of his six guns functioning, Lamb flew formation on them while staying out of range of the 7.7-mm. free guns of their back-seat men. He radioed course and altitude. After getting an acknowledgment he climbed and attacked, claiming three Jills after repeated passes with his one operable gun. Other Hellcats then arrived to scatter the formation.

Also intercepting Jills were Lieutenants William M. Knight and Marvin R. Novak from *Wasp*'s VF-14. That these were the ones chased by Lamb is not clear from their after-action report; probably they were from another formation. Spotting four torpedo planes to port ahead, Knight dove from 6,000 feet. The Jills swerved away, descending to just above the water, skidding and dipping, changing altitude, allowing their rear-seat men to fire. Knight finally hit and dropped one, but Novak found that his target had too good a head start and was too fast to catch. Angered and frustrated after futilely chasing it, he suddenly saw a Judy zip past on an opposite course. Whipping his Hellcat about Novak applied full military power, depressed his water-injection button, pulled 45 inches of manifold pressure, and caught the Judy in only moments. He closed to 300 feet, fired, and held down the button until the plane began to distintegrate. As he pulled up the plane nosed into a 45-degree dive, hit, and exploded, spreading a pool of flame and oil on the heaving, gentle sea.

A handful of the Judys and some Jills got through, attacking Admiral Lee's battleships and Admiral Montgomery's carriers from about 11:50 until a few minutes past high noon. A Jill, imitating a previous attacker at the Battle of Santa Cruz, carried his torpedo into the side of fast battleship *Indiana*. The "fish" did not explode, and in hitting the ship's belt armor at the waterline the pilot merely expended life and plane with but trifling damage to the ship. *Alabama*'s gunners downed two planes trying to line up for runs on the *South Dakota*. The long, lean, and very fast *Iowa* attracted a torpedo that missed.

Six Judys closed Admiral Montgomery's flattops operating on the southern flank of the formation. At exactly noon four planes dove on *Wasp* and two on *Bunker Hill*. The first plane plummeted at *Wasp* from the port quarter. The forward 20-mm. batteries opened up on it just before bomb release. None of the five-inch and 40-mm. batteries fired, the large number of returns having masked the Judy's approach on both fire control and search radars. The bomb hit just clear of the carrier's port bow, exploding on contact and splattering the ship with fragments. A large chunk passed through a 20-mm. director shield and also the back and chest of the gun captain, Gunners Mate 1/c Alfred M. Bridges, killing him instantly. The Judy pulled out of its dive smoking and was seen to crash about 12,000 yards away.

A pair of Judys plunged at *Bunker Hill* two minutes later and crashed without pulling out of their dives. A five-inch shell triggered by a proximity fuse blew one plane in half before it could release, but the other dropped and both plane and bomb hit close alongside the ship's port elevator. Bits of shrapnel spattered the 20- and 40-mm. gun batteries along the entire port side, killing only one man but wounding the remarkable total of 72 others. Most wounds were superficial, a few serious. The *Bunker Hill*'s crew could see the flashes from the wing guns of this plane as it dove, but nobody reported a bullet wound. Damage to the carrier was slight, including minor flooding in a pair of compartments and the start of a small fire in a ready room. Both *Wasp* and *Bunker Hill* throbbed on at 25 knots, fully operational.

Farther to the north several Jills managed to attack Admiral Reeves's TG 58.3. *Princeton* downed one attacking from dead ahead. The light carrier had to swerve to avoid the wreck on the water. *Enterprise*, maneuvering violently, had a torpedo explode in her wake. All American carrier skippers now were taking radical evasive action on first sighting torpedo planes, giving the Japanese pilots much more trouble in trying to line up their attacks.

By 12:30 P.M. all radars in Task Force 58 were clear of enemy planes trying to close, and all CAP Hellcats were either landing to refuel or orbiting their home carriers. Losses to the 601st Air Group in this second major attack of the day had been frightful. Thirty-two Zeros, 42 Judys, and 23 Jills had been destroyed for one non-damaging hit on *Indiana* and a few near misses. In the American fighter squadrons many new aces had been made. But by no means all of the pilots airborne had scored. Lieutenant Commander Bob Winston, the Indiana University graduate and skipper of *Cabot*'s AG 31, had been late getting airborne. He spent his entire time in the air chasing bogies reported by the air controllers, every one of which proved to be a straying friendly plane or flight. *Langley's* VF-32 had similar problems, and its pilots claimed only two enemy planes. The last pilot to score a kill may well have been Ernie Snowden, *Lexington's* Air Group 16 skipper, who chased and downed a stray Judy for his only victory.

Some four hundred miles to the west and south, Admiral Ozawa had only the vaguest notion of how his first two waves of attackers had fared. Nor could he take the time to analyze their scattered radioed messages. From about 9:10 A.M. he had been struggling with a problem quite like that imposed on Frank Jack Fletcher in the Battle of the Coral Sea.

Ozawa's problem came from U. S. submarine *Albacore*. With sisters *Finback*, *Bang*, and *Stingray* the *Albacore* had been patrolling a square of ocean that Vice Admiral C. A. Lockwood, Nimitz's commander of submarines at Pearl Harbor, had correctly estimated that Ozawa would have to transit. After sighting Ozawa's force and getting into position at about 2,000 yards, Commander James W. Blanchard, the skipper, fired a spread of six torpedoes at flagship *Taiho*. Only one hit the 29,300-ton ship, leaving Blanchard bitterly disappointed. He claimed only minor damage. His torpedo data computer had been fed incorrect data, forcing him to ignore it and to fire his spread "by guess and by God."

As had *Lexington* in the Coral Sea, the *Taiho* had rushed on at high speed after the explosion, leaving Blanchard in *Albacore* behind and deep under the sea dodging destroyer depth charges. The "cans" made little effort to hunt seriously, allowing Blanchard to get away unscathed. A thin destroyer screen about *Taiho* had allowed *Albacore* to approach undetected.

The torpedo had struck *Taiho* forward on the starboard side, rupturing fuel lines and a pair of oil bunker tanks. The shock also jammed the forward elevator in the "up" position, but *Taiho* had no list and appeared to be fully capable of handling planes with her after elevators. Admiral Ozawa was confident that his flagship would soon be launching its second strike.

Promise of trouble soon appeared, however, in the form of gasoline and bunker oil seeping into the forward elevator pit. The ruptured fuel tanks had contained the volatile unrefined Tarakan crude. This substance, together with equally volatile avgas, soon released highly explosive vapors. The crew tried to pump overboard free oil from the rent tanks, and when this failed, an inexperienced damage-control officer ordered the hangar deck ventilating duct opened while the ship steamed into the wind at 26 knots. Instead of blowing away the fumes, as he had hoped, this measure spread them throughout the hangar. *Taiho* was now in the same peril that *Lexington* had been in in the Coral Sea; she was a potential inferno awaiting a spark to touch her off. The crew sent away most of her remaining planes to *Zuikaku*, but this did not lessen the extreme danger.

By noon Admiral Ozawa had launched a second strike and was 60 miles beyond the spot where *Taiho* had been torpedoed. Now he crossed the path of another submarine, Commander Herman J. Kossler's *Cavalla*, that had been chasing after his force since reporting it two days earlier. At 11:52 Kossler suddenly discovered the *Shokaku* close at hand. After hastily checking to ensure he was not firing on an American ship—"There was the Rising Sun, big as hell!"—he cut loose with six torpedoes. Four of the six, his torpedo data computer told him, had to hit no matter what the ship did.

Three exploded at 12:20 P.M., causing *Shokaku* to lurch out of formation, listing, burning, and in the same condition that the old *Wasp* had been in after being tagged in Torpedo Junction in 1942. This time, having lost their second carrier charge in one morning and much face in the process, the Japanese destroyer skippers were thoroughly aroused. They kept *Cavalla* down for three hours within a few thousand yards of the burning, drifting *Shokaku*, but failed to sink Kossler's boat.

Shokaku was beyond prospect of salvage. She settled slowly until the forward elevator dipped under. Then she upended and sank. Commander Kossler heard explosions and rumblings and after getting clear radioed home, "That baby sank."

So did the hapless *Taiho*. At 3:32 P.M. a spark ignited the explosive vapors in her hangar to produce a blast as heavy as if a magazine had exploded. Both sides of the hangar blew outward, the armored deck heaved up, and some of the force of the explosion tore holes downward through the engineering spaces and bottom of the ship. The flaming carrier heeled over and foundered with 1,500 of her crew. Admiral Ozawa was unhurt and lucky to get away to destroyer *Wakatsuki*. Thirteen planes sank with *Taiho* and nine with *Shokaku*.

Ozawa's force had continued to launch strikes until almost the moment that *Shokaku* was torpedoed. Also, Admiral Takaji Jojima's Second Carrier Division had gotten away its first strike between 10:00 and 10:15 A.M. This consisted of 16 Zero 52s, 26 Zero fighter-bombers, and seven Jills, all from the 652nd Air Group. The majority of these planes, including the Jills, failed to contact Task Force 58. *Yorktown's* radar spotted a formation that may have been them 108 miles due west at 11:48 A.M. Then they turned southwest. Shortly afterward *Yorktown* picked them up again orbiting at a hundred-mile distance, but two divisions of Hellcats missed contact. The controllers then decided that a heavy cloud must have deceived them. For these Japanese pilots June 19 was no contest; they returned to their Jojima force unmolested.

About 20 planes, Zero fighter-bombers with escorting Zero fighters, had broken off from the formation on radioed orders to head for a contact reported by a recce plane at grid point 3 *ri* on the Japanese charts. This was off the northern rim of TF 58 and evidently had been made by a float plane that had sighted Lee's battleships. The 20 attacking planes spotted two of the battle wagons at the 3 *ri* location but flew on north and east, searching in vain for carriers. Then they turned back and at 12:42, when they were 99 miles north, bearing 320 degrees, they registered on *Yorktown's* radar. Since this ship's CAP was searching to the west, *Hornet's* air controllers assumed the bogie, vectoring out 12 Hellcats accompanied by a section of *Yorktown* night fighters operating in this emergency in a day-intercept mode.

Led by Lieutenant Arthur Van Haren, Jr., the 17 Hellcats tallyhoed at 1:03 P.M. Van Haren counted off 12 to 15 Zekes 4,000 feet below at 15,000 feet. As his wingman, Lieutenant (jg) Carroll L. Carlson, later recalled, "Twelve of us peeled off and everybody picked out a plane. The Zekes pulled up in chandelles, and I started firing at one from eighteen hundred feet, full deflection from above. It burned and went in." Lieutenant Earling Zaeske got another, recording his attack as "a steep run from six o'clock." His Zero tried no evasive action, and when hit it burned readily and fell. *Hornet's* pilots claimed seven kills and the *Yorktown* night fighter pilots a like number, with actual Japanese losses being exactly half of the claimed total of 14.

Several Zeros managed to get free of the melee, and at 1:20 a single plane attacked the *Essex*, dropping a bomb that landed a hundred feet clear of the ship. No other plane made a drop. An apparent navigational error and a timely interception had totally frustrated the third major attack by the Japanese and the first launched from Admiral Jojima's carrier division. The only American damage was a Hellcat hit in the port wing by a 20-mm.

For the American Helldiver and Avenger crews orbiting at economical speed 25 to 30 miles east and south of Task Force 58 the great "Marianas Turkey Shoot," as the American fighter pilots came to call it, was so far a bloody bore. Droning along at 110 knots, watching their slowly sinking gas gauges, nervously eyeing the Hellcats that looked them over when they ventured too close to TF 58, awed by the colossal volume of AA fire that occasionally erupted about the American carrier groups on the horizon in the distance, they realized by noon that there was no prospect of reaching the Japanese fleet. Seven Avenger pilots from *Enterprise's* VT-10 were numbingly tired. They had again taken off, their planes still laden with four 500-pound bombs each with four- to five-second delay fuses, only three hours after returning from a five-hour night search.

Finally, at about 1:00 P.M., Lieutenant Commander Ralph Weymouth, the skipper of Bombing 16 from *Lexington*, decided to act on his own. His SBD-5s, he knew, would soon have to jettison their bombs in order to conserve fuel. Rather than waste them in the ocean he decided to visit Guam's Orote field, 62 miles away, and crater it. Accompanied by 21 *Enterprise* Dauntlesses and Avengers, he set out covered by ten Hellcats. Arriving at 1:30 P.M., the planes tipped into dives only to find that Japanese AA fire was, if anything, better than before. Lieutenant G. L. Marsh's SBD took a light AA hit in the engine. Marsh dropped successfully, pulled out over Orote field, and then headed out to sea to ditch about four miles off Orote Point. With Radioman W. L. Lindsey he successfully inflated his rubber boat and settled down to await rescue. He was grateful to see a four-plane section from *Bunker Hill* arrive a few minutes later and orbit over him. Their presence, he knew, would discourage whatever ideas the Japanese might have about sending a Jake float plane or small boat to pick him up. Ultimately, an American float plane did. The other Dauntless pilots in making their dives had noted Zeros, Judys, and twin-engine Bettys on the field, some of which appeared to be undamaged and operational. But Orote's lightly surfaced coral runway took a good beating. The *Enterprise* Avengers, glide-bombing, scattered their 500-pounders down the strip, their pilots reporting that the four- to five-second delay fuse seemed ideally suited to produce craters.

Other squadrons followed in the *Lex* and *Enterprise* units to hit both Orote and Agana fields. These had been ordered to do so by Mitscher, who recognized and commended Weymouth's initiative. None met fighter opposition, but the AA again took a toll. *Yorktown*'s VB-1 lost an SB2C "Beast" when its pilot tried to strafe Orote after dropping a thousand-pounder on Agana. *Bunker Hill* also lost a Helldiver and crew and *Essex* two planes to barrier crashes on landing. Losses to the attackers were thus reasonably heavy, but one 500-pounder, landing between two parked Bettys, blew apart both. Strafing sieved some Zeros that appeared intact, and fires in a POL dump suggested further loss to the defenders' store of avgas. Both Orote and Agana were badly cratered at the worst possible time from the Japanese standpoint. Already en route and destined to try landings on the fields were planes comprising the fourth and last carrier strike of the day.

This mission consisted of planes from Admiral Jojima's *Junyo, Hiyo,* and *Ryuho,* supplemented by four Jills and four Zeros from *Zuikaku.* These were the only planes ready that *Zuikaku* had left. From the other carriers the aircraft were the normal second strike launched at about 11:00 A.M. Rear Admiral Obayashi's Third Carrier Division, kept busy landing straggling survivors from the earlier raids, failed to launch its second strike. In total numbers this fourth and last mission of the day was formidable; it totaled 27 Vals, ten Zero fighter-bombers, nine Judys, and six Jills, escorted by 30 Zero fighters.

In what proved to be a tragic error these planes were vectored to a contact in the ocean 100 miles southwest of Guam in the 15 *ri* sector of the Japanese battle chart. This was a phantom; nothing was there. One of Ozawa's search pilots had failed to correct for compass deviation in plotting a valid find.

After searching the vicinity of the 15 *ri* position and finding nothing, the Japanese formation split three ways. Eighteen planes, those from *Zuikaku* and the ten Zero fighter-bombers, started back to base. Others, including the nine Judys, headed for the unused airstrip at Rota. The remaining 49 planes, including all 27 of the Val dive bombers, started for just bombed Orote field on Guam. All three formations got into combat, but only the Rota-bound Judys contacted surface targets.

The Judys sighted Admiral Montgomery's TG 58.2 then in the process of taking aboard Helldivers just returned from Guam. Because of clutter radar operators on the *Bunker Hill* and *Wasp* did not identify the Judys as enemy until they were only 53 miles out. This was at 2:13 P.M. The Judys then dropped low and came in under the CAP vectored out at 8,000 feet, much lower than the customary practice of the day. No American, either airborne or afloat, spotted the enemy planes until 2:23 P.M., when a lookout on cruiser *Mobile* spotted the first two planes dashing in low for a glide-bomb run, dive angle 35 degrees.

Captain C. A. F. "Ziggy" Sprague on *Wasp* ordered hard right rudder though the carrier was already in a 15-degree left turn at 22 knots. The *Wasp* spun hard on its stern post as its gunners began to fire. The radar fire-control operators of Sky Aft did a superb job, getting an accurate, quick track on each of three Judys diving in column and giving the 40-mm. and five-inch gunners the chance to splash each in turn. One plane and the bomb it had dropped hit together 200 feet off *Wasp*'s port beam. Evidently, this missile had an instantaneous fuse, for it exploded and sprayed fragments. One chunk hit Captain R. C. Rosacker, USMC, and three of his men from 20-mm. Group Two. A blow on the left shoulder knocked Rosacker down and earphones from his head, but he scrambled up, recovered the earphones with his uninjured right arm, and continued to direct fire. Two other bombs dropped by the second Judy fell 250 feet clear of the ship aft. The third plane released several small bombs, of which one exploded about 300 feet above the flight deck. This missile was a 32-kilogram Japanese Navy-type incendiary cluster filled with small white phosphorus pellets. Three hit and ignited on steel surfaces at Bat II and in gun galleries, doing nothing worse than to scorch paint. Some pellets fell on the flight deck and caught fire when crewmen stepped on them. Presumably, the Japanese pilot had hoped to fire planes on *Wasp*'s flight deck—in theory a good idea, perhaps, but in this case it didn't work.

Two Judys went after *Bunker Hill*. One near missed the carrier with three bombs that hit 50, 100, and 200 feet off her starboard quarter without damage. Gunners picked off the other that flew out over the cruiser-destroyer screen smoking and losing altitude. It geysered in and burned clear of the outermost destroyer.

Just after 4:00 P.M. most of the 652nd Air Group's planes jettisoned their bombs into the ocean off Guam. Then they closed battered and cratered Orote field. The airstrip hardly was in condition to receive them. About 15 minutes before a second strike of Helldivers from *Hornet* had dive-bombed the field through ack-ack that downed one plane and badly damaged another. The rear-seat gunner had bailed out of the damaged

SB2C thinking that the plane would crash. This costly mission had further cratered the strip at a crucial time.

The incoming Japanese flight included all 27 of the 652nd Air Group's Val dive bombers, ten Zero fighter-bombers, two Kate torpedo planes, and ten escorting Zero 51 fighters, in all 49 planes. The Vals were circling the field, flaps down, their pilots unaware that they were about to be bounced by the heaviest concentration of Hellcats vectored over Guam all day. These included sweeps of a dozen each from *Essex* and *Cowpens,* 19 from *Hornet,* including three night fighters, eight from *Enterprise,* and four from *San Jacinto.* Others, including a section from *Princeton,* arrived later to bring the Hellcat count to over 50.

First to spot the incoming Vals was Commander Gaylord B. Brown commanding VF-25 from *Cowpens.* He radioed, "Forty enemy planes circling Orote field at Angels 3 [3,000 feet] some with wheels down." To Lieutenant Russell L. Reiserer of VNF-76 from *Hornet,* "They acted like a carrier air group in their approach and breaking off." Lieutenant (jg) Charles H. Carroll of *Hornet's* VF-2 recalled, "I saw as many as 12 Vals— three flights of three and three breaking up coming into a left-hand turn singly." The protecting Zeros, Lieutenant William K. Blair noted, were orbiting at 2,500 feet above the Vals.

All planes dove, some at the Zeros and some at the Vals, catching the hapless Japanese in a bind. They were trapped as badly as Major Floyd Pell had been with his squadron of P-40s over Port Darwin when the attackers were Commander Itaya's Zeros instead of Hellcats.

Leading the *Essex* pack was Commander Dave McCampbell with Ensign R. L. Nall hugging his wing. McCampbell jumped the leader of a four-plane section of the Zero escort, dropping him on a second pass. He then found himself with little speed in front of a pair of Zeros, one of which put six 7.7-mm. holes in his wing and tail. Nall's Hellcat was also hit, with one elevator shot completely away. McCampbell and Nall ran for it, then scissored into the Thach weave, permitting McCampbell to blast down a Zero with a good burst. The other broke away with McCampbell following. "He attempted to evade," the commander recalled later, "by completing the most beautiful slow roll I ever have seen." It was too good. McCampbell neither changed his point of aim nor discontinued fire. The Zero then dove over Orote field, smoking, and McCampbell broke off, ". . . since I found myself as a lone F-6."

Ensign Wilbur B. Webb of VF-2 flew squarely into the circling ring of Vals. From close range and dead astern he blasted down five and then picked off a sixth from below. Lieutenant Reiserer in his night-fighter Hellcat claimed five more, bringing down his last Val with only one gun working. "I had to let my wheels and flaps down to stay behind the enemy planes."

The overwhelmed Zeros fought bravely and downed two of their tormentors, Ensign T. E. Hallowell from *San Jacinto's* VF-51 and Lieutenant

H. C. Clem from *Enterprise*'s VF-10. Clem committed the error of pulling almost straight up after a Zero and stalling out. The Zero did a snap wingover, made a head-on run, and Clem's Hellcat spun into the ocean. Neither American survived.

For the 652nd Air Group the results of the engagement hardly could have been worse. Twenty-eight Zeros and Vals and—if American plane identification be right—two Kates fell outright. Others crash-landed and the rest flew away from Guam to orbit until—hopefully—the American planes had left the scene and it would be safe to return.

Ill-luck dogged even the 18 planes—ten Zeros and eight Jills—from *Zuikaku* that had elected to turn back. At 3:05 P.M., when some 200 miles due west of Guam, flying at only 500 feet, they encountered a pair of Avengers and a Hellcat. These were planes from *Lexington*'s Air Group 16 flying an unsuccessful 325-mile search for the Japanese fleet. The Zeros climbed and dove and the three American planes turned sharply into the attack. They also radioed a "Hey, Rube!" to a neighboring search team for aid.

What had seemed to be easy pickings for the Zeros proved to be anything but. The Hellcat pilot downed two as they jumped the Avengers, and Ensign E. P. Baker, an Avenger pilot, got another. His burst evidently killed the pilot, for the plane went right into the water. Turret gunner G. L. Stanfill blew up a fourth Zero as it dove from three o'clock above.

The two Avengers and their escort Hellcat from the adjacent sector search team arrived near the end of the fight and also mixed it with the Zeros. They claimed three more for a total of seven of ten Zeros destroyed. That the gunnery training of the Zero pilots left something to be desired is suggested by the damage to the American planes. Just one plane was hit, an Avenger that took a 20-mm. round in its vertical stabilizer and rudder.

As far as can be determined from American records, only one group of planes from a land base bothered Task Force 58 all day. At 1:10 P.M. four Hellcats jumped six Bettys and four Judys at 20,000 feet 40 miles south of the task force. They claimed several planes that may have been from Guam or perhaps Yap.

Repeated sweeps over Rota flown at intervals all afternoon disclosed no enemy activity, suggesting that Captain Arleigh Burke may have been right in surmising that the Japanese had no avgas stocked there. A sweep by seven *Belleau Wood* Hellcats at 5:00 P.M., however, led to a claim of a Val and Judy destroyed, the one plane exploding on the runway, the other burning in a dispersal area. These were either dummies rigged to fool the American pilots or stragglers that had escaped the Turkey Shoot to land at Rota. Probably the latter.

The last big fight of the day developed over Orote field on Guam at about 6:25 P.M. This happened when Commander Charles W. Brewer, skipper of VF-15 from *Essex*, led a sweep over the island. Brewer dove with a four-plane section at a Judy trying to land on the field. But as he did so several Zeros dove on the Americans from above and behind. These must have been planes from the 652nd Air Group now returning, low on fuel, to land. The Japanese pilots fought well, lost several of their number but managed to down Commander Brewer and his wingman, Ensign Thomas Tarr, neither of whom survived. No Japanese pilot, however, landed safely on Orote. A Japanese diarist recorded that all survivors of this final air battle crashed trying to land in gathering darkness on the cratered field.

During June 19 Admiral Ozawa had dispatched about 328 of his 440 combat aircraft against Task Force 58. He lost over 200 of them and 23 of his Kate, Jill, and Jake reconnaissance planes. Destruction of some 50 more land-based planes on Guam and Rota brought the Japanese loss to just short of 300 planes, not far off American claims of 353 planes shot down.

On the American side only 23 planes had been destroyed, including 16 Hellcats lost in air combat. Seven bombers fell to the accurate AA fire from Guam, and eight other planes were lost operationally. The American pilots accepted their victory—the greatest by far in carrier warfare—matter-of-factly. It confirmed their confidence in their training and tactics and especially in the virtues of their Hellcat fighters.

After *Lexington* secured from General Quarters at about 5:30 P.M., war correspondent Busch went below from the bridge to the officers' wardroom. There, another pilot asked a fighter pilot already seated at the clean, cloth-covered table how he had fared. "Not bad—got two," was the calm reply. Then using exactly the same tone of voice, he replied to the mess boy who had asked him how he wanted his steak for supper: "Not too rare."

Several hundred miles to the northwest in his life raft, at almost exactly the same time, Lieutenant Commander Robert H. Price was downing a last morsel of raw fish. Two small basslike fishes, six and four inches long, evidently frightened by larger predators, had jumped into his rubber boat a few minutes before. "I immediately cleaned and ate both, finding them very tasty and refreshing. They were quite juicy and helped to alleviate my thirst to some extent."

As dusk fell, about 7:30 P.M., a few Japanese air crew were still alive in the water. Most had no rafts; none could expect recovery by a Japanese ship. They faced certain death, either from the sea or perhaps at their own hands to escape what most sincerely believed would be the worst fate of all—capture.

26. Battle in the Philippine Sea

Dusk on June 19 found Admiral Ozawa aboard cruiser *Haguro*. He had transferred to it at 4:06 P.M. after losing the *Taiho*. The cruiser lacked commo adequate for use as a flagship, and Ozawa was handicapped by a lack of information. Specifically, not until the next day did he learn that his carriers had only 102 planes—44 Zero fighters, 17 Zero fighter-bombers, 11 Val and Judy dive bombers, and 30 Kate and Jill torpedo planes.

Nor did Ozawa know how much damage he had dealt his enemy. A signal from *Zuikaku* had indicated that an enemy cruiser and carrier had been hit; another from Admiral Obayashi's 3rd Carrier Division had reported four carriers smoking "continuously" after an attack. This sketchy information led Ozawa's staff to make the extremely optimistic guess that Japanese planes had damaged or sunk four or five carriers and a battleship or heavy cruiser. Enemy plane losses, they estimated, must have been about 160. It was therefore conceivable that—except in plane losses—Mitscher's fleet had suffered more damage than their own.

Nevertheless, Ozawa acknowledged that his air strikes had been "insufficient." He knew, too, that he would have to reorganize his depleted squadrons scattered on several carriers before striking again. At 6:08 P.M., therefore, he ordered the entire Mobile Fleet onto a northwesterly course. It held to this course through the night and into the early hours of June 20 at a leisurely speed of 18 knots. In the morning the First Mobile Fleet was to meet six tankers and begin to refuel. After that Ozawa would figure out how to strike again at Mitscher. A GO was to continue despite the dire results of the Turkey Shoot.

As Admirals Mitscher and Spruance viewed them, the results of the Turkey Shoot had been most encouraging. Well before final results were in both realized that Ozawa could not possibly have many planes left. Spruance on the late afternoon of the 19th radioed to Mitscher:

Desire to attack enemy tomorrow if we know his position with sufficient accuracy. . . . Point OPTION should be advanced to the west as much as air operations admit.

Mitscher agreed with his chief. But though he put Task Force 58 about immediately at 3:00 P.M., he could not maintain a westward course because of his need to launch and recover planes. Not until 10:00 P.M. did all ships assume a bearing of 260 degrees at 23 knots, the maximum speed that the fuel-short destroyers dared sustain. Rota Island lay astern 35 miles. Admiral Lee's battleships cruised 25 miles ahead just in case Ozawa should try a night surface strike.

Mitscher considered and rejected the idea of launching a night search to find Ozawa's carriers. He still did not know precisely where they were, because no American planes had seen them during the day. Available for a special long-range search were his F6F and F4U night fighters and the radar-equipped Avengers of Air Group 10 aboard *Enterprise*. But probably because he wanted to spare his air crews, Mitscher decided to wait until morning to search. He elected to rely on long-range PBM flying boats from Saipan to find and track the enemy during the night.

Already, he had detached Admiral Harrill's *Essex* group. It needed fuel and could be usefully employed the next day in keeping Guam pounded down. Mitscher as well as Spruance continued mindful of the need to protect the Saipan beachhead.

Before sunup on June 20 the first Avengers roared off TF 58's decks on a standard search. After rendezvousing they fanned out to either side of due west to 325 miles. But Mitscher's ships were no closer to Ozawa's than they had been the night before. Consequently the nearest plane fell short again by about 50 miles of sighting the Mobile Fleet. The weakness in long-range search continued to deny Mitscher (and Spruance) absolutely vital intelligence.

As the morning of June 20 wore on without word from the search Avengers, Spruance began to lose hope that Ozawa would be found. It seemed reasonable to suppose that with most of his planes gone, the Japanese admiral had hightailed it southwest toward the air cover of the southern Philippines. If so, there was little chance of catching him. But the *Shokaku*-class carrier that the *Cavalla* had torpedoed might still be afloat. If so, she might steam due north for the Japanese home islands. As early as 3:00 A.M. Spruance had radioed to Mitscher:

Damaged *Zuikaku* [*Shokaku*'s sister] may still be afloat . . . heading northwest. [She] must be sunk if we can reach her.

If she could not be, Mitscher was to put about by nightfall and head back toward Saipan.

By noon on June 20 Mitscher was ready to concede that Spruance's staff might have been right. His last search plane was now back with a negative report. He ordered TF 58 to rotate its bearing northwest to 330 degrees in the hope that he could catch the damaged *Shokaku*. He also approved without enthusiasm a daring plan from Fleet Air Officer Gus Widhelm. Widhelm had proposed a special search/strike by Hellcats from

Lexington under the command of Ernie Snowden. Armed with bombs and auxiliary tanks, the big fighters would fly out at 340 degrees for 475 miles to search a 20-degree arc. If they found the damaged carrier they would assemble, attack, and sink her. If not they would jog south and west while returning. At long last Mitscher was making full use of the range capacity of his Hellcats; Snowden's mission would be the longest yet flown from an American carrier, equal in range to standard search missions flown by the Japanese.

Unfortunately, Widhelm's guess as to the possible vector of the Japanese fleet was wrong. Ozawa had progressed more west than north. Consequently, Snowden's planes failed to make contact. But Mitscher's change of course had been well advised; he had begun rapidly to close the First Mobile Fleet that by now was milling about, making little headway west as its ships were trying with a maximum of confusion to rendezvous with their nourishing tankers.

Ozawa should have been aware of the danger in refueling so far to the east. Two Jake seaplanes had encountered American carrier planes at 7:13 A.M. and had gotten off radioed reports. These reached Ozawa after considerable delay, but not until 1:00 P.M. did he order off his first long-range search consisting of three Kates from *Chitose* and *Zuiho*. If launched at dawn these planes might well have found the oncoming Mitscher. They found him anyway, but not until 5:15 P.M., too late to alter the outcome of battle.

Because the *Haguro* was short of commo gear, Ozawa also failed properly to rendezvous his force with the tankers. The First Mobile Fleet arrived piecemeal at the appointed rendezvous, then circled about for hours, signaling back and forth by blinker, flag, and even voice radio. Few if any ships took aboard hoses until late in the day.

At 1:00 P.M. Ozawa transferred to carrier *Zuikaku*, where he finally learned the full extent of his plane losses. Yet he did not stop planning for resumed battle. He still hoped that land-based planes from Japan, staging via Iwo to Guam and Rota, would make good any disparity in air power. A shuttle attack from his carriers against the American fleet and on to Guam and Rota might work if launched the next day. Also, he might be able to try a night surface attack if his search planes located the foe. Limited though they might be, he believed he still had offensive options.

At 1:35 P.M. on the 20th Lieutenant R. S. Nelson of *Enterprise's* radar-equipped VT-10 dipped right and climbed away from the veteran carrier. Nelson's mission, numbered 47AV24, was part of a routine afternoon search consisting of four three-plane teams. Flying wing on Nelson in another TBF was Lieutenant (jg) J. S. Moore. Above them, weaving in escort, was Lieutenant (jg) W. E. Velte, Jr. If the mission encountered an enemy Jake or Kate, it would be Velte's job to shoot it down with his Hellcat.

Nelson flew out 297 degrees true (northwest) from the *Enterprise* at an economical speed of 150 knots. He stayed low because haziness reduced visibility at high altitudes. On spotting an enemy scout at 3:05 P.M., he decided not to have Velte chase it, reasoning that the fighter pilot's six .50s might come in handy if he found the source of the plane and an enemy CAP.

Nelson was nearing the limit of his 325-mile radius at 3:38 P.M. after two hours and three minutes in the air. Then what appeared to be a ripple on the water caught his eye. It was slightly to port and about 30 miles ahead at the limit of visibility. The ripple, the young pilot concluded, could only be Ozawa's fleet. Climbing to 3,000 feet and heading for the edge of a nearby rain squall, the better to close the range to ten miles while remaining unseen, Nelson worked out a position report. At 3:40 P.M. he sent a message, twice by voice, then by dot-dash.

Two groups [of enemy ships], one heading west and one heading east. Ten ships in northern group and 12 in southern. They seem to be fueling. Large CV in northern group.

What Nelson had seen was *Zuikaku*, a pair of heavy cruisers, and a light cruiser and seven destroyers of a northern grouping of ships, and a dozen ships in a southern grouping on a course headed away from him. He could not make out the southern grouping's profile, but he guessed that he had seen two or three carriers, a pair of oilers, one refueling a destroyer, and cruisers and destroyers of a screen. Halfway between the two groups he identified an oiler.

Nelson, Moore, and Velte stayed in contact for a half hour with Nelson radioing several more contact reports. One was a vitally important corrected position report transmitted at 4:06 P.M. His first report had been wrong a full 60 nautical miles due to a plotting error. His corrected report was sound and put the Japanese fleet about 275 miles from Task Force 58. At 4:10 P.M. Nelson broke contact and headed for home. His crew had spotted a float plane from one of the Japanese gunnery ships and also a Zero fighter that appeared to be on a closing heading. When the *Zuikaku* turned broadside and fired an AA burst, which may have been only a routine signal to its CAP, Nelson decided that he had seen enough. "We took departure pronto."

Though badly garbled by static and a simultaneous transmission from another plane, Nelson's first contact report reached *Lexington*'s flag plot. It was clear enough to indicate that he had seen surface ships. Aboard the ship it acted as a tonic that nothing else could have equalled. Prior to its receipt, at 3:30 P.M., Mitscher's staff had abandoned nearly all hope that Ozawa could be found. Snowden's Hellcats had reached the limit of their fruitless search for the mythical "damaged *Shokaku*" and would be turning back after jettisoning bombs and belly tanks. Absence of transmissions indicated that Ernie had drawn a blank. For some minutes Captain Arleigh Burke, cold pipe clenched between his teeth, had been pacing about murmuring softly, "Damn, damn, damn." Gus Widhelm was almost ready to give up on his thousand-dollar bet; it seemed most unlikely that on this cruise an American pilot would bomb the Japanese fleet.

Nelson's garbled message immediately threw flag plot into a flurry of activity. But Nelson's first position report, though short by 60 miles, produced whistles, then silence for a moment as the fleet navigator plotted. Finally, Mitscher, who had come in from the bridge, asked, "Well, can we make it?" Gus Widhelm replied, "We can make it, but it's going to be tight." Mitscher then whispered crisply, "Launch 'em."

Just moments later Admiral Ozawa on *Zuikaku*'s bridge was studying a message from cruiser *Atago*. This contained an intercept of Lieutenant Nelson's corrected position report transmitted at 4:06. Lookouts aboard the Mobile Fleet evidently had not seen Nelson's plane, but the translated voice radio intercept could only mean that the fleet had been sighted. At 4:20 P.M. Ozawa abruptly ordered fueling broken off and instructed all ships to retire northwest at high speed. He must now expect attack from the air. But his mood was still not entirely defensive. If his scouting planes found Mitscher he was prepared to put about and strike.

Mitscher's "Launch 'em" triggered a controlled frenzy in Task Force 58. Already on decks was a full strike of Avengers, Helldivers, Dauntlesses, and Hellcats fully armed and fueled. The Hellcats had 400 gallons each of hundred octane, the SB2Cs 310 gallons, the Dauntlesses 254 gallons, and the Avengers—TBFs and TBMs—330 gallons. This sufficed for the Hellcats, but the other planes would be cutting it very, very close. All planes would be flying five or more hours and must land at night. Other than the night-qualified Air Group 10 few air crew had practiced night landings. With sinking hearts the pilots ran—literally—to their aircraft. They well understood that every minute saved now would mean a minute more of daylight on the return trip home.

Usually, Lieutenant Alex Vraciu was eager to go. But this time he felt tense, reluctant, apprehensive. He dreaded the flight ahead of him. Harry Kelly, an SBD gunner and radioman, noted the *Lexington*'s crew giving him thumbs up and thought, "Thumbs up, hell! What they mean is 'So long, sucker!' "

At 4:21 all carriers swung into the easterly wind, and at 4:24 Lieutenant Henry Kosciusko's Hellcat rose from the *Lexington*. The order of takeoff on big carriers had been altered from the war's early days. Now, the fighters still went first, but the Avenger torpedo planes followed, and the dive bombers took off last. With its superb launch and landing characteristics, a loaded TBF or its General Motors-built twin, the TBM, took off easily fully loaded from less than full-deck length. From aft on the flight decks rolled the heavily laden "Beasts," the SB2Cs, some carrying a belly tank and a pair of 250-pound wing-mounted bombs as well as the customary thousand-pounder in the bomb bay.

The last SBD from the *Lexington* left at 4:36 P.M., just twelve minutes after Kosciusko had launched. Other carriers did slightly better, shaving to record lows the time of takeoff between planes. All skippers wanted this deckload away fast in order to put the wind astern and speed northwest. Every mile gained before the planes returned might spare a pilot a dunking.

The pilots had not received Nelson's corrected report of the First Mobile Fleet's position by takeoff. They learned of it by radio—some by direct radio contact with Nelson—after becoming airborne. The report was a shocker. Another 60 miles to fly! It put the enemy at least 275 miles away when sighted, and the planes would probably have to fly about 300 miles, counting the distance the enemy would travel after their takeoff. (Admiral Spruance's staff put the estimated flight distance at 290 miles at 289 degrees.) The length of flight out was therefore at least 40 to 50 miles beyond the normal maximum 250-mile radius of the Helldivers, Dauntlesses, and Avengers. All pilots gritted their teeth and leaned fuel mixtures until their engines began to smoke.

Mitscher had originally intended to launch a second deckload an hour after the first. But after receiving Nelson's corrected report he decided against it. His reasoning to his staff was sound:

I can't sacrifice any more of these boys' lives, not even for the Japanese fleet. Our Sunday punch tonight ought to do the job, and we'll get the rest in the morning. There's no telling how many planes we'll lose from this first flight. We've got to have something left to hit them with tomorrow.

Mitscher had dispatched 236 planes from all six fleet carriers and from all CVLs except *Princeton*. Few air groups tried to join up, even those from the same task group. Most rendezvoused while flying northwest toward the enemy, holding to courses of about 290 degrees. The planes from the light carriers tagged along behind the strikes from the big ones. Pilots held their air speeds to an economical 130 to 140 knots, while the Hellcats weaved above.

Only one who has been through the experience himself can truly appreciate the emotions of the young pilots, most of them in their early twenties and only a few months out of aviation cadet training. Some were only nineteen years of age. The strain of flying carefully to conserve gas, the constant roar of static on the radio, the need to watch sky and water ahead, eyes endlessly sweeping the horizon, the professional desire to "get a hit," and the nagging worry about the long flight home and a night landing—all of these concerns stretched nerves to the breaking point. Some pilots had to turn back because of rough engines, hydraulic leaks, or other problems, and one could hardly blame them if they felt a surge of relief. Commander Winston aboard *Cabot* did not expect any of the planes to return. All, he thought, would have to ditch in a black and empty sea.

Knowledge that his enemy was stalking him did not affect Admiral Ozawa's cool judgment. At 5:15 P.M. he received word from the pilot of

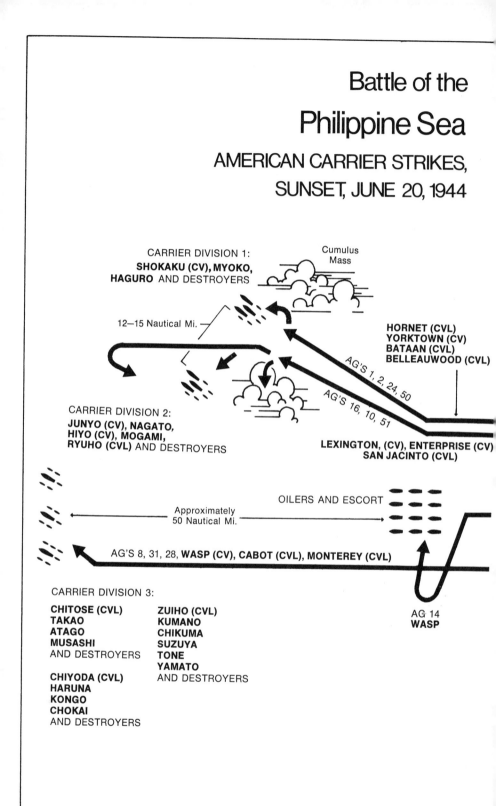

Battle of the
Philippine Sea
AMERICAN CARRIER STRIKES, SUNSET, JUNE 20, 1944

CARRIER DIVISION 1:
SHOKAKU (CV), MYOKO, HAGURO AND DESTROYERS

Cumulus Mass

12—15 Nautical Mi.

**HORNET (CVL)
YORKTOWN (CV)
BATAAN (CVL)
BELLEAUWOOD (CVL)**

AG'S 1, 2, 24, 50

AG'S 16, 10, 51

CARRIER DIVISION 2:

JUNYO (CV), NAGATO, HIYO (CV), MOGAMI, RYUHO (CVL) AND DESTROYERS

LEXINGTON, (CV), ENTERPRISE (CV) SAN JACINTO (CVL)

OILERS AND ESCORT

Approximately 50 Nautical Mi.

AG'S 8, 31, 28, **WASP (CV), CABOT (CVL), MONTEREY (CVL)**

AG 14
WASP

CARRIER DIVISION 3:

**CHITOSE (CVL)
TAKAO
ATAGO
MUSASHI**
AND DESTROYERS

**CHIYODA (CVL)
HARUNA
KONGO
CHOKAI**
AND DESTROYERS

**ZUIHO (CVL)
KUMANO
CHIKUMA
SUZUYA
TONE
YAMATO**
AND DESTROYERS

the searching Kate who had sighted two of Mitscher's carriers. The time of day and distance of flight forbade a round-trip attack mission, but an after-dark torpedo strike with the planes continuing on to land at Guam and Rota might succeed. Ozawa therefore ordered Admiral Obayashi, commanding Carrier Division 3, to dispatch a flight of seven Kates led by three radar-tracking Jill scouts. Obayashi launched this strike at 6:20 P.M. Unfortunately, it failed to find Task Force 58.

Ozawa also issued a preliminary order to Vice Admiral Kurita, commanding the heavy ships escorting Obayashi's carriers, to prepare for a night action as a "diversionary attack force." This he radioed at 5:55 P.M., adding an order to cruiser *Mogami* to join. He did not, however, issue an execute, and in the circumstances it was well that he did not. At 6:25 P.M. a plane patrolling east of the First Mobile Fleet warned, "Enemy aircraft sighted."

By this time the First Mobile Fleet was steaming in four groups, each disposed to meet air attack. Farthest east, steaming due west on course 270 degrees, was the supply force of six oilers escorted by a like number of destroyers. Steaming at 24 knots on course 320 degrees about 25 miles to the north and west was *Zuikaku*, all that remained of Carrier Division 1, escorted by *Myoko*, *Haguro*, light cruiser *Yahagi*, and seven destroyers. Some 12 miles to the southwest of *Zuikaku*, steaming on a course of 300 degrees true, was Admiral Takaji Jojima's Carrier Division 2. It consisted of *Hiyo, Junyo,* and *Ryuho*, escorted by battleship *Nagato*, cruiser *Mogami*, and eight destroyers. Southwest and perhaps 40 to 50 miles almost due west of the oiler force, also on a course of 300 degrees, was Admiral Sueo Obayashi's Carrier Division 3. It comprised light carriers *Chiyoda, Chitose,* and *Zuiho*. These light carriers were on a north-south line of bearing well separated, each a miniature task force surrounded by a screen of powerful surface warships. *Chitose* and *Zuiho* had as escorts super battleships *Yamato* and *Musashi*. *Chiyoda*, operating on the south flank, had as consorts fast battleships *Haruna* and *Kongo* and heavy cruiser *Maya*. Heavy cruisers *Takao* and *Chokai* and light cruiser *Noshiro* and eight destroyers thickened the screens and the density of the antiaircraft.

Ozawa's disposition of forces can be faulted. That the oilers would fall behind was inevitable; they could not muster the 24-knot speed of the warships. But Obayashi's light carriers with their heavy screens should have been at the rear and not at the van of the formation. There, they might have blunted the American attack by luring the Helldivers and Avengers away from the more valuable larger carriers.

In adopting a 20-degree course divergence of *Zuikaku* from the other carriers, Ozawa may have been trying to spare his most valuable ship. If so, he failed, for every one of the four separate groups of his scattered fleet underwent attack. Alone and isolated, *Zuikaku* was vulnerable.

27. Attack at Sundown

At 6:25 P.M. a lookout on CVL *Chiyoda* paused in the rhythmic sweep of his binoculars and peered intently to the southwest. Then he yelled a warning. He had counted off 23 specks approaching at 3,000 meters. Already they were breaking into four distinct groups. From all over the *Chiyoda* force flags shot up, "Repel air attack!" Moments later a single AA shell, deep lavender in color, burst directly above the center of the warship formation. Then all ships put up a barrage of exploding shells at 14,000 feet in a weirdly beautiful variety of colors—red, blue, lavender, black, pink, and yellow. White bursts emitted fountainlike streamers of phosphorus and resembled Fourth-of-July star shells. Battleships *Haruna* and *Kongo* fired their five-inch batteries in salvo, each flash lighting up the entire ship. Ahead on the western horizon the magnified sun was a huge ball, almost as red as the Hinomarus (Rising Suns) on Japanese war planes.

The attackers actually numbered 42 planes, counting escorting fighters, from carriers *Bunker Hill, Monterey,* and *Cabot.* Leading them was Commander Ralph L. Shifley, skipper of Air Group 8, a thirty-four-year-old graduate of the U. S. Naval Academy's Class of 1933. As was rapidly becoming standard practice, Shifley was flying a Hellcat, and his cameras would record the results of the bombing.

Shifley's attackers had flown by his estimate 315 nautical miles, well beyond the combat radius of most of the planes. With the enemy in sight, the commander circled to the west of the force, preparing to swing back for a photographic run. The 12 Helldivers under Lieutenant Commander James D. Arbes, skipper of Bombing 8, continued straight in from the southwest, deploying into diving order. The pilots could see *Zuiho* and *Chitose* to the north, indistinctly, but Arbes led all pilots against the *Chiyoda* and its escorts. *Zuiho* and *Chitose* thus escaped attack. No Zeros appeared to be about, but the bursts of the AA rocked the planes and holed several as they entered the barrage zone.

At 6:32 Commander Arbes dove, hurtling down at 70 degrees, strafing with his two 20-mm. wing guns, releasing his three bombs at about 2,000 feet. He missed *Chiyoda* to starboard as the carrier heeled into a sharp turn to port. Eight other planes followed at precise intervals, while the remaining four, blinded by the smoke about the *Chiyoda,* dove on a battleship and a pair of cruisers. With the exception of a close burst that set afire cruiser *Maya*'s port torpedo tubes, all bombs apparently missed, though the pilots were certain that several had scored. *Chiyoda*'s sharp turn had saved her; very near misses on both sides had violently rocked her, and fragments had inflicted casualties among her crew, but she had no significant material damage. In the four minutes or less of the attack the 13,600-ton flattop had skidded about on her stern post, ending up in the opposite direction with way almost lost.

Following the Helldivers were eight TBM Avengers from the CVLs *Monterey* and *Cabot,* led by Lieutenant R. P. "Rip" Gift from *Monterey*'s Air Group 28. These planes had four 500-pounders each and glide-bombed at 50 degrees at very high speed, dropping from 8,000 feet to release at about 3,500. Four of the planes picked *Chiyoda* as a target; four chose battleship *Haruna.*

As the Avengers began their dives *Chiyoda* recovered from its turn to port and, picking up speed, began to turn to starboard. Diving on her was Gift and his wingman and Lieutenant E. E. Wood, skipper of *Cabot*'s VT-31, and his wingman, Lieutenant (jg) J. B. Russell. To the *Chiyoda*'s crew it seemed as if the enemy had "returned to the attack with increasing fury" to drop "some tens" of bombs. And their enemy scored. At 6:38 P.M. a pair of 500-pounders hit the after end of *Chiyoda*'s flight deck, starting fires, damaging a Jill and Zero in the hangar, and killing 20 and wounding 30 of the crew.

One bomb also scored on *Haruna,* striking this heretofore luckiest of Japanese ships aft. This hit—or other near misses—started seepage into a powder magazine. But according to the First Mobile Fleet's after-action report, the battleship suffered no loss of immediate fighting or steaming capacity though the damage to the hull required drydocking.

Bunker Hill's eight Avengers under Commander Ken Musick each carried an improved Mark 13 torpedo fitted with a "pickle barrel," a circular cover about the warhead that permitted high-speed drops. The squadron flew around the enemy force westward and then began a high-speed run-in from the southwest. By now the *Chiyoda,* still under attack by Gift's Avengers, was swinging into a tight circle. This made impossible the preferred torpedo-plane tactic of an attack from either bow. Coming in at 250 knots and better, Musick's pilots found it difficult even to line up, and only Musick and Lieutenants Carter and Mason appear to have dropped at the carrier. The others released at the gunnery ships of the screen. Though two pilots "saw" pairs of "torpedo explosions," these must have been either phantoms or bombs that near missed, for no Japanese ship took a hit.

By 6:46, only 14 minutes after the first Helldiver had plunged, the last of the torpedo planes was clear of the screen and AA fire ceased.

Chiyoda's crew turned to with a will to douse the fires aft, and all ships resumed station to continue west at 24 knots.

Up to this point the three American attacking flights had come off easily. Several planes had been damaged, but none had fallen to an AA barrage that had been heavy but inaccurate. But on retirement just out of range of the AA, they encountered Zero fighters on CAP from *Chiyoda* and its sisters.

Commander Shifley spotted them first on completing his photo run when a Zero crossed in front of him. He and his wingman, Lieutenant (jg) Gerry Rian, both fired on it, but the Zero did a full loop and disappeared below and behind. Shifley and Rian then tangled with six or seven Zeros at the rendezvous point 20 miles to the east of the scene of attack. The Americans weaved and took pot shots, with Shifley claiming two Zeros, trying to keep the enemy fighters stirred up and away from rendezvousing Avengers and Helldivers. When three Zeros settled on Shifley's tail however, the commander slammed his throttle full forward and pulled away within 30 seconds, drawing 52 inches of manifold pressure at 2,700 rpm.

Other Zeros attacked the Helldivers as they circled to the east of the enemy ships. Five of the "Beasts" were indicating close to 250 knots when four Zeros came in under their tails where the rear-seat gunners could not fire. The Japanese pilots shot down one SB2C and probably another, but nine managed to join up for the long ride home.

The bombing accuracy of the American pilots had been very poor— only three hits and one damaging near miss for 68 bombs dropped. Also, all eight of the torpedoes missed. On the other hand, the Japanese AA defense had been worse, and of the intercepting Zeros seven failed to return and another ditched. Two more crashed on landing. Obayashi's carrier group had had 23 planes operational on the morning of June 20; now, as darkness fell this day, it had almost none.

Out of sight of the *Chiyoda* group from both deck and air but in greater peril was Ozawa's own *Zuikaku* group. Rapidly approaching his Carrier Division 1 was a big flight from four U. S. carriers. In the lead was *Hornet*'s Air Group 2 with *Yorktown*'s Air Group 1 following and AGs 50 and 24 from *Bataan* and *Belleau Wood* last. Leading the formation was Commander Jackson D. Arnold, *Hornet*'s air-group skipper.

A little after 6:00 P.M. Arnold had spotted the oiler force and a few minutes later Ozawa's and Jojima's groups of ships on the horizon west and north. Immediately, he opened his Hellcat's throttle to scout ahead. "My primary concern," he told an intelligence officer afterward, "was to avoid overlooking . . . [any] enemy group of ships so that no ship would get away undamaged." Arnold well recalled the experience of his old Air Group 2 in the Battle of the Coral Sea where this same *Zuikaku* had escaped attack.

As he drew nearer Arnold could make out both Jojima's Carrier Division 2 and Ozawa's Carrier Division 1, separated, he estimated, by ten to 15 miles. Between the two lay a great cumulus cloud rising from about 3,000 feet to above the 14,000-foot altitude of the attackers. Snapping on his voice radio, Arnold ordered all of his "Ripper" (Air Group 2) planes to attack *Zuikaku*. "I told them that that was their ticket home."

Immediately, *Hornet*'s 14 Helldivers of Bombing 2 began to deploy, followed by six Avengers from Torpedo 2 and 13 Helldivers from *Yorktown*'s VB-1. Tailing in behind were ten bomb-carrying Hellcats from *Bataan*'s VF-50. Other planes, including *Hornet*'s fighters and air-group skipper Arnold, peeled off to the south to attack the Jojima group.

At about 6:45 P.M. Lieutenant H. L. Buell led down on *Zuikaku* the first six Helldivers, followed in moments by his squadron commander Lieutenant Commander G. B. Campbell with eight more. Buell's division had been a little ahead of Campbell's and so was ordered by Arnold to dive first. As the planes power-glided to 12,000 feet and then tipped over, they passed into the colorful antiaircraft barrage noting bursts of red, green, orange, and black as well as the beautiful white phosphorus streamers. Lower down, they passed into range of the silver streamers of 37-mm. and 25-mm. light AA rising from the rim of *Zuikaku*'s deck. Arnold, watching from above, thought that Buell's bomb hit and that at least six more pilots scored. Campbell was sure of at least one hit, for he reported afterward that as he dove he could see a "big hole with a fire down inside near the island." Ensign F. E. Looney diving last in plane 68 at 6:50 P.M., seconded his skipper. ". . . I noticed that the CV was afire on the port side amidships. There may have been other fires that I did not see as I was concentrating on dropping my own bombs—believe I scored a hit." Nearly every other pilot and gunner of Campbell's division made similar observations.

Yorktown's Helldivers, led by Lieutenant Commander J. W. Runyan, USNR, had circled to the north as VB-2 was diving. Runyan started down just as Ensign Looney was pulling away over the ships of the screen at better than 250 knots. "The spacing," Runyan recalled afterward, "and the angle of dive were excellent." He saw a hit near the island structure while drawing away and two more aft, "one of which left a large hole rimmed with fire apparently emanating from the hangar deck below." The last two *Yorktown* pilots concluded that the *Zuikaku* was finished and dove on an escort ship they took to be a heavy cruiser.

Lieutenant F. D. Hoover leading *Hornet*'s torpedo planes found the AA fire so heavy that his squadron could not make a coordinated attack. He and three other pilots attacked *Zuikaku* but claimed no more than a "possible" torpedo hit. Hoover thought his own fish porpoised after his drop. Ensign V. G. Stauber found on his run that he had forgotten to open his bomb-bay doors. Banking right and remedying his error, he flew up the side of *Zuikaku* and saw dead ahead a heavy cruiser. He made a good run, released, and his turret gunner watched the fish run hot and true directly into the side of the ship, to explode and toss up a geyser of water and brown smoke twice the height of the mast. A certain hit? Apparently not, for Ozawa's action report lists no damage other than to the carrier. Unless what the three crewmen "saw" was the product of supercharged imaginations or a now rare "premature," the best explanation would appear to be that the explosion was from a near miss by a bomb, possibly from a *Yorktown* plane.

Admiral Ozawa's troubles had not quite ended. Coming in last and diving steeply on *Zuikaku* at about 7:00 P.M. were Hellcats from *Bataan's* Fighting 50. Originally they had numbered ten, but several pilots, including flight leader Lieutenant C. E. Fanning, had tangled with Zeros that had jumped them from out of cloud cover. Lieutenant Wiley A. Stoner was missing after the attack and presumably was shot down.

The other pilots, led by Lieutenant C. M. Hinn, dove from 8,000 feet at *Zuikaku* and her cruiser escort. The flattop, all agreed, was burning "furiously." All pilots released and pulled out sharply and so were unable to see the results of their dives. One watched the bomb dropped by Ensign F. F. Francis, minus its tail fin, tumble down end over end.

As Hinn and his mates reformed at 12,000 feet, circling north of *Zuikaku* for a few minutes before heading east for base, they could see smoke coming from the entire length of the carrier's flight deck. *Zuikaku* had received seven hits or damaging near misses by Japanese admission. Had the carrier had aboard a full load of planes, she probably would have been lost, for water mains had failed and the crew had to resort to hand-carried CO_2 extinguishers to check the flames. At one point the bridge passed an order to abandon ship, only to cancel it minutes later when the firefighters began to report progress.

That most of *Zuikaku's* flight deck remained intact after her ordeal may be attributed to the use of delay-fuse bombs in most of the Helldivers. Had they been carrying 1/100th second bombs they might either have sunk *Zuikaku* or completely destroyed her flight deck and put her out of the war. As it was none of the semiarmor-piercing bombs penetrated deeply enough to sunder her bottom. The carrier, the Japanese said, had no trouble steaming "under combat conditions" once her fires had been extinguished. But *Zuikaku* had to go immediately to Kure for drydocking and extensive repair.

While *Hornet's* dive bombers bored west and north, Commander Arnold had turned left with the carrier's fighters to head for Admiral Jojima's Second Carrier Group. Arnold could see *Junyo*, *Hiyo*, and *Ryuho* and also far to the southwest the massive superstructures and masts of *Yamato* and *Musashi*. His bomb-carrying Hellcats dove on a ship they took to be a CVL—probably the *Ryuho* if their identification was up to snuff. Commander W. A. Dean, skipper of *Hornet's* VF-2, thought he hit the carrier with his bomb, but Japanese sources do not support the claim. In this phase of the battle a definitive answer to the question "who hit what?" probably is impossible. *Ryuho* was only slightly damaged by near misses; hence it seems certain that VF-2 did not hit her if she was, indeed, the outfit's target. It is also not possible to determine the order in which planes from the various air groups attacked the 2nd Carrier Group. The authors are reasonably certain, however, that only ships of the 2nd Carrier Division and not *Zuiho* and *Chitose* of the 3rd Carrier Division underwent attack.

Yorktown also had sent out bomb-carrying fighters of VF-1, 12 of them, under Commander Strean. Strean did not dive immediately but for some minutes swept the area between the Ozawa and Jojima groups and also to the west, looking for enemy fighters. Finding none, he picked a big flattop in the Jojima group that from the shape of its island and its slanting funnel he identified as of the *Hiyo* class. All planes dove, released at 2,000 feet, and claimed three "confirmed" hits and five near misses. One bomb, the pilots thought, went through the edge of the carrier's flight deck before exploding in the water. On pullout Ensign Reinert made a head-on pass at a Val dive bomber, this quick, inconclusive exchange of fire being the only aerial combat for VF-1. In looking back at about 7:10 P.M., Strean could see that his target had begun evasive action and was turning sharply to the south. All three of Jojima's carriers still were in sight, each surrounded by a circular screen of warships. There appears to be no way to verify or deny VF-1's claim of hits. Both *Junyo* and *Hiyo* received bomb damage, but not necessarily in this attack. Strean also saw attacking planes from another carrier; these may have been from *Lexington* or *Enterprise*.

When Commanders Arnold and Strean turned left to attack the Jojima group, so also did nine torpedo planes, five from *Yorktown* and four from *Belleau Wood*. Lieutenant Charles W. Nelson, leading the *Yorktown*'s planes, turned sharply left into the cumulus mass lying between the Ozawa and Jojima carrier groups. Emerging at 2,500 feet, he found his division approaching a ship he took to be a light carrier—it must have been Jojima's *Ryuho*. On pullout at 220 knots and 300 feet AA fire caught his Avenger in its main fuel tanks, sending the plane blazing into the ocean. The other pilots dropped at 1,000 yards and claimed to see two fish hit the flattop and another a destroyer, "blowing it up." Unless the carrier was the *Hiyo,* it seems certain that all planes missed. Certainly, no destroyer was hit, and it is probable that the *Yorktown* pilots fell victim to what was almost a universal impulse among American pilots— the compulsion to believe that their attacks, made at such risk, were successful.

Commander James M. Peters, skipper of *Yorktown*'s Air Group 1, flying a Hellcat, stayed at high altitude to observe the results of his pilots' attacks. He was skeptical of all bomb-hit claims. He recorded afterward:

Observations made by pilots of attacking planes are almost totally unreliable. The camera is the only good observer. From the air, a bomb hit doesn't appear much different from the AA fire of the ship during the plane's approach. Hits can be estimated more by the lack of splashes in the water than by any other method. Naturally, if a fire is started it is readily visible.

Peters concluded:

The AA fire from scattered ships and the wide area in which forces were involved made it comparable to watching a ten-ring circus with a sniper shooting at you from behind the lion's cage.

The four *Belleau Wood* Avengers with Lieutenant (jg) G. P. Brown leading had followed in the *Yorktown* group at 12,000 feet. On seeing no planes apparently heading for Jojima's carriers, they turned left through 180 degrees from the west of the warship formation and in a 50-degree dive began a run with the sun partly behind them. Breaking through some scattered cumulus at 2,000 feet, they approached *Hiyo* operating on the northern flank, scattering widely to "anvil" the ship. Lieutenant Brown was approaching on the bow, slightly to port, Lieutenant (jg) B. C. Tate was broad on the starboard bow, and Lieutenant (jg) W. R. Omark was on the starboard quarter. Ensign W. D. Luton, flying the fourth plane, lost contact temporarily, and then circled left to attack the Jojima group from the east.

As Brown was letting down to attack altitude, antiaircraft knocked off a section of his Avenger's port wing and set the big-bellied craft afire. Flames and smoke filling the rear section forced radioman E. C. Babcock and gunner G. H. Platz immediately to bail out. Both drifted into the water in their chutes in the middle of the enemy fleet. Brown stayed with the plane, the fire died out, and he continued his run, bleeding profusely from a wound.

Hiyo was turning sharply to port when Brown released, followed closely by Tate. The run of both fish was good, but both apparently missed. But the *Hiyo* was committed in a turn when Omark came in, flashing past battleship *Nagato,* pride of the prewar Japanese fleet, to drop at 400 feet altitude and 240 knots. As he banked sharply away his gunner and radioman saw the fish run squarely into the carrier to explode about a quarter of the length of the ship from the bow. This hit was no phantom; the hole torn by the blast flooded *Hiyo's* engine rooms. Within a few minutes the ship had drifted to a stop within sight of Babcock and Platz floating in their lifejackets in the water.

Ensign Luton attacked a carrier—without an island, he thought. His fish made a normal run but scored no hit, and because he retired in a violent 180-degree turn he could see nothing further.

As Omark pulled away a Zero dove on him to get a hot reception from J. E. Prince, his turret gunner. Two Vals also attacked, evidently planes out on antisub patrol, but Prince discouraged them, too, hitting one. While flying east Omark joined another TBF that had been horribly shot up, its belly rent and blackened by fire. It was the wounded Brown, doggedly trying to get home. Omark stayed with Brown until long after dark but lost him when he vanished in a cloud. Nobody saw him again; *Belleau Wood* carried him as "missing in action."

Possibly because their Dauntlesses cruised a little more slowly than the Helldivers, Air Groups 16 and 10 from *Lexington* and *Enterprise* arrived somewhat later than the others. Both, it seems certain, attacked the Jojima carrier group. *Lexington*'s strike consisted of nine Hellcats without bombs, 14 Dauntless dive bombers, and six Avengers. *Enterprise* had sent 12 fighters, 11 Dauntlesses, and six Avengers laden with bombs and not torpedoes. Light carrier *San Jacinto* contributed what it could—two Avengers. Like the *Lexington* and *Enterprise* VT, they each carried four 500-pounders.

Lexington's planes were about 20 minutes ahead of those from *Enterprise*. They came abreast and to the north of the oiler group at about 6:40. For a time the big cumulus cloud blocked the view of flight commander Ralph Weymouth, skipper of VB-16, but at length he could see both the Ozawa and Jojima groups. Noting that *Zuikaku* was still under attack, Weymouth led his Dauntlesses and Avengers due west past both carrier groups. His plan was to dive on the two *Hiyos* with the sun behind him, a sun that now was just touching the rim of the horizon. Then by pulling out to the east he would reduce to the minimum the distance of flight home. Weymouth was a savvy veteran; he had seen Japanese carriers before in the Battle of the Eastern Solomons.

In an unfortunate mistake seven of Weymouth's 11 escorting Hellcats, none toting a bomb, climbed to engage some supposed Zeros but found only some F6Fs. Only four remained low enough to give support, and in the event only two did, the pilot of one plane being Alex Vraciu.

At 6:48 P.M. a flight of Zero 52s from *Zuikaku* suddenly dove from the rear on Weymouth's Dauntlesses and Avengers. One hit Lieutenant (jg) Warren E. McLellan's torpedo plane in the main fuel tank, setting it and the port side of the crew compartment instantly ablaze. McLellan, his gunner, J. S. Hutchinson, and his radioman, Selbie Greenhalgh, all climbed out immediately and jumped. The chutes of all three opened, and they drifted into the ocean not far from Babcock and Platz, Lieutenant Brown's crewmen. None could see the others; all were in life jackets.

Alex Vraciu spotted some Zeros diving on the tail of his squadron mate, Ensign H. W. Brockmeyer. Vraciu fired two bursts that exploded a Zero, but Brockmeyer already was spiraling down toward the water, trailing a cloud of thickening black smoke. He became an MIA, missing in action.

After recovery the Zeros attacked again, this time Weymouth's SBDs. Repeating a pattern that had held good throughout the war, the rear-seat gunners gave them a hot reception with their twin .30s. None of the SBDs fell, and the gunners smoked several Zeros. One of these dropped a wheel and was seen to glide down to alight near a destroyer. This may have been the Number 4 plane from *Zuikaku*'s fighter squadron that the Japanese record as ditching after attacking an SBD section.

The Zeros gave up and pulled away when the First Mobile Fleet's AA began to put out its peculiar form of color display—green, yellow, black, blue, purple, and white with those flaming streamers. SBD driver Don Reichel, who had been a commercial artist, was especially taken with the beauty of some bursts of reddish purple.

When the Zeros attacked, Weymouth had put the formation into a dive from 12,000 to 10,000 feet that carried the Dauntlesses well to the west of Jojima's carriers. At his attack signal all planes put about, deployed into diving order, and with Weymouth leading started down at exactly 7:04 P.M. just as the sun was sliding below the horizon.

Weymouth had selected the southernmost of the two *Hiyos* as his target—almost certainly Jojima's flagship *Junyo*. The flattop was turning violently left from 330 to 290 degrees and so Weymouth dived very low, heeding the refrain that kept drumming in his head, "Gotta get a hit! Gotta get a hit! Gotta get a hit!" He released and pulled out sharply, and his gunner, McElhinney, thought he saw a puff of black smoke from the carrier's deck close to the island. Eleven more planes followed Weymouth down, claiming at least three more hits. Probably some pilots scored. *Junyo* was hit twice near the stack and six more bombs near missed in the course of the action.

Two planes dove on the northern carrier, almost certainly *Hiyo*, since it seemed to be dead in the water with a fire on its deck. Both pilots claimed hits and on retirement noted that the ship was smoking badly. One SBD suffered windshield fogging problems, the curse of old *Yorktown*'s Bombing 5 in the Coral Sea. This was because the plane was so elderly that it lacked the hot-air windshield defroster standard on all newer Dash 5 models.

Following in the dive bombers was Lieutenant Norman A. Sterrie, who had replaced the deceased Bob Isely as skipper of *Lexington*'s VT-16. With his own six planes and two from *San Jacinto* he glide-bombed the *Junyo,* claiming several hits for 20 bombs dropped. The planes continued east at very high speed—over 300 knots—to form up in a tight defensive V.

It was well they did, for Zeros again appeared just clear of AA range to attack both the Sterrie's Avengers and Weymouth's Dauntlesses. They scored—and were scored upon. Three attacked a trio of SBDs being led by Weymouth. Gunners Lemay, Maggio, and McElhinney opened up and two Zeros pulled away. The third bored in determinedly from the side of the formation despite being hit repeatedly in the engine, tracers sparkling off indicating the accuracy of the .30-caliber fire. It closed, fired with its 7.7s and then with its 20-mm. cannons directly into the Dauntless of Lieutenant (jg) Jay A. Shields. Shields' wingman and roommate, Lieutenant Tom Sedell, saw his friend jerk violently as bullets apparently entered his right side, his goggles flew off, his head fell back, and his mouth opened as if he were screaming. Then he plunged forward over the stick, the plane nosed down, and with gunner Lemay still firing, it crashed into the ocean with a great splash and disappeared. But the Zero pilot perished, too. His Model 52 plane with a bulbous cowling new to the Americans pulled up, then toppled off with propeller windmilling idly to plummet steeply into the ocean near the grave of Shields' SBD. At least one Zero fell to the Avengers, too. Lieutenant Sterrie's turret gunner, J. W. Webb, put 20 .50-caliber slugs into its belly and wing as it tried a half roll and recovery after a run from dead astern. It blazed and went into the water in a 45-degree dive. Minus three of their number, one each from the fighter, bomber, and torpedo squadrons, all of the *Lexington* planes finally assembled for the long ride home.

The *Enterprise* planes came in directly behind those of *Lexington*. Flight leader W. R. Kane, Air Group 10's skipper, sighted the First Mobile Fleet at 6:45. His formation consisted of a dozen SBD-5s and five TBF-1Cs, escorted by a dozen F6F-3s of VF-10 that stayed close to their charges and were not carrying bombs.

Coming in directly from the east at 15,000 feet after sighting the oilers, Kane noticed that *Ryuho*, which by this time had maneuvered several miles to the southeast of *Hiyo* and *Junyo*, was lined up perfectly for a bomb run. Kane was in a Hellcat, and diving steeply from 12,000 feet a little after 7:00 P.M., he led down his division of four Hellcats in a steep firing run. After him came six Dauntlesses and all five Avengers. Lieutenant Commander J. D. Ramage, Bombing 10's skipper, thought his thousand-pounder missed *Ryuho* just astern but close enough to cause some damage, and he may have been right. Lieutenant (jg) A. A. Schaal, diving last, thought his SAP bomb hit the stern, but his missile, too, probably registered no better than a near miss. Smoke and some flame seen on fantail suggested that *Ryuho* may have been ablaze from a plane or gasoline, but the First Mobile Fleet's action report admits to no more than "Small damage due to near miss; no trouble in cruising or participating in combat."

Leading in the five *Enterprise* Avengers at 7:15 P.M. was Lieutenant Van V. Eason. By this time *Ryuho* was now turning violently to port. All planes glide-bombed in trail, releasing bombs at between 3,000 and 4,000 feet. The pilots claimed eight hits scattered about the bow of the carrier, and Lieutenant E. J. Lawton reported a tremendous explosion on the ship with flames shooting 200 to 300 feet high. But *Ryuho* was not hit, and the explosion—if indeed there was one—was not fatal.

On retirement Kane's fighters tangled with some Zeros that also harried Eason's Avengers. Kane knocked down a landing wheel from one that his wingman Ensign J. L. Wolf finished off. Wolf got another, too, with the VF-10 pilots claiming eight in all. Ensign J. I. Turner had an oil line severed by a Zero bullet but managed to fly 30 miles to the east of the Japanese fleet before ditching. A float plane found him 24 hours later. Kane's cryptic story of the fight recorded: "Usual story. Folly to dogfight Zekes. Jap pilots on this occasion better than those previously encountered, but our VF had no difficulty shooting them down if division and section tactics followed."

Lieutenant L. L. Bangs, second-in-command of *Enterprise*'s Bombing

10, maintained a westerly heading with his section after Kane and Ramage had peeled off after *Ryuho*. He had decided to drop on *Zuikaku*, which he had seen, but changed his mind when he spotted around the edge of the great cumulus cloud carrier *Hiyo* not then under attack. Followed by the remaining *Enterprise* Dauntlesses, he plunged steeply on the ship from 9,000 feet. His squadron mates saw his bomb hit the stern of *Hiyo*, now listing and dead in the water. The missile exploded and flung overside a group of planes on the fantail. Lieutenants Mester and Lewis, following, likewise claimed hits after strafing the ship all the way down with their forward-firing .50 and pulling out at 1,000 feet. It is possible that their claims were correct, for the downed American airmen in the water noted tremendous explosions aboard *Hiyo* at about this time, after which the carrier became a roaring mass of flame. An aggressive Zero made a close run on Bangs during the latter's retirement, smacking a 20-mm. shell into his wing and punching 20 7.7-mm. holes through his canopy. But Bangs and his gunner were unhurt.

As they formed up and flew eastward, the *Enterprise* airmen noted that smoke and flames were coming from the oiler group. Someone, they guessed, had decided that the enemy's tanker force was fair game. They were right. The attackers were from *Wasp*'s Air Group 14.

Wasp had launched 16 fighters, none with bombs, 12 Helldiver dive bombers, and seven torpedo planes loaded with 500-pound bombs. Leading was Lieutenant Commander J. D. Blitch, skipper of Bombing 14. At an estimated 310 miles from his carrier, Blitch spotted directly to the west the Japanese supply force of six oilers and six destroyers. Knowing that he was coming in behind *Bunker Hill*'s planes and failing to see the Jojima and Ozawa groups to the north and west, apparently because of intervening clouds, Blitch made a bad guess: Just before he reached the oilers he turned south. After flying for 50 miles on a course of 170 degrees and finding nothing, Blitch decided to put about and attack the oilers. He dared not search further in view of the gas shortage in his planes, and he reasoned that if he destroyed the oilers he might delay the retirement of the enemy's carriers. They might be forced to cruise at economical speed to conserve fuel. All the oilers were deep in the water, indicating that little of their precious cargo had as yet been transferred.

Approaching from the southeast, Blitch assigned three Helldivers each to four of the oilers and four Avengers to a fifth. The other four Avengers, coming in last, were to attack targets of opportunity. He divided the escorting fighters, sending half to strafe the destroyers and reduce AA and the other half to a rendezvous point ten miles due west of the oilers.

When the American planes drew in range, the oilers that had been steaming in two columns of three each split, one column turning to port and the other to starboard, each ship turning as tightly as it could, maintaining a speed of between 12 and 15 knots. All ships put up extremely heavy AA, particularly light 25-mm. and 37-mm. stuff in red, blue, and yellow tracer that contrasted with the purple and black puffs of the heavier caliber flak. The fire was very accurate, too, certainly as good and perhaps better than any put up by the Japanese carrier groups.

The Helldivers ran the gantlet in steep plunges, some taking light-caliber hits on the way down. Their interval was good, their releases low. Torpedo 14 followed, dropping bombs in an expertly timed attack about 15 seconds after the last SB2C had released. The pilots claimed numerous hits, and in fact their bombing accuracy was the best of any American air group, probably because their targets were slower and less agile. Several bombs started a huge fire on *Seiyo Maru,* forcing its abandonment. *Hayasui Maru* took a direct hit and two near misses, but managed to put out her fires and continue. *Genyo Maru* took three near misses that split her seams, flooded her engine rooms, stopped her, and forced destroyer *Yukikaze* to scuttle her with torpedoes after removing her crew. Blitch's decision had been very wise; at this stage of the war fleet oilers were as valuable as major warships, perhaps more so, for Japan's fleet could not leave port without this "black gold."

Retribution was waiting for *Wasp*'s Air Group 14 in the form of mottled brown Zeros that jumped the planes as they retired west toward their rendezvous point. Fighting 14 got into quite a scrap, claiming five Zeros but losing Lieutenant E. E. Cotton. In making head-on passes at each other neither a Zero pilot nor Cotton swerved and the two planes collided head on. Probably also downed by Zeros was a Helldiver that vanished before reaching the rendezvous point. By 7:35 P.M., in rapidly darkening twilight, all planes had shaken off the Zeros and were homeward bound.

A record of three ships sunk and seven damaged by an attack force of 216 aircraft that reached the target cannot be regarded as impressive. The reader need only compare this score with that posted by Admiral Nagumo's First Air Fleet in the opening months of the war. Yet the relatively poor American bombing is understandable. All pilots were rusty at attacking fast-moving targets. Also, the American air groups were very low on fuel; about all they had time for was a single, quick pass and then to head for home. They had no time to orbit and attack at leisure. Moreover, in shooting down or otherwise damaging or destroying about 65 more Japanese planes, they performed a service as valuable as destroying carriers. At the day's end on June 20 Admiral Ozawa had only 35 planes operational. He was out of business, and Japan's painfully accumulated store of carrier-qualified pilots had been destroyed.

28. Landing by Night

Between 7:00 and 7:30 P.M. on June 20, while his air groups were attacking the enemy, Pete Mitscher smoked three cigarettes. He had but one radioed report, that from Ralph Weymouth, who recorded (mistakenly) two *Hiyo* class carriers as sunk and two others, one a *Zuikaku* class, as on fire. Now he was "sweating out" the return of his boys.

By 8:00 P.M. darkness was nearly total, with no moon and no horizon discernible to the pilots. The few who had cruised rapidly to beat the darkness had wasted their gas. By 8:30 TF 58's radars had picked up some of the planes that had been homing on the carriers with YE, YJ, and Racon beacon gear. Some of the Avengers and Helldivers used their airborne radars to find the fleet and to maintain their bearings as they began orbiting and looking for a flight deck. Random flying suggested that other pilots could not see the blacked-out carriers below. Sliding down from his chair, Mitscher walked into *Lexington*'s flag plot. Sitting down carefully at the end of a leather transom, he lighted another cigarette, looked up, and said softly, "Turn on the lights." "Thirty-One Knot" Burke leaped for the TBS.

From every carrier a searchlight beam shot straight into the air and glow lights blinked the outline of flight decks. Tuck lights lit up on cruisers and destroyers. Mitscher was taking the deliberate chance that no Japanese submarine would be about to save the lives of his pilots. He added, "Tell 'em to land on any carrier."

Lexington's landing signal officer guided in the first six planes smoothly with minimum of wave-offs, but the seventh, piloted by a frightened young man in a battle-damaged Helldiver, ignored a wave-off and piled into the barrier, fouling the deck. The same happened on most of the other big carriers as more and more planes arrived to circle overhead, jamming the circuits with their reports of low fuel.

Hard-luck ship for deck crashes was *Bunker Hill*. Her air group had returned first and the first plane landed at 8:33 P.M. Then 23 minutes later an SB2C from *Hornet* came in, missed the arrester wires, crashed the barrier, and nosed up, lodging its propeller into the teakwood deck. The crash crew still was struggling to clear the plane when a *Cabot* pilot, ignoring both the LSO and red Very pistol flares, landed, bounded over the barrier, hit the Helldiver, and then the ship's island. The severely burned young ensign survived, but his runaway Avenger had killed Commander Wayne Smith, the air officer, and two of his crash crew. By 9:44 P.M. *Bunker Hill's* deck was clear again, to stay open for 52 minutes, closing at 10:36 when a *Wasp* fighter hit the barrier. The crew quickly jettisoned this wreck overside, and at 11:05 P.M. the carrier took aboard her last plane.

Of *Bunker Hill's* air group only one fighter had to water-land (pilot lost), but five of her eight Avengers failed to make it. Two Avengers had to pick CVL decks, and Lieutenant Le Compte made *Enterprise* at 9:45 with his gas gauge reading exactly zero. Of the *Bunker Hill's* 12 Helldivers just one landed safely. Nine others water-landed, one crew lost, and two more went down over the target. The "Beasts" had arrived back over TF 58 with an average of 15 gallons of gas remaining. Four, nevertheless, had managed landing passes at carriers only to get the wave-off because of foul decks. Most pilots then decided to ditch while they had power and could make controlled landings. The experience of Ensign Adam Berg was typical of scores of other air crew that night:

[Being nearly out of fuel] . . . I scanned the horizon and sighted a searchlight which I judged to be 20 miles away. I made for the light. . . . I had approximately 15 minutes of fuel left and spent 11 minutes of it circling the destroyer from which the light was coming trying to force open my hatch that had been jammed closed by a 20-mm. hit. Finally, in desperation, I pulled on the handle of the hatch release until I broke the cable and it left the plane. My gunner blinked his lamp at the DD since we had no lights. I put down full flaps and power stalled into the sea 1,400 yards ahead and to starboard of the destroyer. The plane floated for four minutes during which time my air crewman removed the rubber raft and the two of us climbed aboard. We fired three tracer bullets [from Berg's .38-caliber pistol] and I flashed my pocket light. . . . Fifteen minutes later we were aboard the U. S. S. *Monssen*.

Every carrier using SB2Cs reported heavy losses. *Hornet* lost 11 of 14, eight to water landings and three to barrier crashes. *Yorktown* lost nine, one to a crash and eight in the water. Had the crews had the time to jettison the 250-pound bombs that the Helldivers had carried and to replace them with wing tanks, most probably would have had enough fuel to orbit until decks were clear. By contrast, night-trained Air Group 10 from *Enterprise* flying SBDs did much better. Only five *Enterprise* planes had to ditch, only one a Dauntless.

Air discipline broke down in the landing circles. Pilots cut each other out, ignored wave-offs, and did things they never would have dreamed of doing in ordinary circumstances. To Lieutenant (jg) E. J. Lawton from *Enterprise* the scene about Task Force 58, viewed from above, "was a weird kaleidoscope of fast-moving lights forming intricate trails in the darkness." Giving up on the big carriers as hopeless because of the traffic jam circling each, Lawton set his Avenger down at 10:05 on CVL *Princeton* that had sent out no planes but had asked for permission to land them. His was the last plane she had room for. "Small as that deck had been I was awfully glad to see it."

Many overeager gunnery ships, anxious to help, turned on so many lights that the pilots mistook them for carriers. This circumstance and how to resolve it became a major topic of review afterward in action reports. Lawton's squadron mate, Lieutenant (jg) C. B. Collins, circled a ship showing a vertical searchlight, slid into the groove, and was pulling the nose of his plane high about to touch down when he suddenly realized that he was trying to land on a destroyer. Frantically gunning his big Cyclone engine and pulling away, he checked his fuel and found that he had only five minutes more. Rather than try to find a carrier, he gave it up and ditched ahead of the "can."

Ensign E. G. Wendorf of *Lexington*'s VF-16 was a very lucky young man. When over the *Lex* and orbiting at 110 knots, he glanced to the right and saw the glowing exhaust stacks of another plane approaching fast. As he dived to dodge his Hellcat's left landing wheel dipped into the water. The left wing hooked, and the fighter cartwheeled in, snapping off its right wing, flipping onto its back, and driving the nose eight to ten feet under. Water poured in as Wendorf pried back the broken canopy and upside down, started out.

I got halfway out when the hood slid forward and caught my chute and [seat-pack] raft. I slashed back at it with my fist, knocking it free, and was able to get out. I was out of the plane but underneath it, and it was sinking fast. . . . The pressure was building up in my ears before I was finally able to kick myself free. I was about 20 feet under. Upon reaching the surface I inflated my Mae West [lifejacket] and rested.

It took Wendorf an hour to get his seat-pack life raft inflated and three tries before he was able to get into the raft, utterly spent. Repeatedly he vomited, sick from swallowing salt water spiked with oil from the plane. Later, he noted with alarm the fins of several large sharks, "but they never actually attacked me." He fired his pistol with tracers to attract several destroyers that passed him by, but it was a light carrier that saw him and tossed over a smoke float. At 4:14 A.M. a destroyer finally took Wendorf aboard after investigating the float, hearing his shout, and turning a search-light on him.

Given the location of his crash, away from the heart of TF 58, Wendorf probably was lucky to get picked up. *Wasp* had five crews known to have ditched that nobody rescued. How long the hapless men may have floated, in lifejackets or rafts, it may be better not to know. *Yorktown* had Lieutenant M. M. Tomme killed after he had landed successfully on the carrier. A plane coming in close behind hit, bounced high, and landed atop Tomme's Hellcat before he could get out of it. By way of contrast Ensign H. G. Lewis, who had made only 23 carrier landings prior to this eventful mission, got aboard the *Hornet* on his first pass, landing smoothly and easily in his gas-shy Helldiver. Finally, luckiest of all were the two air crews that simultaneously landed on *Enterprise*. One caught a forward wire, the other a rear wire with no damage to either plane.

Task Force 58's first try at a mass night landing had been a failure. Even with plenty of fuel plane losses probably would have been inacceptably high because of the lack of night-landing training of most pilots. By Admiral Mitscher's reckoning only 6 fighters, ten dive bombers, and four torpedo planes, 20 aircraft altogether, had been lost in combat. But 17 fighters, 35 dive bombers, and 28 Avengers had been lost in deck crashes and water landings. Exactly 100 planes of 216 reaching the target area had been lost. Yet personnel losses had hardly been greater than in the Turkey Shoot the day before. The final count came to 16 pilots, 22 air crew, two deck officers, and four ships' enlisted crewmen killed or missing. Probably TF 58's loss in air crew was less than that suffered by pilots of Admiral Ozawa's First Mobile Fleet in defending their carriers.

In military terms Mitscher's decision to strike the enemy late in the day had paid off, though not as handsomely as he had hoped. He might have done better to have kept shadowing Ozawa and to have deferred launching until morning. But his further decision to "turn on the lights" reduced what admittedly were heavy plane and pilot losses and proved to be of lasting benefit to the morale of his hard-worked air crew.

During a landing process that had taken nearly four hours, Task Force 58 had steamed steadily into an easterly wind at 22 knots. Every turn of the ships' screws carried them farther from Ozawa's battered First Mobile Fleet. Also, after putting about at around midnight Admiral Mitscher elected to steam along the bearing of the returning air crews rather than directly toward the projected "Point Option" of Ozawa's fleet in order to save as many downed airmen as possible. He had also to hold down his speed of advance because of destroyer fuel shortages and consequently could not gain sufficient ground to get within striking range by morning. Ozawa, for his part, had abandoned all hope of having Admiral Kondo and the surface ships seek a night battle. He headed directly for Nakagusuku Bay, a Japanese fleet anchorage on Okinawa.

At 2:29 A.M. on June 21 Lieutenant R. S. Nelson of VT-10 from *Enterprise* went aloft again on another search mission. This time his duty was to find Ozawa's retreating fleet, especially any crippled ships that might be lagging behind. Flying wing on him in a second TBF was Lieutenant J. S. Moore. Nelson and Moore had plenty of gas for this trip. Both Avengers carried 270-gallon droppable bomb-bay tanks in addition to regular tankage. Each plane had 605 gallons of fuel, enough to get it out more than 400 miles. In fact, Nelson flew out 390 miles and back 290 and was in the air 7.6 hours. Though physically exhausted by the mission, he still had 150 gallons of gas in his tanks on return.

At 4:40 A.M. Nelson registered on his radar the rear ships of Ozawa's force and soon sighted visually an oil slick. Following it, he found six destroyers and ahead of them in a diamond formation on a course of 300 degrees Admiral Obayashi's Carrier Division 3. He spotted *Chitose, Zuiho,* and *Chiyoda,* the latter trailing oil, *Kongo, Haruna,* and the two giants *Yamato* and *Musashi.* Nelson radioed home his second find in two days, and because the Japanese were tossing AA fire at him and the carriers acted as if they might be turning to launch planes, he started back to the *Enterprise* at 6:55 A.M. To make certain he had not overlooked a cripple he took a homeward course 20 miles northward of his outbound route.

While Nelson was returning Mitscher launched a strike. But mindful of the range limitation of the Helldivers and Avengers, he gave the air crew strict orders to go no farther than 250 miles. Nelson overheard transmissions between some planes, broke in, and gave the pilots the position of his sighting. He then heard a flight leader call base and report, "Enemy position out of range." Nelson was, as he recorded in his after-action report, bitterly disappointed "by the realization that our striking planes would not be able to reach these sitting-duck targets."

The strike planes found no cripples—there were none—and at the limit of their missions, perhaps a little beyond, they found only some wreckage on the water. But in scouting carefully the locale of the previous day's battle, seaplanes and PBM "Dumbos" from Saipan found McLellan and his crew, air crewmen Babcock and Platz, and several others.

At 7:20 P.M. on the 21st, after further day-long searches had failed to contact Ozawa's ships, Ray Spruance decided that further pursuit would be useless. An hour later *Lexington* put about and Task Force 58 headed east for a rendezvous set up with a tanker force to take on critically needed fuel.

Having defeated his main enemy, Spruance was convinced that little threat remained to the amphibious forces about Saipan and Tinian. Strikes by Harrill's *Essex* group, TG 58.4, on Guam on June 20 had effectively completed the mangling of that island's airfields and what planes were left. Three task groups, therefore, departed the Marianas to Eniwetok for rest and replenishment, but the ever-aggressive "Jocko" Clark decided that prudence required one more slap at Iwo Jima. After fueling his *Hornet, Yorktown, Belleau Wood,* and *Bataan,* he started north for the Bonins. In so doing he picked up a passenger en route.

Commander Price, still in his life raft, had spent June 21 and 22 fishing without success. He finished the last of his water on the 22nd but did not give up hope because "I felt that at least the law of averages should give me rain shortly as showers were around me invariably each morning and evening. I still felt no great desire for food and was surprised at the relative amount of strength I retained."

By the next day, however, Price began to note the effects of dehydration. "The inside of my mouth and tongue were very dry and covered with a salty scale and my tongue felt slightly swollen and prickly." In the late afternoon he was sitting on the gunwale of his raft, bailing it, when he suddenly noticed a ship approaching him from behind. "I was quite startled because it took me completely by surprise." It was a destroyer only 300 yards away. Price eyed it suspiciously, fearing that it might be Japanese, but when it had closed to 75 yards he heard, "Can you take a heaving?" He waved an affirmative, caught a line, and pulled himself to the U. S. S. *Boyd,* one of Jocko's destroyers. Within an hour he was transferred to the *Hornet,* where in sick bay he was given some soup "and a half glass of water at intervals which seemed much too long." In 11 days at sea Price had lost 28 pounds, but he quickly gained weight and on July 6 went back to *Cowpens* and command of Air Group 25. The sea had released one of its lone waifs.

The next day, June 24, *Hornet, Yorktown,* and *Bataan* launched 51 bomb-laden Hellcats to sweep and attack Iwo's airfields. Given radar warning, Admiral Sadaichi Matsunaga's newly arrived squadrons of the 27th Air Flotilla got airborne and intercepted the fighters, forcing all but four to jettison their bombs. A terrific battle followed with the outcome again going heavily against the inexperienced Japanese. Twenty-four Zeros and five Judys fell by Japanese admission against six Hellcats lost. Most heavily engaged of Clark's planes were Lieutenant Commander J. C. Strange's 17 fighters from *Bataan.* The pilots claimed 17 kills and three probables but lost two of their own men.

In the meantime, two strikes had gotten airborne from Iwo against Jocko's carriers. Twenty torpedo planes came in alone without escort, and every plane fell to AA or CAP. A second strike of nine Jills, nine Judys, and 23 Zeros was intercepted by CAP well out from the carriers, lost 17 planes, failed to sight the carriers, and made no attacks. Again *Bataan* planes were heavily engaged, claiming nine downed against the loss of Lieutenant Commander R. S. Lemmon, skipper of VF-50.

The next day found the *Bataan* and the rest of TG 58.1 steadied on course 125 degrees en route to Eniwetok. For the fast carriers Operation Forager was over. For *Bataan* everything had gone smoothly. Commander Strange said cryptically in his report dated June 27, "Commander Air Group FIFTY has no comments or recommendations," to which his skipper, Captain V. H. Schaeffer, endorsed only "Forwarded."

The decisive Battle of the Philippine Sea fulfilled prophecy. In an American war game in the 1930s centering around the concept of a decisive clash between battleships, the contest had occurred within a thousand-mile radius of Guam. In World War II on June 19 and 20, 1944, it had taken place within the prescribed area between rival carrier task forces.

It would have been as well-nigh impossible for the Americans to have lost the battle as for the Japanese to have won it. Admiral Spruance had committed a terrible blunder, neglecting the hard experience of carrier war, in failing to close his enemy on the night before the clash. In so doing he granted to Ozawa the priceless opportunity of launching full strikes while still out of reach. But the outcome had been all the worse for Japan. Not only had Ozawa's airmen failed to score a single direct hit on a carrier, but three-fourths had lost their lives. And they constituted Japan's only team of carrier airmen. Had Mitscher been able to close and strike first, the Japanese carriers might have been sunk, but most of the airmen would probably have survived. This way, shot down hundreds of miles from their own ships, they perished nearly to a man. As it was, two submarines had cost Ozawa more dearly in ships by sinking two of his best carriers than had Mitscher's lone strike launched late in the day.

On July 6, 1944, as American ground forces were nearing the tip of Marpi Point, the last Japanese stronghold on the island, Vice Admiral Chuichi Nagumo, the former commander of Japan's fast carriers and attacker of Pearl Harbor, assembled what was left of his Saipan naval command. He now had no ships, not so much as a sampan, and was crowded with his men into a cave not far from another occupied by General Saito, the local Japanese Army commander. With Nagumo were about 60 faithful staff officers and yeomen. Knowing he soon might face capture, Nagumo slowly raised a pistol to his temple and fired. This faithful servant of his Emperor had performed his last duty. He had, as Japanese custom required, taken his own life. Writes historian Morison, his was a "strange and appropriate fate!" He and Japan's carrier fleet had perished together.

Epilogue

With the defeat of Japan's carrier force and the fall of Saipan, many thoughtful Japanese leaders in the Navy and in Japan's higher civil government ranks realized that the Empire could not win the war. The Naval Staff knew that it could not again restore Japan's carrier groups. Enough men might be trained to fly, but carrier qualifications demanded skills in landing and navigation that they would not have time to master. Moreover, a growing bunker oil shortage caused by a lack of tankers soon would prevent large-scale fleet operations.

The Japanese Navy would come out in force one more time in the Battle of Leyte Gulf in October 1944. The result would be utter defeat because of a lack of carrier air power. In a final desperate try to win Navy air leaders would adopt Kamikaze tactics, the mounting from land bases of attacks by manned suicide planes bent on crash-diving into American ships. Kamikazes would cause terrible hurt to Task Force 58 and its successor, Task Force 38, but they would not be decisive. Only one more U. S. fleet carrier, CVL *Princeton,* would join the old *Lex, Yorktown, Wasp,* and *Hornet* on the bottom of the Pacific, it being the victim of a bomb, not a Kamikaze. Both of the remaining veterans, *Enterprise* and *Saratoga,* would suffer Kamikaze hits to add to their numerous scars and accumulation of hard-won glory.

In truth, World War II at sea in the Pacific had been won by the United States at least six months before the Battle of the Philippine Sea. It had been won by America's naval aviation training fields that implemented a soundly conceived training plan, by her shipyards, and—to be specific—by such aircraft manufacturing plants as the Bethpage, Long Island, works of the Grumman Aircraft Company, where the F6F-3 Hellcat was built. Still better Japanese resistance would not have mattered in the long run, because in no way could Japan have matched America's massive output of pilots, planes, and flattops. As the North submerged the South in the American Civil War, so the United States submerged Japan under a tidal wave of carrier air power.

In fighting a new type of naval war, one that even veteran airmen had not clearly foreseen and one that some traditional naval officers on both sides were never able to fathom, both sides made mistakes. But the United States could afford to make mistakes and win, while Japan's errors materially hastened her defeat. Japan's greatest blunder was Yamamoto's at Midway in failing to mass his carriers. Of almost equal proportions was the Naval Staff's failure to equip combat planes with armor and self-sealing tanks until nearly the end of the war. And again, Japan's naval air training program on the outbreak of war and for months thereafter was too small and elitist.

In contrast, after the debacle of Pearl Harbor the United States made no errors of comparable magnitude. The U. S. Navy soon adopted good combat tactics, acquired high-performance and well-protected planes, converted cruisers into carriers, and quickly relegated its battleships to the secondary roles of shore bombardment and carrier escort. Shaken by defeat, the Americans became rapid learners; afflicted by "victory disease" —and perhaps by the overwhelming personality of Yamamoto—the Japanese learned more slowly.

After mid-1943, however, American conduct of the carrier war may well have been excessively conservative. At no timely date did Admiral Nimitz apparently consider the possibility of trying a surprise raid on Truk. Had he done so while Koga's Combined Fleet was still anchored in the lagoon, then an extremely damaging blow might have been struck to aid greatly Halsey's campaign in the Solomons and MacArthur's in New Guinea. The first Truk strike came too late. It is ironic that the most daring American carrier strike of the war was the first one—Halsey's on the Marshall Islands in early 1942.

Yet the greatest American military achievement of World War II may have been neither tactical, nor material, nor strategic but intellectual, the cracking of Japan's high-security naval code and the development of extremely sophisticated methods of communications intelligence. That the Battles of the Coral Sea and Midway were victories of intelligence is now well recognized. Less well understood is how important was communications intelligence for the Guadalcanal campaign following and for the Battles of the Eastern Solomons and Santa Cruz. For the rest of the war, too, "comint" remained vital, though the specifics still are shrouded—perhaps with reason—by dictates of security.

In one area of carrier war the U. S. Navy never equalled its adversary's performance—air search. Throughout, the failure to have on carriers specially trained and equipped scouts capable of searching out to at least 600 miles resulted in contacts missed and opportunities lost, especially in the Battle of the Philippine Sea. Mitscher's late-afternoon strike should not have been necessary. Because of communications problems long-range search from land bases never was an effective substitute for long-range search from carriers.

That the United States tolerated for so long the Mark 13 torpedo is difficult to fathom. The defects of this miserable weapon that made torpedo-plane attack well-nigh worthless until the Philippine Sea battle (and perhaps not good then) were recognized but not soon remedied. Why could not the United States Navy, by reverse lease-lend, have acquired British 18-inch aerial torpedoes of the type that hit the *Bismarck?* Though smaller, these weapons had at least one virtue—they exploded. However galling it might have been to Admiral King to adopt a British weapons system, it would have made as much sense as bringing H. M. S. *Victorious* to the South Pacific.

On the other hand, the Mark 13 is almost the only weapons failure not quickly remedied. Even the SB2C "Beast" was tamed and, after the Battle of the Philippine Sea, was passionately defended by Lieutenant Commander J. D. Blitch, skipper of *Wasp's* Bombing 14. "Overall operation," Blitch wrote, "of the SB2C-1C and SB2C-3 airplanes in combat has been excellent." Good maintenance in his squadron, he insisted, had ended the problem of engine loss of power on takeoff. The plane was steady in a dive, could stand the stress of 9-G pullouts, and with wing tanks could operate with bombs to a 400-mile radius. With wing *and* belly tanks, Blitch insisted, "the scouting radius can safely be assumed to be about 650 miles." In the Curtiss, Blitch was convinced, Admiral Mitscher had a solution to the problem of long-range scouting from a carrier deck.

Yet the Battle of the Philippine Sea presaged the demise of the dive bomber as a weapon in both the American and Japanese navies. The Japanese had found that the bomb-carrying Zero had better range than even the fast Judy and could more easily penetrate enemy defenses. The Americans had found that the Hellcat could carry a bomb farther and dive-bomb as accurately as a Helldiver. But except when used by Admiral Nagumo's veterans, the dive bomber had not been very accurate. It remains a mystery, then, why the U. S. Navy did not early adopt skip-bombing by Hellcats. Had these fine airplanes used this tactic in the Philippine Sea a dozen or more of Ozawa's ships might have been sunk or crippled.

Finally, throughout World War II American antiaircraft fire was vastly more effective than Japanese. Persistent effort finally paid off in the perfection of radar fire control, negating the mask of darkness. Combined with the VT proximity fuse it converted the threat of night-flying Betty torpedo planes from a grave danger into a nuisance.

More than two years of experimentation and naval construction finally had enabled Admiral Nimitz in late 1943 and early 1944 to perfect the carrier task force in the form of TF 58. He had massed his fast carriers, had placed in charge an airmen's airman, and had made proper use of the naval principle of concentration of force in strategy. The Japanese had started the war with the correct use of this principle at Pearl Harbor, had continued it during the "grand tour" of Nagumo's carriers in the war's opening months, then had abandoned it in losing the Battles of the Coral Sea and Midway. Only twice more did they properly use it, first in the Battle of

Santa Cruz and then in the Philippine Sea, where it was invalidated by American naval air supremacy.

The aircraft carrier task force had been born in the strike of H. M. S. *Furious* against a pair of German airship sheds in World War I. It had been developed into a usable and effective weapon in both the Japanese and American navies in the 1920s and 1930s. It had emerged full-blown in its most awesome form at Pearl Harbor, had faded as both sides lost carriers, then had re-emerged in Mitscher's overwhelming powerful Task Force 58. Today one may see it again in San Diego harbor in the form of a new U. S. S. *Enterprise*, a nuclear-powered, jet-plane-equipped flattop of 90,000 tons—a carrier task force in itself. In both the Korean and Vietnam wars the carrier task force was used as in World War II to bring effective attack power on specific land targets.

To see carrier air power as it was between 1941 and 1945, one today must go to Pensacola. Stopping at the Naval Air Museum there, one can view and touch a Wildcat, a Hellcat, and an Avenger. In the nearby bay he can view the Lady *Lex*, now a training carrier, but still the same ship, CV-16, that fought in the Battle of the Philippine Sea. If the day is right and broken clouds are scuttling low overhead at 2,000 feet, in his mind's eye one can see passing overhead Air Group 16 with Commander Ernie Snowden in the lead, followed by the Hellcats, Dauntlesses, and Avengers of his fighting, bombing, and torpedo squadrons. Or, imagining still more, he can look at the *Lex* again and see her become transformed into a longer, more massive flattop, with huge funnel and island and with paired eight-inch turrets fore and aft. Glancing up, one can see the chubby little Wildcats of VF-2, followed by SBD-3s and ungainly TBD Devastators. But deep thunder from the nearby airfield and the boom of cut-in after-burners brings one to reality. An F4H Phantom is taking off to tilt almost vertically and climb out of sight in a moment, a reminder that more than 30 years have passed since that eventful day in the Coral Sea. The old *Lex*, CV-2, is but a memory.

Sources

Chapter 1. Pearl Harbor

Documentary sources, American

After-action reports. Commander, Aircraft Battle Force (W. F. Halsey) on operations December 7–8, 1941. U. S. S. *Enterprise,* December 7–8, 1941. U. S. S. *Northampton,* "Engagement between enemy and *Northampton* aircraft, December 7, 1941."

U. S. Congress, Congressional Investigation of Pearl Harbor Attack, *Hearings,* Parts 13 and 22.

Documentary sources, Japanese

International Military Tribunal, Far East, Exhibit No. 1127(a), Interrogation of Admiral Nagano.

Japanese Monograph No. 113, *Task Force Operations* (covers operations of First Air Fleet from November 1941 to April 1942). Japanese Monograph No. 97, *Pearl Harbor Operations.* These and all other Japanese monographs listed below were prepared for U. S. occupation forces, Japan.

U. S. Strategic Bombing Survey, Pacific, Naval Analysis Division, *The Campaigns of the Pacific War* (1946), and *Interrogations of Japanese Officials* (2 vols., 1946). See interrogations of Minoru Genda, Mitsuo Fuchida, Kintaro Miura, and Y. Watanabe.

Books

Barker, A. J., *Pearl Harbor* (New York, 1969). Ballantine series on World War II.

Burns, Eugene, *Then There Was One: The U. S. S. Enterprise and the First Year of the War* (New York, 1944).

Caidin, Martin, *The Ragged Rugged Warriors* (New York, 1966).

Coffey, Thomas M., *Imperial Tragedy* (New York, 1970).

Dickinson, Clarence, *The Flying Guns* (New York, 1942).

Fuchida, Mitsuo, and Masatake Okumiya, edited by Clarke H. Kawakami and Roger Pineau, *Midway: the Battle That Doomed Japan* (Annapolis, 1955).

Halsey, Fleet Admiral William F., *Admiral Halsey's Story* (New York, 1947).

Haugland, Vern, *The AAF Against Japan* (New York, 1948).

Karig, Walter, and Wellbourn Kelley, *Battle Report: Pearl Harbor to Coral Sea* (New York, 1944).

Morison, Samuel Eliot, *History of United States Naval Operations in World War II,* Vol. 3, *The Rising Sun in the Pacific* (Boston, 1948).

Okumiya, Masatake, and Jiro Horikoshi with Martin Caidin, *Zero!* (New York, 1956).

Potter, John Deane, *Yamamoto* (New York, 1970).

Reports of General MacArthur. Japanese Operations in the Southwest Pacific Area, Vol. 2, Part 1 (Washington, D.C., 1966). This is the so-called "MacArthur History" published originally by the U. S. Army, Far East Command.

Sakamaki, Kazuo, *I Attacked Pearl Harbor* (New York, 1949).

Sherrod, R., *History of Marine Corps Aviation in World War II* (Washington, D.C., 1952).

Toland, John, *The Rising Sun* (New York, 1970).

Wallin, Vice Admiral Homer N., USN (ret.), *Pearl Harbor Why, How, and Final Appraisal* (Washington, D.C., 1968).

Articles

Fuchida, Mitsuo, "I Led the Air Attack on Pearl Harbor," U. S. Naval Institute, *Proceedings,* September 1952.

Fukudome, Vice Admiral Shigeru, "Hawaii Operation," U. S. Naval Institute, *Proceedings,* December 1955.

Ward, Robert E., "The Inside Story of the Pearl Harbor Plan," U. S. Naval Institute, *Proceedings,* December 1951.

"Pearl Harbor," Part 25 of *History of the Second World War,* BPC Publishing (1973).

Chapters 2 and 3. Sticks, Wires, and Former Battle Cruisers; American, Japanese, and British Naval Air Power

Documentary sources, American

U. S. Navy, Deputy Chief of Naval Operations (Air), Naval Aviation History Office, *Monographs on the History of Naval Aviation, 1898–1939,* 16 vols., Clifford L. Lord, *The History of Naval Aviation, 1898–1939* (1946).

Documentary sources, Japanese

Japanese Monographs No. 118, *Operational History of Naval Communications,* Nos. 146, 149, and 160, *Outline of Naval Armament and Preparations for War,* Parts I, II, and III, No. 166, *History of Naval Air Operations, First Phase, China Incident, July–November 1937.*

Books

Aireview, *General View of Japanese Military Aircraft in the Pacific War* (3rd rev. ed., Tokyo, 1958).

Aireview, *Fifty Years of Japanese Aviation, 1910–1960* (Tokyo, 1961).

Bowers, Peter M., *Boeing Aircraft Since 1916* (New York, 1968).

Brown, J. D., *Carrier Operations in World War II* (London, 1968).

Bueschel, Richard M., *Mitsubishi A6M1/2/2N Zero-Sen in Japanese Naval Service,* Arco-Aircam Aviation Series No. 18 (New York, 1970).

Caidin, Martin, *Zero Fighter* (New York, 1969).

Cameron, Ian, *Wings of the Morning: The Story of the Fleet Air Arm in the Second World War* (London, 1962).

Douglas Aircraft Company, *Service Information Summary, 50th Naval Anniversary* (El Segundo, California, 1962).

Fahey, James C., *Ships and Aircraft of the United States Fleet,* Victory edition (Washington, D.C., 1945).

Francillon, R. J., *Japanese Aircraft of the Pacific War* (New York, 1970).

Green, William, *Warplanes of the Second World War,* 9 vols. (Garden City, 1960–67).

Jameson, Sir William S., *Ark Royal* (London, 1957).

Jane's All the World's Aircraft, 1919–1946 eds. (London, 1919–1946).

Jane's Fighting Ships, 1919–1944/5 eds. (London, 1919–1945).

Kemp, P. K., *Fleet Air Arm* (London, 1954).

MacDonald, Scot, *Evolution of Aircraft Carriers* (Washington, D.C., 1964). Issued by Office of the Chief of Naval Operations, U. S. Department of the Navy. Originally appeared as series of articles in *Naval Aviation News.*

Macintyre, Donald, *Aircraft Carrier: the Majestic Weapon* (New York, 1968).

Mehorn, Charles Mason, *Lever for Rearmament: the Rise of the Carrier.* Unpublished doctoral dissertation, University of California, San Diego (1973).

Miller, Lieutenant Harold Blane, USN, *Navy Wings* (rev. ed., New York, 1942).

Mizrahi, J. V., *U. S. Navy Carrier Fighters* (Northridge, California, 1969) and *U. S. Navy Dive and Torpedo Bombers* (Northridge, California, 1967).

Newton, Don, and A. Cecil Hampshire, *Taranto* (London, 1959).

Polmar, Norman, *Aircraft Carriers* (Garden City, 1969).

Potter, E. B., and C. W. Nimitz, eds., *The Great Sea War* (Englewood Cliffs, 1960) and *Sea Power* (Englewood Cliffs, 1960).

Reynolds, Clark G., *The Fast Carriers: The Forging of an Air Navy* (New York, 1968). Focuses on command relationships.

Roskill, S. W., *The War at Sea, 1939–1945,* 3 vols. (London, 1954–1961).

Schofield, Vice Admiral B. B., *The Attack on Taranto* (London, 1973).

Skiera, Joseph A., *Aircraft Carriers in Peace and War* (New York, 1964).

Swanborough, F. G., and P. M. Bowers, *United States Navy Aircraft Since 1911* (New York and London, 1968).

Turnbull, Archibald D., and Clifford L. Lord, *History of United States Naval Aviation* (New Haven, 1949). Official history based on Lord monograph above. Sketchy on period of 1930s.

United States Naval Aviation, 1910–1970 (Washington, D.C., 1970). A chronology issued by U. S. Navy, Deputy Chief of Naval Operations (Air) and Naval Systems Air Command.

Watts, A. J., *Japanese Warships of World War II* (Garden City, 1966).

Watts, A. J., and B. G. Gordon, *The Imperial Japanese Navy* (Garden City, 1971).

Wilson, Eugene, *Slipstream* (New York, 1950).

Articles

Fukaya, Hajime, "The *Shokakus:* Pearl Harbor to Leyte Gulf," and "Japan's Wartime Carrier Construction," U. S. Naval Institute, *Proceedings,* June 1952 and September 1955.

Genda, General Minoru, JSDF (ret.), "Tactical Planning in the Imperial Japanese Navy," *Naval War College Review,* October 1969. Also "Evolution of Aircraft Carrier Tactics of the Imperial Japanese Navy," unpublished Ms.

Jordan, D. S., "Fisher's Folly: The Fabulous *Furious,*" U. S. Naval Institute, *Proceedings,* June 1955.

O'Hara, Robert, "H. M. S. *Furious:* the First Aircraft Carrier," *Sea Classics,* January 1969.

Robinson, Waltron L., "Akagi," U. S. Naval Institute, *Proceedings,* May 1948.

Stokes, Sergeant C. Ray, and Sergeant Tad Darling, USMC, "Yokosuka Naval Air Base and Japanese Naval Aviation," U. S. Naval Institute, *Proceedings,* March 1948.

Tate, Rear Admiral J. R., USN (ret.), "Covered Wagon Days" and "The Cinderella Ships," *Naval Aviation News,* December 1970 and March 1972. Story of the old *Langley, Lexington,* and *Saratoga.*

Newspaper

The New York Times, files.

Chapter 4. Sledgehammer at Rabaul

Documentary sources

See Japanese Monograph No. 113, *Task Force Operations,* cited above. Also Japanese Monograph No. 107, *Malaya Invasion Naval Operations,* revised edition.

Interrogations of Mitsuo Fuchida and Captain Kameo Sonokawa in USSBS, *Interrogations of Japanese Officials.*

"The Southern Cross," diary of seaman Iki Kuramoti of *Akagi,* U. S. Congress, Pearl Harbor Attack, *Hearings,* Pt. 13.

Books

See Roskill, *War at Sea,* Vol. I, for official British account of loss of *Repulse* and *Prince of Wales.* Also Ash, Bernard, *Someone Had Blundered: The Story of the Repulse and the Prince of Wales* (Garden City, 1960).

Bennett, Geoffrey, *The Loss of the Prince of Wales and Repulse* (Annapolis, 1973).

Churchill, Sir Winston, *The Grand Alliance* (Boston, 1950).

Gillison, Douglas, *Royal Australian Air Force 1939–1942* (Canberra, 1962).

Grenfell, Russell, *Main Fleet to Singapore* (London, 1951).

Article

Mason, David, "Japanese Victory: the Sinking of Force Z," in Part 26 of *History of the Second World War,* BPC Publishing (1973).

Chapter 5. Riposte in the Marshalls

Documentary sources, American

After-action reports. Commanders Task Force 8 (Halsey) and Task Force 17 (Fletcher). U. S. S. *Enterprise* and U. S. S. *Yorktown.*

War diaries of *Enterprise, Yorktown, Lexington,* and *Saratoga* for period December 7, 1941–February 5, 1942.

Documentary sources, Japanese

After-action report. Report on Marshalls raid by Japanese 6th Fleet, WDC translation 160268.

Japanese Monographs No. 102, *Submarine Operations,* December 1941–April 1942, No. 116, *The Imperial Japanese Navy in World War II . . . ,* Part VIII, *Monthly Losses of Combatant and Non-Combatant Vessels,* December 1941–August 1945, No. 161, *Inner South Seas Islands Area Operations,* Part I, *Gilbert Islands,* No. 173, *Inner South Seas Area Naval Operations,* Part II, *Marshall Islands.*

Joint Army-Navy Assessment Committee, *Japanese Naval and Merchant Shipping Losses During World War II by All Causes* (1947). The authors have used this document and Monograph 116 above to establish Japanese losses in this volume.

Books

See works of Burns, Dickinson, Halsey, and Morison cited above. Also Stafford, E. P., *The Big E* (New York, 1962).

Articles

Riley, William A., "The Chiefs of Fighting Two," and James V. Sanders, "The Brewsters of Fighting Two," in American Aviation Historical Society, *Journal,* Vol. 14, No. 3, 3rd quarter, 1969.

Wilds, Thomas, "How Japan Fortified the Islands," U. S. Naval Institute, *Proceedings,* April 1955.

Newspaper

Osaka Mainichi, files.

Chapter 6. Darwin, Marcus, New Guinea

Documentary sources, American

After-action reports. Of U. S. S. *Enterprise, Lexington,* and *Yorktown.*
Deputy Chief of Naval Operations (Air), *Essays in the History of Naval Air Operations,* Vol. I, *Carrier Warfare.* Also DCNO (Air), *Aircraft Availability in Early Carrier Raids—Pacific.*

Documentary sources, Japanese

Japanese Monographs No. 113, *Task Force Operations,* and No. 101, *Naval Operations in the Invasion of the Netherlands East Indies.*
Diary of Air Warrant Officer Kumesaka Nemoto, seaplane tender *Kiyokawa Maru,* U. S. Navy translation.

Books

See Gillison, *Royal Australian Air Force,* cited above. Also Edmonds, Walter D., *They Fought With What They Had* (Boston, 1951).
Lockwood, Douglas, *Australia's Pearl Harbour, 1942* (Melbourne, 1966).

Chapter 7. Ceylon and Tokyo

Documentary sources, American

After-action report. Commander Task Force 16 (Halsey) on Tokyo raid, April 28, 1942.
Bureau of Aeronautics, U. S. Navy. Interview with Lieutenant Commander John S. Thach, commander, VF-3, August 26, 1942.

Documentary sources, Japanese

Japanese Monographs No. 113, *Task Force Operations,* No. 109, *Homeland Defense Naval Operations,* Part I, No. 120, *Southeast Area Naval Air Operations,* Part I.
After-action report. Battle Report No. 9 of *Hiryu, Indian Ocean Maneuvers,* WDC translation 160467.
Kuramoti, "The Southern Cross," cited above.

Books

Griffin, A. R., *A Ship to Remember: the Saga of the Hornet* (New York, 1943).
Jackson, Robert, *Strike from the Sea: A Survey of British Naval Air Operations* (London, 1970).
Merrill, James M., *Target Tokyo* (Chicago, 1964).

Popham, Hugh, *Sea Flight: A Fleet Air Arm Pilot's Story* (London, 1954).

Roskill, Captain S. W., *The War at Sea, 1939–1945,* Vol. II, *The Period of Balance* (London, 1956).

Russell, Wing Commander W. W., *Forgotten Skies: The Story of the Air Forces in India and Burma* (London, 1945).

Sherman, F. C., *Combat Command* (New York, 1950).

Articles

Elsegood, A. G., "The Epic of the *Dorsetshire*," *Dorset Year Book,* No. 39 (1945–46).

Thach, Lieutenant Commander John S., "The Red Rain of Battle," in Maude Owens Walters, ed., *Combat in the Air* (1944).

Chapter 8. The Coral Sea

Documentary sources, American

After-action reports. Of Commander Task Force 17 (Fletcher), *Lexington,* and *Yorktown,* plus supporting ships.

Naval War College, *The Battle of the Coral Sea, Strategical and Tactical Analysis* (1947).

Office of the Chief of Naval Operations, report of interview party empaneled to investigate loss of U. S. S. *Lexington.*

Documentary sources, Japanese

After-action reports. *Records of Aircraft Carrier Operations,* WDC translation 160677. War Diary of the *Shoho,* WDC 160465. War Diary of the 25th Air Flotilla, April–May 11, 1942, WDC translation 161725.

Diary of Kumesaka Nemoto, *Kiyokawa Maru. Battle of the Coral Sea According to the Notebook of Ensign Toshio Nakamura,* JINCPOA item no. 4986.

Japanese Monographs No. 120, *Southeast Area Naval Air Operations,* Part I, and 96, *Eastern New Guinea Invasion Operations.*

Interrogations of Tadaichi Hara, Kikunori Kijima, Keizo Komura, Takeo Kurita, Kintaro Miura, Takashi Miyazaki, T. Ohmae, Toshitane Takata, M. Yamioka, and Y. Watanabe in USSBS, *Interrogations of Japanese Officials.*

USSBS, *Campaigns of the Pacific War.*

Books

See Fuchida and Okumiya, *Midway,* cited above.

Barker, A. J., *Midway: The Turning Point* (New York, 1971).

Hoehling, A. A., *The Lexington Goes Down: the Last Seven Hours of a Fighting Lady* (Englewood Cliffs, 1971).

Johnson, Stanley, *Queen of the Flattops* (New York, 1942).

Kahn, David, *The Code-Breakers* (New York, 1967).

Karig, Walter, and Eric Purdon, *Battle Report: Pacific War Middle Phase* (New York, 1947).

Lord, Walter, *Incredible Victory* (New York, 1967).

Morison, S. E., *History of United States Naval Operations in World War II*, Vol. 4, *Coral Sea, Midway and Submarine Actions* (Boston, 1949).

Newspaper

Osaka Mainichi, article by Navy reporter Amefugi, June 16, 1942.

Chapters 9 and 10. Midway: The Battle Joined; Midway: Climax and Pursuit

Documentary sources, American

After-action reports. Task Force 16 (Spruance) and 17 (Fletcher), commander-in-chief, Pacific Fleet (Nimitz), *Enterprise, Hornet, Yorktown,* and attached ships, Commanding Officer (C. T. Simard) of U. S. Naval Air Station, Midway Island, Marine Air Group 22. Also see Lieutenant Robert E. Laub, "Torpedo Plane Operations in the Air Battle of Midway," and Ensign George H. Gay, Torpedo Squadron Eight, "Personal Account of Attacks on Japanese Carriers, June 4, 1942."

Deputy Chief of Naval Operations (Air), Naval Air History Unit, *Battle of Midway Island, A Résumé . . . Prepared by the Fighter Director School, Navy Yard, Pearl Harbor,* April 3, 1943. Also see by this office Lieutenant William L. Bryant and Lieutenant Heith I. Herman, *Essays in the History of Naval Air Operations . . . History of Naval Fighter Direction.*

Bureau of Aeronautics, interview with Rear Admiral George D. Murray, November 25, 1942.

Division of Naval History, *War Record of VF-6,* Captain James S. Gray, *Decision at Midway,* and Rear Admiral C. C. Ray, *Personal Recollections of Certain Events of the Battle of Midway.*

Naval War College, *The Battle of Midway: Strategical and Tactical Analysis* (1947).

Documentary sources, Japanese

Report of Commander, First Air Fleet (Nagumo) *Midway Operation,* June 15, 1942. This document has been translated and reprinted in full in Office of Naval Intelligence, U. S. Navy, *ONI Review,* June 1947.

Japanese Monographs No. 93, *Midway Operations,* and No. 88, *Aleutian Naval Operations.*

Action reports of *Akagi, Kaga, Soryu, Hiryu* translated and published by Office of Naval Intelligence, U. S. Navy.

Interrogations of Tarijiro Aoki, Susumu Kawaguchi, H. Ohara, M. Okumiya, Akira Soji, and T. Takata, USSBS, *Interrogations of Japanese Officials.*

Interrogations of prisoners of war from *Hiryu* and *Mikuma,* Office of Naval Intelligence, U. S. Navy.

Books

See works of Barker, Fuchida and Okumiya, Karig, Lord, and Morison listed in sources for Chapter 8. Also Dickinson, *Flying Guns,* listed in sources for Chapter 1. Also Forrestel, E. P., *Admiral Raymond A. Spruance, USN, A Study in Command* (Washington, D.C., 1966).

Frank, Pat, and J. D. Harrington, *Rendezvous at Midway* (New York, 1967).

Mears, Lieutenant Frederick, USNR, *Carrier Combat* (New York, 1944).

Smith, Vice Admiral William W. ("Poco"), *Midway: Turning Point of the Pacific* (New York, 1966).

Tuleja, Thaddeus V., *Climax at Midway* (New York, 1960).

Werstein, Irving, *The Battle of Midway* (New York, 1961).

Articles

Ainsworth, Michael, "The Rising Sun at Midway . . . ," *Sea Classics,* March 1970.

Morison, S. E., "Two Minutes That Changed the Pacific War," *New York Times Magazine,* June 1, 1952.

Prange, Gordon W., "Miracle at Midway," *Reader's Digest,* November 1972. Condensation of a forthcoming book.

Tillman, Barrett, " 'Go in and get a hit!' " *Airpower,* July 1973.

Van Wyen, Adrian O., "In Retrospect: the Battle of Midway," *Naval Aviation News,* June 1962.

Newspaper

Osaka Mainichi, files, June–July 1942.

Chapter 11. The Eastern Solomons

Documentary sources, American

After-action reports. Of Commander, Pacific Fleet (Nimitz), of Task Force 11 (Fletcher), of *Enterprise, Saratoga,* and *Wasp,* plus supporting ships of screens. Also see war diaries of these ships.

Office of Naval Records and History. Narratives of Lieutenant Commander Louis J. Kirn, Commander E. B. Mott, and George W. Polk.

Documentary sources, Japanese

Japanese Monographs No. 98, *Southeast Area Naval Operations,* Part I, and No. 122, *Southeast Area Naval Air Operations,* Part II.

USSBS, *Campaigns of the Pacific War.*

Outline of Citations for Naval Units in Greater East Asia War, WDC translation 161709. See for carriers *Ryujo, Shokaku,* and *Zuikaku* and CVS *Chitose.* Not action reports as such, these summaries were prepared to support individual citations of meritorious service. Useful for Midway battle and other carrier actions as well.

Books

See works of Burns, Stafford, and Sherrod, cited above. Also De Chant, John A., *Devilbirds* (New York, 1947).

Griffith, Samuel B., *The Battle for Guadalcanal* (New York, 1963).

Hara, Captain Tameichi, *Japanese Destroyer Captain* (New York, 1961).

Hough, F. O., V. E. Ludwig, and H. I. Shaw, Jr., *History of United States Marine Corps Operations in World War II*, Vol. I, *Pearl Harbor to Guadalcanal*. Published by Historical Branch, H.Q., U. S. Marine Corps, Washington, D.C., n.d.

Miller, Thomas G., *The Cactus Air Force* (New York, 1969).

Morison, S. E., *History of United States Naval Operations in World War II*, Vol. 5, *The Struggle for Guadalcanal* (Boston, 1949).

Sakai, Saburo, with Martin Caidin and Fred Saito, *Samurai* (New York, 1957).

Toland, John, *The Rising Sun* (New York, 1970).

Zimmerman, Major John L., *The Guadalcanal Campaign* (Washington, D.C., 1949). Monograph published by Historical Division, H.Q., U. S. Marine Corps.

Article

Macintyre, Captain Donald, "Guadalcanal: The Sea Battles," in Part 40 of *History of the Second World War*, BPC Publishing (1974).

Chapters 12 and 13. Santa Cruz; "Then There Was One"

Note: The sources listed for Chapter 11 apply also to these chapters.

Documentary sources, American

After-action reports. Commander Pacific Fleet (Nimitz), Commander South Pacific Area and South Pacific Force (Halsey), Commander TF 61 (Kinkaid), Commander TF 17 (Murray), *Hornet, Enterprise, South Dakota, Smith, Portland* and other ships of TF 61. Also see war diaries of these ships.

Bureau of Aeronautics, interview with Rear Admiral George D. Murray, November 25, 1942.

Office of Naval Records and History, narrative of Lieutenant Robin Lindsey, Landing Signal Officer, U. S. S. *Enterprise,* September 17, 1943.

Documentary sources, Japanese

After-action reports. Cruiser Division 8, WDC translation 161270, Destroyer Division 10, WDC translation 160985.

Campaigns of the Pacific War, USSBS.

Interrogations of Kikunori Kijima, Keizo Komura, and Yasumi Toyama, *Interrogations of Japanese Officials,* USSBS.

Books

Okumiya and Horikoshi, *Zero,* previously cited.

Chapter 14. Finale at Guadalcanal

Documentary sources, American

After-action reports. U. S. S. *Enterprise,* U. S. S. *Washington,* U. S. S. *South Dakota,* and escorting ships. Also see war diaries of these vessels.

Documentary sources, Japanese

After-action report. Carrier *Junyo,* WDC translation 171709.
Campaigns of the Pacific War, USSBS.
Interrogations of T. Ohmae, Horishi Tokuno, Tadashi Yamamoto, and S. Yunoki, *Interrogations of Japanese Officials,* USSBS.
Japanese Monographs No. 98, *Southeast Area Naval Operations,* Part I, and 122, *Southeast Area Naval Air Operations,* Part III.

Books

See cited above works of Miller, Morison, *Struggle for Guadalcanal,* Potter and Nimitz, *Great Sea War.* Also Bulkley, John J., Jr., *At Close Quarters: PT Boats in the United States Navy* (Washington, D.C., 1962).

Articles

Macintyre, Captain Donald, "Guadalcanal: the Final Actions," in Part 46 of *History of the Second World War,* BPC Publishing (1974).
Tanaka, Raizo, "The Struggle for Guadalcanal," and Toshikazu Ohmae, "The Battle of Savo Island," in U. S. Naval Institute, *The Japanese Navy in World War II* (1969).

Chapter 15. New Georgia and Points North

Documentary sources, American

War diaries of U. S. S. *Saratoga* and U. S. S. *Enterprise.*

Documentary sources, Japanese

Japanese Monographs Nos. 98, 99, and 100. *Southeast Area Naval Operations,* Parts I, II, and III, No. 122, *Southeast Area Naval Air Operations,* Part III.
Campaigns of the Pacific War, USSBS.

Books

See already cited Karig *et. al., Battle Report: Pacific War Middle Phase,* and Potter and Nimitz, *The Great Sea War.*

Davis, Burke, *Get Yamamoto* (New York, 1969).

Morison, S. E., *History of United States Naval Operations in World War II,* Vol. VI, *Breaking the Bismarcks Barrier* (Boston, 1950).

Potter, John Deane, *Yamamoto* (New York, 1965).

Pratt, Fletcher, *Night Work: the Story of Task Force 39* (New York, 1946).

Article

Wible, John T., "The Yamamoto Mission," American Aviation Historical Society, *Journal,* Vol. 12, No. 3, 3rd Quarter, 1967.

Chapter 16. The New Fast Carriers

Documentary sources, American

War diaries of following new carriers from dates of commissioning to commencement of combat service: *Bataan, Belleau Wood, Bunker Hill, Cowpens, Essex, Independence, Intrepid, Lexington* (CV-16), *Hornet* (CV-12), *Wasp* (CV-18), *Yorktown* (CV-10).

Cruise books of *Belleau Wood, Saratoga, Independence, Essex,* and *Bunker Hill* (informal records written for ships' crews).

Documentary sources, Japanese

Japanese Monographs Nos. 160, 169, 172, and 174, *Outline of Naval Armament and Preparations for War,* Parts III, IV, V, and VI.

Log of Japanese carrier movements, July 1942–1945, WDC translation 160677. Records arrivals and departures of all carriers with some important gaps. Records also commissionings of new and converted carriers.

U. S. Strategic Bombing Survey, Pacific War, Report No. 53, *The Effects of Strategic Bombing on Japan's War Economy,* Table 8, "Aircraft and Engine Production, Fiscal Years 1942–1944."

Books

See already cited under Chapters 2 and 3 works by Fahey, Francillon, Fukaya article, "Japan's Wartime Carrier Construction," MacDonald, Macintyre, Polmar, Watts, and Watts and Gordon. Also Bryan, Joseph, *Aircraft Carrier* (New York, 1954).

Francillon, Rene J., *Japanese Navy Bombers of World War II* (Garden City, 1969).

Olds, Robert, *Helldiver Squadron: The Story of Bombing Squadron 17 with Task Force 58* (New York, 1944).

Pawlowski, G. L., *Flattops and Fledglings* (South Brunswick, 1969).
Profile Publications No. 124. *The Curtiss SB2C Helldiver*, n.p., n.d.

Chapter 17. "Makee Learn"

Documentary sources, American

After-action reports. Commander TF 15 (Pownall) for attacks on Marcus,
August 31, 1943, and Tarawa, September 18, 1943. U. S. S. *Belleau Wood,
Lexington,* and *Princeton,* for Tarawa attack. U. S. S. *Essex, Independence* and
Yorktown for Marcus attack. Commander TF 14 (Montgomery) for raid on
Wake Island, October 4–5, 1943. U. S. S. *Essex, Yorktown, Lexington, In-
dependence, Cowpens, Belleau Wood* for Wake attack.

Pacific Fleet. *Notes on a Conference held in Admiral Towers' Office,*
Monday, August 10, 1943.

U. S. Office of the Secretary of Defense. Weapons Systems Evaluation
Study Group No. 4, *Operational Experience of Fast Carrier Task Forces,*
August 15, 1951.

U. S. Strategic Bombing Survey, Pacific, *The Reduction of Wake Island.*

Documentary sources, Japanese

Japanese Monographs No. 99, *Southeast Area Naval Operations,* Part II,
No. 127, *Southeast Area Operations Record [Japanese Army],* Part IV, Novem-
ber 1942–August 1945, No. 140, *Outline of Southeast Area Naval Air Opera-
tions,* Part IV, July–November 1943, No. 161, *Inner South Sea Islands Area
Naval Operations,* Part I, *Gilbert Islands,* No. 173, *Inner South Seas Area
Naval Operations,* Part II, *Marshall Islands.*

Books

See already cited Morison, *Breaking the Bismarcks Barrier,* and Reynolds,
Fast Carriers. Also Clark, J. J. "Jocko," and Clark G. Reynolds, *Carrier Admiral* (New York, 1967).

Article

Wilds, Thomas, "The Admiral Who Lost His Fleet [Koga]," U. S. Naval
Institute, *Proceedings,* November 1951.

Chapter 18. Rabaul Interlude

Documentary sources, American

After-action reports. Commander Task Force 38 (Sherman) of Rabaul
strike, November 5, 1943. Commander Task Force 50.3 of Rabaul strike November 11, 1943, U. S. S. *Saratoga* and *Princeton, Independence, Essex,* and

Bunker Hill of Rabaul strikes, Commander Fighting Squadron 17 (Lieutenant Commander J. T. Blackburn) of action on November 11, 1943.

U. S. Strategic Bombing Survey, Pacific, *The Allied Campaign Against Rabaul.*

Documentary sources, Japanese

After-action report. 751st Naval Air Group, WDC translation 161634.
Diary of Japanese airman stationed Rabaul, ATIS CT 122.
Japanese Monograph Nos. 100 and 127, *Southeast Area Naval Operations,* Parts II and III, 140, *Outline of Southeast Area Naval Air Operations,* Part IV.
Interrogation of Tsuneo Shiki, USSBS, *Interrogations of Japanese Officials.*
USSBS, *Campaigns of the Pacific War.*

Books

See cited above Hara, *Japanese Destroyer Captain,* and Morison, *Breaking the Bismarcks Barrier.*

Article

Burns, Eugene, "We Avenge Pearl Harbor," *Saturday Evening Post,* July 22, 1944.

Chapter 19.   Tarawa and Makin

Documentary sources, American

After-action reports. Commander Task Forces 50.1 (Pownall), 50.2 (Radford), 50.3 (Montgomery), 50.4 (Sherman), U. S. S. *Saratoga, Princeton, Essex, Belleau Wood, Independence, Enterprise, Yorktown,* and *Lexington.*

Documentary sources, Japanese

Action reports of 24th Air Flotilla and 755th Naval Air Group (Roi).
Diary of Takizawa, eyewitness of Taroa attack, January 3–4, 1944.
Japanese Monographs No. 100, *Southeast Area Naval Operations,* Part III, Nos. 161 and 173, *Inner South Sea Islands Area Naval Operations,* Parts I and II.
Log of Japanese carrier movements, WDC translation 160677.
Campaigns of the Pacific War, USSBS.
Interrogations of G. Matsura, C. Nakajima, S. Nabeshima, and Hiroshi Tokuno, USSBS, *Interrogations of Japanese Officials.*

Books

See Clark and Reynolds, *Carrier Admiral,* Morison, *Aleutians, Gilberts and Marshalls,* and Potter and Nimitz, *Great Sea War.* Also Karig, Captain Walter, *et. al., Battle Report: The End of an Empire* (New York, 1948).

Article

Trousdale, Lieutenant Commander James H., Jr., "The Birth of the Navy's Night Fighters," U. S. Naval Institute, *Proceedings,* June 1952.

Chapter 20. The Marshalls and Truk

Documentary sources, American

After-action reports. Commander, Task Force 58 (Mitscher) on Marshalls operation and Truk raid. Commanders, Task Groups 58.1 (Reeves), 58.2 (Montgomery), 58.3 (Sherman), and 58.4 (Ginder) on Marshalls operation and Truk raid. *Intrepid, Monterey, Bunker Hill, Enterprise,* and *Yorktown.*

U. S. Strategic Bombing Survey, Pacific, Report No. 77, *The Reduction of Truk.*

U. S. Navy, Pacific Fleet, Vice Admiral Mitscher to Vice Admiral Towers, *Report of Night Radar Minimum Altitude Bombing Attack on Enemy Shipping in Truk Atoll, March 8, 1944.*

Documentary sources, Japanese

After-action report. *War Records and Battle Reports of the 101st Air Base,* December 1, 1943–March 10, 1944.

Diary of Second Lieutenant Kakino, 1st Amphibious Brigade, Eniwetok, Jincpoa translation, March 10, 1944.

Interrogations of Chikataka, Nakajima and Mitsuo Fuchida, USSBS, *Interrogations of Japanese Officials.*

USSBS, *Campaigns of the Pacific War.*

Japanese Monograph No. 173, *Inner South Seas Area Naval Operations,* Part II, *The Marshalls.*

Books

See Karig *et. al., Battle Report: End of an Empire,* Morison, *Aleutians, Gilberts,* and *Marshalls,* Potter and Nimitz, *The Great Sea War,* Reynolds, *Fast Carriers,* and Taylor, *Magnificent Mitscher.* Also Boyington, Major Gregory ("Pappy"), USMCR, *Baa Baa Black Sheep* (New York, 1958).

Winston, Commander Robert A., USN, *Fighter Squadron* (New York, 1946).

Jensen, O. O., *Carrier War* (New York, 1945).

Articles

See already cited Wilds, "The Admiral Who Lost His Fleet."

Gulliver, Louis J., "Truk in the Carolines," U. S. Naval Institute, *Proceedings,* December 1943.

Chapter 21. The Carolines and Hollandia

Documentary sources, American

Action reports. Commander TF 58 (Mitscher) on Palau & Hollandia operations and second Truk raid. *Bataan, Belleau Wood, Bunker Hill, Cabot, Cowpens, Hornet, Enterprise, Langley, Lexington, Princeton,* and *Yorktown* on same operations. Commander, U. S. S. *Tang* (Richard H. O'Kane), on lifeguard mission in support of 2nd Truk raid, Commanders TG 58.1 (Reeves), 58.2 (Montgomery), and 58.3 (Ginder) on above operations.

Cruise book, U. S. S. *Saratoga.*

War diary, U. S. S. *Saratoga.*

Documentary Sources, Japanese

Interrogations of Takao Suzuki, 751st Air Group, and Sumitaka Sakaguchi, 761st Air Group, Joint Intelligence Center, Pacific Ocean Areas.

Japanese Monographs No. 112, *Southeast Area Naval Operations,* Part IV, February–April 1944, and No. 142, *Outline of Southeast Area Naval Air Operations,* Part V, December 1943–May 1944.

Campaigns of the Pacific War, USSBS.

Books

See already cited Clark and Reynolds, *Carrier Admiral,* Karig *et. al., Battle Reports: The End of an Empire,* Potter and Nimitz, *Great Sea War,* and Taylor, *Magnificent Mitscher.* Also Morison, Samuel Eliot, *History of United States Naval Operations in World War II,* Vol. VIII, *New Guinea and the Marianas* (Boston, 1953).

Article

See previously cited Wilds, "The Admiral Who Lost His Fleet." Also Reynolds, Clark G., "*Sara* in the East," U. S. Naval Institute, *Proceedings,* December 1961.

Chapter 22. Operation A GO

Documentary sources, Japanese

Campaigns of the Pacific War, USSBS.

Japanese Monographs No. 90, *A GO Operations,* May–June 1944, No. 91, *A GO Operations Log, Supplement,* May–June 1944, No. 112, *Southeast Area Naval Operations,* Part IV, February–April, 1944, No. 117, *Outline of Third Phase Operations,* February 1943–August 1945, No. 142, *Outline of Southeast Area Naval Air Operations,* Part V, December 1943–May 1944, Nos.

171 and 184, *Submarine Operations in Third Phase Operations,* Parts II, III, IV, and V, November 1943–August 1945.

Interrogations of Mitsuo Fuchida, Shigeru Fukudome, Takeo Kurita, Toshikazu Ohmae, Jisaburo Ozawa, and Momochio Shimanoichi, USSBS, *Interrogations of Japanese Officials.*

Log of Japanese carrier movements, WDC translation 160677.

Book

See already cited Morison, *New Guinea and the Marianas.*

Article

See already cited Wilds, "The Admiral Who Lost His Fleet."

Chapters 23. Operation Forager; 24. Mitscher, Spruance, Ozawa; 25. The Marianas Turkey Shoot; 26. Battle in the Philippine Sea; 27. Attack at Sundown; 28. Landing by Night; Epilogue. These chapters cover the Marianas conquest and the Battle of the Philippine Sea, June 19–20, 1944.

Documentary sources, American

After-action reports. Commander, Fifth Fleet (Spruance) on Operation Forager. Commander TF 58 (Mitscher) on Operation Forager. Commander TG 58.1 (Clark) on Forager operation. U. S. S. *Bataan, Belleau Wood, Cabot, Cowpens, Enterprise, Essex, Bunker Hill, Hornet, Langley, Lexington, Monterey, Princeton, San Jacinto, Wasp,* and *Yorktown* on Forager operations.

Deputy Chief of Naval Operations (Air), Lieutenant (jg) A. O. Van Wyen and Lieutenant (jg) W. G. Land, *Naval Air Operations in the Marianas, June 11–20, 1944.*

Office of Naval Records and Library, recorded narratives on Marianas campaign by Commodore Arleigh Burke, Commander David McCampbell, Lieutenant Bert Morris, and Commander Robert A. Winston recorded in 1944–45.

U. S. Naval Academy, Neville T. Kirk, ed., *Problems in the History of Sea Power,* No. 13, *Battle of the Philippine Sea.*

U. S. Navy, Pacific Fleet, *Account of Being Shot Down and Rescued at Saipan by Commander I. Martin, USN, June 13, 1944.*

Documentary sources, Japanese

After-action reports. *A GO Operations of the 601st Naval Air Group,* WDC translation 161642. CVL *Chitose, A GO Operations from 15 to 22 June 1944,* WDC translation 161135. CVL *Chiyoda, A GO Operations from 15 to 22 June 1944,* WDC translation 161635. First Mobile Fleet, *Detailed Battle Report of A GO Operations,* September 5, 1944, WDC translation 161517. CV *Shokaku, A GO Operations from 15 to 20 June 1944,* WDC translation 161635.

652nd Air Group, *Battle Report No. 1*, WDC translation 161642. Imperial Naval Headquarters, Tokyo, *Impressions and Battle Lessons (Air) in the "A" Operations*, WDC translation 239992. *War Diary of Destroyer Squadron 10, 1–30 June 1944*, WDC translation 161517.

Interrogations of Mitsuo Fuchida, Takeo Kurita, and Jisaburo Ozawa, USSBS, *Interrogation of Japanese Officials*.

Japanese Monographs No. 49, *Central Pacific Operations Record* (of Japanese Army), 90 and 91, *A GO Operations* and *A GO Operations Log*, No. 117, *Outline of Third Phase Operations*, and No. 136, *North of Australia Operations Record* (of Japanese Army).

Interrogations of Norizo Ikeda, Toshio Sakuraba, Zenkichi Uda, and Masaji Oe, Joint Intelligence Center, Pacific Ocean Areas.

Books

See already cited Karig *et. al.*, *Battle Report: End of an Empire*, Morison, *New Guinea and the Marianas*, Potter and Nimitz, *Great Sea War*, Reynolds, *Fast Carriers*, Okumiya and Horikoshi, *Zero*, Stafford, *The Big E*, and Winston, *Fighter Squadron*. Also Ballantine, D. S., *U. S. Naval Logistics in the Second World War* (Princeton, 1947).

Blassingame, Wyatt, *The Navy's Fliers in World War II* (Philadelphia, 1967).

Bryan, J., and P. G. Reed, *Mission Beyond Darkness* (New York, 1945).

Crowl, Philip A., *The United States Army in World War II, The War in the Pacific, Campaign in the Marianas*, Office of the Chief of Military History, U. S. Department of the Army (Washington, 1960).

Lockwood, C. A., and H. C. Adamson, *Battles of the Philippine Sea* (New York, 1967).

Olds, Robert, *Helldiver Squadron: The Story of Bombing Squadron 17 with Task Force 58* (New York, 1944).

Shaw, Henry I., B. C. Nalty, and E. T. Turnbladh, *History of U. S. Marine Corps Operations in World War II*, Vol. III, *Central Pacific Drive*, Headquarters, U. S. Marine Corps, G-3 Division, Historical Branch (Washington, 1966).

Sims, Edward H., *Greatest Fighter Missions of the Top Navy and Marine Aces of World War II* (New York, 1962).

Articles

Brown, J. D., "Fox Six: The Grumman Hellcat with the U. S. Fleet," *Aircraft Illustrated*, November 1968.

Busch, Noel F., "Task Force 58," *Life*, July 17, 1944.

Miller, Thomas G., Jr., "Anatomy of an Air Battle," American Aviation Historical Society, *Journal*, Spring 1970.

Appendix A

Japanese aircraft carrier commissionings during World War II (CV, CVL)

Shoho (CVL), 11,200 tons, January 26, 1942
Junyo (CV), 24,140 tons standard (merchant-ship tonnage), May 3, 1942
Hiyo (CV), 24,140 tons standard (merchant-ship tonnage), July 31, 1942
Ryuho (CVL), 13,360 tons, November 28, 1942
Chiyoda (CVL), 11,190 tons, October 31, 1943
Chitose (CVL), 11,190 tons, January 1, 1944
Taiho (CV), 29,300 tons, March 7, 1944
Unryu (CV), 17,150 tons, August 6, 1944
Amagi (CV), 18,300 tons, August 10, 1944
Katsuragi (CV), 17,400 tons, October 15, 1944
Shinano (CV), 62,000 tons, November 19, 1944
Kasagi (CV), 18,300 tons, launched, never commissioned
Aso (CV), 17,150 tons, launched, never commissioned
Ikoma (CV), 18,300 tons, launched, never commissioned
Ibuki (CVL), 12,500 tons, launched as cruiser, conversion never completed

Japanese escort carriers commissioned during World War II (CVEs)

Taiyo (CVE), 17,830 tons standard, September 5, 1941 (ex-*Kasuga Maru*)
Unyo (CVE), 17,830 tons standard, May 31, 1942 (ex-*Yawata Maru*)
Chuyo (CVE), 17,850 tons standard, November 25, 1942 (ex-*Nitta Maru*)
Kaiyo (CVE), 13,600 tons standard, November 23, 1943 (ex-*Argentina Maru*)
Shinyo (CVE), 17,500 tons standard, December 15, 1943 (ex-*Scharnhorst*)
Brazil Maru, scheduled to be converted as CVE, sunk before conversion could
    be started by U. S. submarine attack

Japanese aircraft carriers completed prior to World War II (CV, CVL)

Hosho (1922), 7,470 tons
Akagi (1927), 36,500 tons
Kaga (1928), 38,200 tons
Ryujo (1933), 10,600 tons
Soryu (1937), 15,900 tons
Hiryu (1939), 17,300 tons
Shokaku (1941), 25,625 tons
Zuikaku (1941), 25,625 tons

Commissionings of Independence (CVL) and Essex (CV) class carriers were as follows:

1943

Essex (CV-9), December 31, 1942
Independence (CVL-22), January 1, 1943
Lexington (CV-16), February 17, 1943
Princeton (CVL-23), February 25, 1943
Belleau Wood (CVL-24), March 31, 1943
Yorktown (CV-10), April 15, 1943
Bunker Hill (CV-17), May 25, 1943
Cowpens (CVL-25), May 28, 1943
Monterey (CVL-26), June 17, 1943
Cabot (CVL-28), July 24, 1943
Intrepid (CV-11), August 16, 1943
Langley (CVL-27), August 31, 1943
Bataan (CVL-29), November 17, 1943
Wasp (CV-18), November 24, 1943
Hornet (CV-12), November 29, 1943

San Jacinto (CVL-30), December 15, 1943

Total 1942–43, 9 CVL, 7 CV

1944–45

Franklin (CV-13), January 31, 1944
Hancock (CV-19), April 15, 1944
Ticonderoga (CV-14), May 8, 1944
Bennington (CV-20), August 6, 1944
Shangri-La (CV-38), September 15, 1944
Randolph (CV-15), October 9, 1944
Bon Homme Richard (CV-31), November 26, 1944
Antietam (CV-36), January 28, 1945
Boxer (CV-21), April 16, 1945
Lake Champlain (CV-39), June 3, 1945

Total 1944–45, 10 CV

Carriers completed prior to World War II

Langley (1922), 11,050 tons, CV-1
Saratoga (1927), 36,000 tons, CV-3
Lexington (1927), 36,000 tons, CV-2
Ranger (1934), 14,500 tons, CV-4

Yorktown (1937), 19,800 tons, CV-5
Enterprise (1938), 19,800 tons, CV-6
Wasp (1940), 14,700 tons, CV-7
Hornet (1941), 19,800 tons, CV-8

Postwar completions, 1945–50

Midway (CVB-41), September 10, 1945
Franklin D. Roosevelt (CVB-42), October 27, 1945
Princeton (CV-37), November 18, 1945
Tarawa (CV-40), December 8, 1945
Kearsarge (CV-33), March 2, 1946
Leyte (CV-32), April 11, 1946
Philippine Sea (CV-47), May 11,

1946

Saipan (CVL-48), July 14, 1946
Valley Forge (CV-45), November 3, 1946
Wright (CVL-49), February 9, 1947
Coral Sea (CVB-48), October 1, 1947
Oriskany (CV-34), September 25, 1950

Total postwar, 3 CVB, 2 CVL, and 7 CV

Appendix B

Note: The popular, common, or code designation is given first.

Albacore   Fairey biplane carrier torpedo bomber (Britain).

Avenger   Grumman monoplane carrier torpedo bomber (U. S.).

Betty   Mitsubishi G4M Type 1 and 2 twin-engine Navy medium bomber (Japan).

Buffalo   Brewster monoplane carrier fighter (U. S.)

Camel   Sopwith biplane World War I fighter (Britain).

Catalina   Consolidated PBY flying boat (U. S., Canada).

Claude   Mitsubishi A5M Type 96 monoplane carrier fighter (Japan).

Corsair   Vought F4U monoplane carrier fighter (U. S.).

Dauntless   Douglas SBD monoplane carrier dive bomber (U. S.).

Dave   Nakajima E8N biplane reconnaissance float plane (Japan).

Devastator   Douglas TBD monoplane carrier torpedo bomber (U. S.).

Emily   Kawanishi H8K four-engine flying boat (Japan).

F2B, F3B, F4B   Boeing biplane carrier fighter (U. S.).

F2F, F3F   Grumman biplane carrier fighter (U. S.).

Flying Fortress   Boeing B-17 four-engine Army heavy bomber (U. S.).

Frances   Yokosuka P1Y Ginga (Milky Way) twin-engine Navy light bomber (Japan).

Fulmar   Fairey two-seat monoplane reconnaissance/fighter (Britain).

Hellcat   Grumman F6F monoplane carrier fighter (U. S.).

Helldiver   Curtiss SB2C "Beast" monoplane carrier dive bomber (U. S.).

Hurricane   Hawker monoplane fighter (Britain).

Jack   Mitsubishi J2M Raiden (Thunderbolt) carrier fighter (Japan).

Jake   Aichi E13A Type O reconnaissance float plane (Japan).

Jill   Nakajima B6N Tenzan (Heavenly Mountain) carrier torpedo bomber (Japan).

Judy   Yokosuka D4Y Suisei (Comet) carrier dive bomber (Japan).

Kate   Nakajima B5N Type 97 carrier torpedo bomber (Japan).

Kingfisher   Vought OS2U monoplane reconnaissance float plane (U. S.).

Lightning   Lockheed twin-engine Army P-38 fighter (U. S.).

Marauder   Martin B-26 twin-engine Army medium bomber (U. S.).

Mavis   Kawanishi H6K Type 97 four-engine flying boat (Japan).

Mitchell   North American B-25 twin-engine Army medium bomber (U. S.).

Nell   Mitsubishi G3M twin-engine Navy medium bomber (Japan).

P-36   Curtiss monoplane Army fighter (U. S.).

P-40   Curtiss monoplane Army fighter (U. S.).

Seagull   Curtiss SOC biplane reconnaissance float plane (U. S.).

Swordfish   Fairey biplane carrier torpedo bomber (Britain).

TG-2   Great Lakes biplane pre-World War II carrier torpedo bomber (U. S.).

Type 89   Mitsubishi biplane prewar carrier torpedo bomber (Japan).

Type 90   Nakajima biplane prewar carrier fighter (Japan).

Type 96   Yokosuka B4Y1 biplane carrier torpedo bomber (Japan).

Val   Aichi D3A monoplane carrier dive bomber (Japan).

Vindicator   Vought SB2U monoplane carrier dive bomber (U. S.).

Wildcat   Grumman F4F monoplane carrier fighter (U. S.).

Wirraway   North American-design monoplane fighter-bomber/trainer (Australia).

Zero   Mitsubishi A6M monoplane fighter—Allied code name Zeke (Japan).

Index

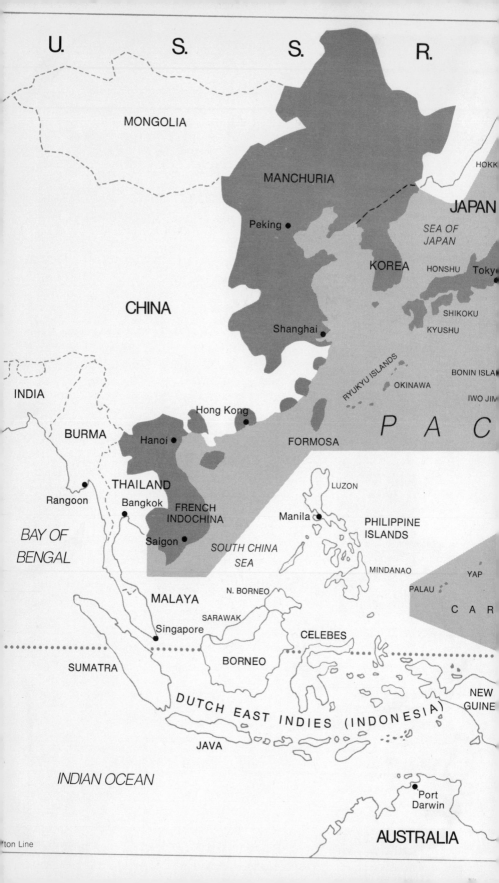